CRY HAVOC

MYTHING IN ACTION

words
SIMON SPURRIER

pictures
RYAN KELLY

colors

NICK **FILARDI** | LEE **LOUGHRIDGE** | MATT **WILSON**
London   The Red Place   Afghanistan

letters   design

SIMON **BOWLAND**   EMMA **PRICE**

additional inks

BARBARA **GUTTMAN** | MIGUEL **MONTENEGRO**

volume cover

RYAN **KELLY** | EMMA **PRICE** | CAMERON **STEWART**

IMAGE COMICS, INC.
Robert Kirkman – Chief Operating Officer
Erik Larsen – Chief Financial Officer
Todd McFarlane – President
Marc Silvestri – Chief Executive Officer
Jim Valentino – Vice-President

Eric Stephenson – Publisher
Corey Murphy – Director of Sales
Jeff Boison – Director of Publishing Planning & Book Trade Sales
Jeremy Sullivan – Director of Digital Sales
Kat Salazar – Director of PR & Marketing
Branwyn Bigglestone – Senior Accounts Manager
Sarah Mello – Accounts Manager
Drew Gill – Art Director
Jonathan Chan – Production Manager
Meredith Wallace – Print Manager
Briah Skelly – Publicist
Sasha Head – Sales & Marketing Production Designer
Randy Okamura – Digital Production Designer
David Brothers – Branding Manager
Ally Power – Content Manager
Addison Duke – Production Artist
Vincent Kukua – Production Artist
Tricia Ramos – Production Artist
Jeff Stang – Direct Market Sales Representative
Emilio Bautista – Digital Sales Associate
Leanna Caunter – Accounting Assistant
Chloe Ramos-Peterson – Library Market Sales Representative
IMAGECOMICS.COM

CRY HAVOC, VOL 1: MYTHING IN ACTION. First printing. August 2016. Copyright © 2016 SIMON SPURRIER & RYAN KELLY. All rights reserved. Published by Image Comics, Inc. Office of publication: 2001 Center Street, Sixth Floor, Berkeley, CA 94704. Contains material originally published as Cry Havoc #1-6. CRY HAVOC™ its logos, and the likenesses of all characters herein are trademarks of Simon Spurrier & Ryan Kelly, unless otherwise noted. "Image" and the Image Comics logos are registered trademarks of Image Comics, Inc. No part of this publication may be reproduced or transmitted, in any form or by any means (except for short excerpts for journalistic or review purposes), without the express written permission of Simon Spurrier & Ryan Kelly or Image Comics, Inc. All names, characters, events, and locales in this publication are entirely fictional. Any resemblance to actual persons (living or dead), events, or places, without satiric intent, is coincidental. Printed in the USA. For information regarding the CPSIA on this printed material call: 203-595-3636 and provide reference #RICH-690206.

ISBN: 978-1-63215-833-8

For international rights, contact: foreignlicensing@imagecomics.com

CRY HAVOC™

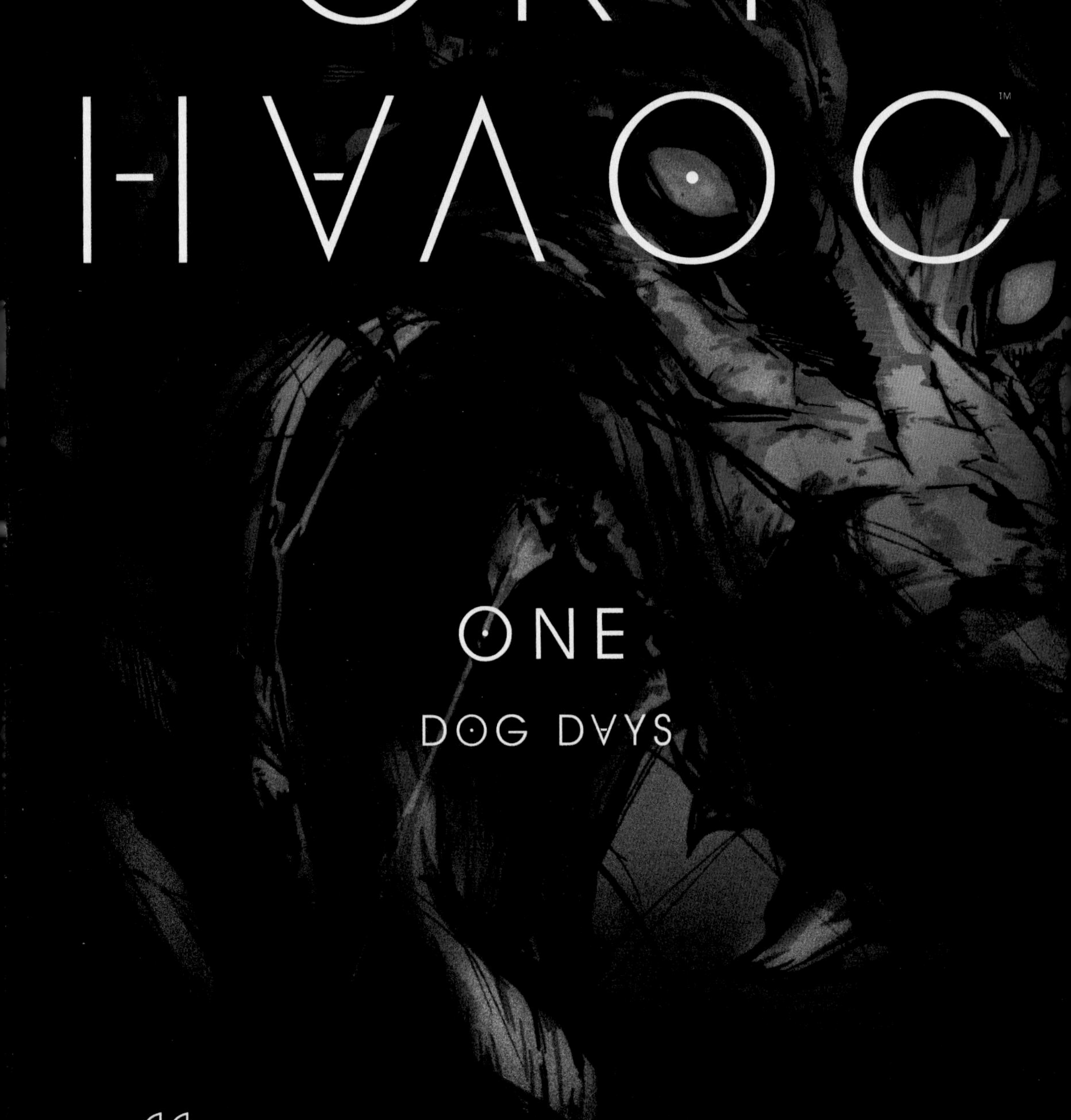

ONE

DOG DAYS

"For a time I would feel I belonged still to a world of straightforward facts; but the feeling would not last long. Something would turn up to scare it away."

JOSEPH CONRAD, *HEART OF DARKNESS*

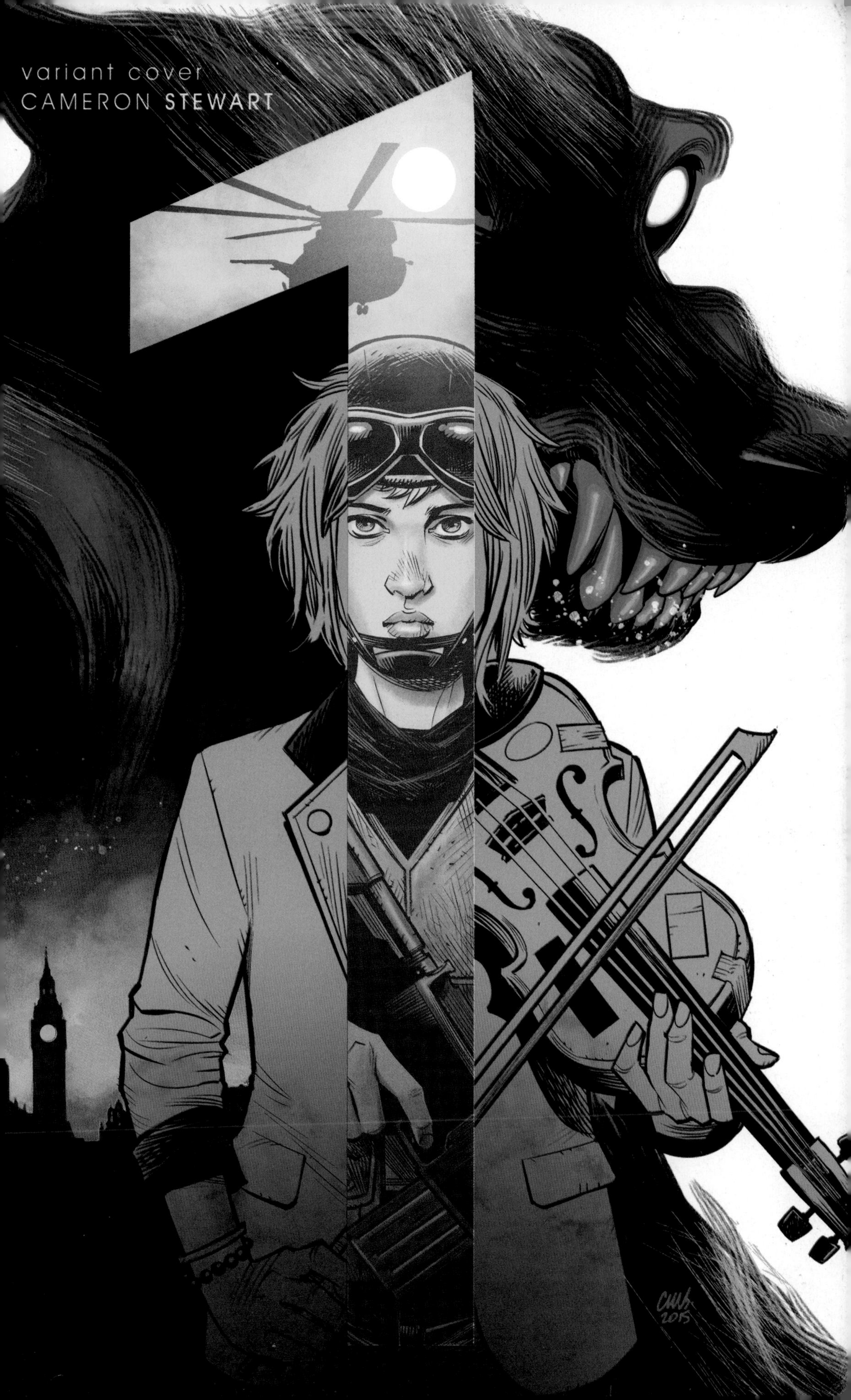

variant cover
CAMERON **STEWART**

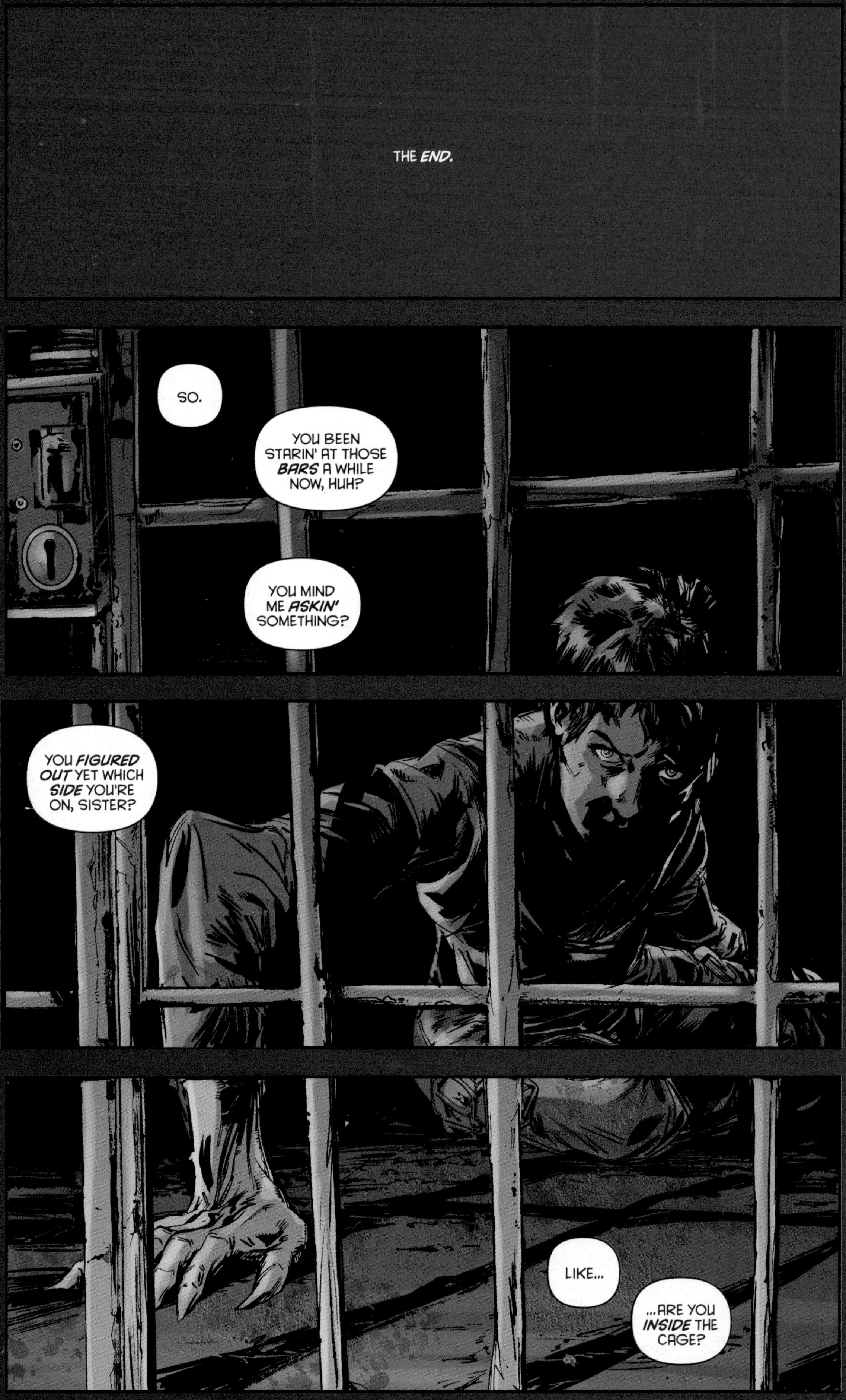
THE *END.*
SO.
YOU BEEN STARIN' AT THOSE *BARS* A WHILE NOW, HUH?
YOU MIND ME *ASKIN'* SOMETHING?
YOU *FIGURED OUT* YET WHICH *SIDE* YOU'RE ON, SISTER?
LIKE...
...ARE YOU *INSIDE* THE CAGE?

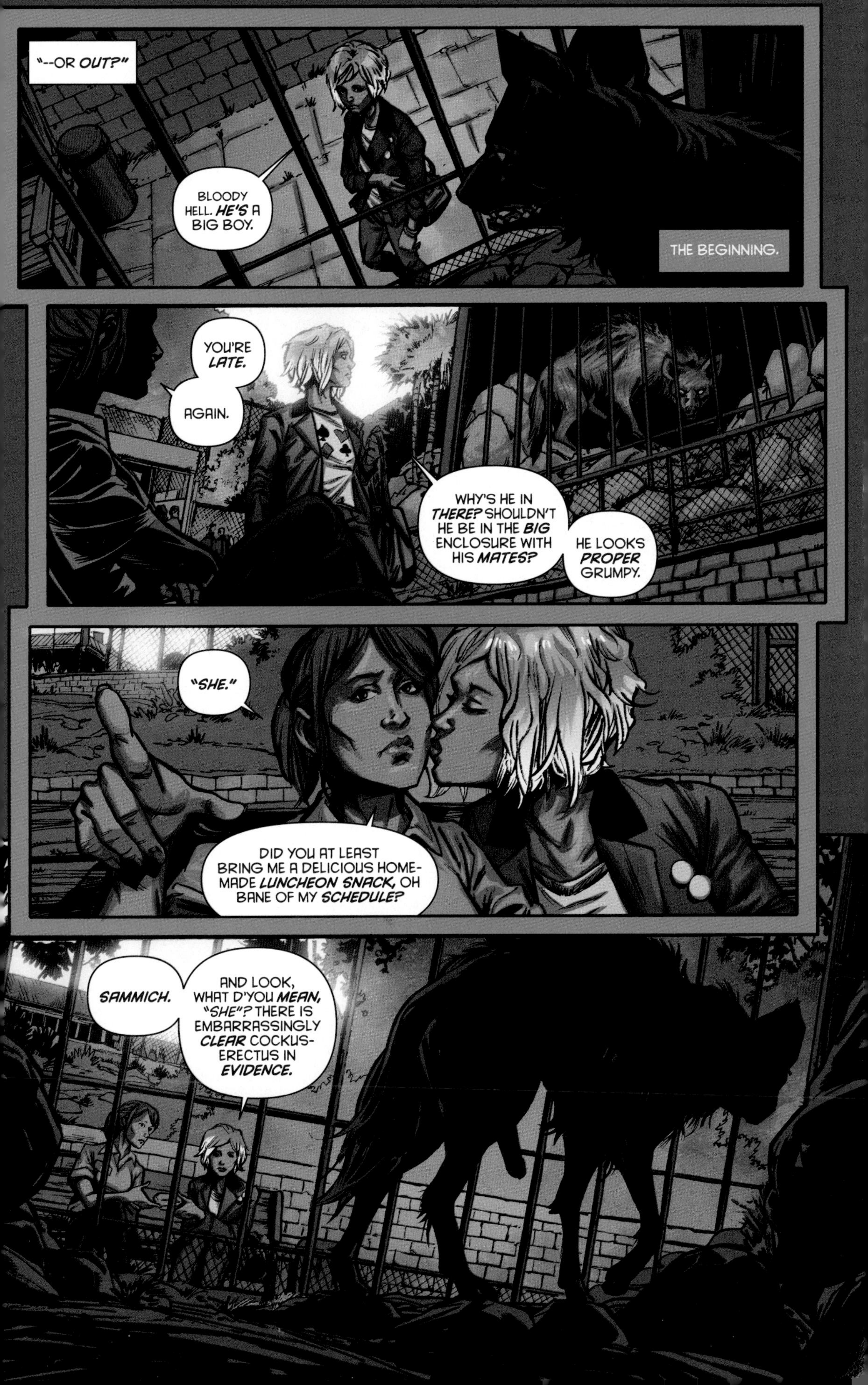
"--OR *OUT?*"
BLOODY HELL. ***HE'S*** A BIG BOY.
THE BEGINNING.
YOU'RE ***LATE.***
AGAIN.
WHY'S HE IN ***THERE?*** SHOULDN'T HE BE IN THE ***BIG*** ENCLOSURE WITH HIS ***MATES?***
HE LOOKS ***PROPER*** GRUMPY.
"SHE."
DID YOU AT LEAST BRING ME A DELICIOUS HOME-MADE ***LUNCHEON SNACK,*** OH BANE OF MY ***SCHEDULE?***
SAMMICH.
AND LOOK, WHAT D'YOU ***MEAN,*** ***"SHE"?*** THERE IS EMBARRASSINGLY ***CLEAR*** COCKUS-ERECTUS IN ***EVIDENCE.***

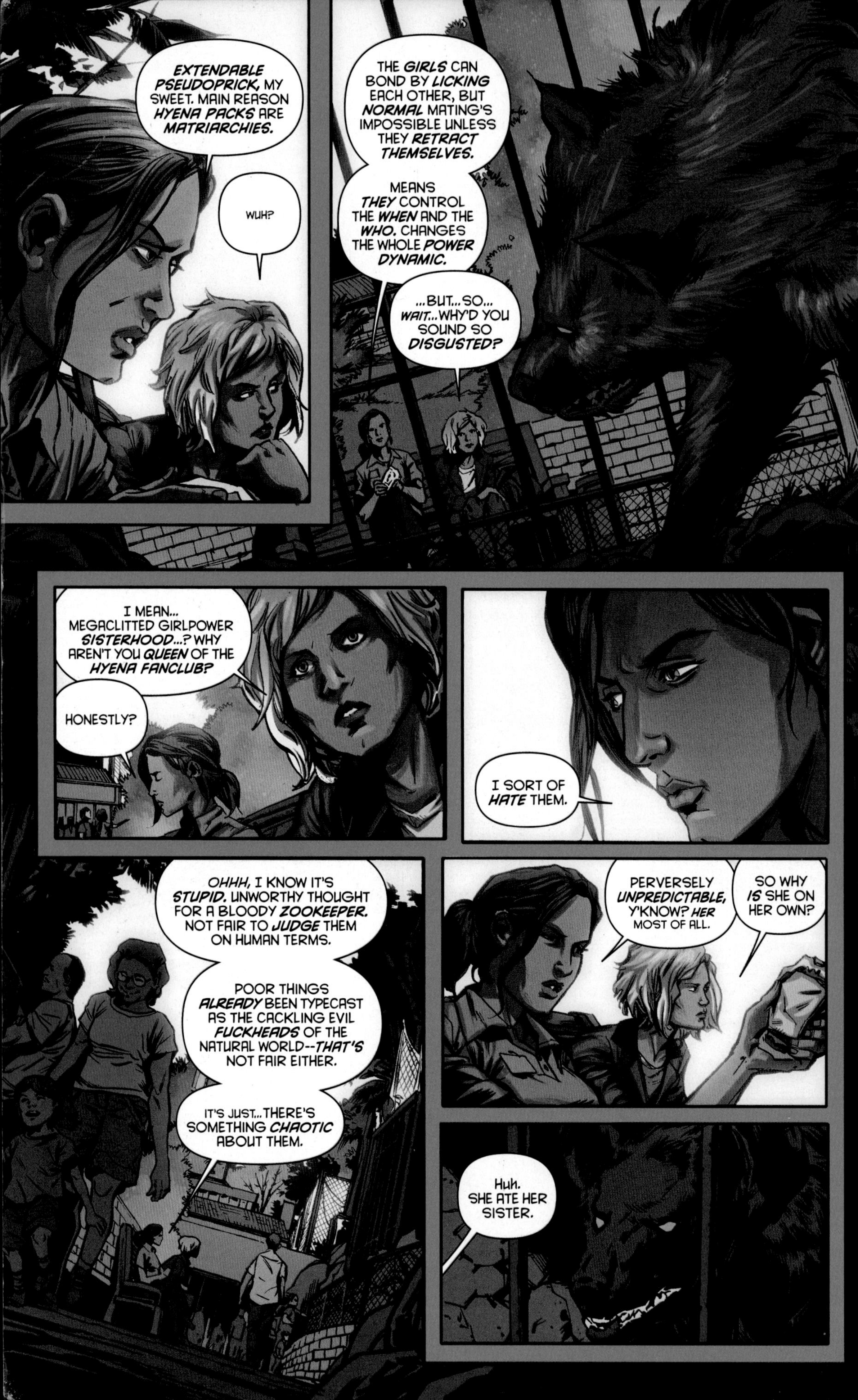

EXTENDABLE PSEUDOPRICK, MY SWEET. MAIN REASON HYENA PACKS ARE MATRIARCHIES.
WUH?
THE GIRLS CAN BOND BY LICKING EACH OTHER, BUT NORMAL MATING'S IMPOSSIBLE UNLESS THEY RETRACT THEMSELVES.
MEANS THEY CONTROL THE WHEN AND THE WHO. CHANGES THE WHOLE POWER DYNAMIC.
...BUT...SO... WAIT...WHY'D YOU SOUND SO DISGUSTED?
I MEAN... MEGACLITTED GIRLPOWER SISTERHOOD...? WHY AREN'T YOU QUEEN OF THE HYENA FANCLUB?
HONESTLY?
I SORT OF HATE THEM.
OHHH, I KNOW IT'S STUPID. UNWORTHY THOUGHT FOR A BLOODY ZOOKEEPER. NOT FAIR TO JUDGE THEM ON HUMAN TERMS.
POOR THINGS ALREADY BEEN TYPECAST AS THE CACKLING EVIL FUCKHEADS OF THE NATURAL WORLD--THAT'S NOT FAIR EITHER.
IT'S JUST...THERE'S SOMETHING CHAOTIC ABOUT THEM.
PERVERSELY UNPREDICTABLE, Y'KNOW? HER MOST OF ALL.
SO WHY IS SHE ON HER OWN?
Huh. SHE ATE HER SISTER.

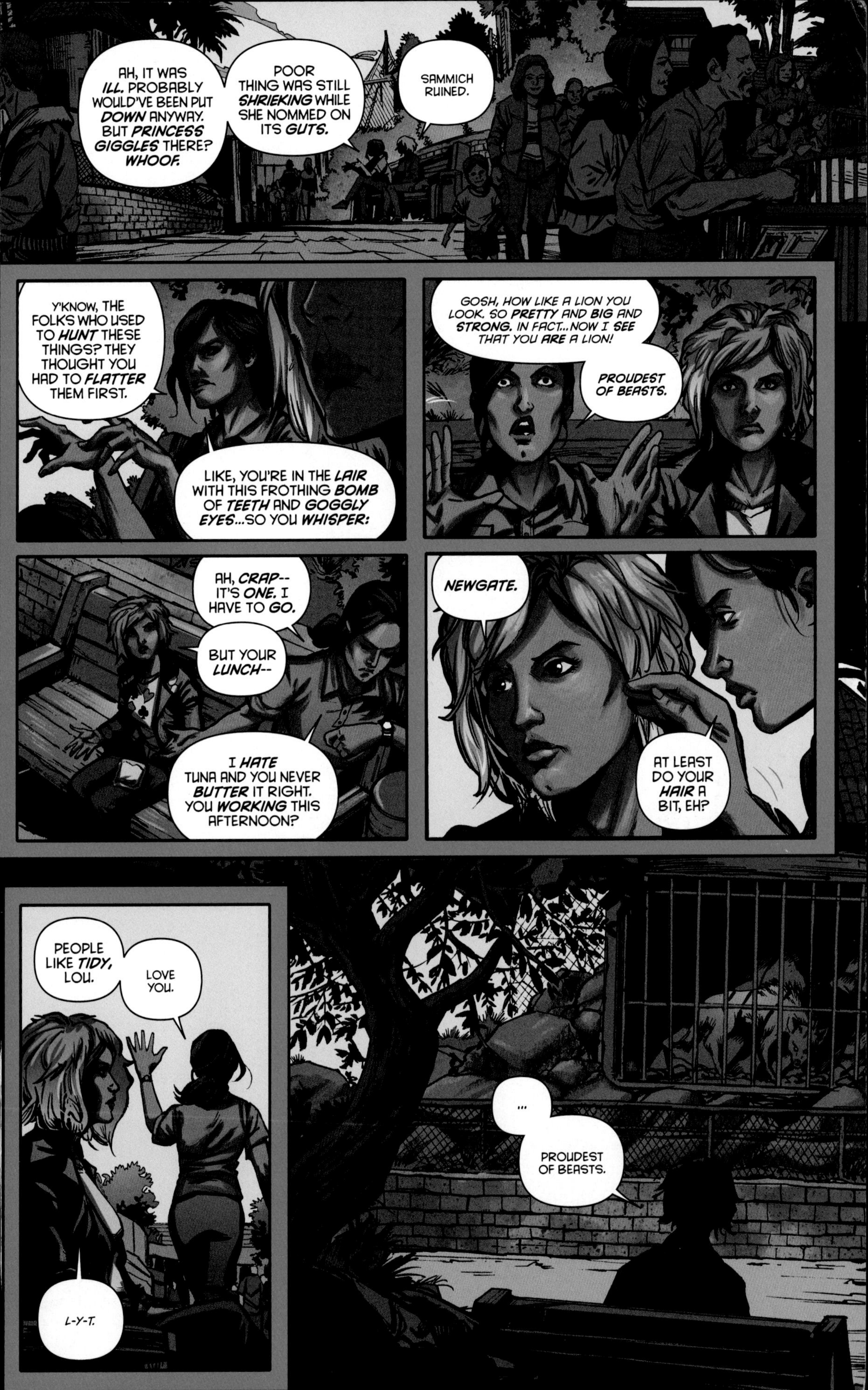

AH, IT WAS ILL. PROBABLY WOULD'VE BEEN PUT DOWN ANYWAY. BUT PRINCESS GIGGLES THERE? WHOOF.
POOR THING WAS STILL SHRIEKING WHILE SHE NOMMED ON ITS GUTS.
SAMMICH RUINED.
Y'KNOW, THE FOLKS WHO USED TO HUNT THESE THINGS? THEY THOUGHT YOU HAD TO FLATTER THEM FIRST.
LIKE, YOU'RE IN THE LAIR WITH THIS FROTHING BOMB OF TEETH AND GOGGLY EYES...SO YOU WHISPER:
GOSH, HOW LIKE A LION YOU LOOK. SO PRETTY AND BIG AND STRONG. IN FACT...NOW I SEE THAT YOU ARE A LION!
PROUDEST OF BEASTS.
AH, CRAP-- IT'S ONE. I HAVE TO GO.
BUT YOUR LUNCH--
I HATE TUNA AND YOU NEVER BUTTER IT RIGHT. YOU WORKING THIS AFTERNOON?
NEWGATE.
AT LEAST DO YOUR HAIR A BIT, EH?
PEOPLE LIKE TIDY, LOU.
LOVE YOU.
L-Y-T.
...
PROUDEST OF BEASTS.

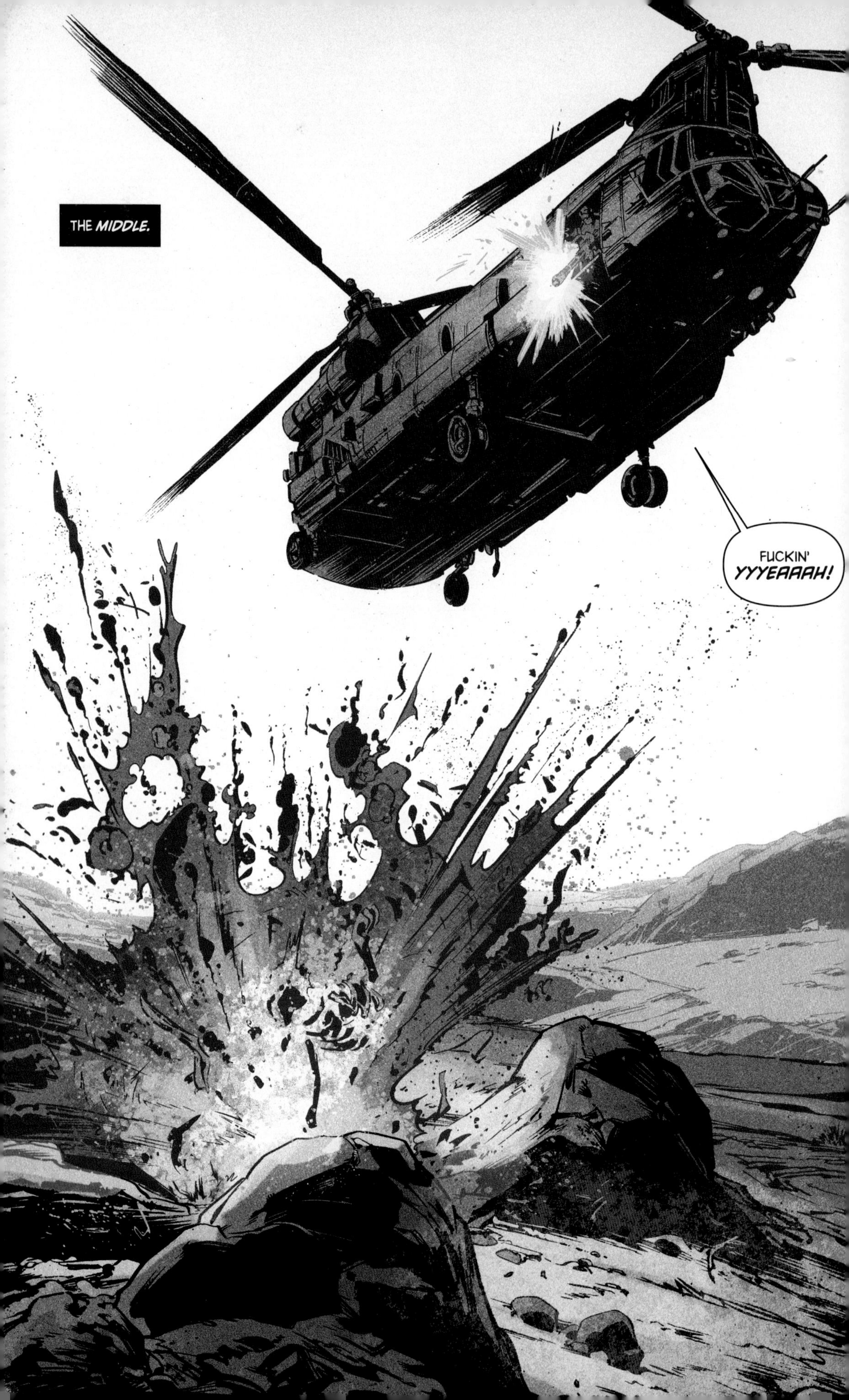
THE MIDDLE.
FUCKIN' YYYEAAAH!

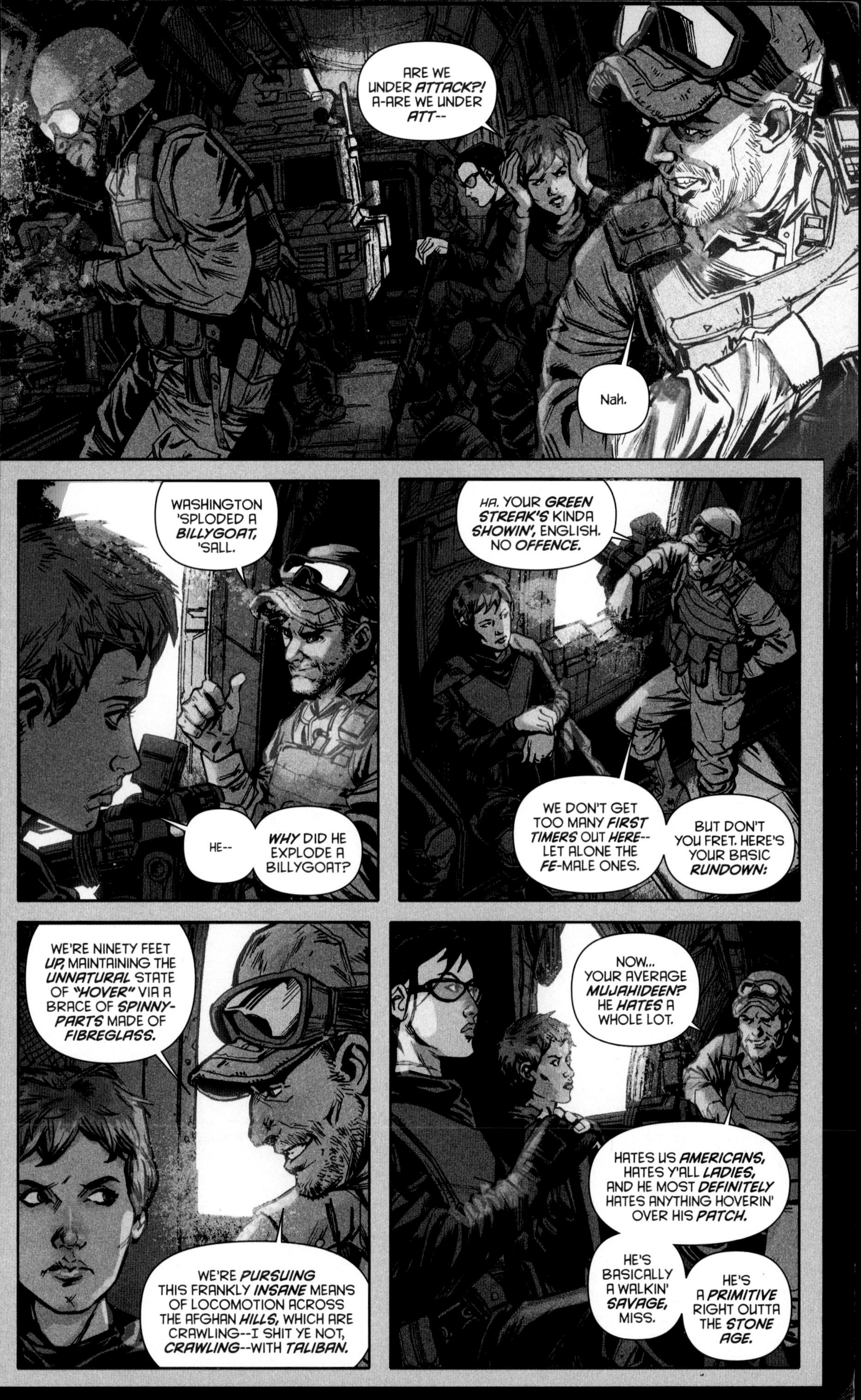
ARE WE UNDER ATTACK?! A-ARE WE UNDER ATT--
Nah.
WASHINGTON 'SPLODED A BILLYGOAT, 'SALL.
HE--
WHY DID HE EXPLODE A BILLYGOAT?
HA. YOUR GREEN STREAK'S KINDA SHOWIN', ENGLISH. NO OFFENCE.
WE DON'T GET TOO MANY FIRST TIMERS OUT HERE-- LET ALONE THE FE-MALE ONES.
BUT DON'T YOU FRET. HERE'S YOUR BASIC RUNDOWN:
WE'RE NINETY FEET UP, MAINTAINING THE UNNATURAL STATE OF "HOVER" VIA A BRACE OF SPINNY-PARTS MADE OF FIBREGLASS.
WE'RE PURSUING THIS FRANKLY INSANE MEANS OF LOCOMOTION ACROSS THE AFGHAN HILLS, WHICH ARE CRAWLING--I SHIT YE NOT, CRAWLING--WITH TALIBAN.
NOW... YOUR AVERAGE MUJAHIDEEN? HE HATES A WHOLE LOT.
HATES US AMERICANS, HATES Y'ALL LADIES, AND HE MOST DEFINITELY HATES ANYTHING HOVERIN' OVER HIS PATCH.
HE'S BASICALLY A WALKIN' SAVAGE, MISS.
HE'S A PRIMITIVE RIGHT OUTTA THE STONE AGE.

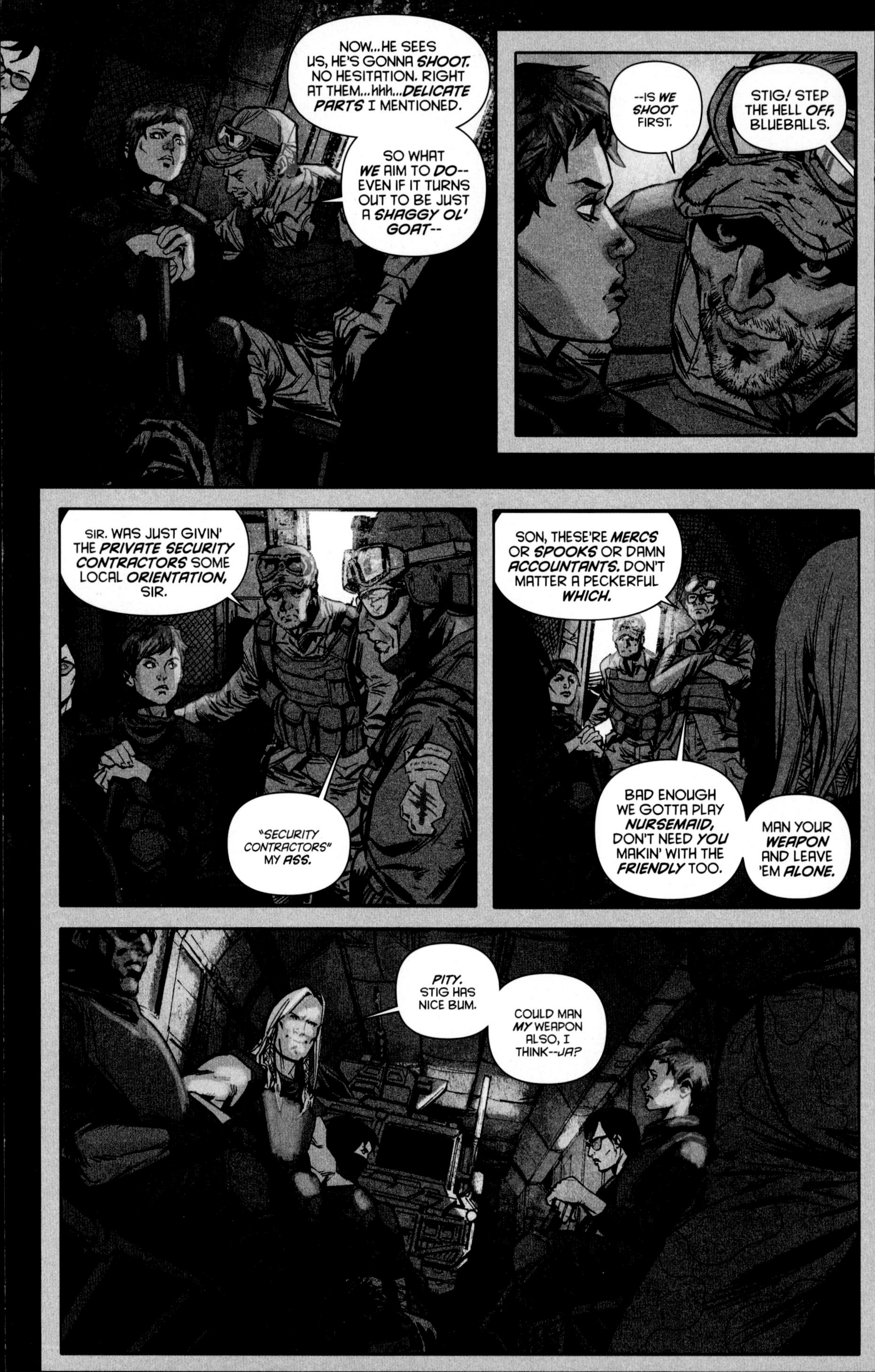
NOW...HE SEES US, HE'S GONNA SHOOT. NO HESITATION. RIGHT AT THEM...hhh...DELICATE PARTS I MENTIONED.
SO WHAT WE AIM TO DO-- EVEN IF IT TURNS OUT TO BE JUST A SHAGGY OL' GOAT--
--IS WE SHOOT FIRST.
STIG! STEP THE HELL OFF, BLUEBALLS.
SIR. WAS JUST GIVIN' THE PRIVATE SECURITY CONTRACTORS SOME LOCAL ORIENTATION, SIR.
"SECURITY CONTRACTORS" MY ASS.
SON, THESE'RE MERCS OR SPOOKS OR DAMN ACCOUNTANTS. DON'T MATTER A PECKERFUL WHICH.
BAD ENOUGH WE GOTTA PLAY NURSEMAID, DON'T NEED YOU MAKIN' WITH THE FRIENDLY TOO.
MAN YOUR WEAPON AND LEAVE 'EM ALONE.
PITY. STIG HAS NICE BUM.
COULD MAN MY WEAPON ALSO, I THINK--JA?

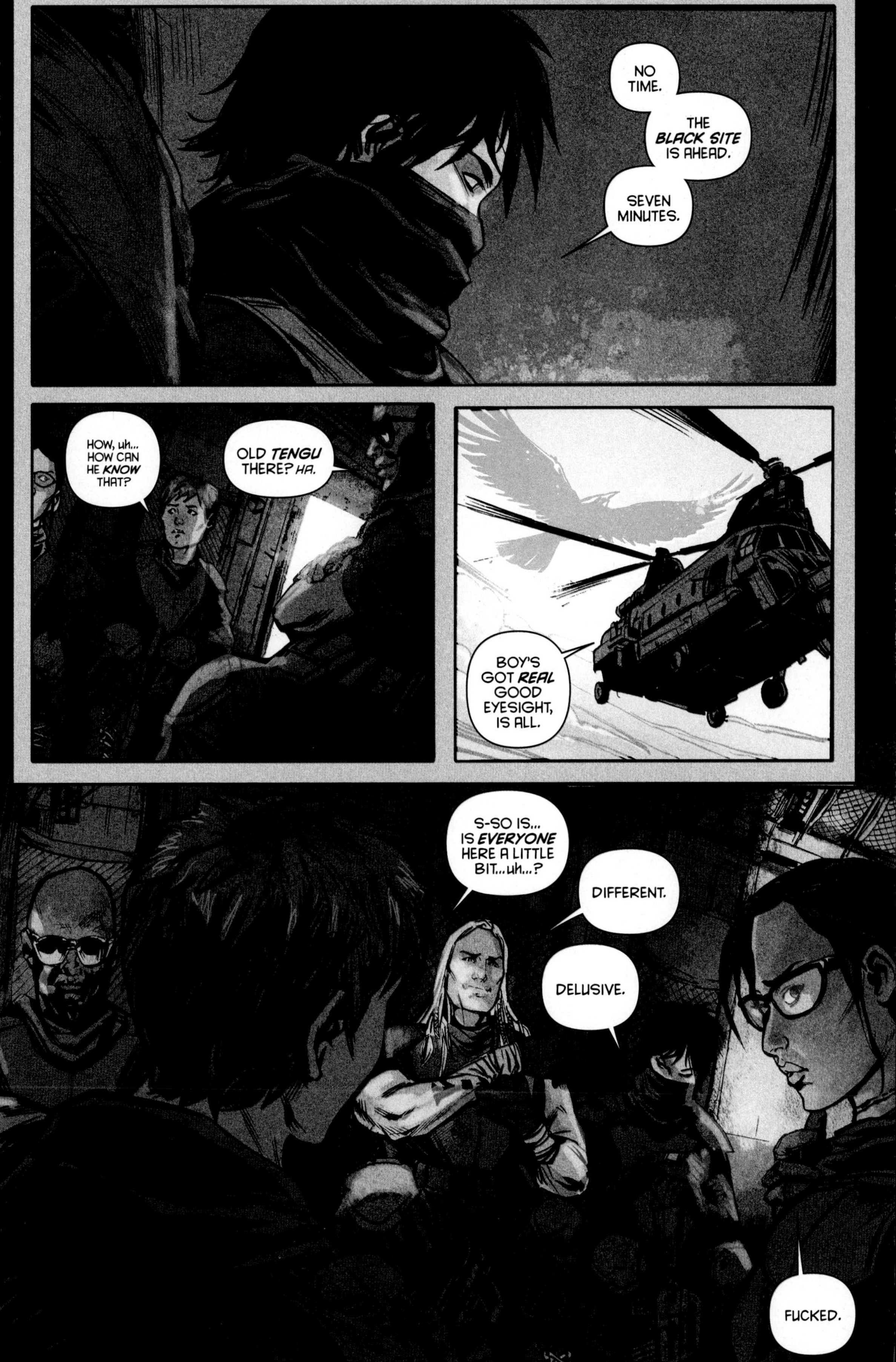
NO TIME.
THE BLACK SITE IS AHEAD.
SEVEN MINUTES.
HOW, uh... HOW CAN HE KNOW THAT?
OLD TENGU THERE? HA.
BOY'S GOT REAL GOOD EYESIGHT, IS ALL.
S-SO IS... IS EVERYONE HERE A LITTLE BIT...uh...?
DIFFERENT.
DELUSIVE.
FUCKED.

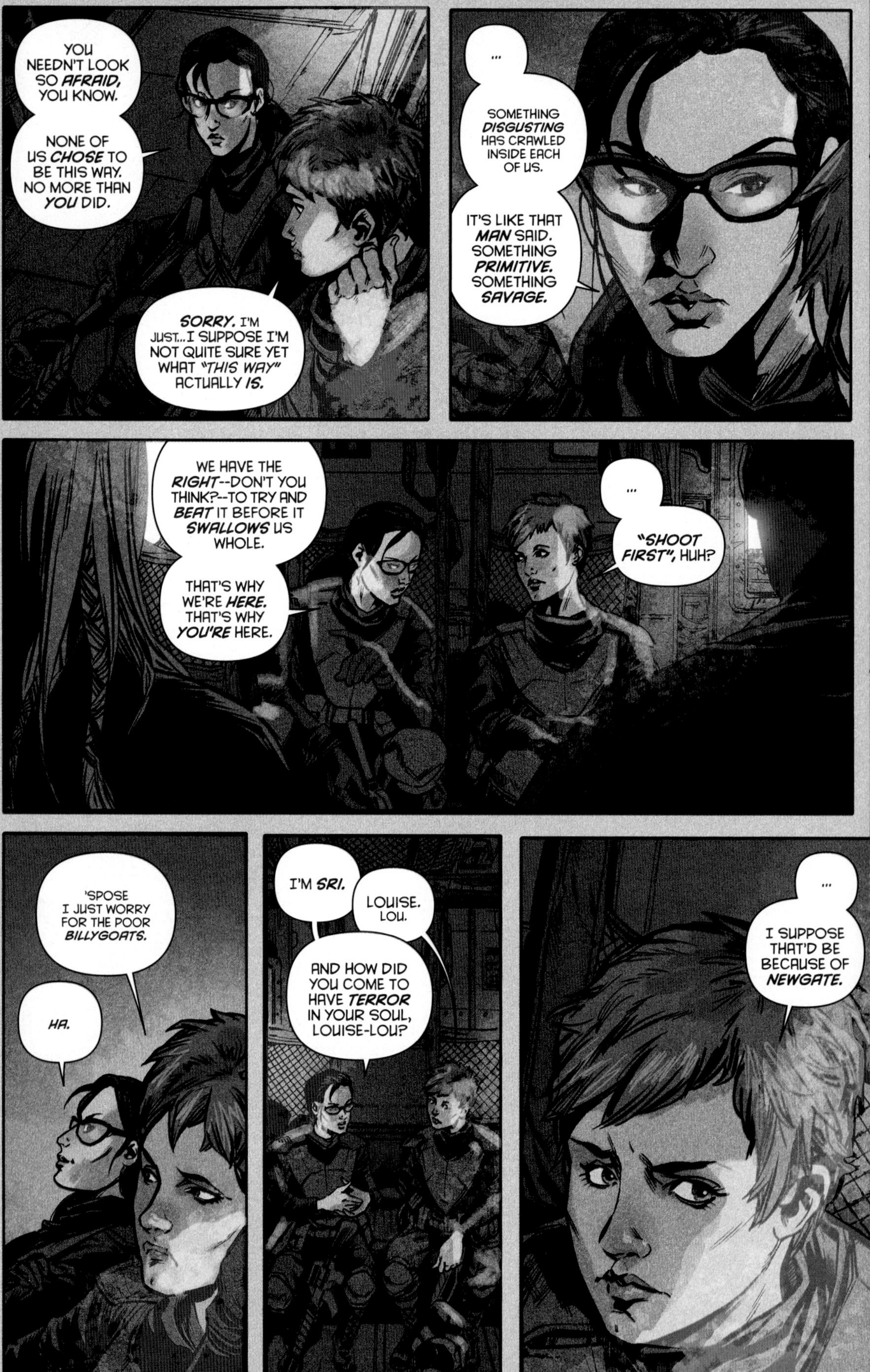
YOU NEEDN'T LOOK SO AFRAID, YOU KNOW.
NONE OF US CHOSE TO BE THIS WAY. NO MORE THAN YOU DID.
SORRY. I'M JUST...I SUPPOSE I'M NOT QUITE SURE YET WHAT "THIS WAY" ACTUALLY IS.
...
SOMETHING DISGUSTING HAS CRAWLED INSIDE EACH OF US.
IT'S LIKE THAT MAN SAID. SOMETHING PRIMITIVE. SOMETHING SAVAGE.
WE HAVE THE RIGHT--DON'T YOU THINK?--TO TRY AND BEAT IT BEFORE IT SWALLOWS US WHOLE.
THAT'S WHY WE'RE HERE. THAT'S WHY YOU'RE HERE.
...
"SHOOT FIRST", HUH?
'SPOSE I JUST WORRY FOR THE POOR BILLYGOATS.
HA.
I'M SRI.
LOUISE. LOU.
AND HOW DID YOU COME TO HAVE TERROR IN YOUR SOUL, LOUISE-LOU?
...
I SUPPOSE THAT'D BE BECAUSE OF NEWGATE.

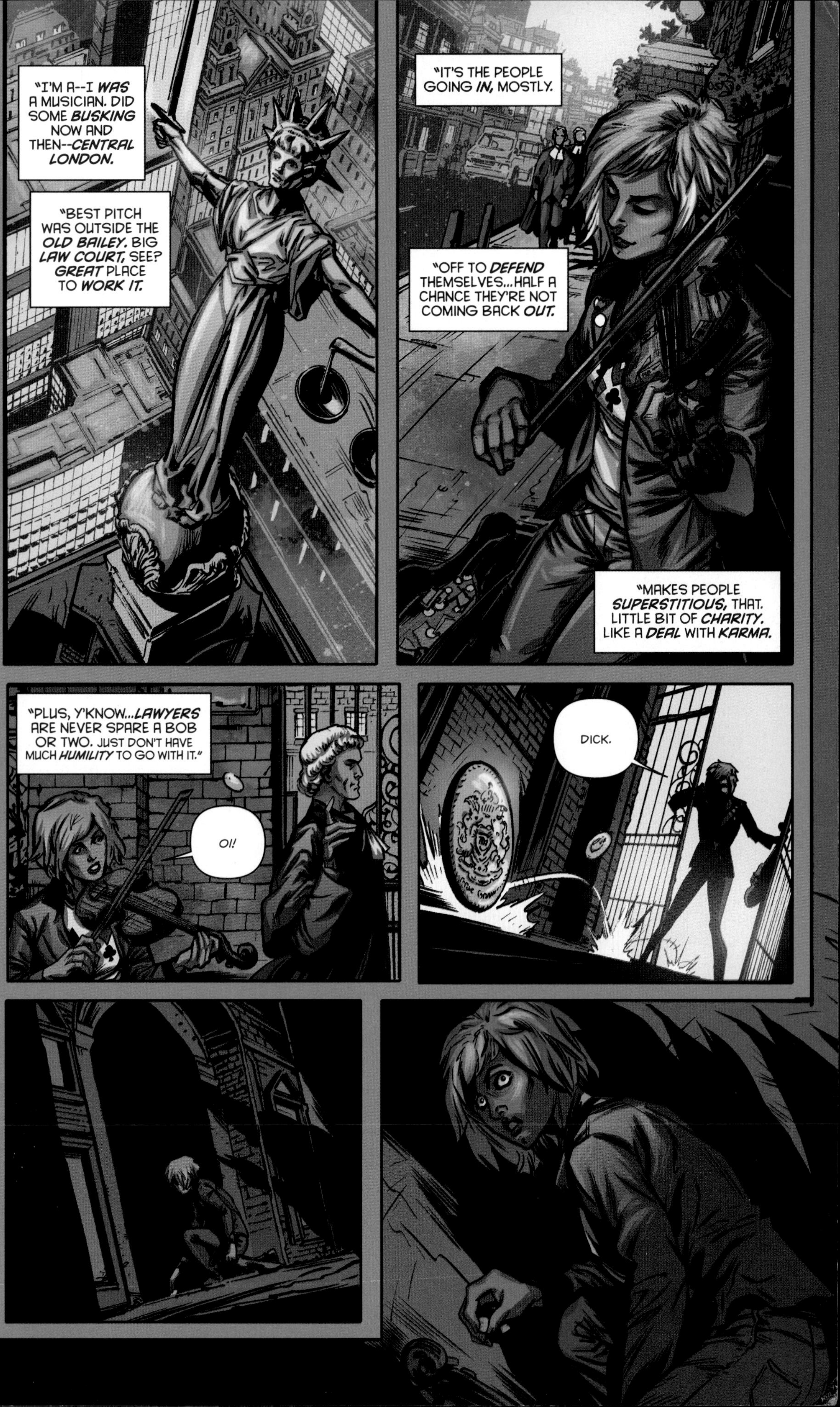
"I'M A--I WAS A MUSICIAN. DID SOME BUSKING NOW AND THEN--CENTRAL LONDON.
"BEST PITCH WAS OUTSIDE THE OLD BAILEY. BIG LAW COURT, SEE? GREAT PLACE TO WORK IT.
"IT'S THE PEOPLE GOING IN, MOSTLY.
"OFF TO DEFEND THEMSELVES...HALF A CHANCE THEY'RE NOT COMING BACK OUT.
"MAKES PEOPLE SUPERSTITIOUS, THAT. LITTLE BIT OF CHARITY. LIKE A DEAL WITH KARMA.
"PLUS, Y'KNOW...LAWYERS ARE NEVER SPARE A BOB OR TWO. JUST DON'T HAVE MUCH HUMILITY TO GO WITH IT."
OI!
DICK.

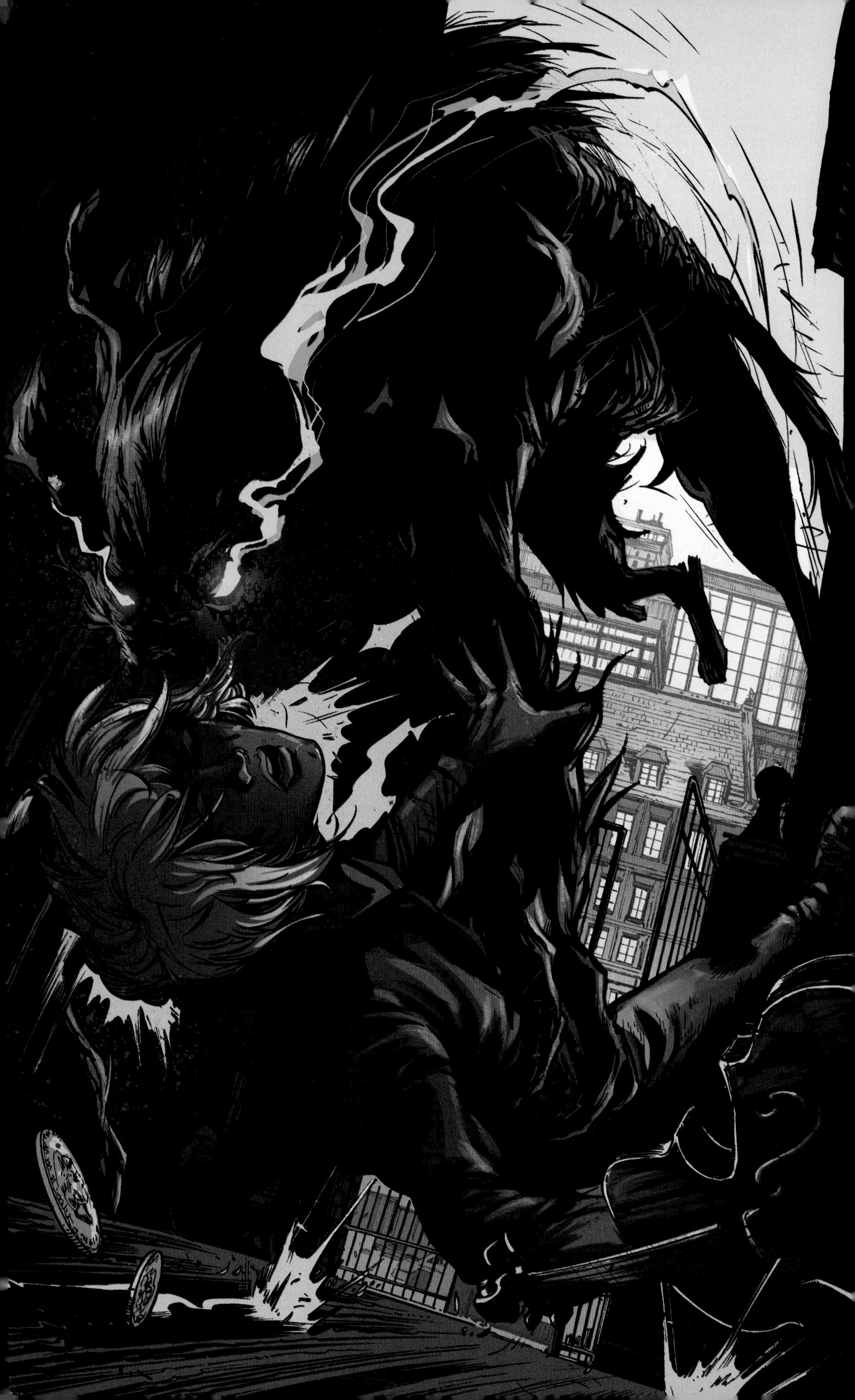

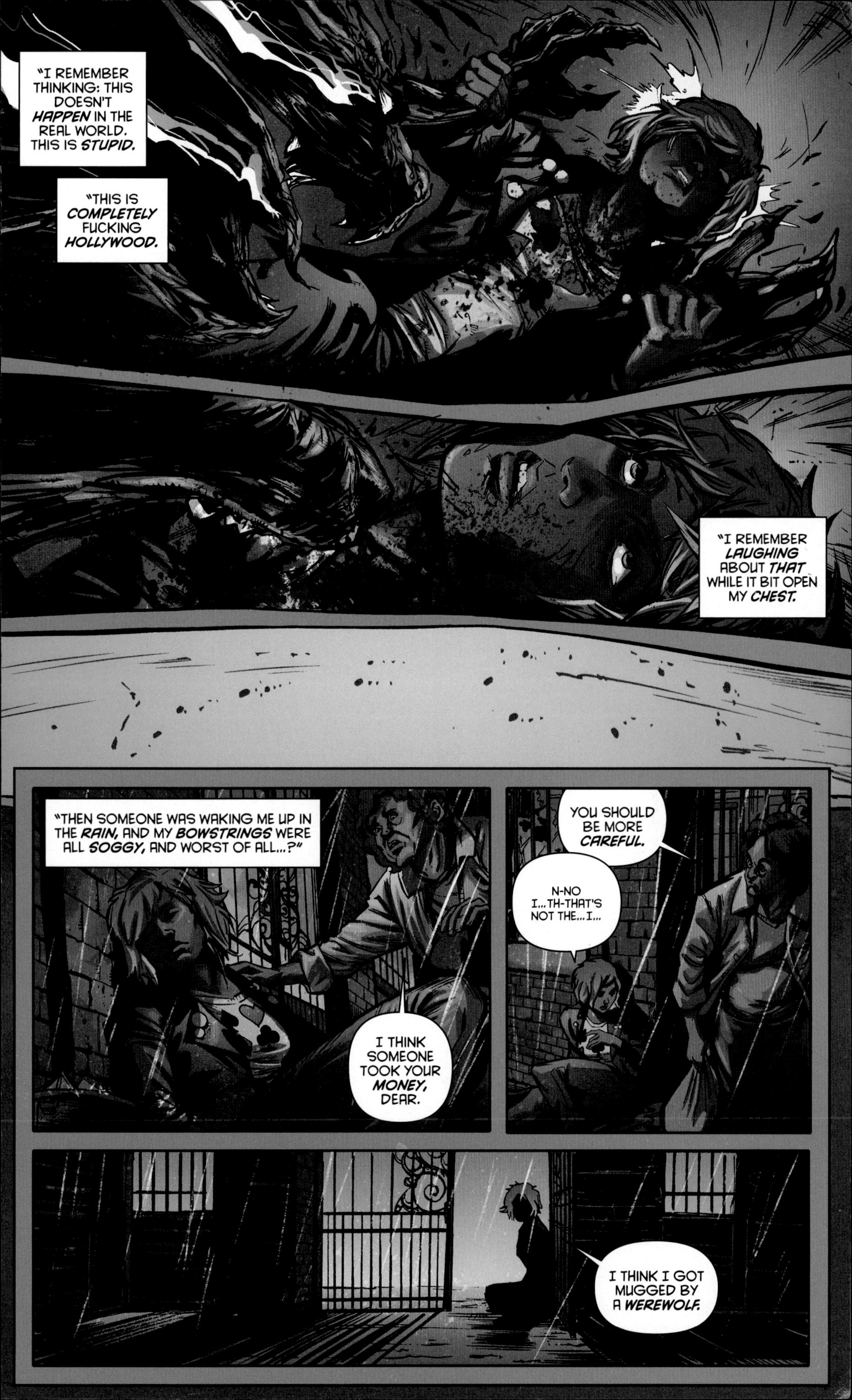
"I REMEMBER THINKING: THIS DOESN'T *HAPPEN* IN THE REAL WORLD. THIS IS *STUPID.*
"THIS IS *COMPLETELY* FUCKING *HOLLYWOOD.*
"I REMEMBER *LAUGHING* ABOUT *THAT* WHILE IT BIT OPEN MY *CHEST.*
"THEN SOMEONE WAS WAKING ME UP IN THE *RAIN,* AND MY *BOWSTRINGS* WERE ALL *SOGGY,* AND WORST OF ALL...?"
I THINK SOMEONE TOOK YOUR *MONEY,* DEAR.
YOU SHOULD BE MORE *CAREFUL.*
N-NO I...TH-THAT'S NOT THE...I...
I THINK I GOT MUGGED BY A *WEREWOLF.*

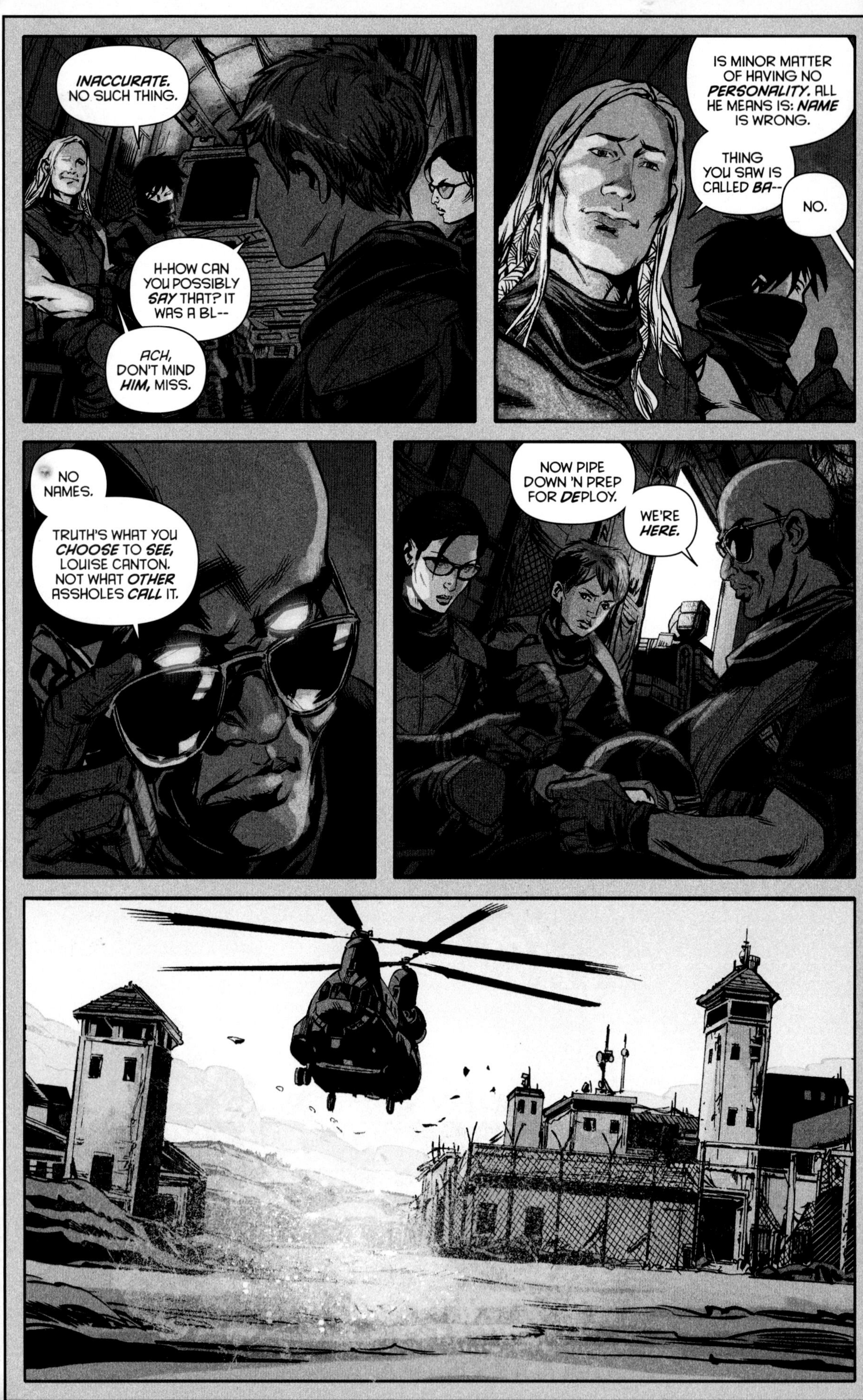
INACCURATE. NO SUCH THING.
H-HOW CAN YOU POSSIBLY SAY THAT? IT WAS A BL--
ACH, DON'T MIND HIM, MISS.
IS MINOR MATTER OF HAVING NO PERSONALITY. ALL HE MEANS IS: NAME IS WRONG.
THING YOU SAW IS CALLED BA--
NO.
NO NAMES.
TRUTH'S WHAT YOU CHOOSE TO SEE, LOUISE CANTON. NOT WHAT OTHER ASSHOLES CALL IT.
NOW PIPE DOWN 'N PREP FOR DEPLOY.
WE'RE HERE.

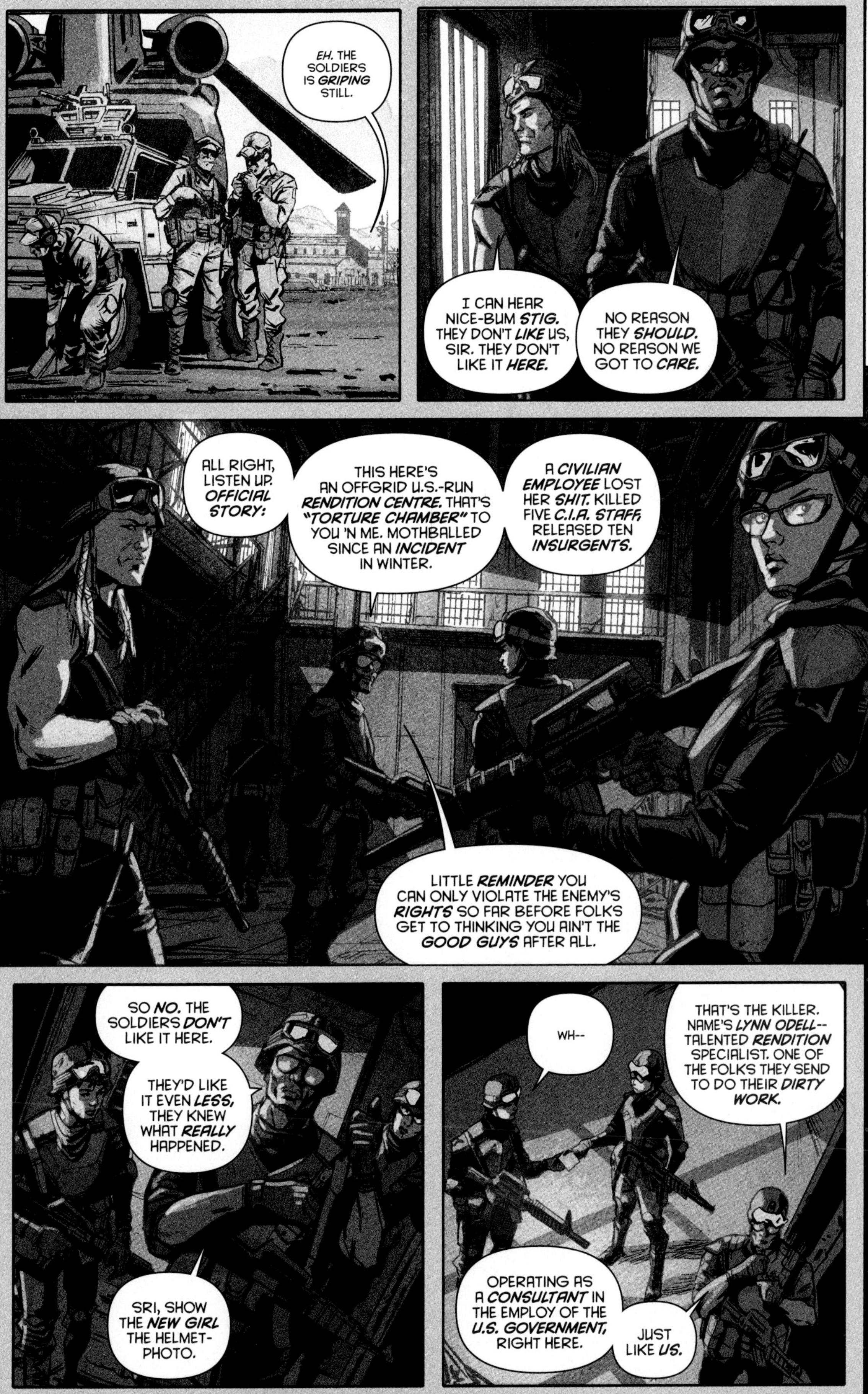

EH. THE SOLDIERS IS GRIPING STILL.
I CAN HEAR NICE-BUM STIG. THEY DON'T LIKE US, SIR. THEY DON'T LIKE IT HERE.
NO REASON THEY SHOULD. NO REASON WE GOT TO CARE.
ALL RIGHT, LISTEN UP. OFFICIAL STORY:
THIS HERE'S AN OFFGRID U.S.-RUN RENDITION CENTRE. THAT'S "TORTURE CHAMBER" TO YOU 'N ME. MOTHBALLED SINCE AN INCIDENT IN WINTER.
A CIVILIAN EMPLOYEE LOST HER SHIT. KILLED FIVE C.I.A. STAFF, RELEASED TEN INSURGENTS.
LITTLE REMINDER YOU CAN ONLY VIOLATE THE ENEMY'S RIGHTS SO FAR BEFORE FOLKS GET TO THINKING YOU AIN'T THE GOOD GUYS AFTER ALL.
SO NO. THE SOLDIERS DON'T LIKE IT HERE.
THEY'D LIKE IT EVEN LESS, THEY KNEW WHAT REALLY HAPPENED.
SRI, SHOW THE NEW GIRL THE HELMET-PHOTO.
WH--
THAT'S THE KILLER. NAME'S LYNN ODELL-- TALENTED RENDITION SPECIALIST. ONE OF THE FOLKS THEY SEND TO DO THEIR DIRTY WORK.
OPERATING AS A CONSULTANT IN THE EMPLOY OF THE U.S. GOVERNMENT, RIGHT HERE.
JUST LIKE US.

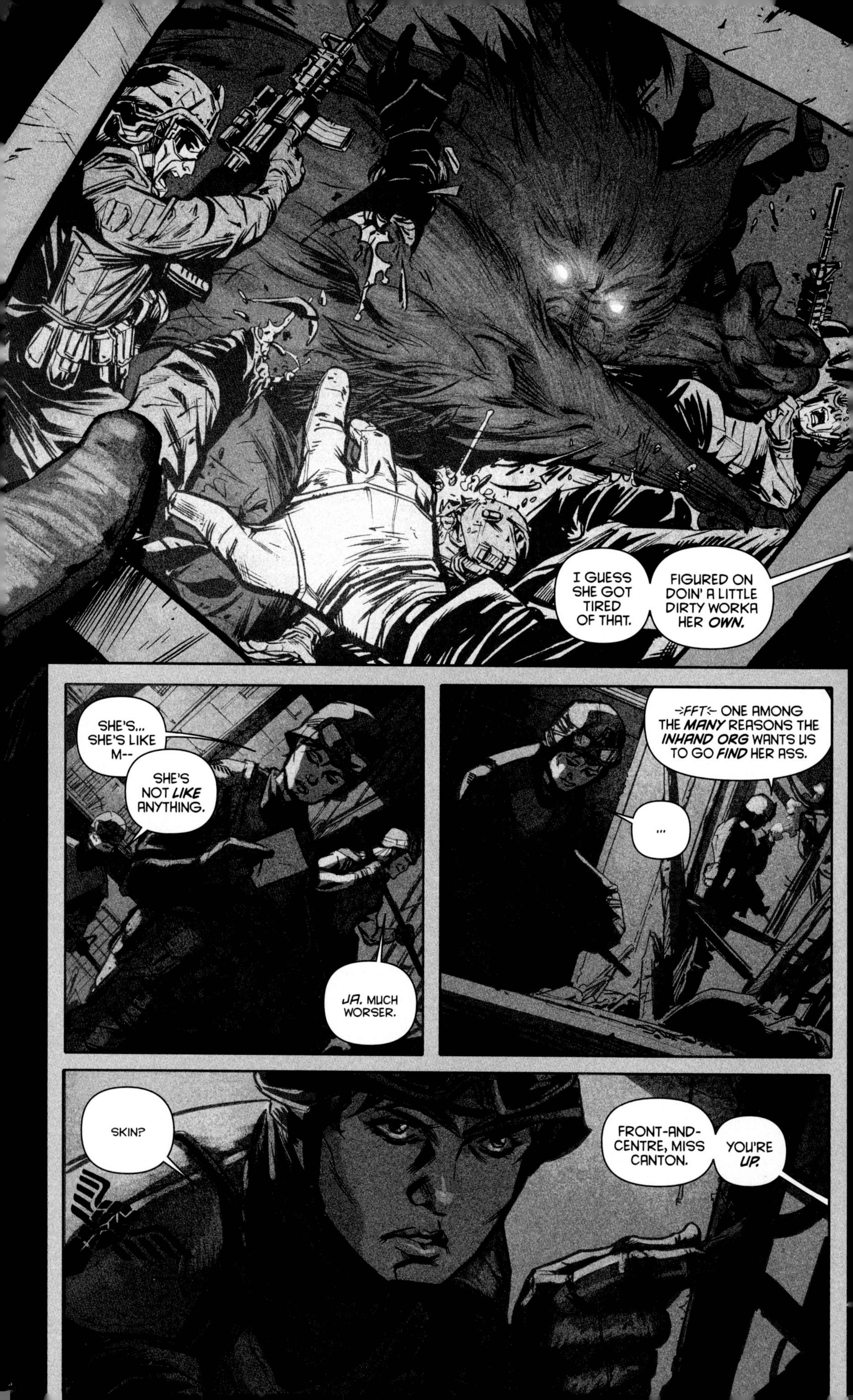
I GUESS SHE GOT TIRED OF THAT.
FIGURED ON DOIN' A LITTLE DIRTY WORKA HER OWN.
SHE'S... SHE'S LIKE M--
SHE'S NOT LIKE ANYTHING.
JA. MUCH WORSER.
FFT ONE AMONG THE MANY REASONS THE INHAND ORG WANTS US TO GO FIND HER ASS.
...
SKIN?
FRONT-AND-CENTRE, MISS CANTON.
YOU'RE UP.

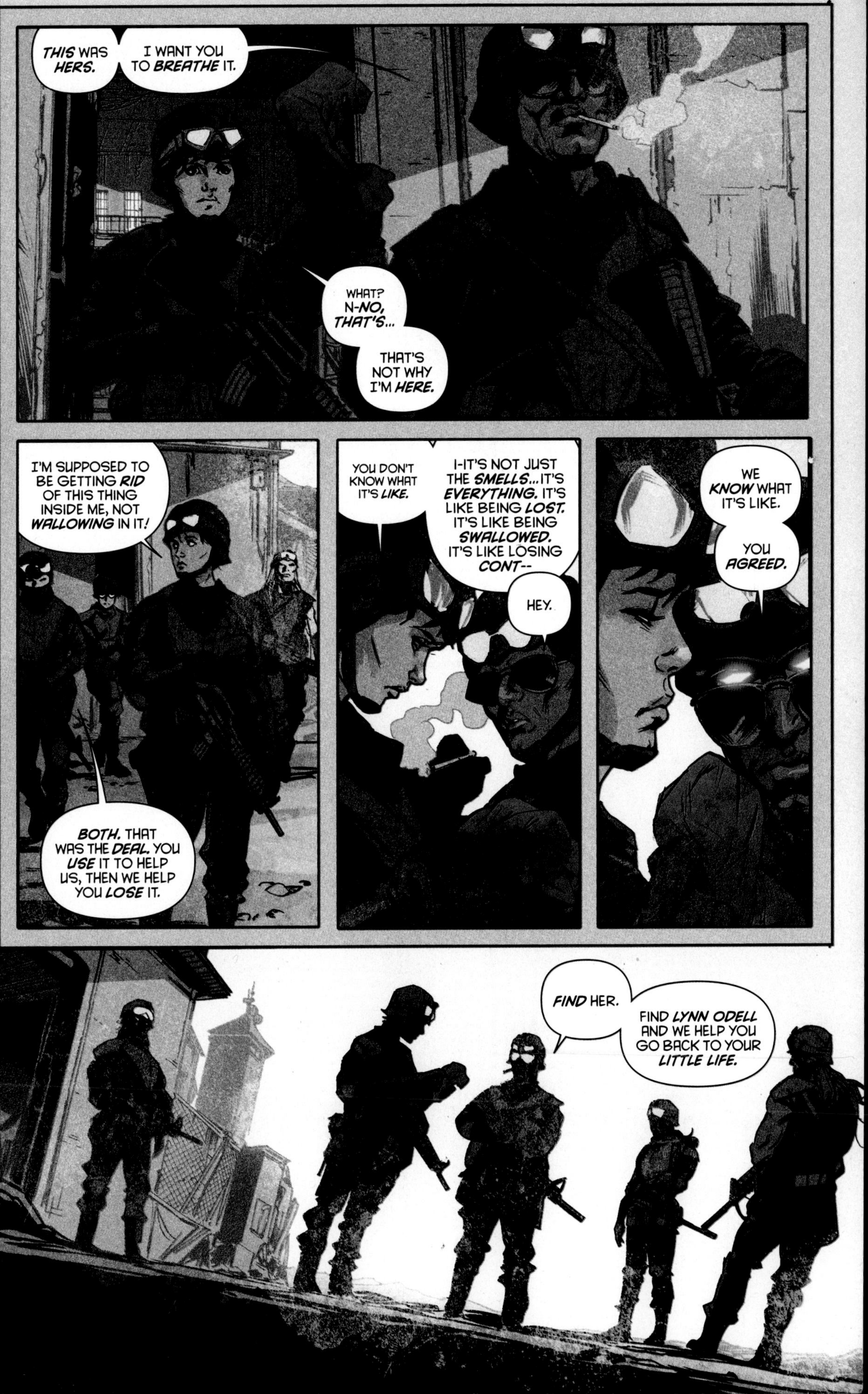
THIS WAS HERS.
I WANT YOU TO BREATHE IT.
WHAT? N-NO, THAT'S...
THAT'S NOT WHY I'M HERE.
I'M SUPPOSED TO BE GETTING RID OF THIS THING INSIDE ME, NOT WALLOWING IN IT!
BOTH. THAT WAS THE DEAL. YOU USE IT TO HELP US, THEN WE HELP YOU LOSE IT.
YOU DON'T KNOW WHAT IT'S LIKE.
I-IT'S NOT JUST THE SMELLS...IT'S EVERYTHING. IT'S LIKE BEING LOST. IT'S LIKE BEING SWALLOWED. IT'S LIKE LOSING CONT--
HEY.
WE KNOW WHAT IT'S LIKE.
YOU AGREED.
FIND HER.
FIND LYNN ODELL AND WE HELP YOU GO BACK TO YOUR LITTLE LIFE.

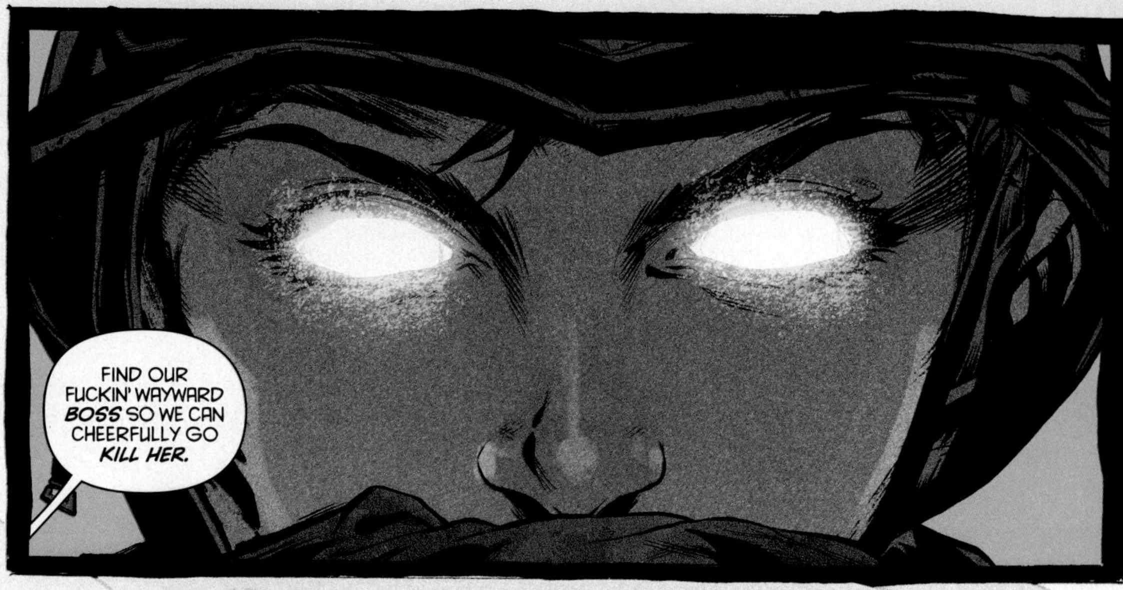
FIND OUR FUCKIN' WAYWARD **BOSS** SO WE CAN CHEERFULLY GO **KILL HER.**

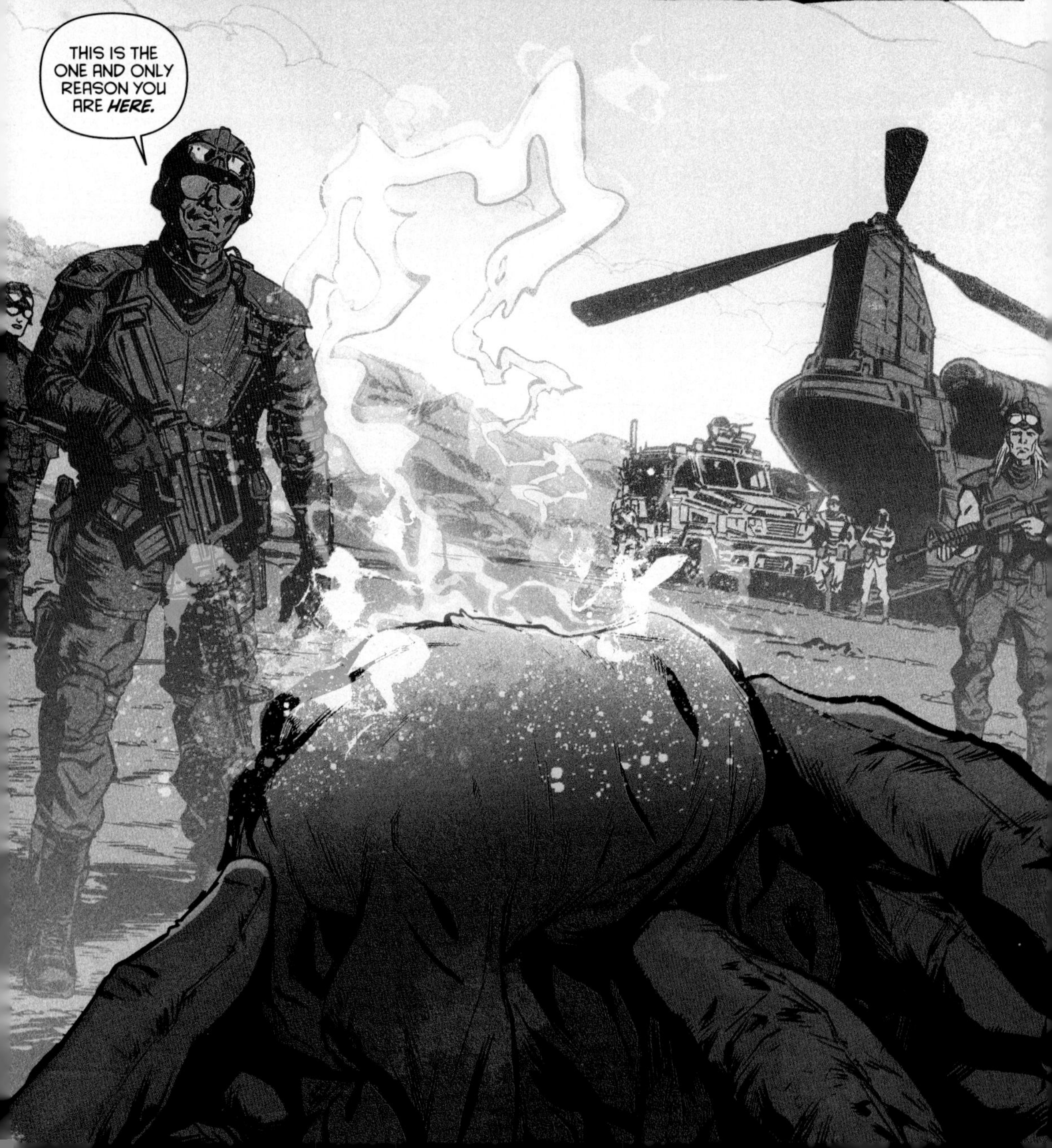
THIS IS THE ONE AND ONLY REASON YOU ARE **HERE.**

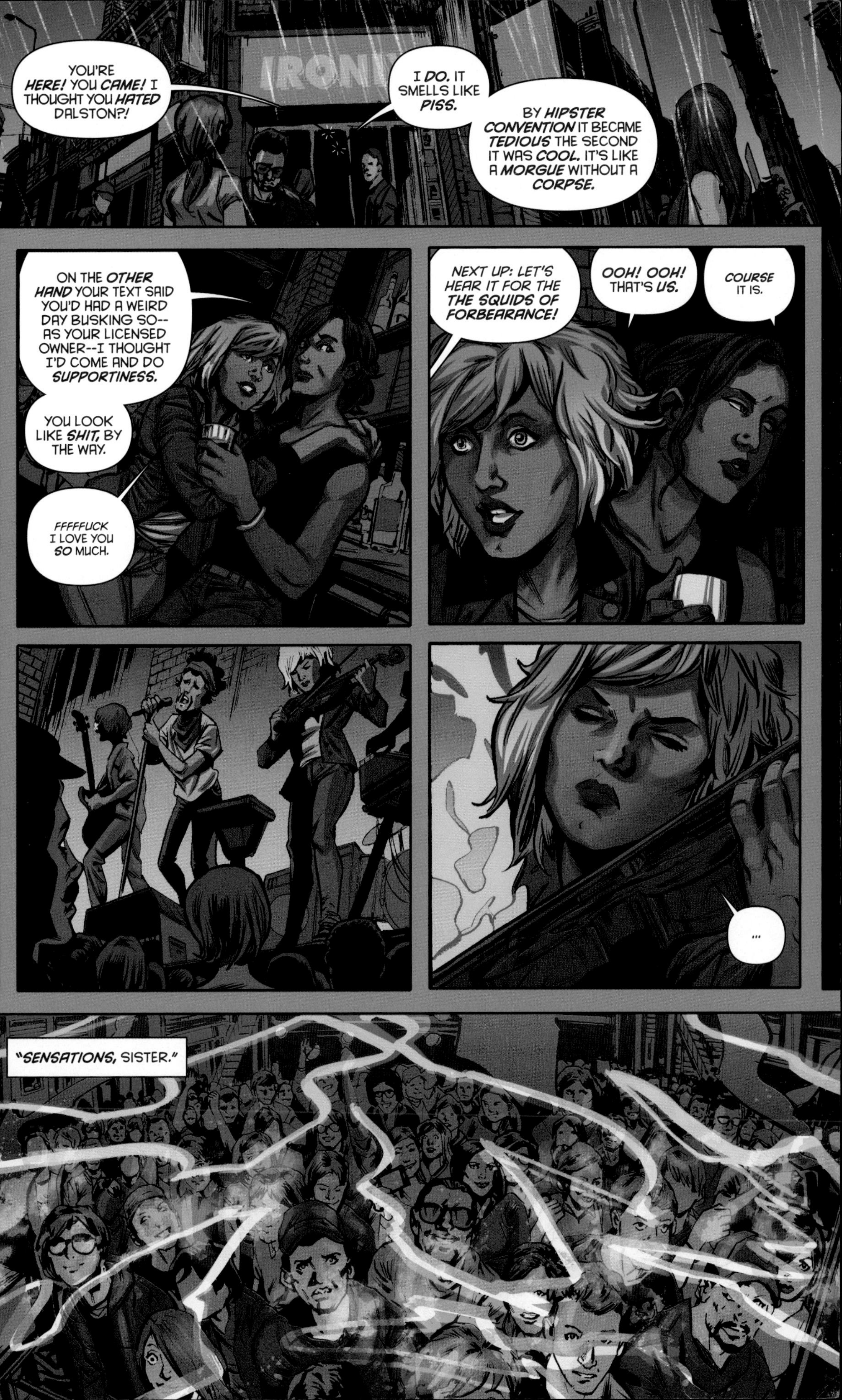

IRON
YOU'RE HERE! YOU CAME! I THOUGHT YOU HATED DALSTON?!
I DO. IT SMELLS LIKE PISS.
BY HIPSTER CONVENTION IT BECAME TEDIOUS THE SECOND IT WAS COOL. IT'S LIKE A MORGUE WITHOUT A CORPSE.
ON THE OTHER HAND YOUR TEXT SAID YOU'D HAD A WEIRD DAY BUSKING SO--AS YOUR LICENSED OWNER--I THOUGHT I'D COME AND DO SUPPORTINESS.
YOU LOOK LIKE SHIT, BY THE WAY.
FFFFFUCK I LOVE YOU SO MUCH.
NEXT UP: LET'S HEAR IT FOR THE THE SQUIDS OF FORBEARANCE!
OOH! OOH! THAT'S US.
COURSE IT IS.
...
"SENSATIONS, SISTER."

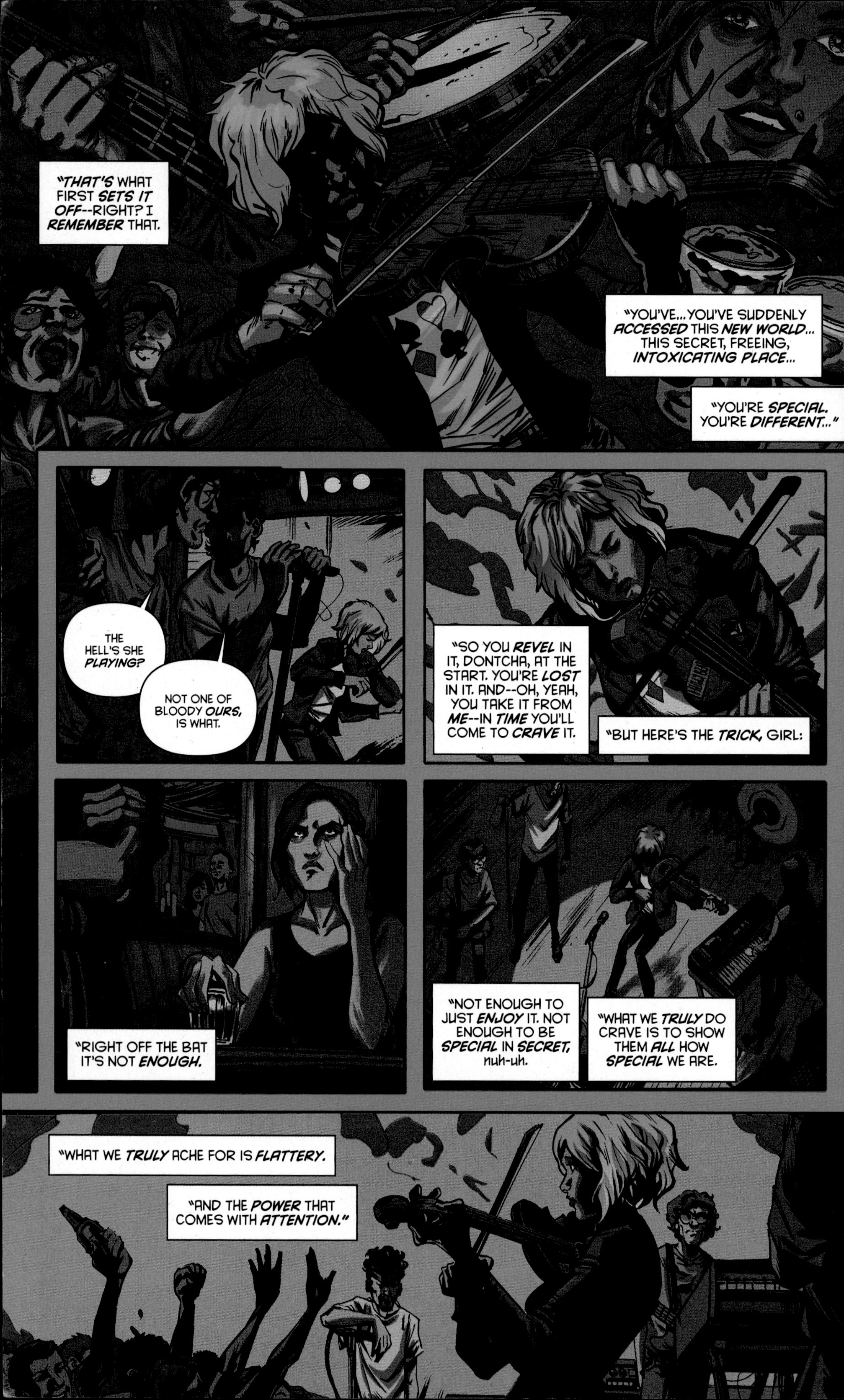
"THAT'S WHAT FIRST SETS IT OFF--RIGHT? I REMEMBER THAT.
"YOU'VE... YOU'VE SUDDENLY ACCESSED THIS NEW WORLD... THIS SECRET, FREEING, INTOXICATING PLACE...
"YOU'RE SPECIAL. YOU'RE DIFFERENT..."
THE HELL'S SHE PLAYING?
NOT ONE OF BLOODY OURS, IS WHAT.
"SO YOU REVEL IN IT, DONTCHA, AT THE START. YOU'RE LOST IN IT. AND--OH, YEAH, YOU TAKE IT FROM ME--IN TIME YOU'LL COME TO CRAVE IT.
"BUT HERE'S THE TRICK, GIRL:
"RIGHT OFF THE BAT IT'S NOT ENOUGH.
"NOT ENOUGH TO JUST ENJOY IT. NOT ENOUGH TO BE SPECIAL IN SECRET, nuh-uh.
"WHAT WE TRULY DO CRAVE IS TO SHOW THEM ALL HOW SPECIAL WE ARE.
"WHAT WE TRULY ACHE FOR IS FLATTERY.
"AND THE POWER THAT COMES WITH ATTENTION."

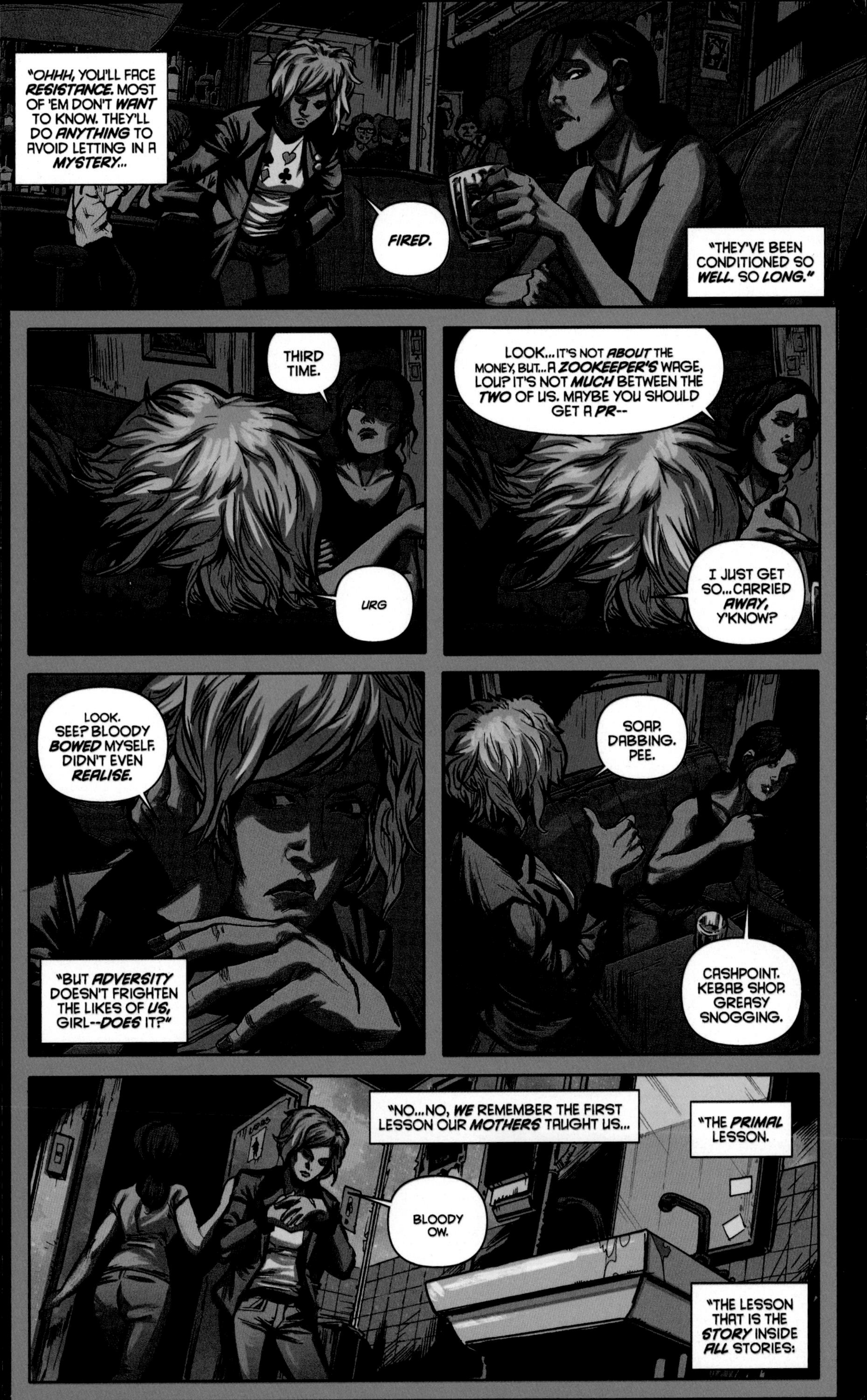
"OHHH, YOU'LL FACE RESISTANCE. MOST OF 'EM DON'T WANT TO KNOW. THEY'LL DO ANYTHING TO AVOID LETTING IN A MYSTERY...
FIRED.
"THEY'VE BEEN CONDITIONED SO WELL. SO LONG."
THIRD TIME.
URG
LOOK...IT'S NOT ABOUT THE MONEY, BUT...A ZOOKEEPER'S WAGE, LOU? IT'S NOT MUCH BETWEEN THE TWO OF US. MAYBE YOU SHOULD GET A PR--
I JUST GET SO...CARRIED AWAY, Y'KNOW?
LOOK. SEE? BLOODY BOWED MYSELF. DIDN'T EVEN REALISE.
"BUT ADVERSITY DOESN'T FRIGHTEN THE LIKES OF US, GIRL--DOES IT?"
SOAP. DABBING. PEE.
CASHPOINT. KEBAB SHOP. GREASY SNOGGING.
"NO...NO, WE REMEMBER THE FIRST LESSON OUR MOTHERS TAUGHT US...
"THE PRIMAL LESSON.
BLOODY OW.
"THE LESSON THAT IS THE STORY INSIDE ALL STORIES:

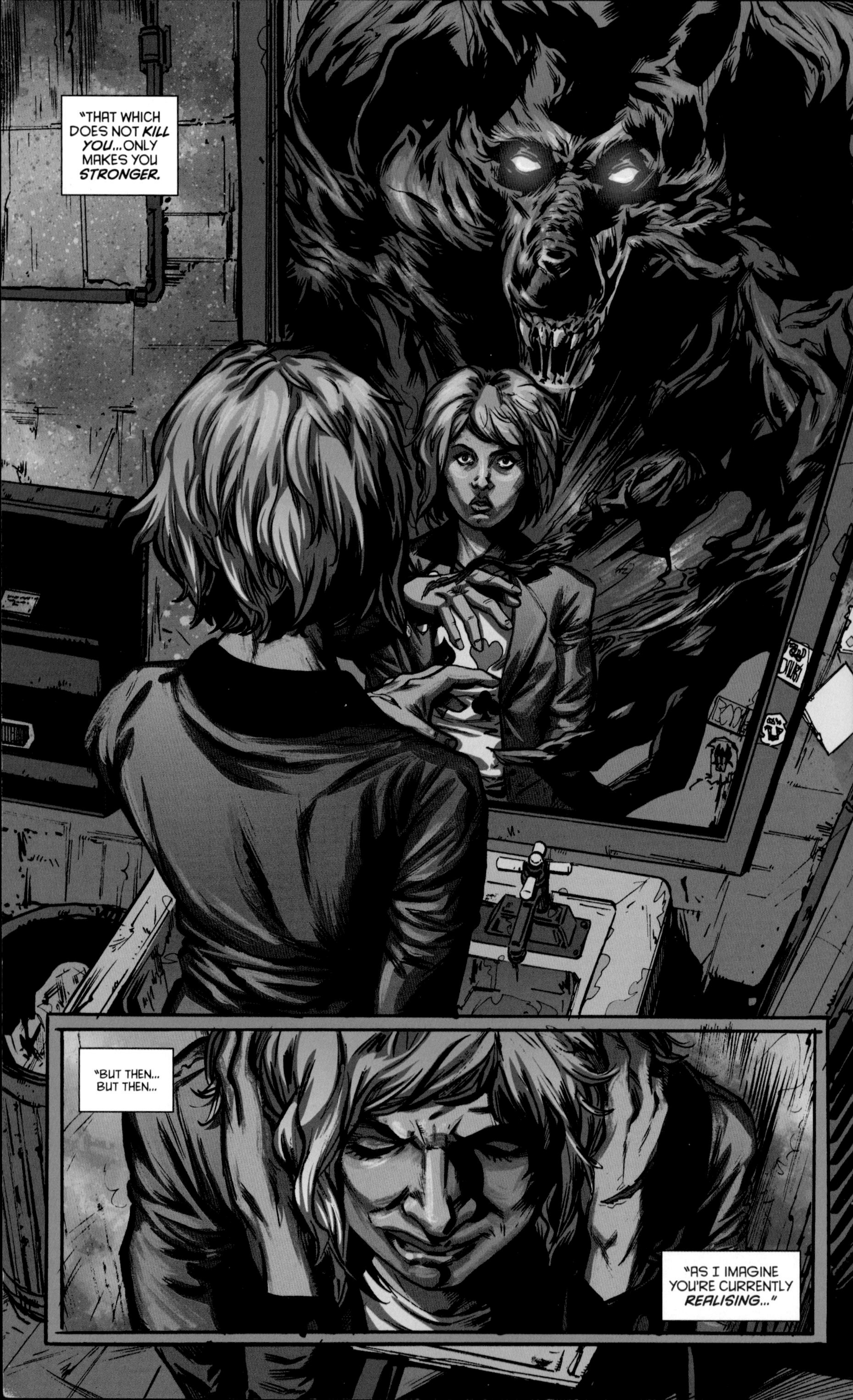
"THAT WHICH DOES NOT *KILL YOU*...ONLY MAKES YOU *STRONGER.*
"BUT THEN... BUT THEN...
"AS I IMAGINE YOU'RE CURRENTLY *REALISING*..."

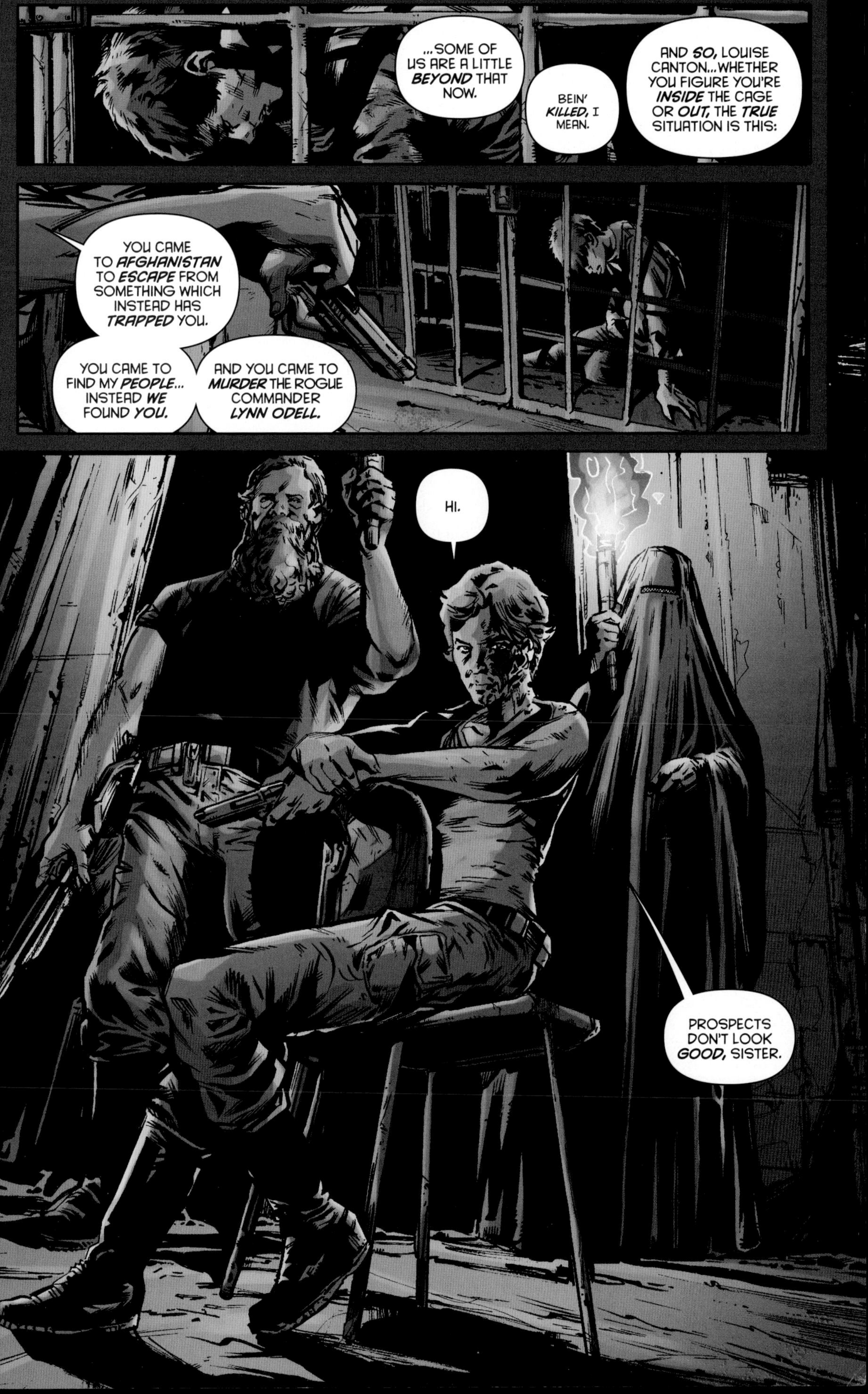
...SOME OF US ARE A LITTLE BEYOND THAT NOW.
BEIN' KILLED, I MEAN.
AND SO, LOUISE CANTON...WHETHER YOU FIGURE YOU'RE INSIDE THE CAGE OR OUT, THE TRUE SITUATION IS THIS:
YOU CAME TO AFGHANISTAN TO ESCAPE FROM SOMETHING WHICH INSTEAD HAS TRAPPED YOU.
YOU CAME TO FIND MY PEOPLE... INSTEAD WE FOUND YOU.
AND YOU CAME TO MURDER THE ROGUE COMMANDER LYNN ODELL.
HI.
PROSPECTS DON'T LOOK GOOD, SISTER.

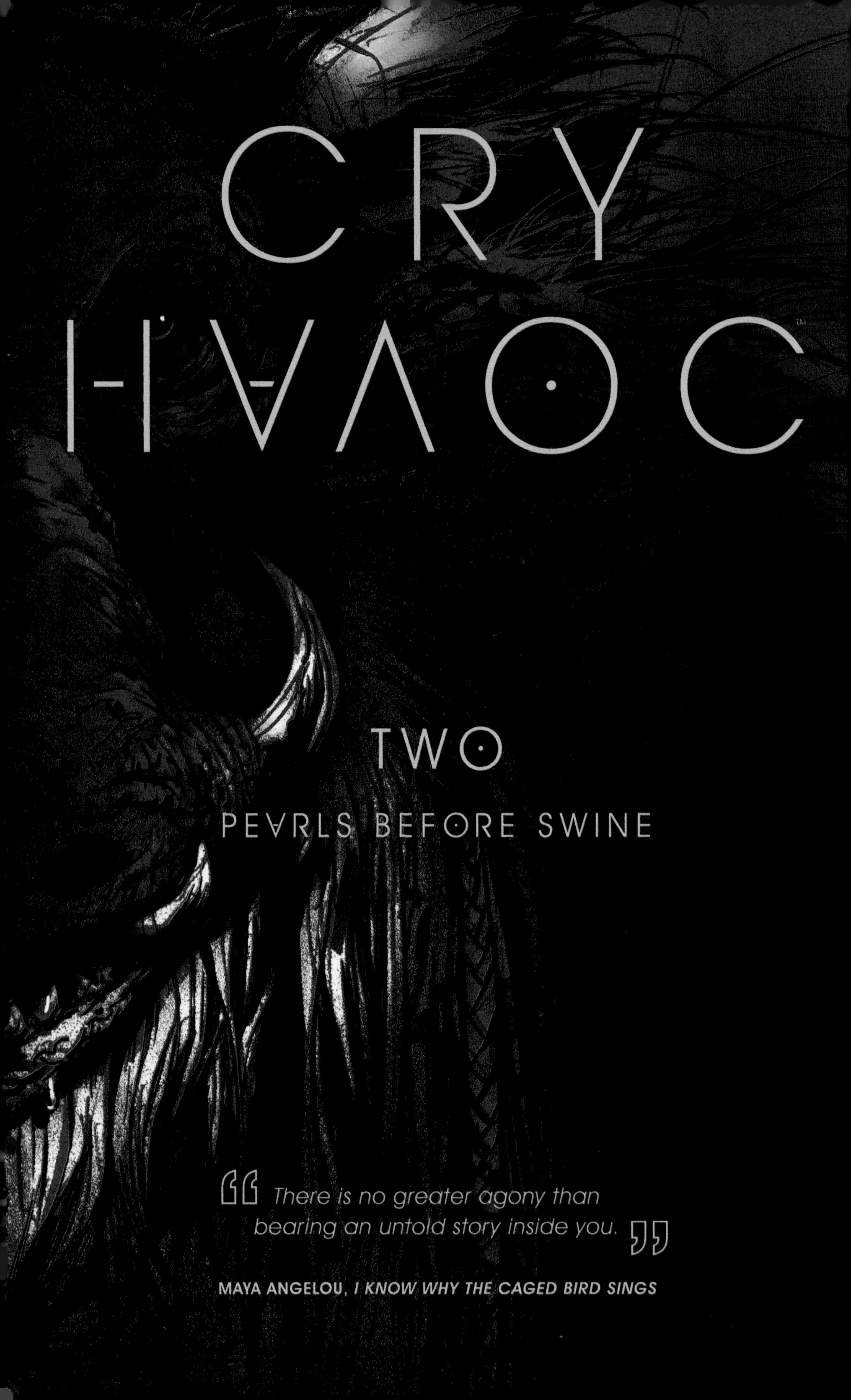

CRY HAVOC

TWO

PEARLS BEFORE SWINE

"There is no greater agony than bearing an untold story inside you."

MAYA ANGELOU, *I KNOW WHY THE CAGED BIRD SINGS*

variant cover
FIONA **STAPLES**

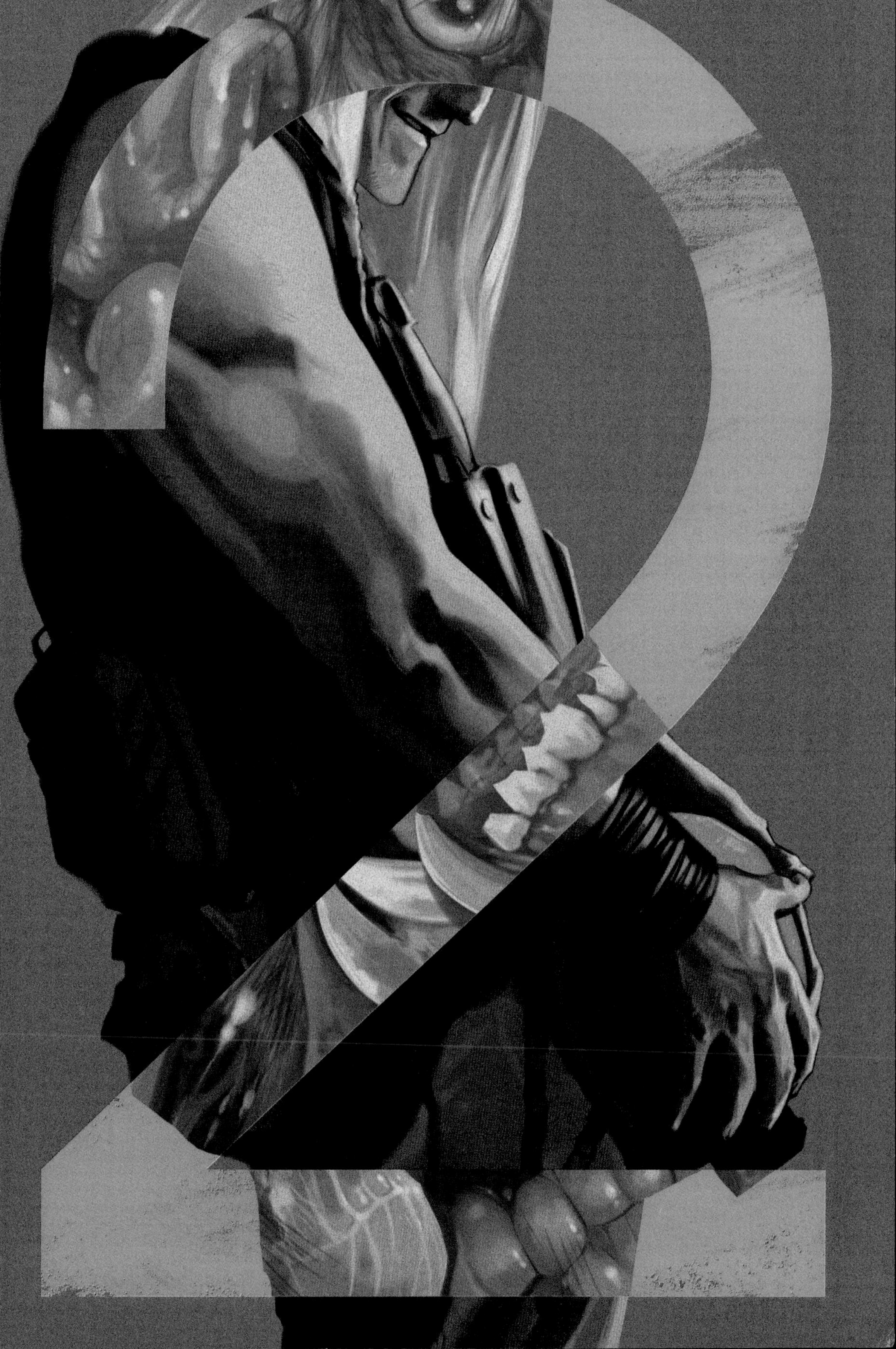

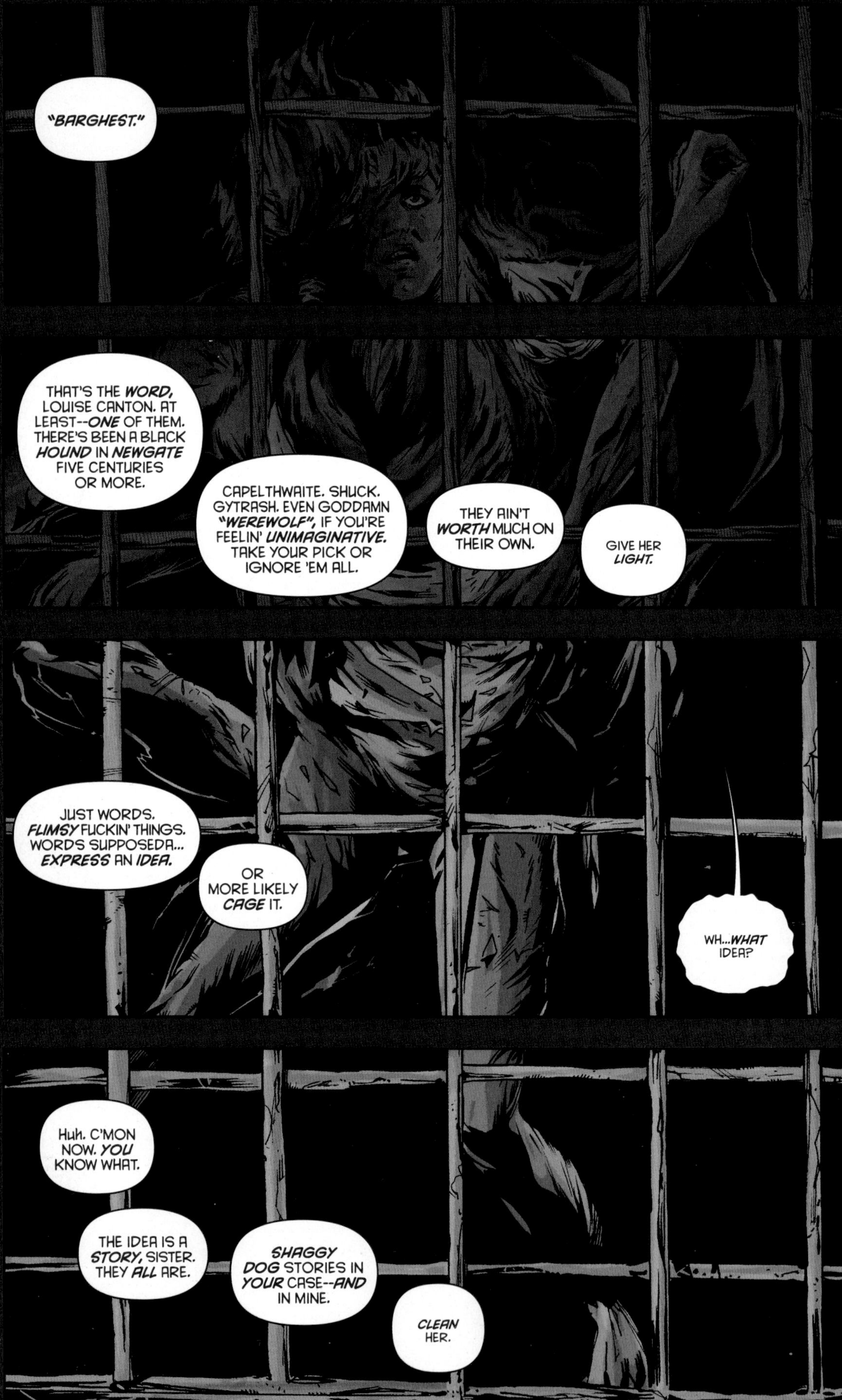
"BARGHEST."
THAT'S THE WORD, LOUISE CANTON. AT LEAST--ONE OF THEM. THERE'S BEEN A BLACK HOUND IN NEWGATE FIVE CENTURIES OR MORE.
CAPELTHWAITE. SHUCK. GYTRASH. EVEN GODDAMN "WEREWOLF", IF YOU'RE FEELIN' UNIMAGINATIVE. TAKE YOUR PICK OR IGNORE 'EM ALL.
THEY AIN'T WORTH MUCH ON THEIR OWN.
GIVE HER LIGHT.
JUST WORDS. FLIMSY FUCKIN' THINGS. WORDS SUPPOSEDA... EXPRESS AN IDEA.
OR MORE LIKELY CAGE IT.
WH...WHAT IDEA?
Huh. C'MON NOW. YOU KNOW WHAT.
THE IDEA IS A STORY, SISTER. THEY ALL ARE.
SHAGGY DOG STORIES IN YOUR CASE--AND IN MINE.
CLEAN HER.

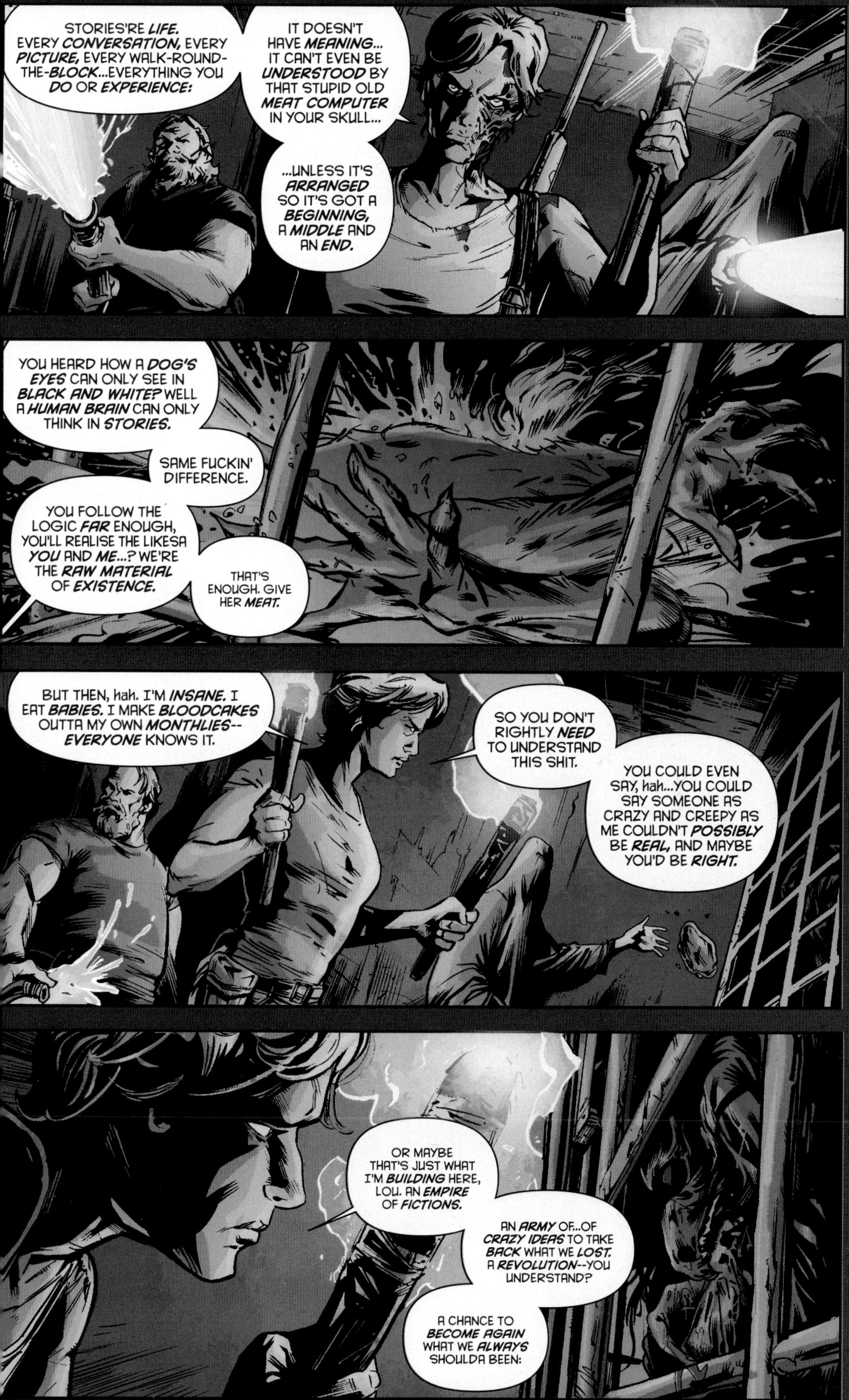
STORIES'RE LIFE. EVERY CONVERSATION, EVERY PICTURE, EVERY WALK-ROUND-THE-BLOCK...EVERYTHING YOU DO OR EXPERIENCE:
IT DOESN'T HAVE MEANING... IT CAN'T EVEN BE UNDERSTOOD BY THAT STUPID OLD MEAT COMPUTER IN YOUR SKULL...
...UNLESS IT'S ARRANGED SO IT'S GOT A BEGINNING, A MIDDLE AND AN END.
YOU HEARD HOW A DOG'S EYES CAN ONLY SEE IN BLACK AND WHITE? WELL A HUMAN BRAIN CAN ONLY THINK IN STORIES.
SAME FUCKIN' DIFFERENCE.
YOU FOLLOW THE LOGIC FAR ENOUGH, YOU'LL REALISE THE LIKESA YOU AND ME...? WE'RE THE RAW MATERIAL OF EXISTENCE.
THAT'S ENOUGH. GIVE HER MEAT.
BUT THEN, hah. I'M INSANE. I EAT BABIES. I MAKE BLOODCAKES OUTTA MY OWN MONTHLIES--EVERYONE KNOWS IT.
SO YOU DON'T RIGHTLY NEED TO UNDERSTAND THIS SHIT.
YOU COULD EVEN SAY, hah...YOU COULD SAY SOMEONE AS CRAZY AND CREEPY AS ME COULDN'T POSSIBLY BE REAL, AND MAYBE YOU'D BE RIGHT.
OR MAYBE THAT'S JUST WHAT I'M BUILDING HERE, LOU. AN EMPIRE OF FICTIONS.
AN ARMY OF...OF CRAZY IDEAS TO TAKE BACK WHAT WE LOST. A REVOLUTION--YOU UNDERSTAND?
A CHANCE TO BECOME AGAIN WHAT WE ALWAYS SHOULDA BEEN:

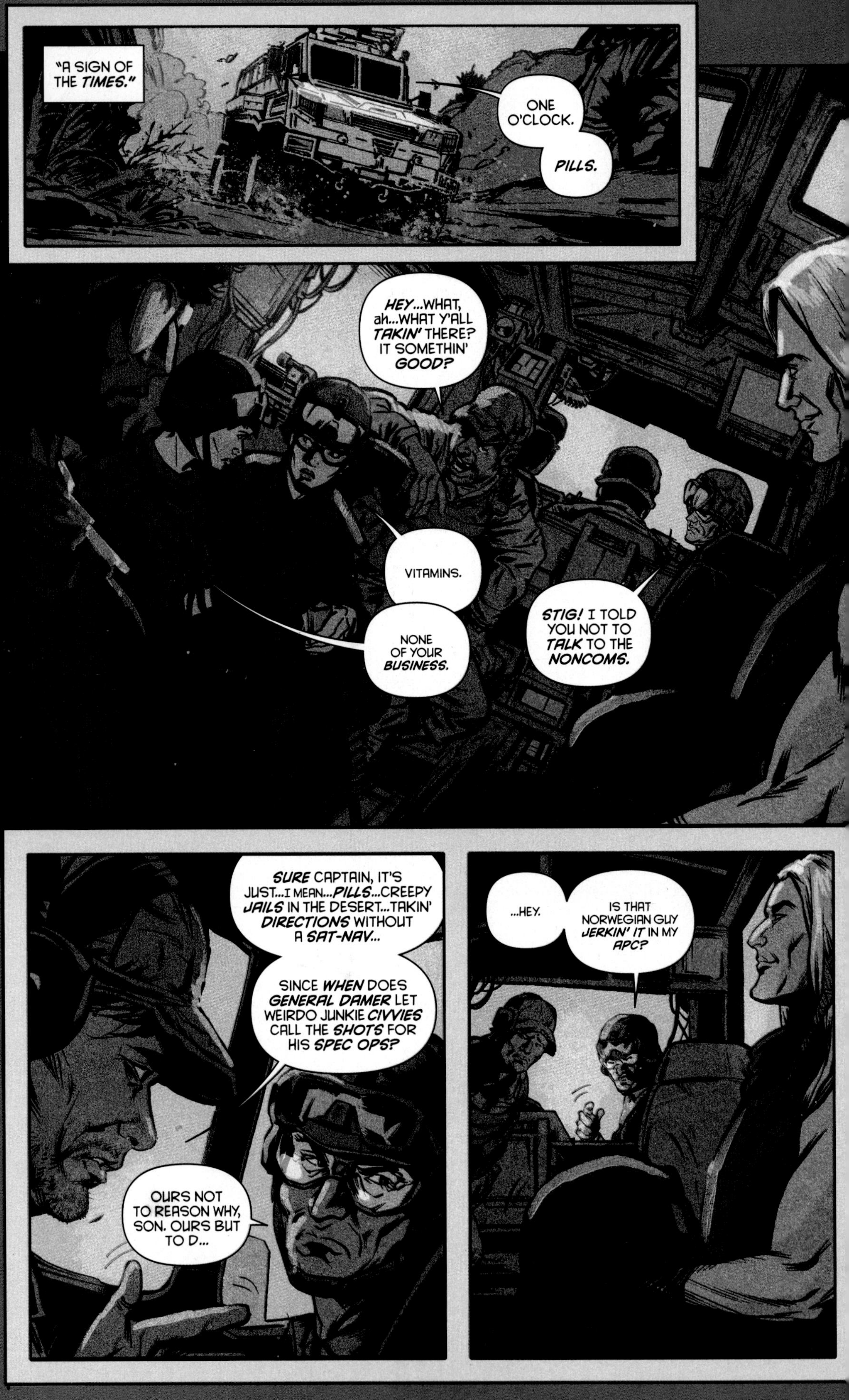
"A SIGN OF THE *TIMES.*"
ONE O'CLOCK.
PILLS.
HEY...WHAT, ah...WHAT Y'ALL *TAKIN'* THERE? IT SOMETHIN' *GOOD?*
VITAMINS.
NONE OF YOUR *BUSINESS.*
STIG! I TOLD YOU NOT TO *TALK* TO THE *NONCOMS.*
SURE CAPTAIN, IT'S JUST...I MEAN...*PILLS*...CREEPY *JAILS* IN THE DESERT...TAKIN' *DIRECTIONS* WITHOUT A *SAT-NAV*...
SINCE *WHEN* DOES *GENERAL DAMER* LET WEIRDO JUNKIE *CIVVIES* CALL THE *SHOTS* FOR HIS *SPEC OPS?*
OURS NOT TO REASON WHY, SON. OURS BUT TO D...
...HEY.
IS THAT NORWEGIAN GUY *JERKIN' IT* IN MY *APC?*

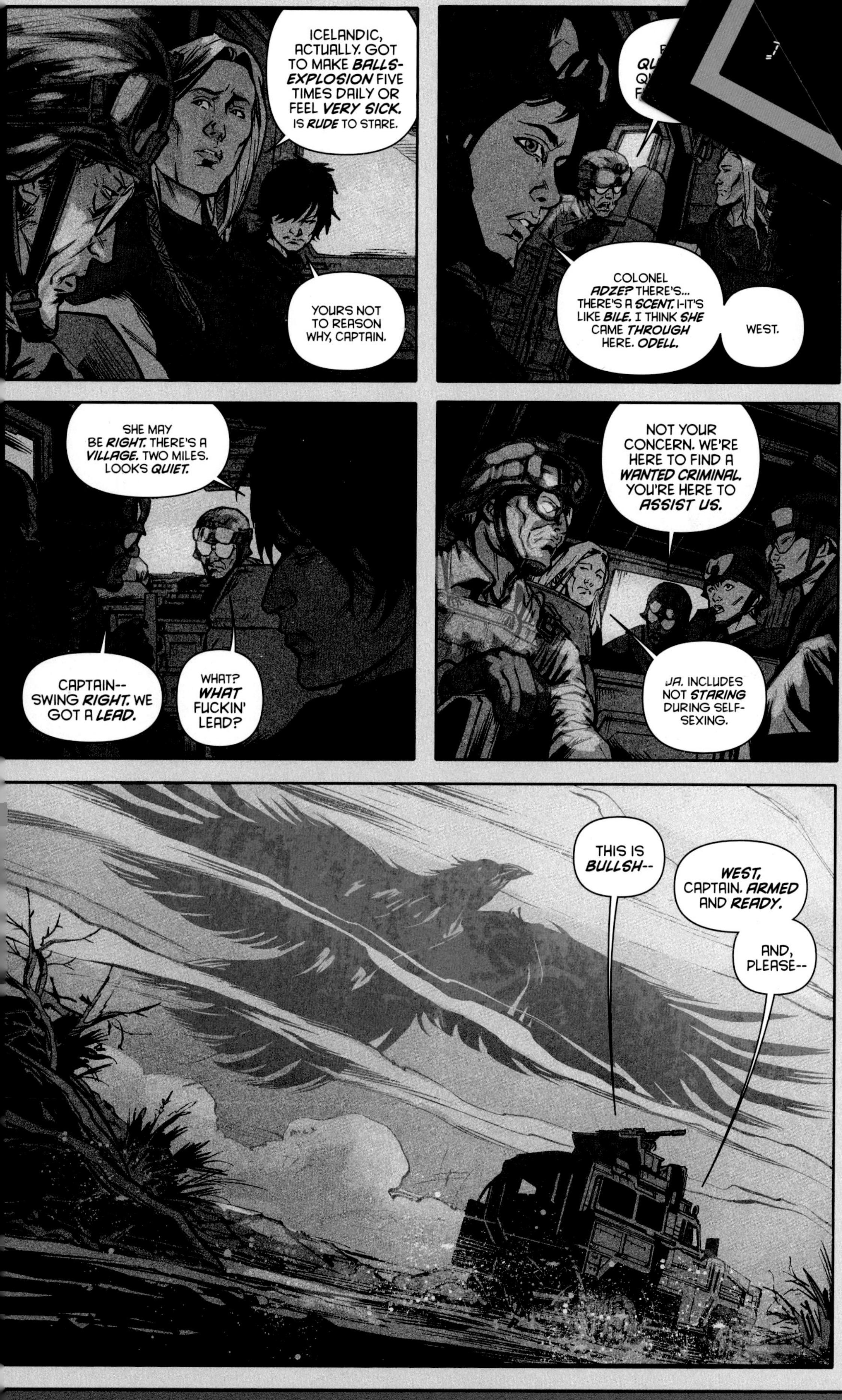
ICELANDIC, ACTUALLY. GOT TO MAKE BALLS-EXPLOSION FIVE TIMES DAILY OR FEEL VERY SICK. IS RUDE TO STARE.
YOURS NOT TO REASON WHY, CAPTAIN.
COLONEL ADZE? THERE'S... THERE'S A SCENT. I-IT'S LIKE BILE. I THINK SHE CAME THROUGH HERE. ODELL.
WEST.
SHE MAY BE RIGHT. THERE'S A VILLAGE. TWO MILES. LOOKS QUIET.
CAPTAIN-- SWING RIGHT. WE GOT A LEAD.
WHAT? WHAT FUCKIN' LEAD?
NOT YOUR CONCERN. WE'RE HERE TO FIND A WANTED CRIMINAL. YOU'RE HERE TO ASSIST US.
JA. INCLUDES NOT STARING DURING SELF-SEXING.
THIS IS BULLSH--
WEST, CAPTAIN. ARMED AND READY.
AND, PLEASE--

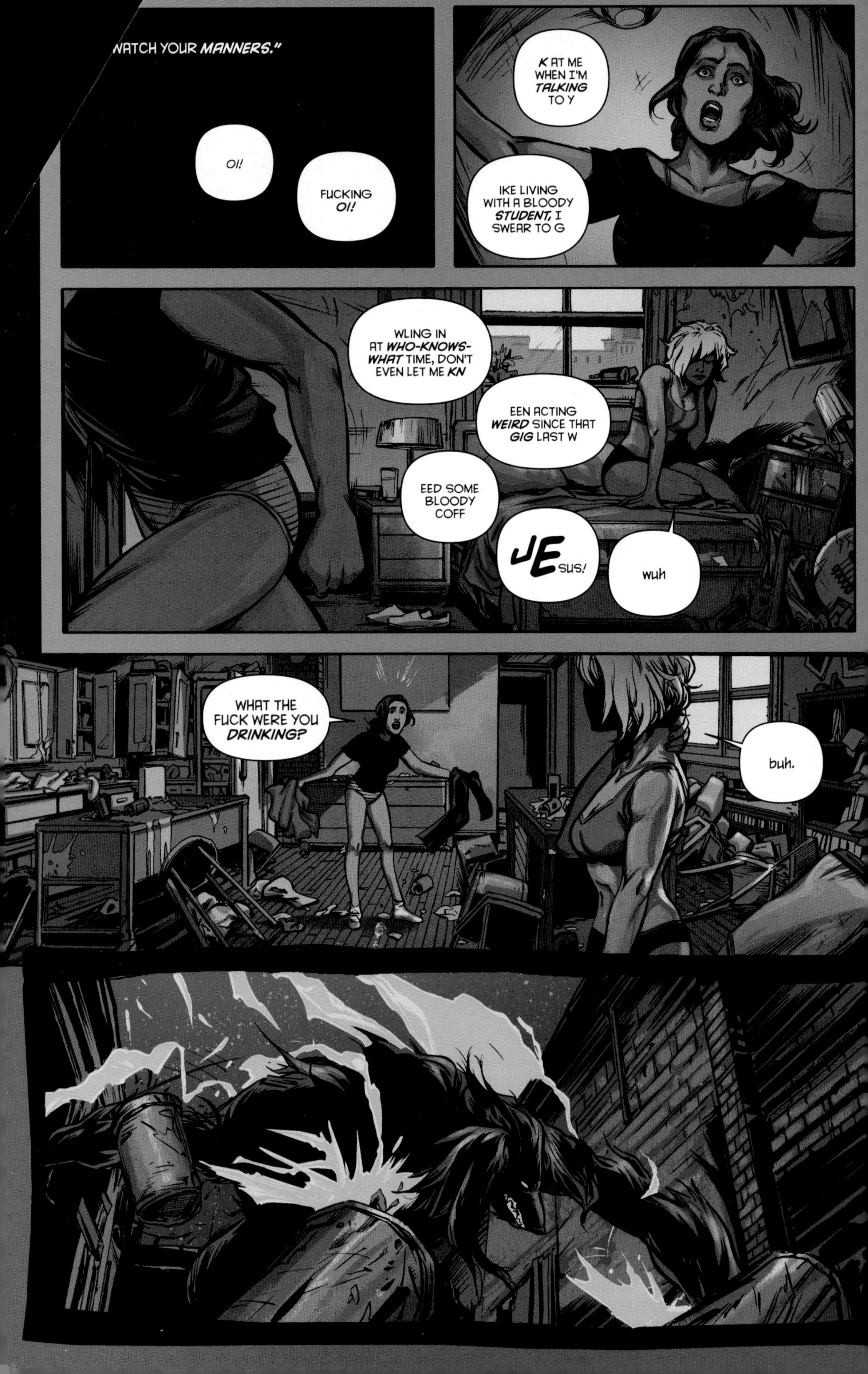
WATCH YOUR *MANNERS.*"
OI!
FUCKING *OI!*
K AT ME WHEN I'M *TALKING* TO Y
IKE LIVING WITH A BLOODY *STUDENT,* I SWEAR TO G
WLING IN AT *WHO-KNOWS-WHAT* TIME, DON'T EVEN LET ME *KN*
EEN ACTING *WEIRD* SINCE THAT *GIG* LAST W
EED SOME BLOODY COFF
JEsus!
wuh
WHAT THE FUCK WERE YOU *DRINKING?*
buh.

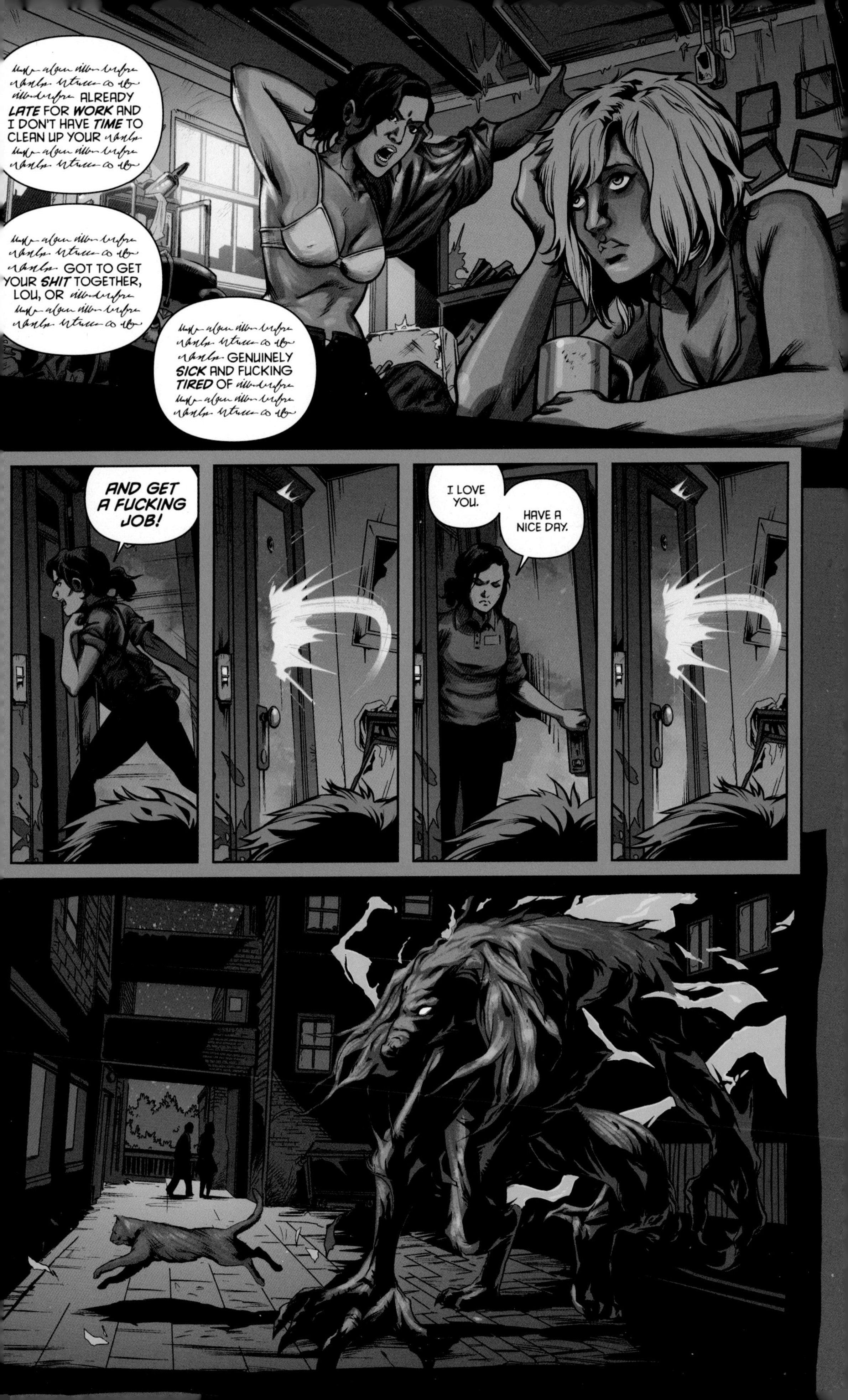
ALREADY LATE FOR WORK AND I DON'T HAVE TIME TO CLEAN UP YOUR
GOT TO GET YOUR SHIT TOGETHER, LOU, OR
GENUINELY SICK AND FUCKING TIRED OF
AND GET A FUCKING JOB!
I LOVE YOU.
HAVE A NICE DAY.

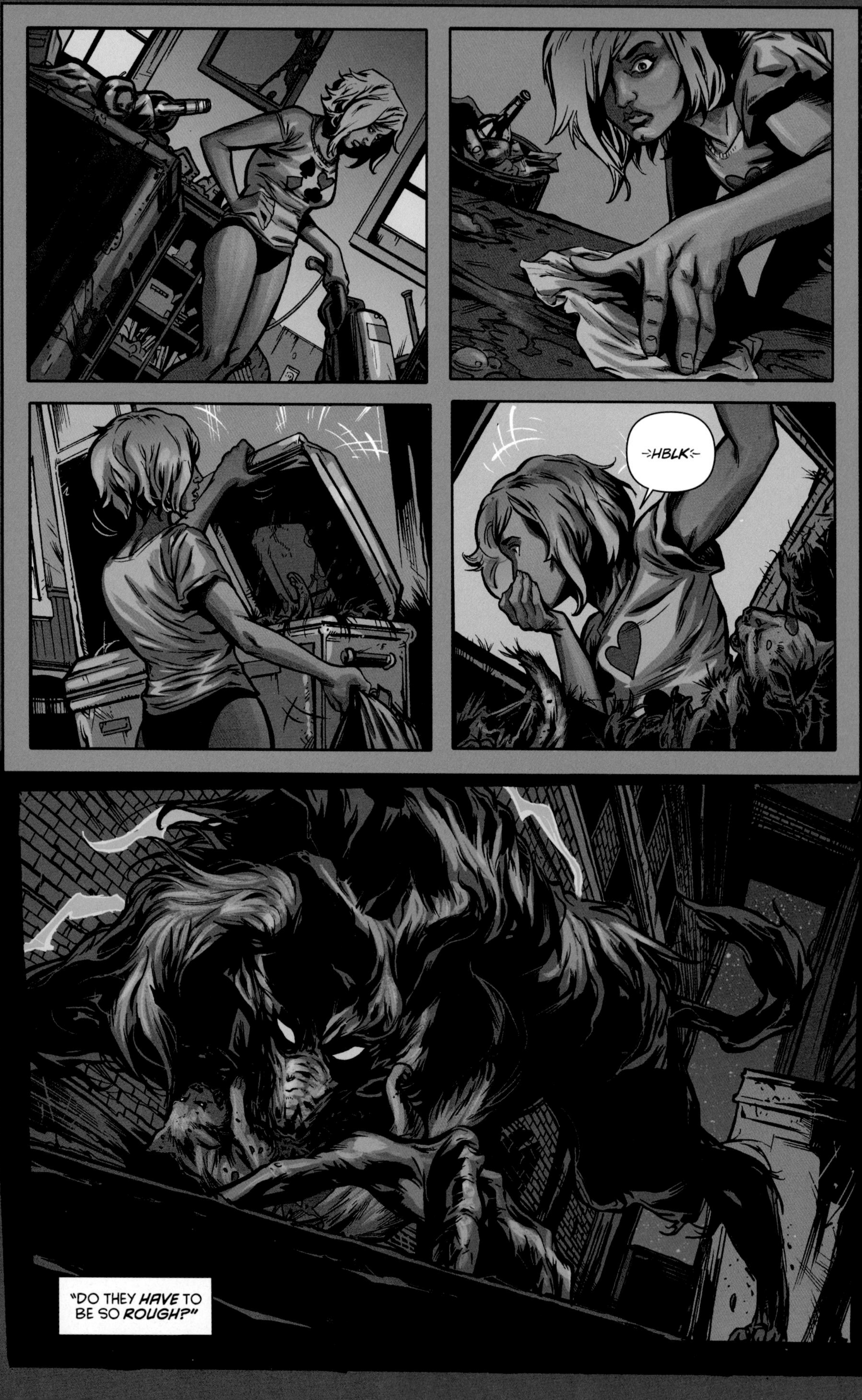

HBLK
"DO THEY *HAVE* TO BE SO *ROUGH?*"

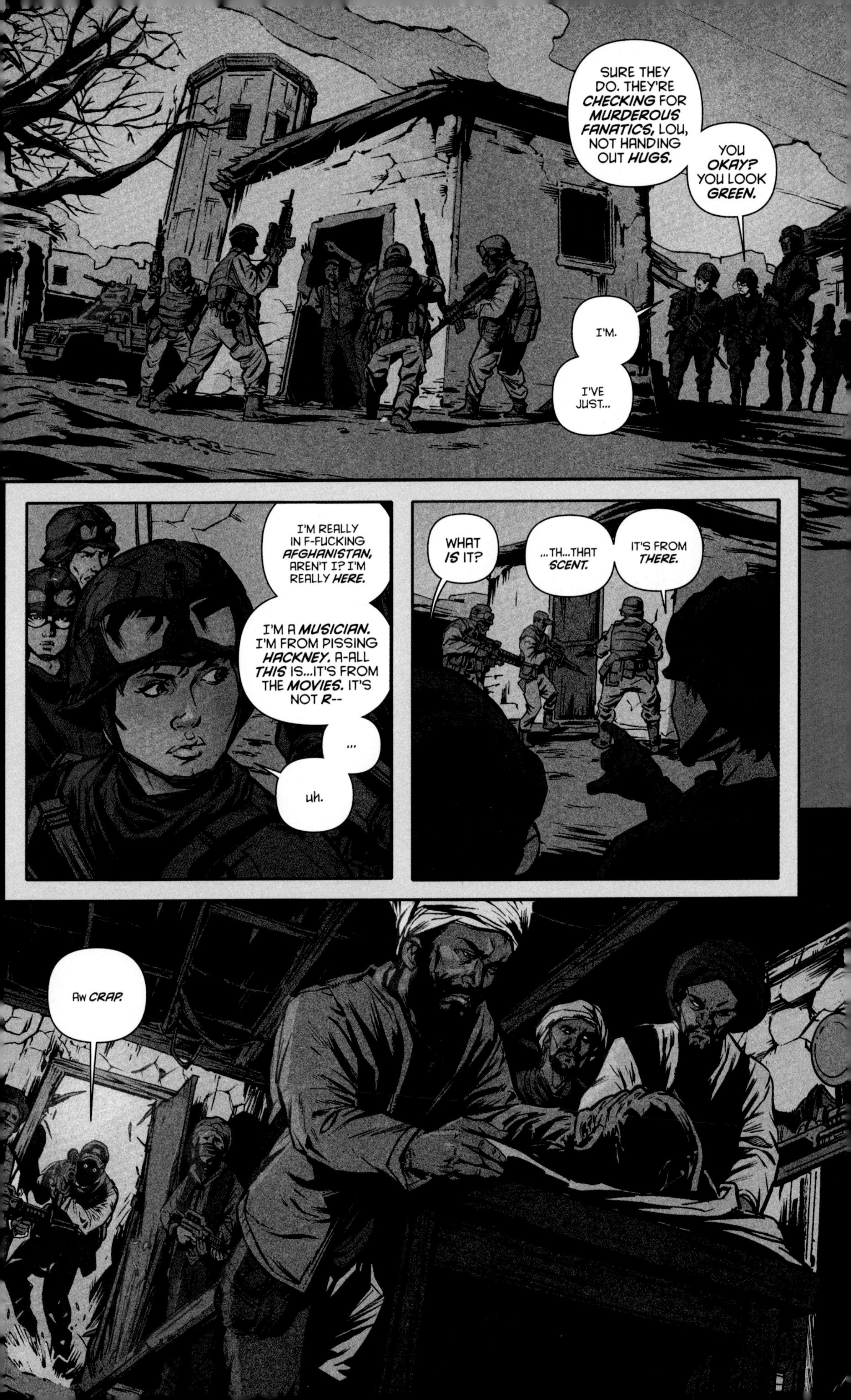

SURE THEY DO. THEY'RE CHECKING FOR MURDEROUS FANATICS, LOU, NOT HANDING OUT HUGS.
YOU OKAY? YOU LOOK GREEN.
I'M.
I'VE JUST...
I'M REALLY IN F-FUCKING AFGHANISTAN, AREN'T I? I'M REALLY HERE.
I'M A MUSICIAN. I'M FROM PISSING HACKNEY. A-ALL THIS IS...IT'S FROM THE MOVIES. IT'S NOT R--
...
UH.
WHAT IS IT?
...TH...THAT SCENT.
IT'S FROM THERE.
AW CRAP.

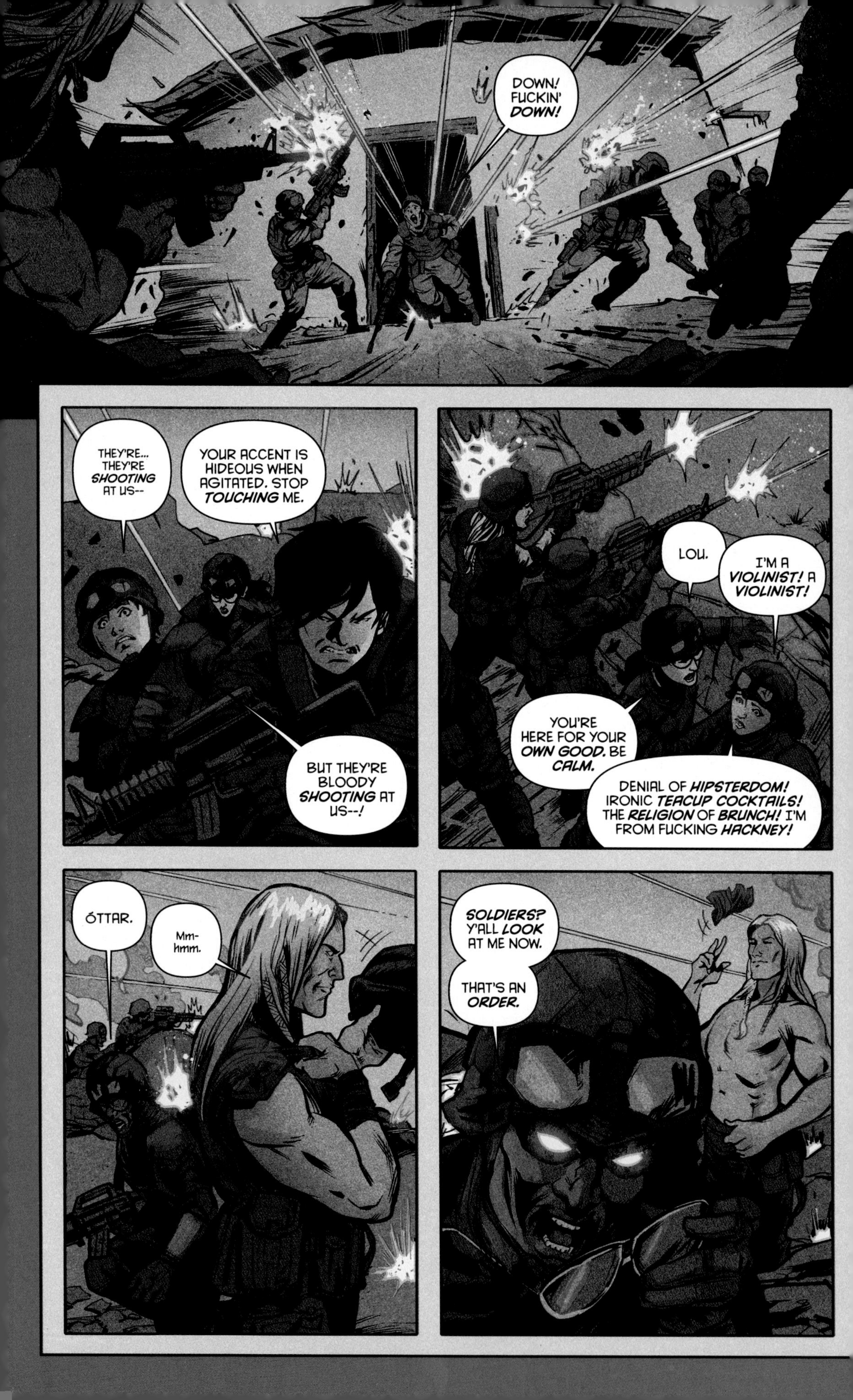
DOWN! FUCKIN' DOWN!
THEY'RE... THEY'RE SHOOTING AT US--
YOUR ACCENT IS HIDEOUS WHEN AGITATED. STOP TOUCHING ME.
BUT THEY'RE BLOODY SHOOTING AT US--!
LOU.
I'M A VIOLINIST! A VIOLINIST!
YOU'RE HERE FOR YOUR OWN GOOD. BE CALM.
DENIAL OF HIPSTERDOM! IRONIC TEACUP COCKTAILS! THE RELIGION OF BRUNCH! I'M FROM FUCKING HACKNEY!
ÓTTAR.
Mm-hmm.
SOLDIERS? Y'ALL LOOK AT ME NOW.
THAT'S AN ORDER.

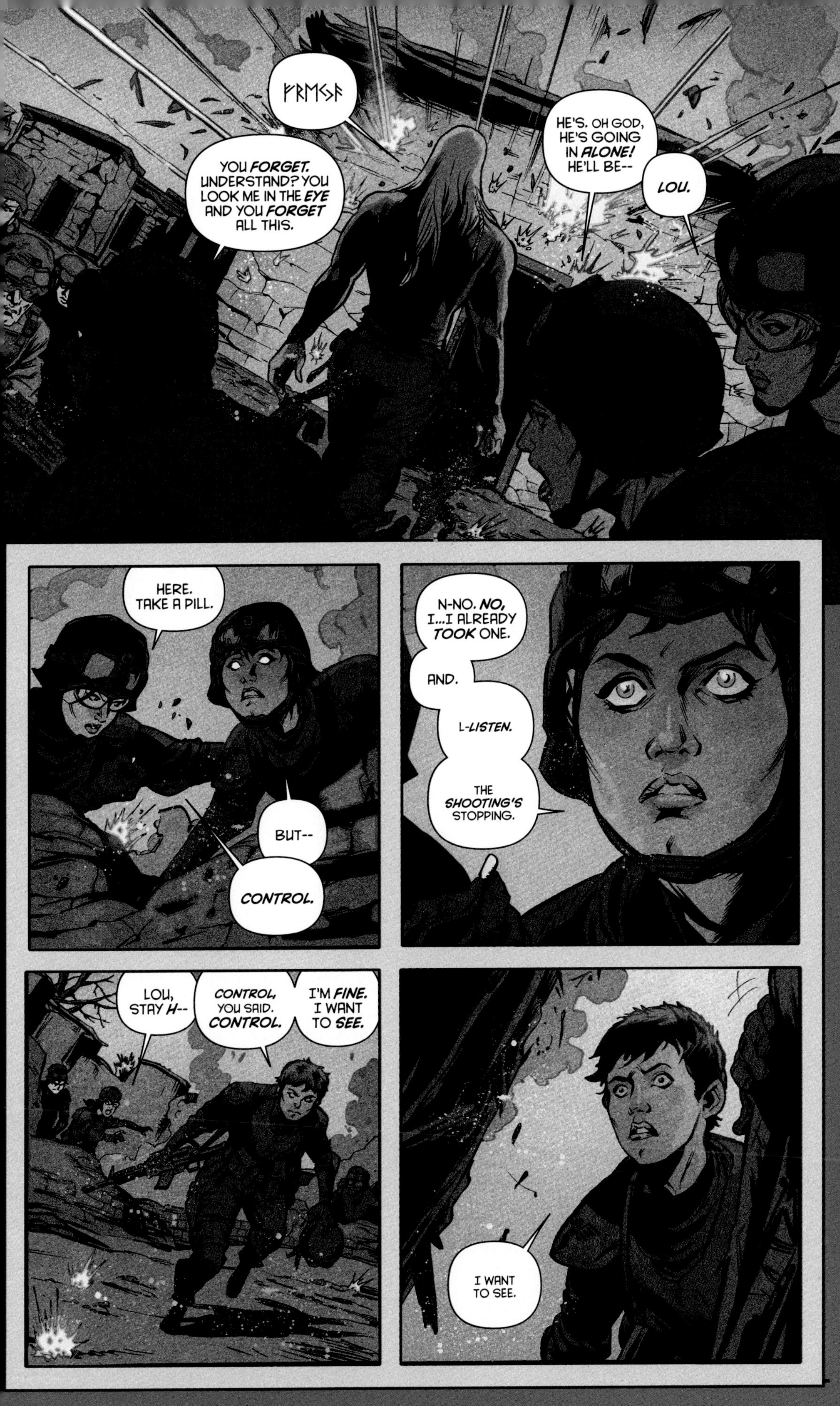

YOU FORGET. UNDERSTAND? YOU LOOK ME IN THE EYE AND YOU FORGET ALL THIS.
HE'S. OH GOD, HE'S GOING IN ALONE! HE'LL BE--
LOU.
HERE. TAKE A PILL.
BUT--
CONTROL.
N-NO. NO, I...I ALREADY TOOK ONE.
AND.
L-LISTEN.
THE SHOOTING'S STOPPING.
LOU, STAY H--
CONTROL, YOU SAID. CONTROL.
I'M FINE. I WANT TO SEE.
I WANT TO SEE.

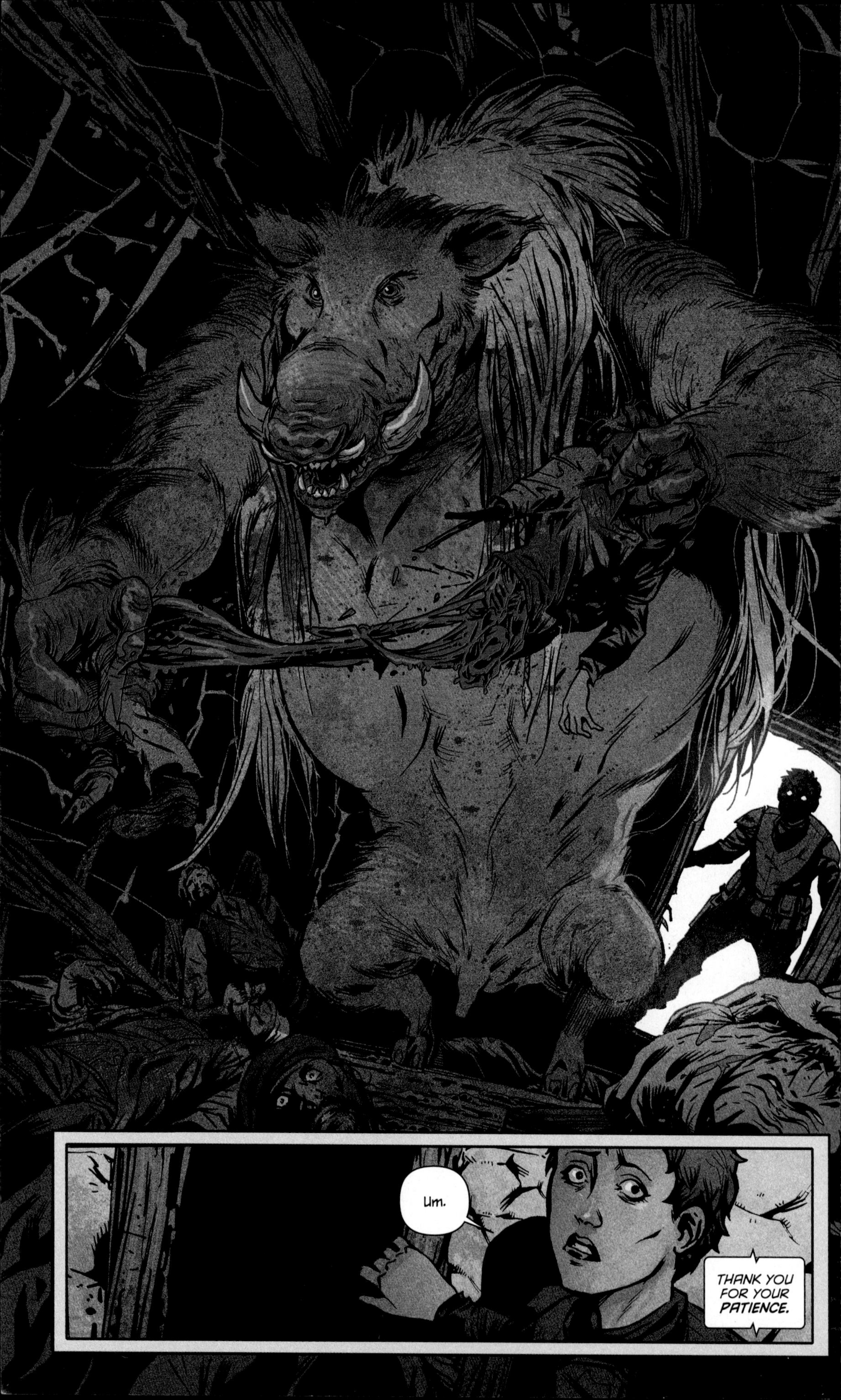
Um.
THANK YOU FOR YOUR PATIENCE.

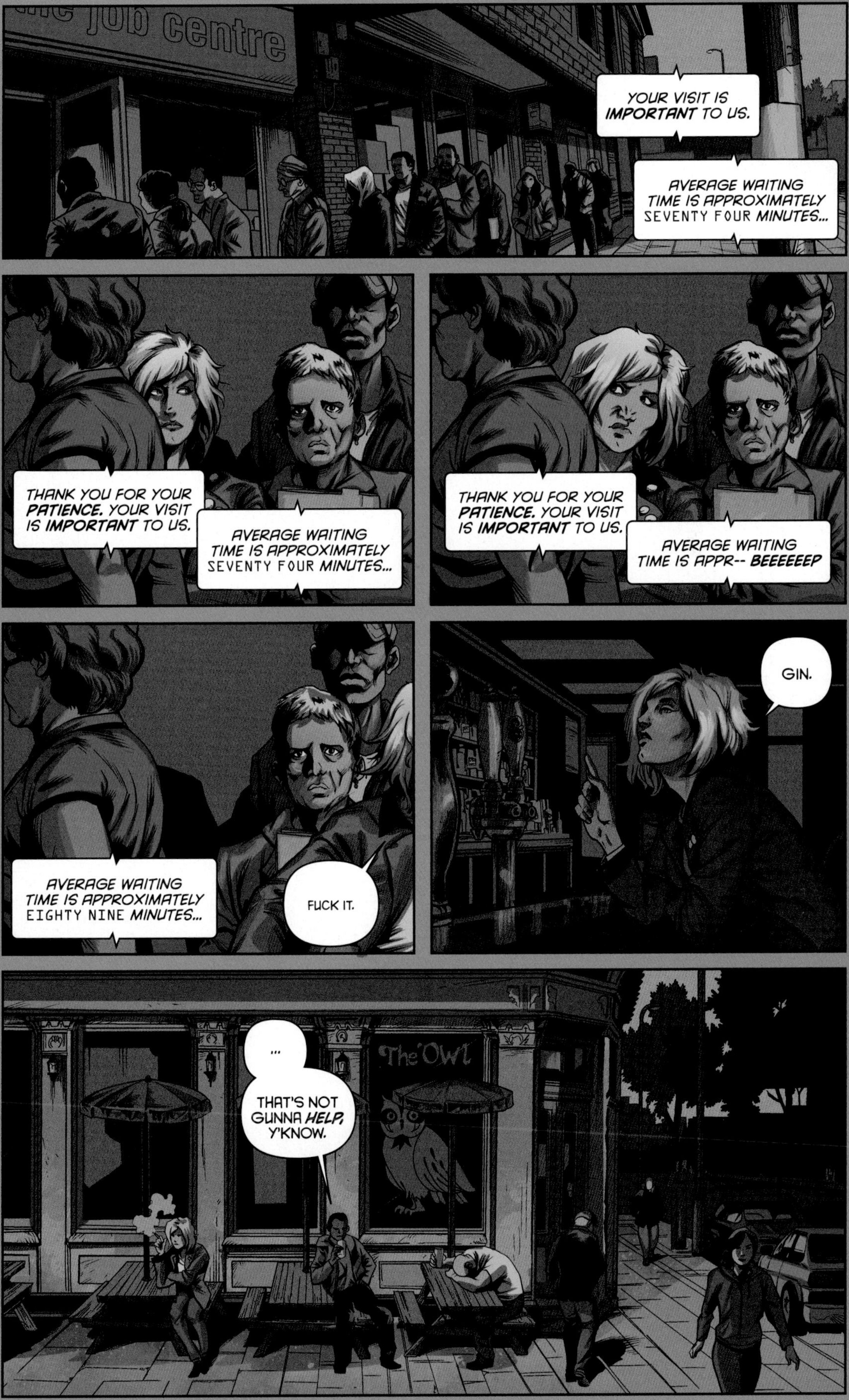
the job centre
YOUR VISIT IS IMPORTANT TO US.
AVERAGE WAITING TIME IS APPROXIMATELY SEVENTY FOUR MINUTES...
THANK YOU FOR YOUR PATIENCE. YOUR VISIT IS IMPORTANT TO US.
AVERAGE WAITING TIME IS APPROXIMATELY SEVENTY FOUR MINUTES...
THANK YOU FOR YOUR PATIENCE. YOUR VISIT IS IMPORTANT TO US.
AVERAGE WAITING TIME IS APPR-- BEEEEEEP
AVERAGE WAITING TIME IS APPROXIMATELY EIGHTY NINE MINUTES...
FUCK IT.
GIN.
The OWL
...
THAT'S NOT GUNNA HELP, Y'KNOW.

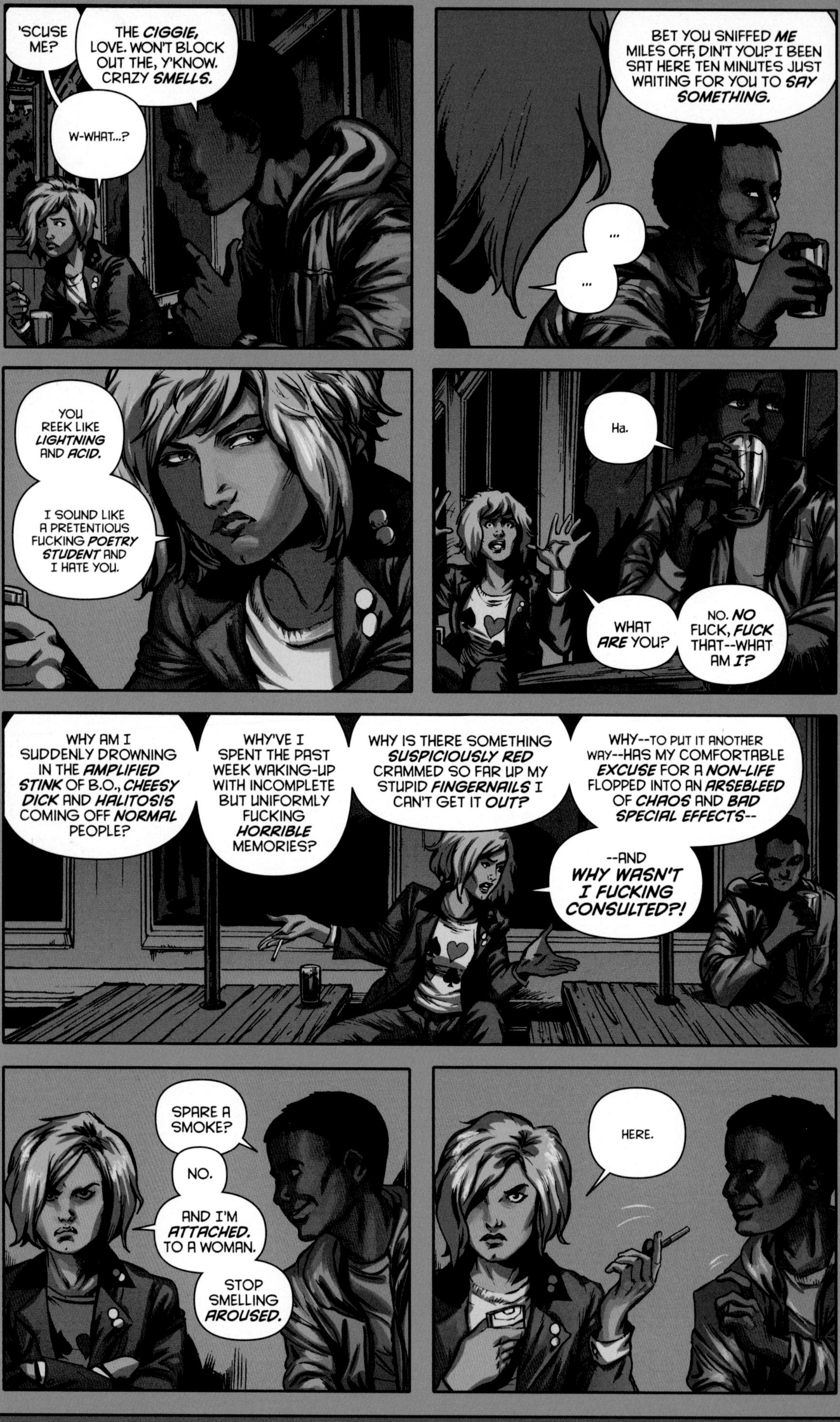
'SCUSE ME?
THE CIGGIE, LOVE. WON'T BLOCK OUT THE, Y'KNOW. CRAZY SMELLS.
W-WHAT...?
BET YOU SNIFFED ME MILES OFF, DIN'T YOU? I BEEN SAT HERE TEN MINUTES JUST WAITING FOR YOU TO SAY SOMETHING.
...
...
YOU REEK LIKE LIGHTNING AND ACID.
I SOUND LIKE A PRETENTIOUS FUCKING POETRY STUDENT AND I HATE YOU.
Ha.
WHAT ARE YOU?
NO. NO FUCK, FUCK THAT--WHAT AM I?
WHY AM I SUDDENLY DROWNING IN THE AMPLIFIED STINK OF B.O., CHEESY DICK AND HALITOSIS COMING OFF NORMAL PEOPLE?
WHY'VE I SPENT THE PAST WEEK WAKING-UP WITH INCOMPLETE BUT UNIFORMLY FUCKING HORRIBLE MEMORIES?
WHY IS THERE SOMETHING SUSPICIOUSLY RED CRAMMED SO FAR UP MY STUPID FINGERNAILS I CAN'T GET IT OUT?
WHY--TO PUT IT ANOTHER WAY--HAS MY COMFORTABLE EXCUSE FOR A NON-LIFE FLOPPED INTO AN ARSEBLEED OF CHAOS AND BAD SPECIAL EFFECTS--
--AND WHY WASN'T I FUCKING CONSULTED?!
SPARE A SMOKE?
NO.
AND I'M ATTACHED. TO A WOMAN.
STOP SMELLING AROUSED.
HERE.

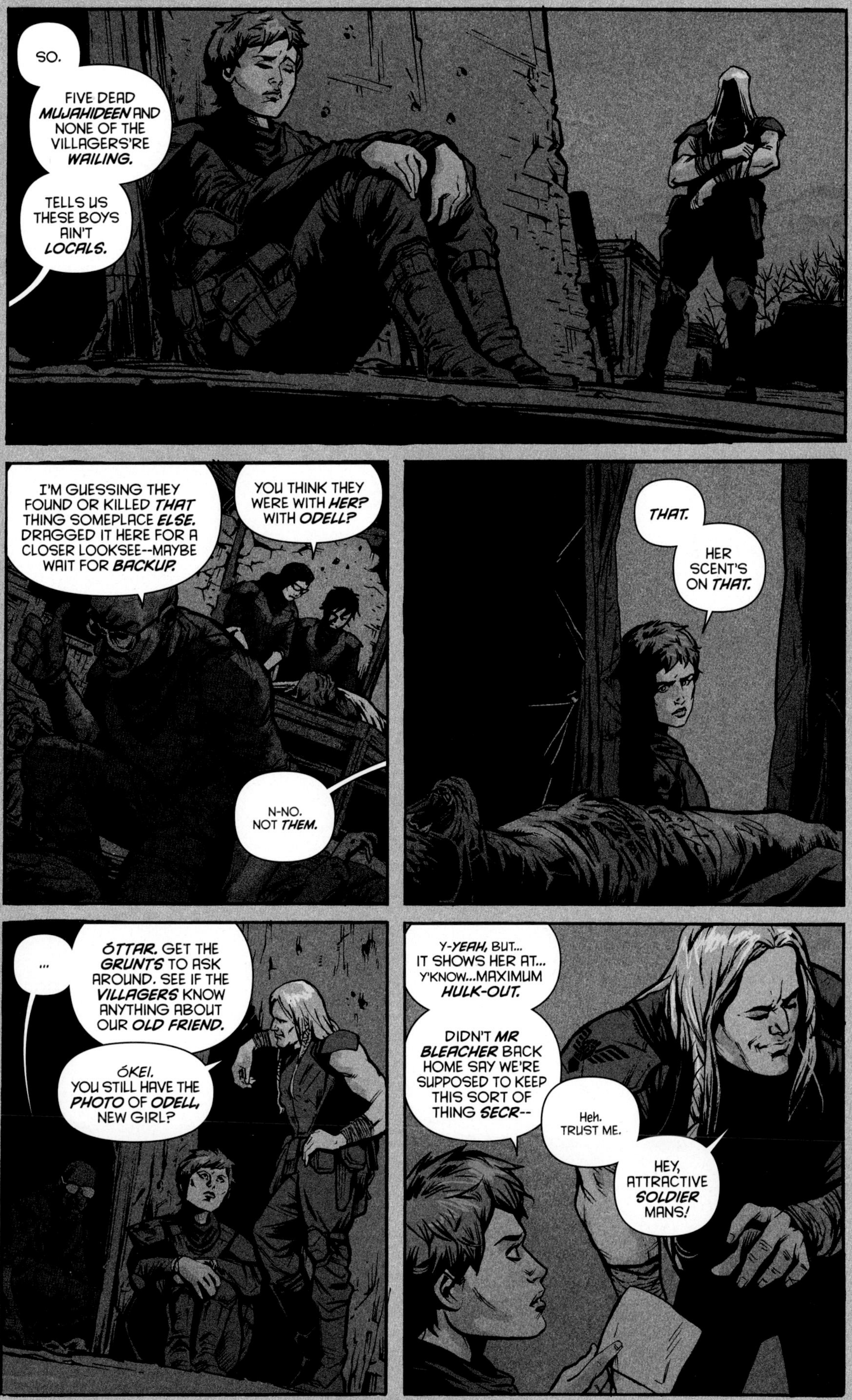
SO.
FIVE DEAD MUJAHIDEEN AND NONE OF THE VILLAGERS'RE WAILING.
TELLS US THESE BOYS AIN'T LOCALS.
I'M GUESSING THEY FOUND OR KILLED THAT THING SOMEPLACE ELSE. DRAGGED IT HERE FOR A CLOSER LOOKSEE--MAYBE WAIT FOR BACKUP.
YOU THINK THEY WERE WITH HER? WITH ODELL?
N-NO. NOT THEM.
THAT.
HER SCENT'S ON THAT.
...
ÓTTAR. GET THE GRUNTS TO ASK AROUND. SEE IF THE VILLAGERS KNOW ANYTHING ABOUT OUR OLD FRIEND.
ÓKEI. YOU STILL HAVE THE PHOTO OF ODELL, NEW GIRL?
Y-YEAH, BUT... IT SHOWS HER AT... Y'KNOW...MAXIMUM HULK-OUT.
DIDN'T MR BLEACHER BACK HOME SAY WE'RE SUPPOSED TO KEEP THIS SORT OF THING SECR--
Heh. TRUST ME.
HEY, ATTRACTIVE SOLDIER MANS!

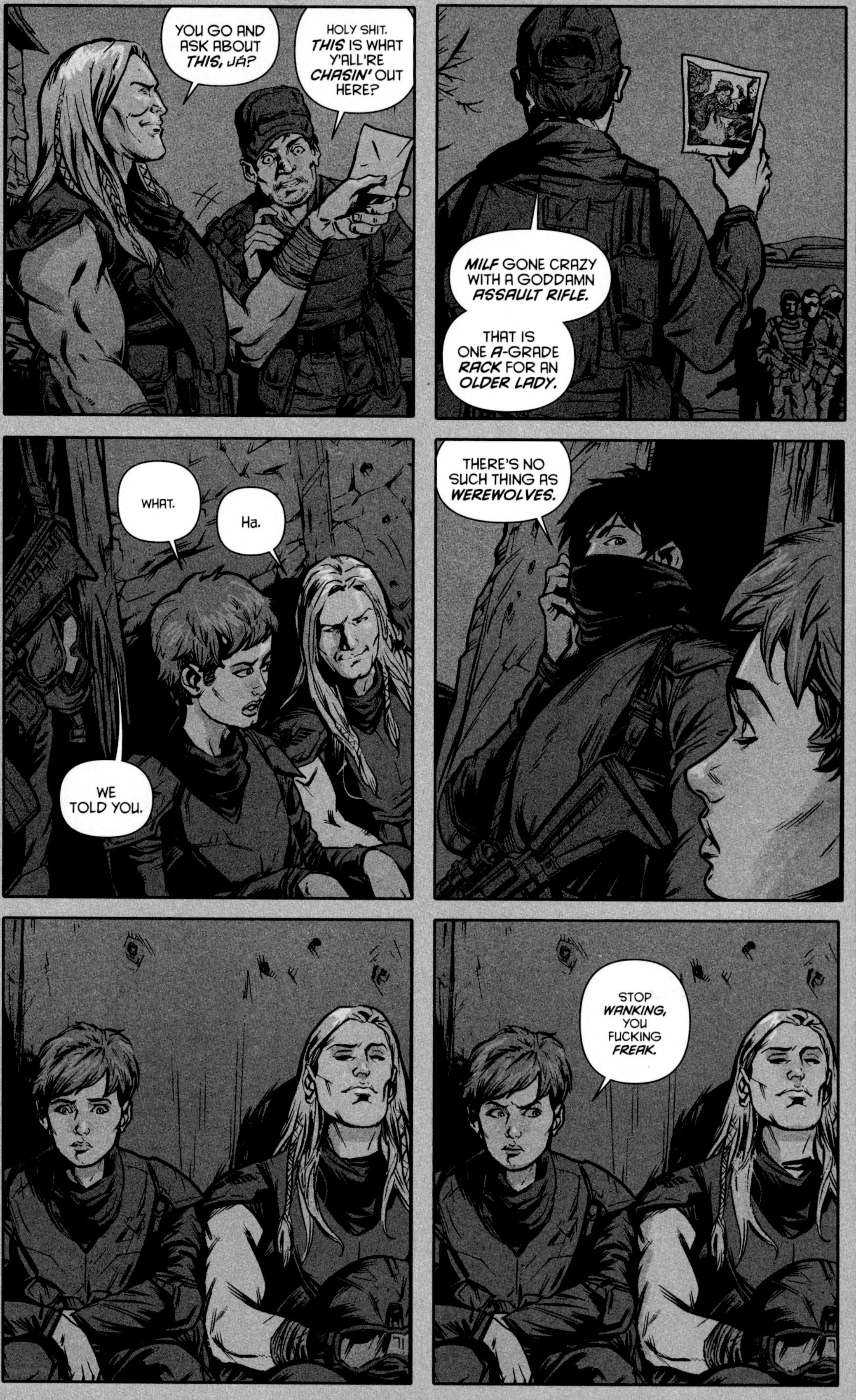
YOU GO AND ASK ABOUT THIS, JÁ?
HOLY SHIT. THIS IS WHAT Y'ALL'RE CHASIN' OUT HERE?
MILF GONE CRAZY WITH A GODDAMN ASSAULT RIFLE.
THAT IS ONE A-GRADE RACK FOR AN OLDER LADY.
WHAT.
Ha.
WE TOLD YOU.
THERE'S NO SUCH THING AS WEREWOLVES.
STOP WANKING, YOU FUCKING FREAK.

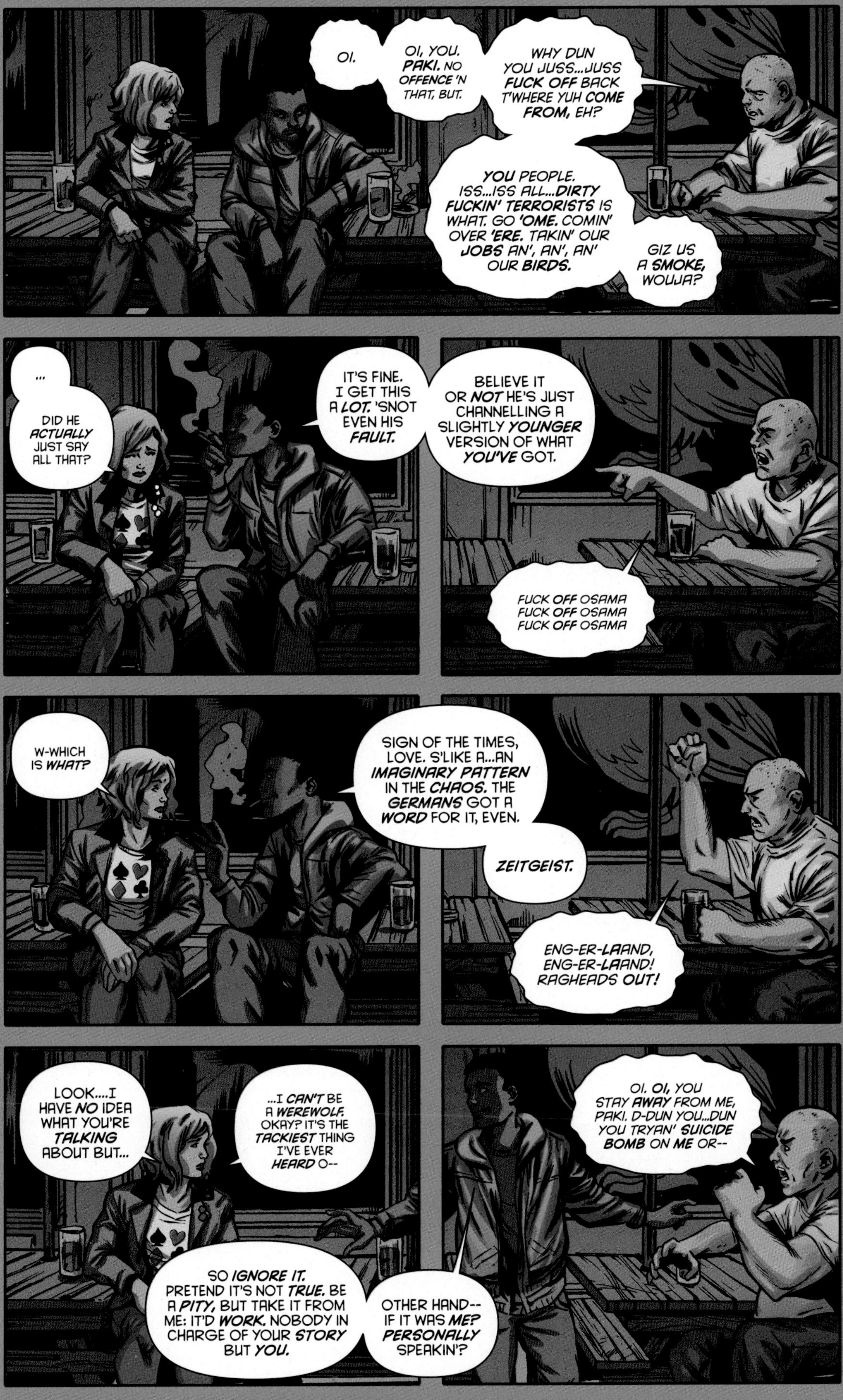

OI.
OI, YOU. PAKI. NO OFFENCE 'N THAT, BUT.
WHY DUN YOU JUSS...JUSS FUCK OFF BACK T'WHERE YUH COME FROM, EH?
YOU PEOPLE. ISS...ISS ALL...DIRTY FUCKIN' TERRORISTS IS WHAT. GO 'OME. COMIN' OVER 'ERE. TAKIN' OUR JOBS AN', AN', AN' OUR BIRDS.
GIZ US A SMOKE, WOUJA?
...
DID HE ACTUALLY JUST SAY ALL THAT?
IT'S FINE. I GET THIS A LOT. 'SNOT EVEN HIS FAULT.
BELIEVE IT OR NOT HE'S JUST CHANNELLING A SLIGHTLY YOUNGER VERSION OF WHAT YOU'VE GOT.
FUCK OFF OSAMA FUCK OFF OSAMA FUCK OFF OSAMA
W-WHICH IS WHAT?
SIGN OF THE TIMES, LOVE. S'LIKE A...AN IMAGINARY PATTERN IN THE CHAOS. THE GERMANS GOT A WORD FOR IT, EVEN.
ZEITGEIST.
ENG-ER-LAAND, ENG-ER-LAAND! RAGHEADS OUT!
LOOK....I HAVE NO IDEA WHAT YOU'RE TALKING ABOUT BUT...
...I CAN'T BE A WEREWOLF. OKAY? IT'S THE TACKIEST THING I'VE EVER HEARD O--
SO IGNORE IT. PRETEND IT'S NOT TRUE. BE A PITY, BUT TAKE IT FROM ME: IT'D WORK. NOBODY IN CHARGE OF YOUR STORY BUT YOU.
OTHER HAND-- IF IT WAS ME? PERSONALLY SPEAKIN'?
OI. OI, YOU STAY AWAY FROM ME, PAKI. D-DUN YOU...DUN YOU TRYAN' SUICIDE BOMB ON ME OR--

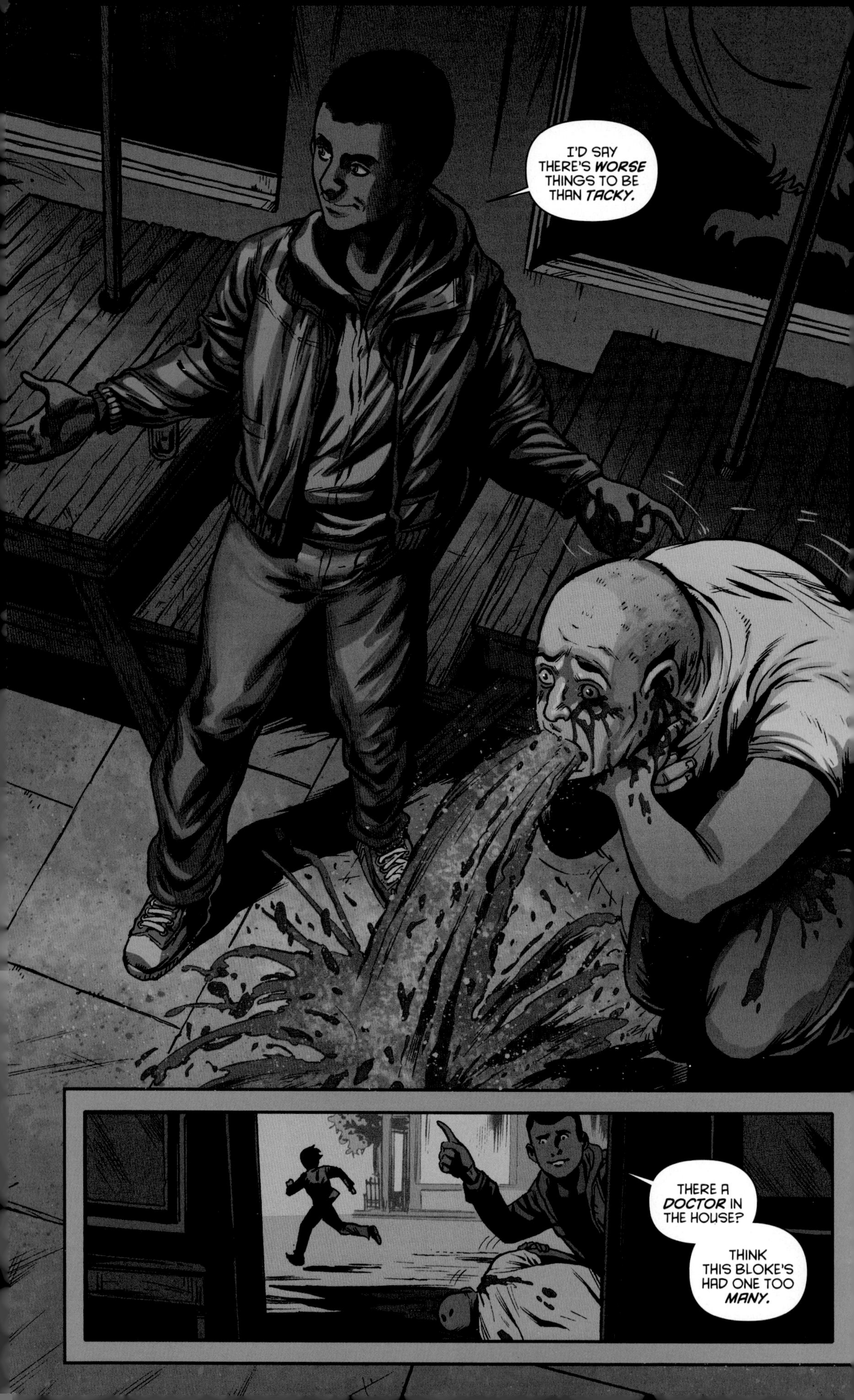
I'D SAY THERE'S WORSE THINGS TO BE THAN TACKY.
THERE A DOCTOR IN THE HOUSE?
THINK THIS BLOKE'S HAD ONE TOO MANY.

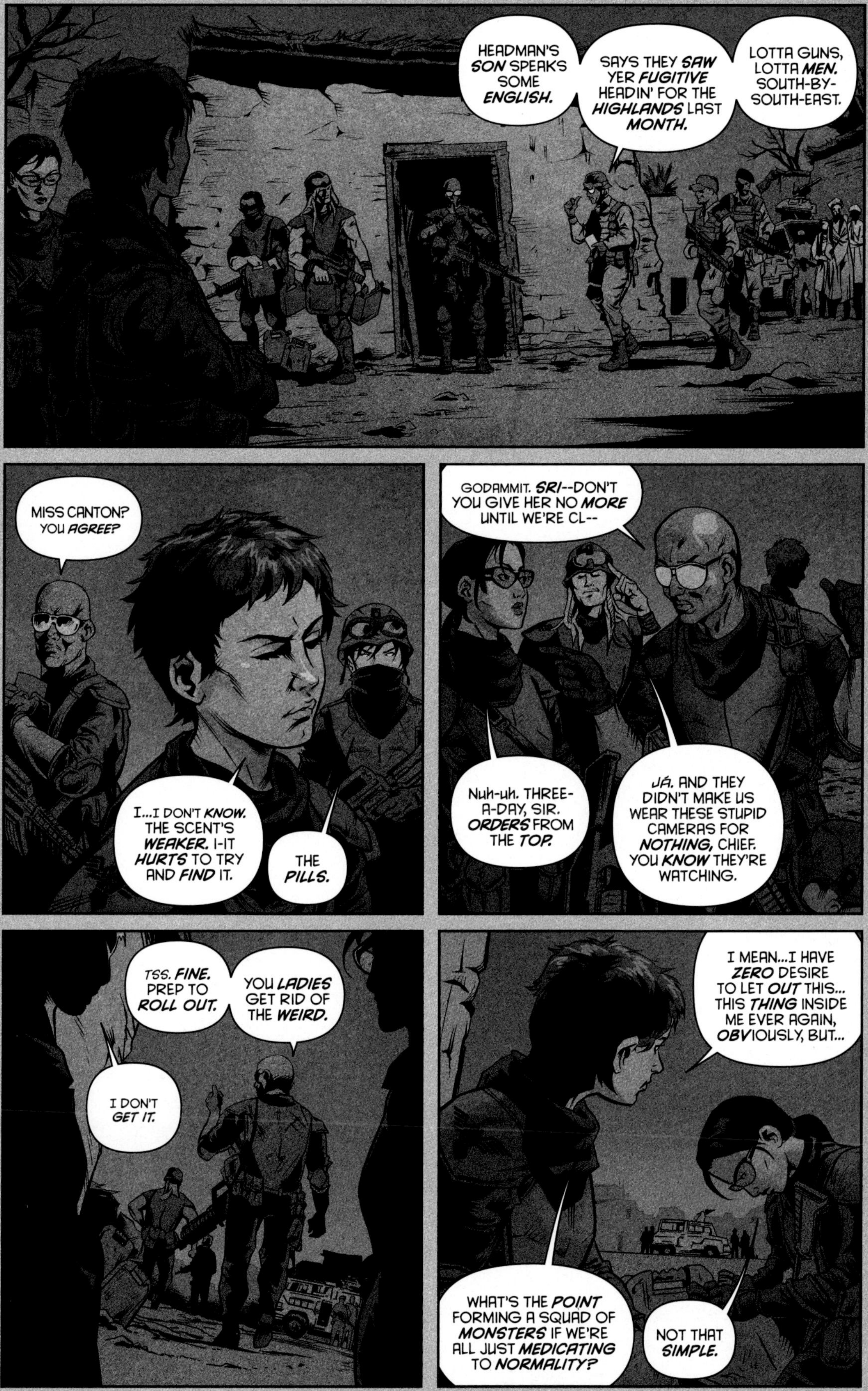
HEADMAN'S SON SPEAKS SOME ENGLISH.
SAYS THEY SAW YER FUGITIVE HEADIN' FOR THE HIGHLANDS LAST MONTH.
LOTTA GUNS, LOTTA MEN. SOUTH-BY-SOUTH-EAST.
MISS CANTON? YOU AGREE?
I...I DON'T KNOW. THE SCENT'S WEAKER. I-IT HURTS TO TRY AND FIND IT.
THE PILLS.
GODAMMIT. SRI--DON'T YOU GIVE HER NO MORE UNTIL WE'RE CL--
Nuh-uh. THREE-A-DAY, SIR. ORDERS FROM THE TOP.
JÁ. AND THEY DIDN'T MAKE US WEAR THESE STUPID CAMERAS FOR NOTHING, CHIEF. YOU KNOW THEY'RE WATCHING.
TSS. FINE. PREP TO ROLL OUT.
YOU LADIES GET RID OF THE WEIRD.
I DON'T GET IT.
I MEAN...I HAVE ZERO DESIRE TO LET OUT THIS... THIS THING INSIDE ME EVER AGAIN, OBVIOUSLY, BUT...
WHAT'S THE POINT FORMING A SQUAD OF MONSTERS IF WE'RE ALL JUST MEDICATING TO NORMALITY?
NOT THAT SIMPLE.

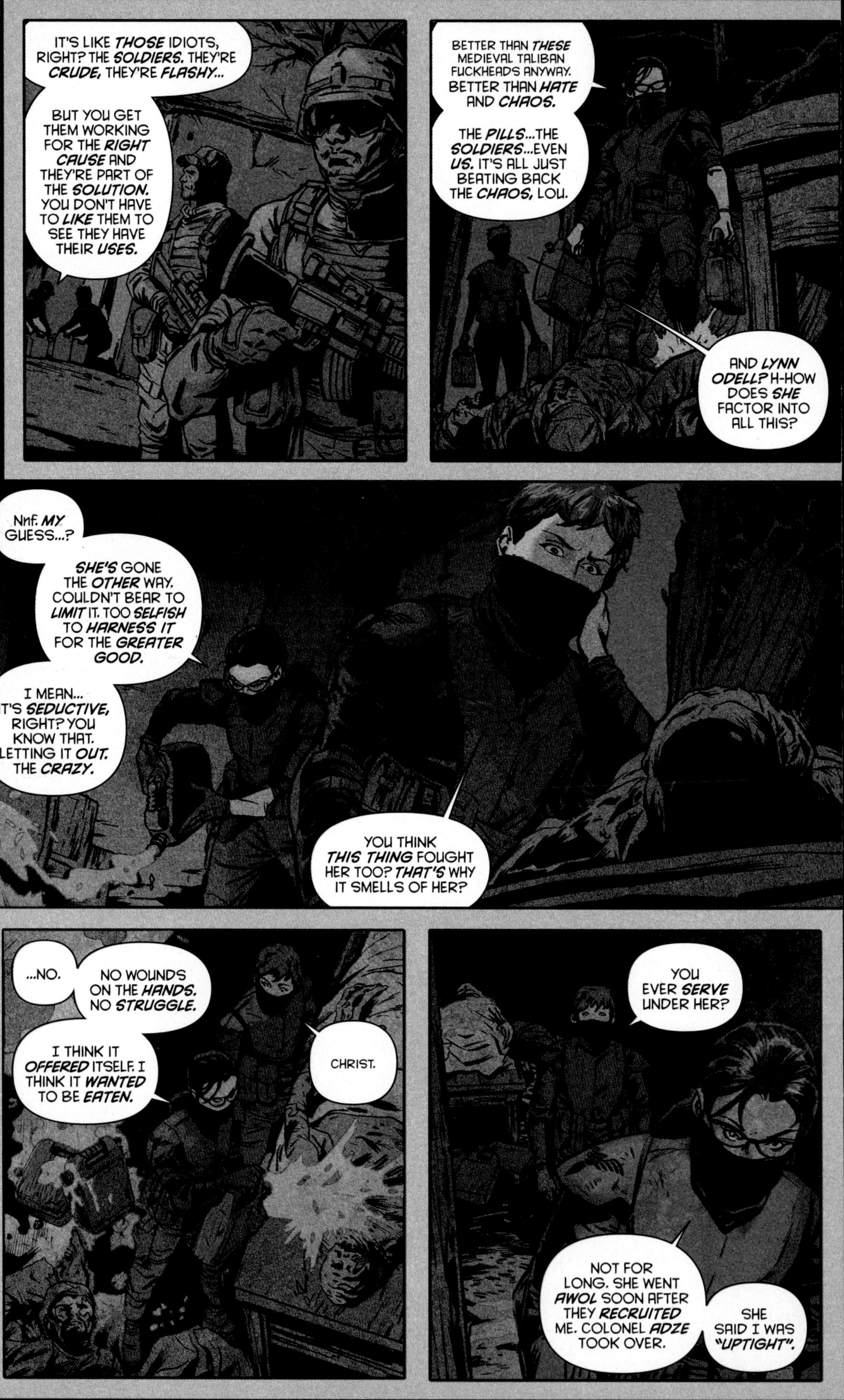
IT'S LIKE THOSE IDIOTS, RIGHT? THE SOLDIERS. THEY'RE CRUDE, THEY'RE FLASHY...
BUT YOU GET THEM WORKING FOR THE RIGHT CAUSE AND THEY'RE PART OF THE SOLUTION. YOU DON'T HAVE TO LIKE THEM TO SEE THEY HAVE THEIR USES.
BETTER THAN THESE MEDIEVAL TALIBAN FUCKHEADS ANYWAY. BETTER THAN HATE AND CHAOS.
THE PILLS...THE SOLDIERS...EVEN US. IT'S ALL JUST BEATING BACK THE CHAOS, LOU.
AND LYNN ODELL? H-HOW DOES SHE FACTOR INTO ALL THIS?
Nnf. MY GUESS...?
SHE'S GONE THE OTHER WAY. COULDN'T BEAR TO LIMIT IT. TOO SELFISH TO HARNESS IT FOR THE GREATER GOOD.
I MEAN... IT'S SEDUCTIVE, RIGHT? YOU KNOW THAT. LETTING IT OUT. THE CRAZY.
YOU THINK THIS THING FOUGHT HER TOO? THAT'S WHY IT SMELLS OF HER?
...NO.
NO WOUNDS ON THE HANDS. NO STRUGGLE.
I THINK IT OFFERED ITSELF. I THINK IT WANTED TO BE EATEN.
CHRIST.
YOU EVER SERVE UNDER HER?
NOT FOR LONG. SHE WENT AWOL SOON AFTER THEY RECRUITED ME. COLONEL ADZE TOOK OVER.
SHE SAID I WAS "UPTIGHT".

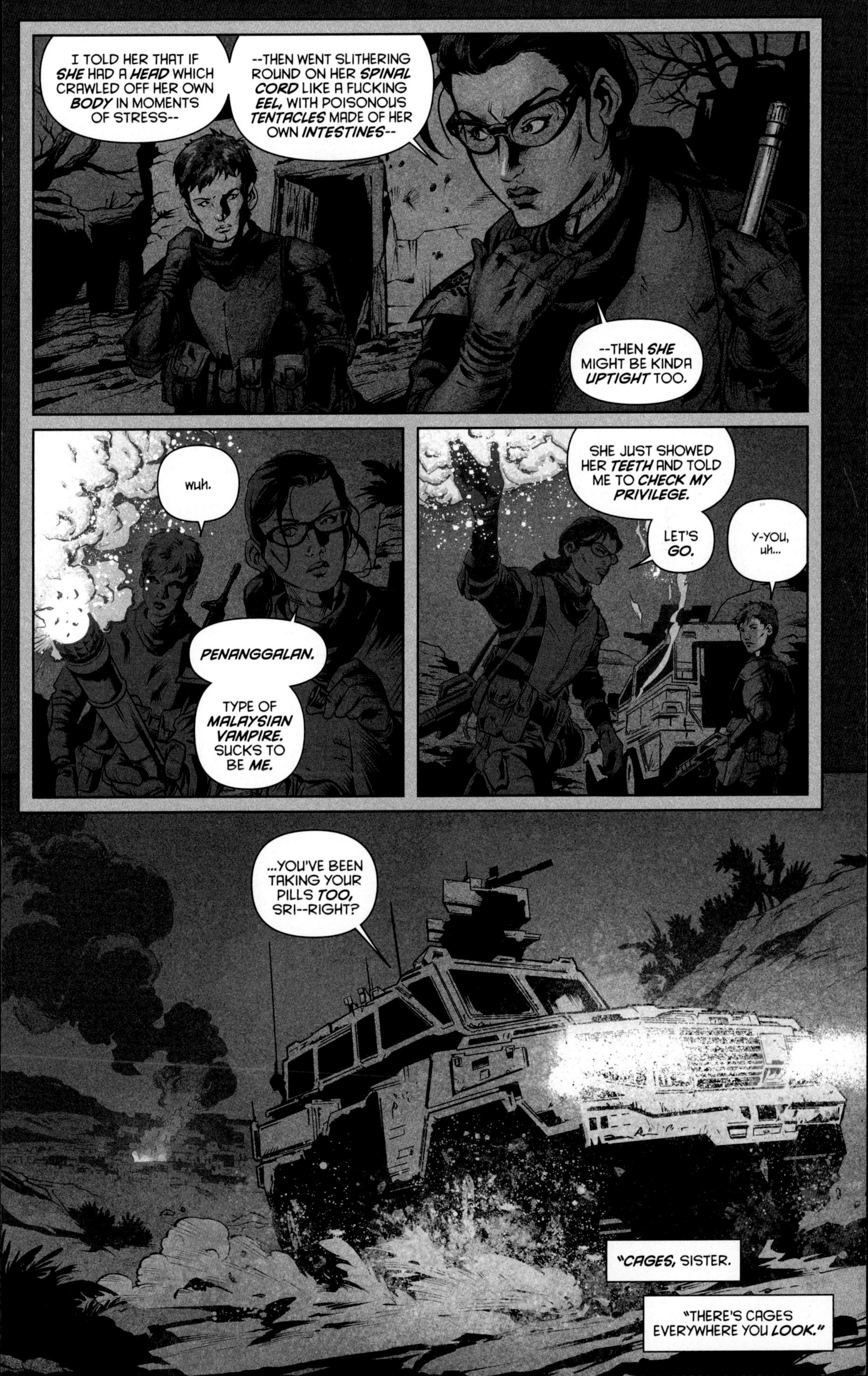
I TOLD HER THAT IF *SHE* HAD A *HEAD* WHICH CRAWLED OFF HER OWN *BODY* IN MOMENTS OF STRESS--
--THEN WENT SLITHERING ROUND ON HER *SPINAL CORD* LIKE A FUCKING *EEL,* WITH POISONOUS *TENTACLES* MADE OF HER OWN *INTESTINES*--
--THEN *SHE* MIGHT BE KINDA *UPTIGHT* TOO.
wuh.
PENANGGALAN.
TYPE OF *MALAYSIAN VAMPIRE.* SUCKS TO BE *ME.*
SHE JUST SHOWED HER *TEETH* AND TOLD ME TO *CHECK MY PRIVILEGE.*
LET'S *GO.*
Y-YOU, uh...
...YOU'VE BEEN TAKING YOUR PILLS *TOO,* SRI--RIGHT?
"*CAGES,* SISTER.
"THERE'S CAGES EVERYWHERE YOU *LOOK.*"

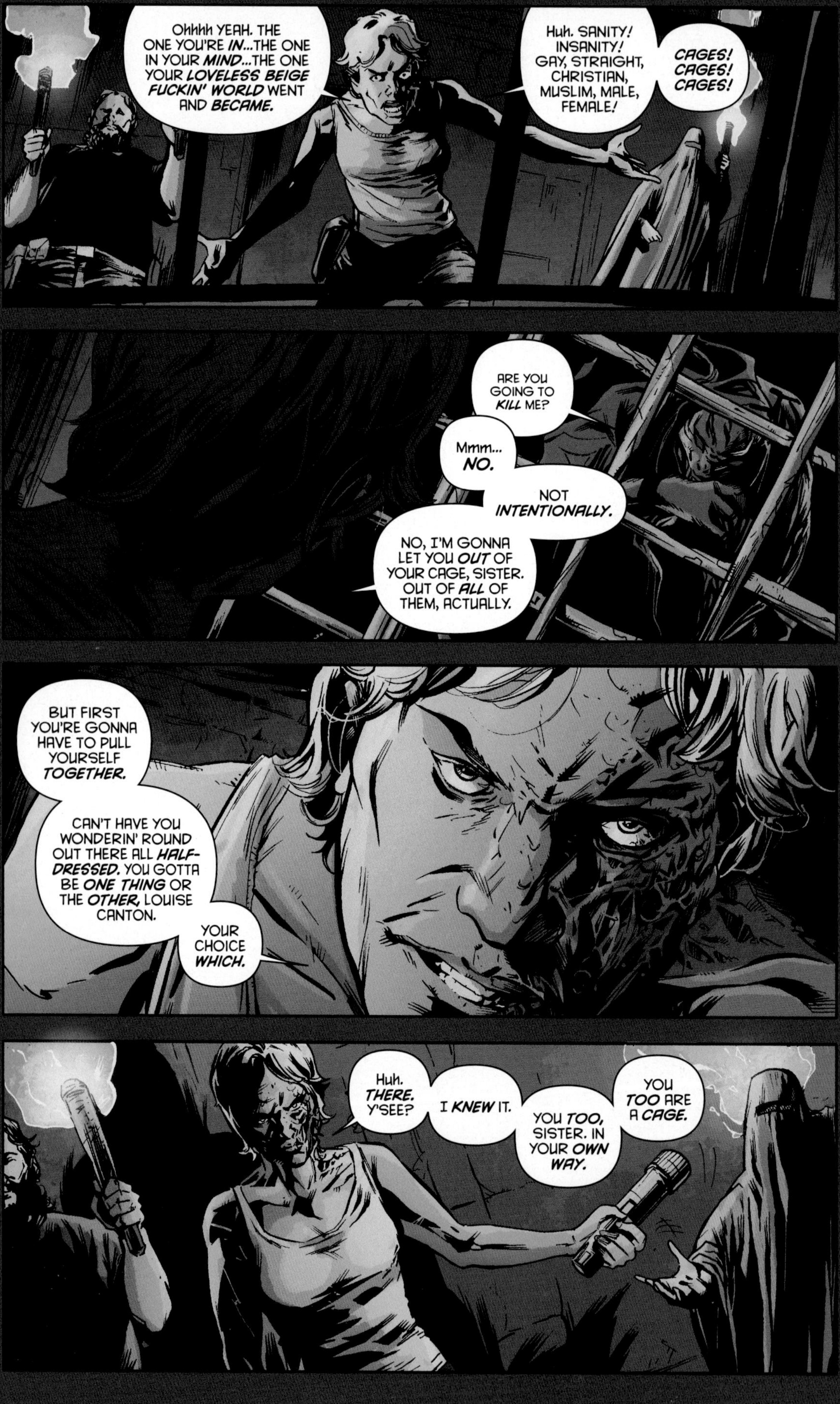
Ohhhh YEAH. THE ONE YOU'RE IN...THE ONE IN YOUR MIND...THE ONE YOUR LOVELESS BEIGE FUCKIN' WORLD WENT AND BECAME.
Huh. SANITY! INSANITY! GAY, STRAIGHT, CHRISTIAN, MUSLIM, MALE, FEMALE!
CAGES! CAGES! CAGES!
ARE YOU GOING TO KILL ME?
Mmm... NO.
NOT INTENTIONALLY.
NO, I'M GONNA LET YOU OUT OF YOUR CAGE, SISTER. OUT OF ALL OF THEM, ACTUALLY.
BUT FIRST YOU'RE GONNA HAVE TO PULL YOURSELF TOGETHER.
CAN'T HAVE YOU WONDERIN' ROUND OUT THERE ALL HALF-DRESSED. YOU GOTTA BE ONE THING OR THE OTHER, LOUISE CANTON.
YOUR CHOICE WHICH.
Huh. THERE. Y'SEE?
I KNEW IT.
YOU TOO, SISTER. IN YOUR OWN WAY.
YOU TOO ARE A CAGE.

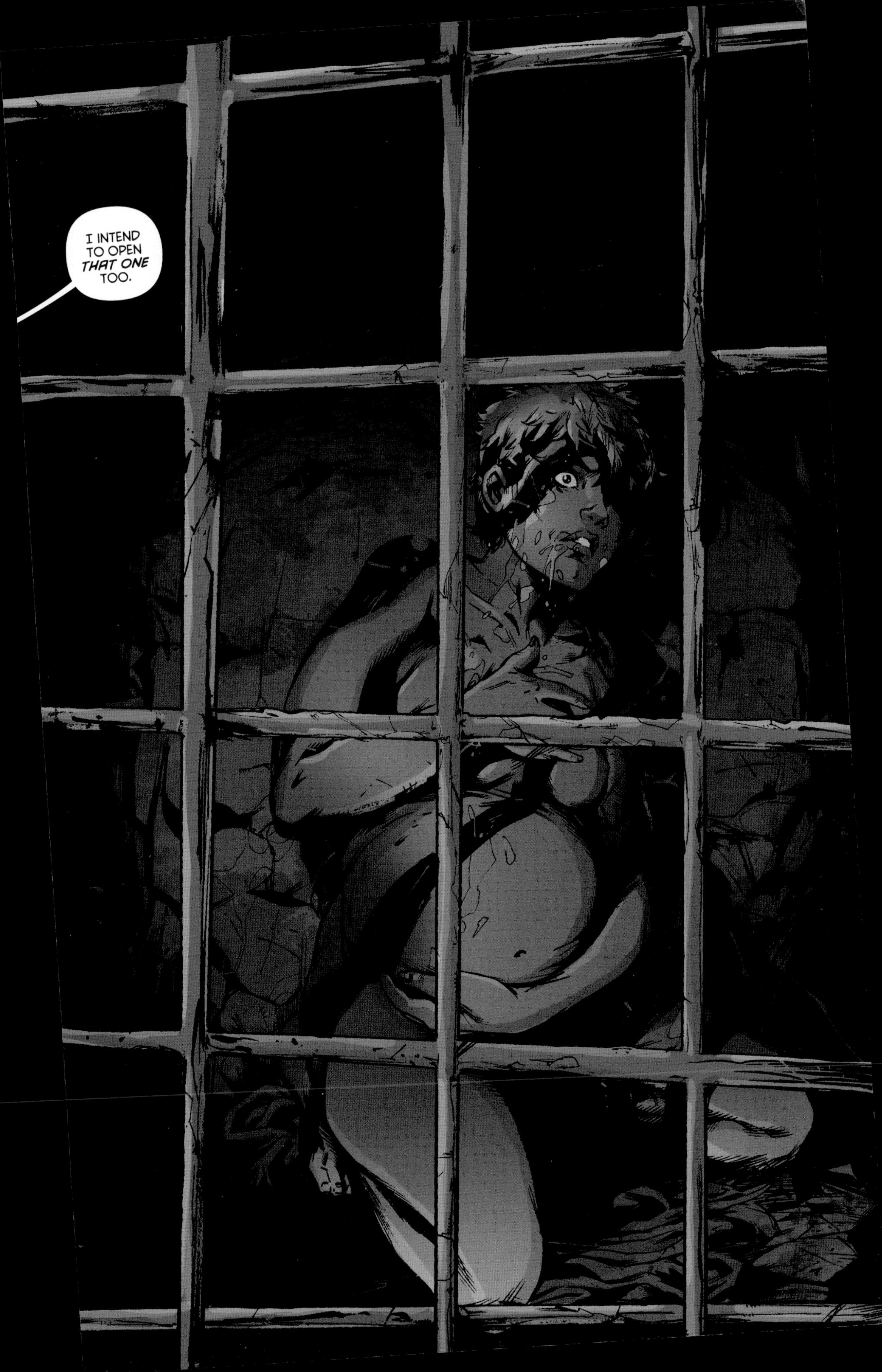
I INTEND TO OPEN *THAT ONE* TOO.

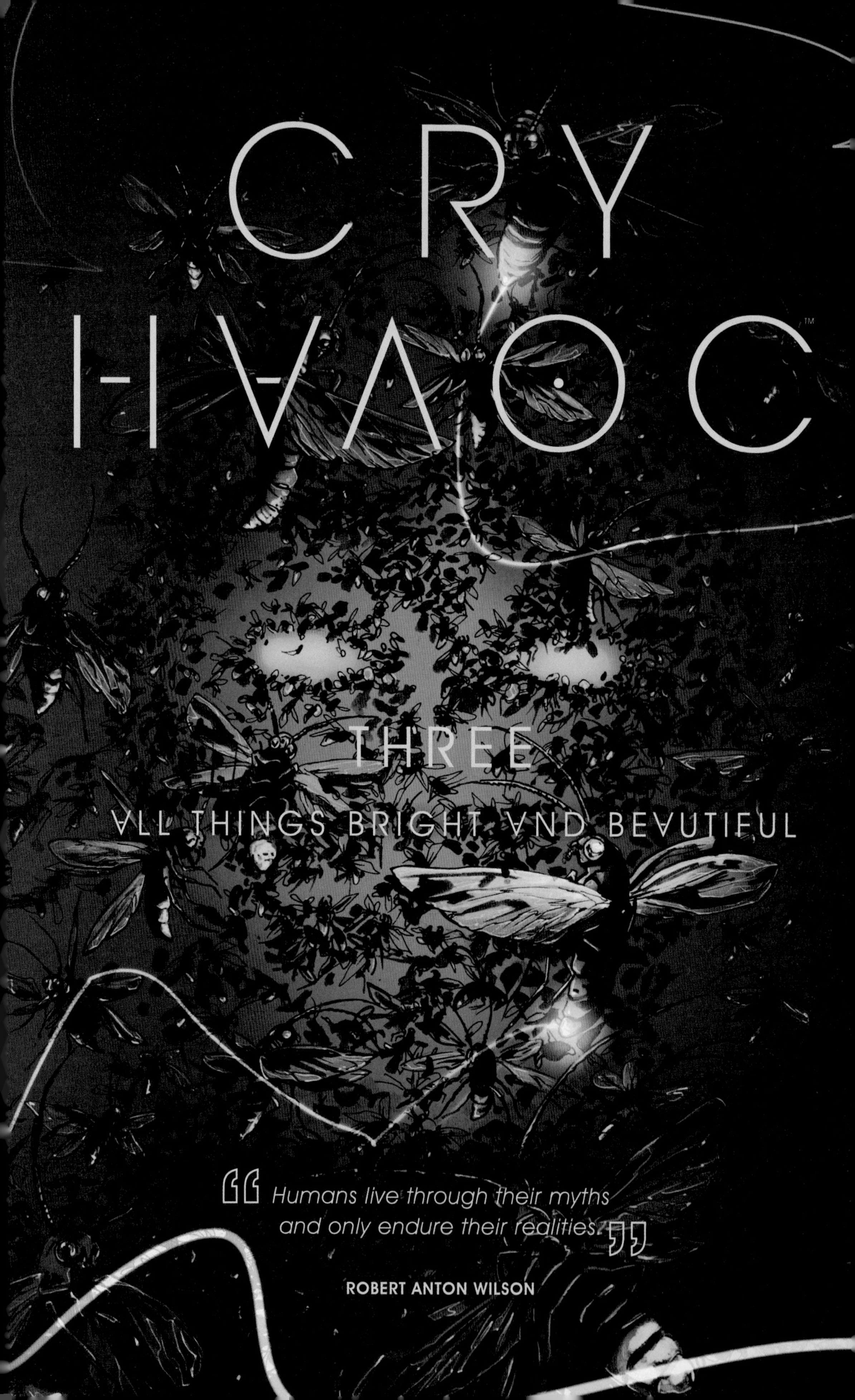
CRY
HAVOC™
THREE
ALL THINGS BRIGHT AND BEAUTIFUL
"Humans live through their myths and only endure their realities."
ROBERT ANTON WILSON

variant cover
SI **GANE**

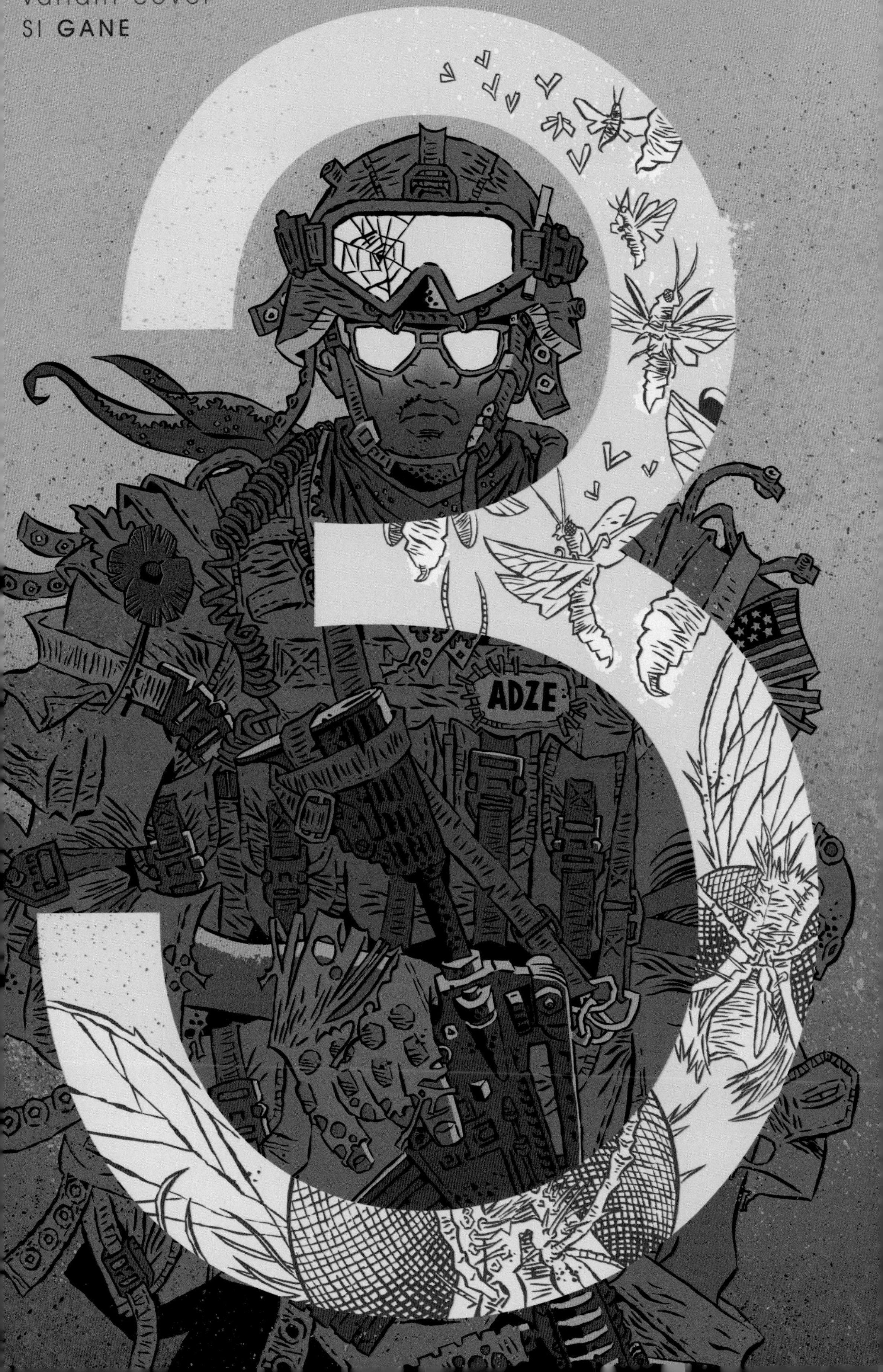

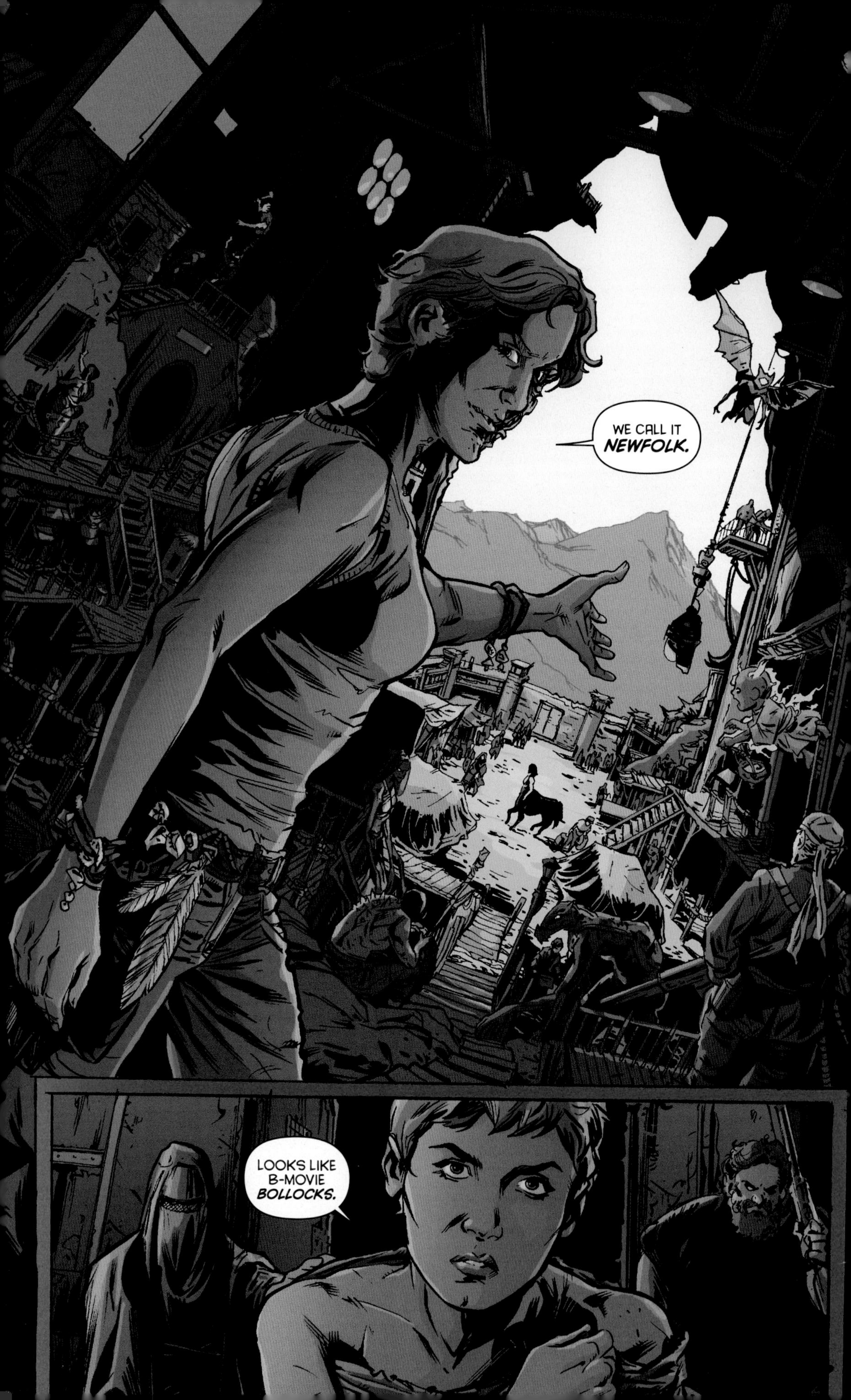
WE CALL IT NEWFOLK.
LOOKS LIKE B-MOVIE BOLLOCKS.

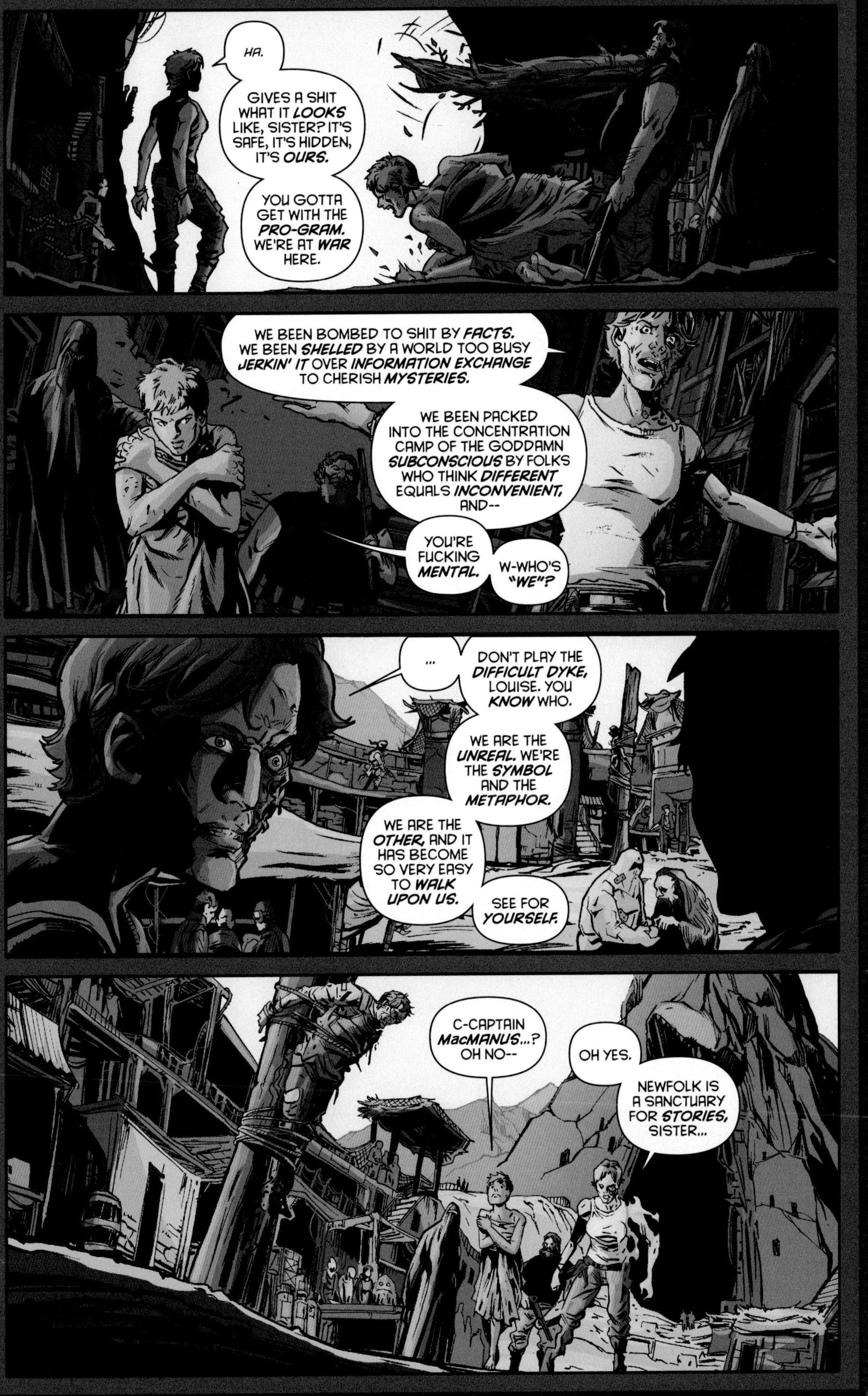
HA.
GIVES A SHIT WHAT IT LOOKS LIKE, SISTER? IT'S SAFE, IT'S HIDDEN, IT'S OURS.
YOU GOTTA GET WITH THE PRO-GRAM. WE'RE AT WAR HERE.
WE BEEN BOMBED TO SHIT BY FACTS. WE BEEN SHELLED BY A WORLD TOO BUSY JERKIN' IT OVER INFORMATION EXCHANGE TO CHERISH MYSTERIES.
WE BEEN PACKED INTO THE CONCENTRATION CAMP OF THE GODDAMN SUBCONSCIOUS BY FOLKS WHO THINK DIFFERENT EQUALS INCONVENIENT, AND--
YOU'RE FUCKING MENTAL.
W-WHO'S "WE"?
...
DON'T PLAY THE DIFFICULT DYKE, LOUISE. YOU KNOW WHO.
WE ARE THE UNREAL. WE'RE THE SYMBOL AND THE METAPHOR.
WE ARE THE OTHER, AND IT HAS BECOME SO VERY EASY TO WALK UPON US.
SEE FOR YOURSELF.
C-CAPTAIN MacMANUS...? OH NO--
OH YES.
NEWFOLK IS A SANCTUARY FOR STORIES, SISTER...

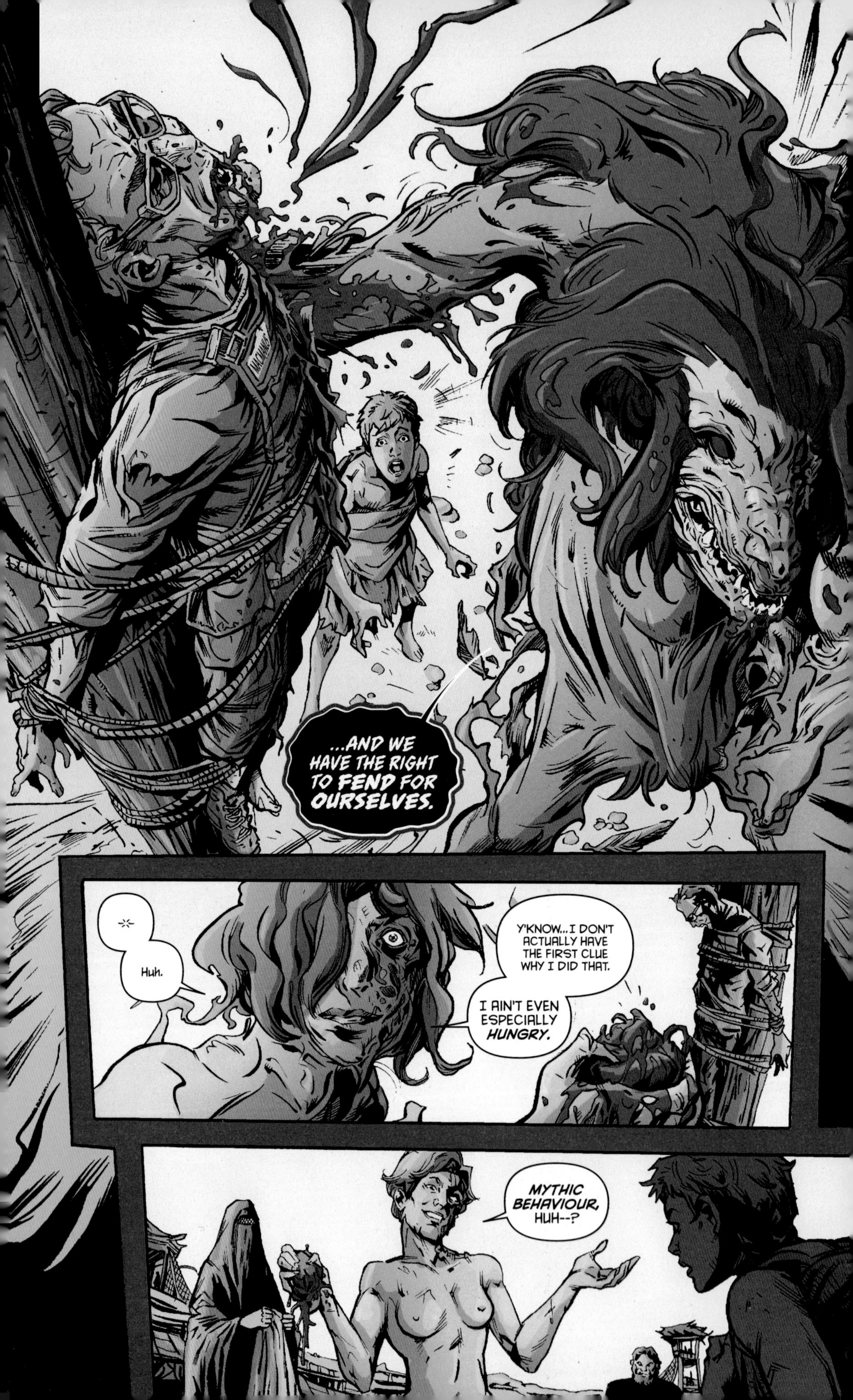

...AND WE HAVE THE RIGHT TO FEND FOR OURSELVES.
*
Huh.
Y'KNOW... I DON'T ACTUALLY HAVE THE FIRST CLUE WHY I DID THAT.
I AIN'T EVEN ESPECIALLY HUNGRY.
MYTHIC BEHAVIOUR, HUH--?

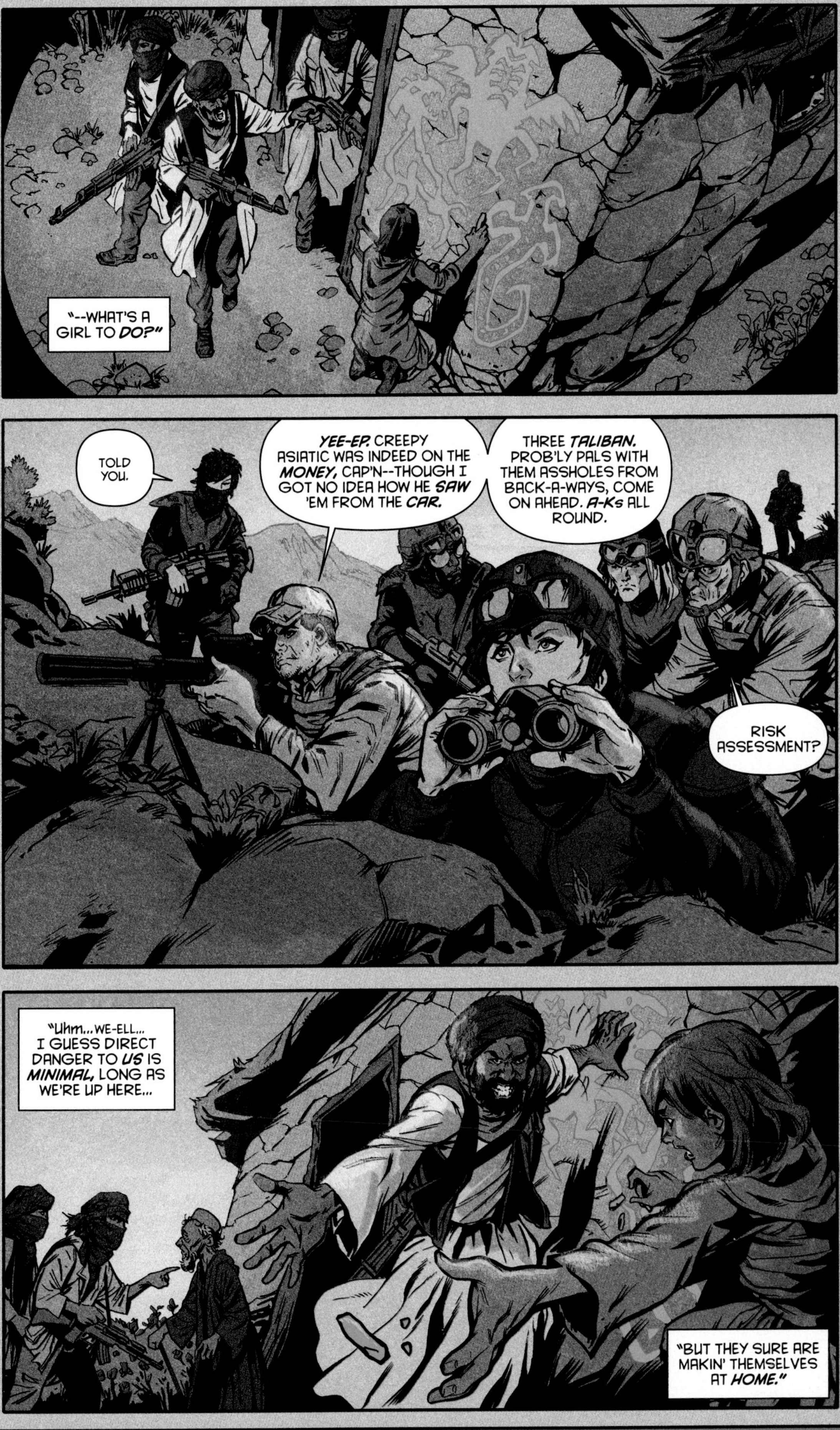
"--WHAT'S A GIRL TO *DO?*"
TOLD YOU.
YEE-EP. CREEPY ASIATIC WAS INDEED ON THE *MONEY,* CAP'N--THOUGH I GOT NO IDEA HOW HE *SAW* 'EM FROM THE *CAR.*
THREE *TALIBAN.* PROB'LY PALS WITH THEM ASSHOLES FROM BACK-A-WAYS, COME ON AHEAD. *A-Ks* ALL ROUND.
RISK ASSESSMENT?
"Uhm... WE-ELL... I GUESS DIRECT DANGER TO *US* IS *MINIMAL,* LONG AS WE'RE UP HERE...
"BUT THEY SURE ARE MAKIN' THEMSELVES AT *HOME.*"

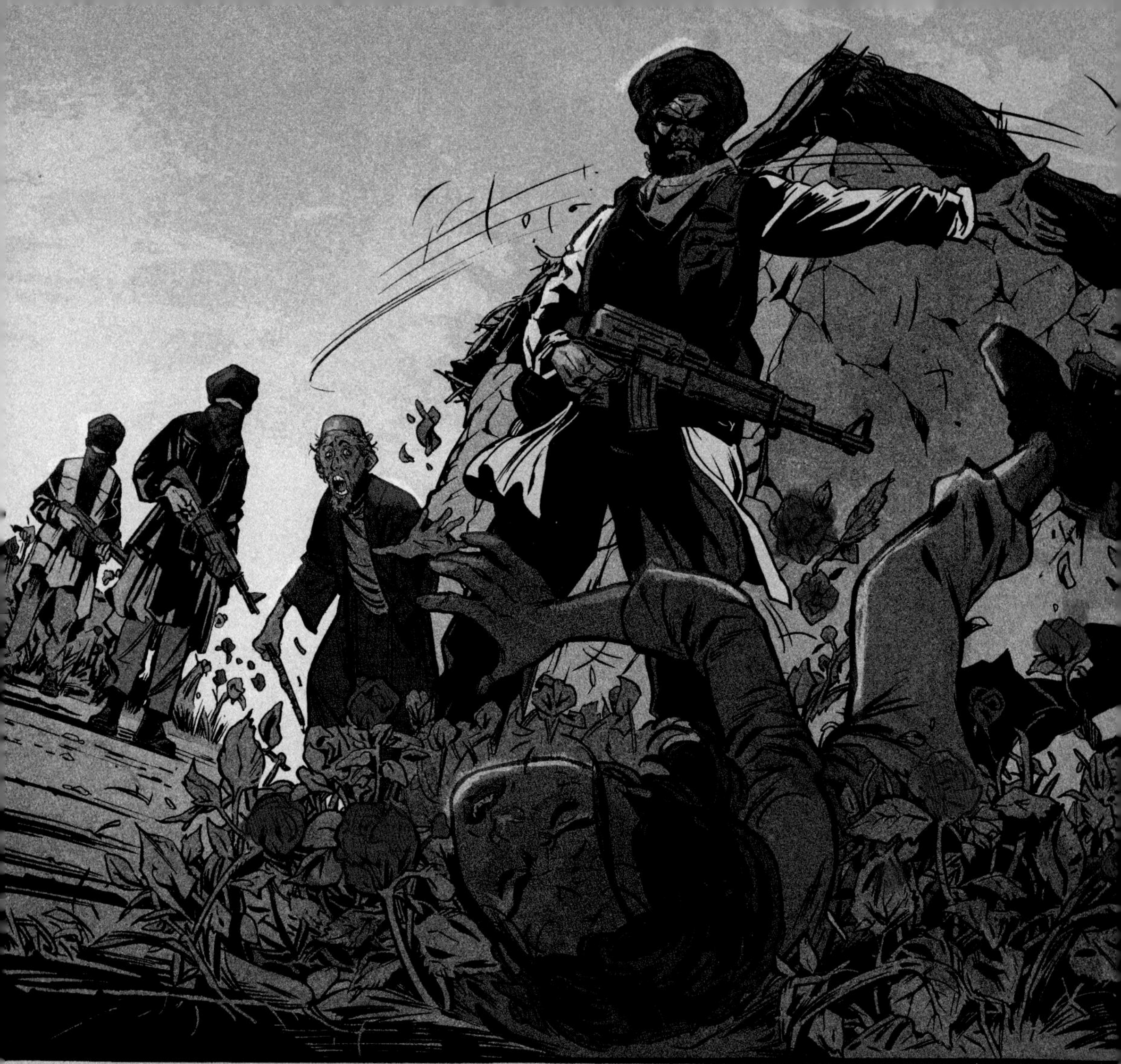

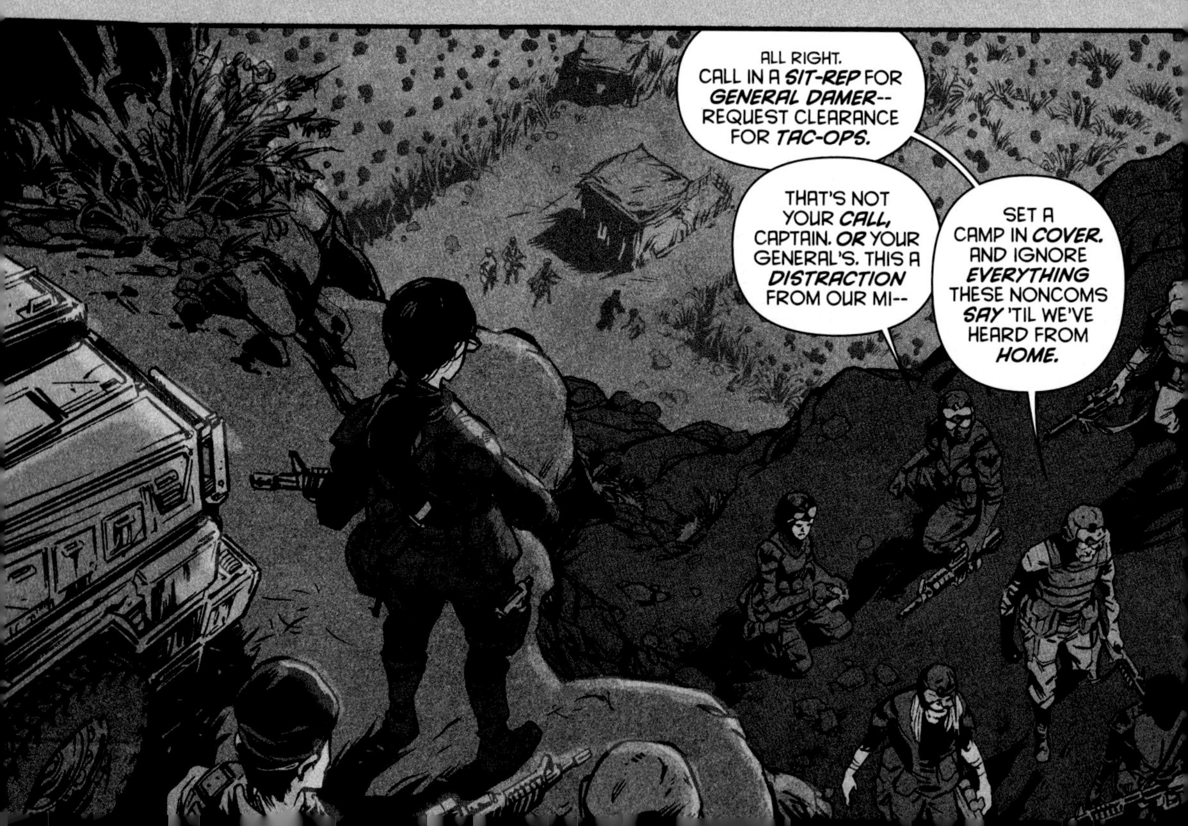
ALL RIGHT. CALL IN A SIT-REP FOR GENERAL DAMER-- REQUEST CLEARANCE FOR TAC-OPS.
THAT'S NOT YOUR CALL, CAPTAIN. OR YOUR GENERAL'S. THIS A DISTRACTION FROM OUR MI--
SET A CAMP IN COVER. AND IGNORE EVERYTHING THESE NONCOMS SAY 'TIL WE'VE HEARD FROM HOME.

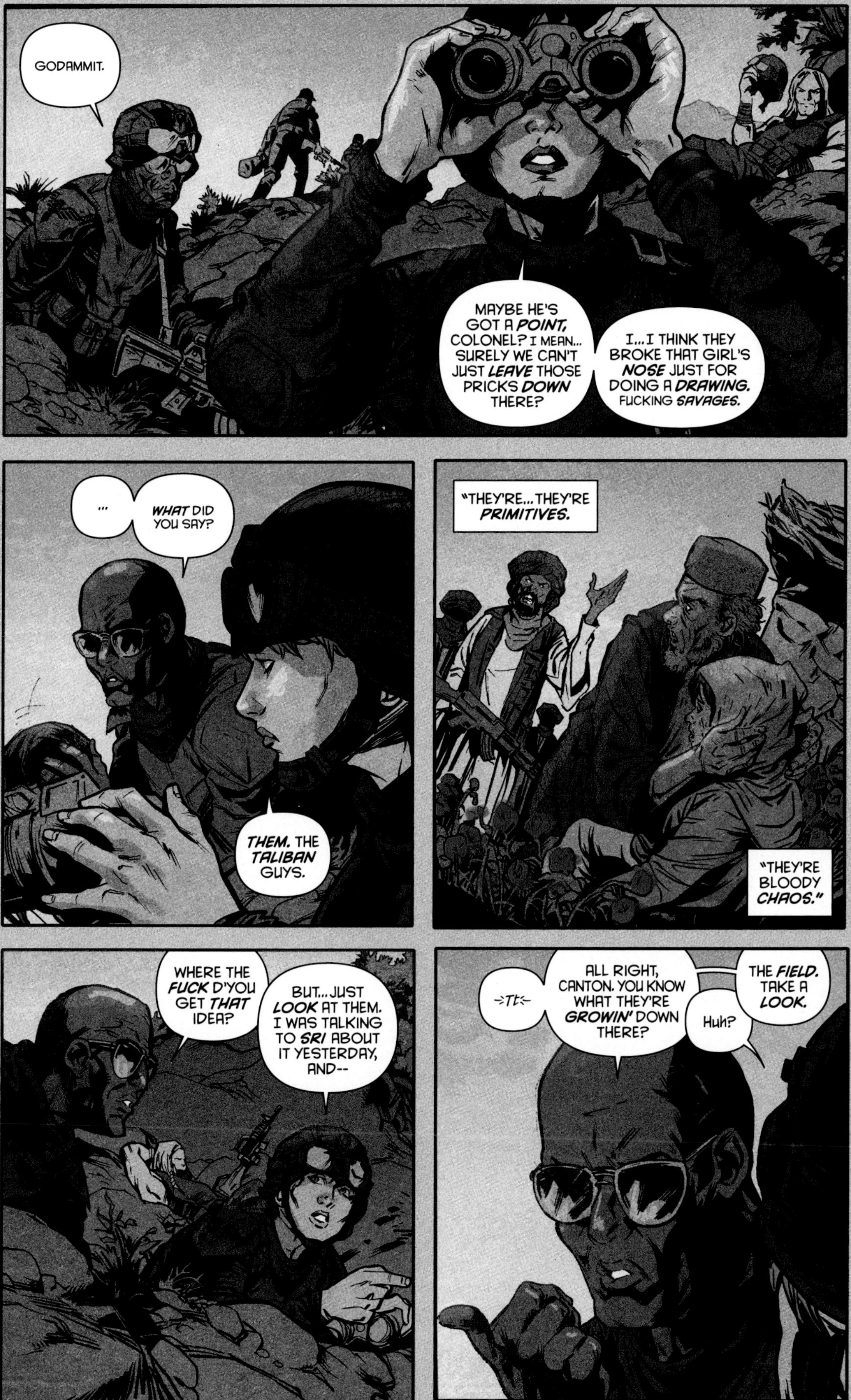
GODAMMIT.
MAYBE HE'S GOT A POINT, COLONEL? I MEAN... SURELY WE CAN'T JUST LEAVE THOSE PRICKS DOWN THERE?
I...I THINK THEY BROKE THAT GIRL'S NOSE JUST FOR DOING A DRAWING. FUCKING SAVAGES.
...
WHAT DID YOU SAY?
THEM. THE TALIBAN GUYS.
"THEY'RE...THEY'RE PRIMITIVES.
"THEY'RE BLOODY CHAOS."
WHERE THE FUCK D'YOU GET THAT IDEA?
BUT...JUST LOOK AT THEM. I WAS TALKING TO SRI ABOUT IT YESTERDAY, AND--
-TT-
ALL RIGHT, CANTON. YOU KNOW WHAT THEY'RE GROWIN' DOWN THERE?
Huh?
THE FIELD. TAKE A LOOK.

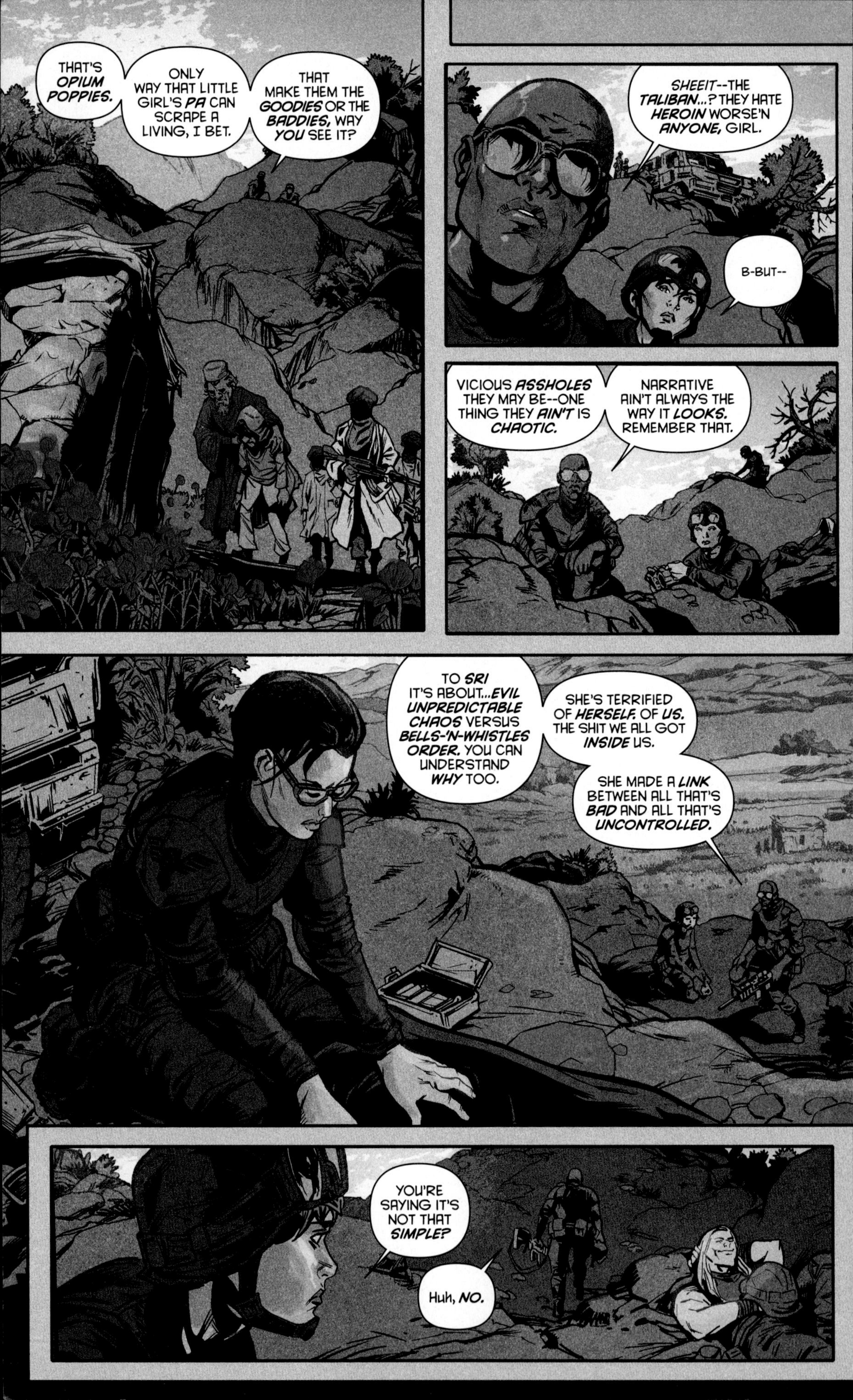
THAT'S OPIUM POPPIES.
ONLY WAY THAT LITTLE GIRL'S PA CAN SCRAPE A LIVING, I BET.
THAT MAKE THEM THE GOODIES OR THE BADDIES, WAY YOU SEE IT?
SHEEIT--THE TALIBAN...? THEY HATE HEROIN WORSE'N ANYONE, GIRL.
B-BUT--
VICIOUS ASSHOLES THEY MAY BE--ONE THING THEY AIN'T IS CHAOTIC.
NARRATIVE AIN'T ALWAYS THE WAY IT LOOKS. REMEMBER THAT.
TO SRI IT'S ABOUT...EVIL UNPREDICTABLE CHAOS VERSUS BELLS-'N-WHISTLES ORDER. YOU CAN UNDERSTAND WHY TOO.
SHE'S TERRIFIED OF HERSELF. OF US. THE SHIT WE ALL GOT INSIDE US.
SHE MADE A LINK BETWEEN ALL THAT'S BAD AND ALL THAT'S UNCONTROLLED.
YOU'RE SAYING IT'S NOT THAT SIMPLE?
Huh, NO.

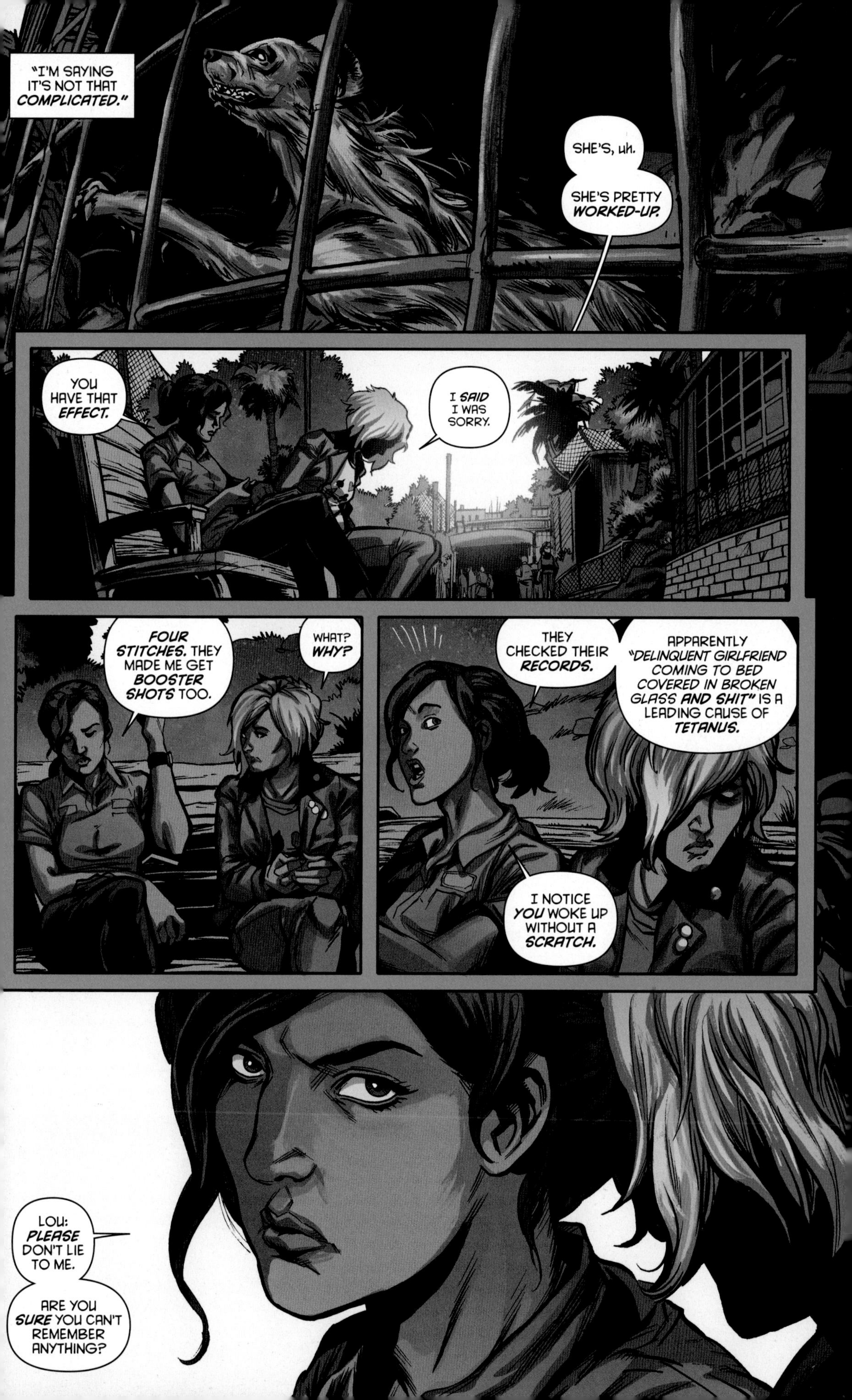
"I'M SAYING IT'S NOT THAT COMPLICATED."
SHE'S, uh.
SHE'S PRETTY WORKED-UP.
YOU HAVE THAT EFFECT.
I SAID I WAS SORRY.
FOUR STITCHES. THEY MADE ME GET BOOSTER SHOTS TOO.
WHAT? WHY?
THEY CHECKED THEIR RECORDS.
APPARENTLY "DELINQUENT GIRLFRIEND COMING TO BED COVERED IN BROKEN GLASS AND SHIT" IS A LEADING CAUSE OF TETANUS.
I NOTICE YOU WOKE UP WITHOUT A SCRATCH.
LOU: PLEASE DON'T LIE TO ME.
ARE YOU SURE YOU CAN'T REMEMBER ANYTHING?

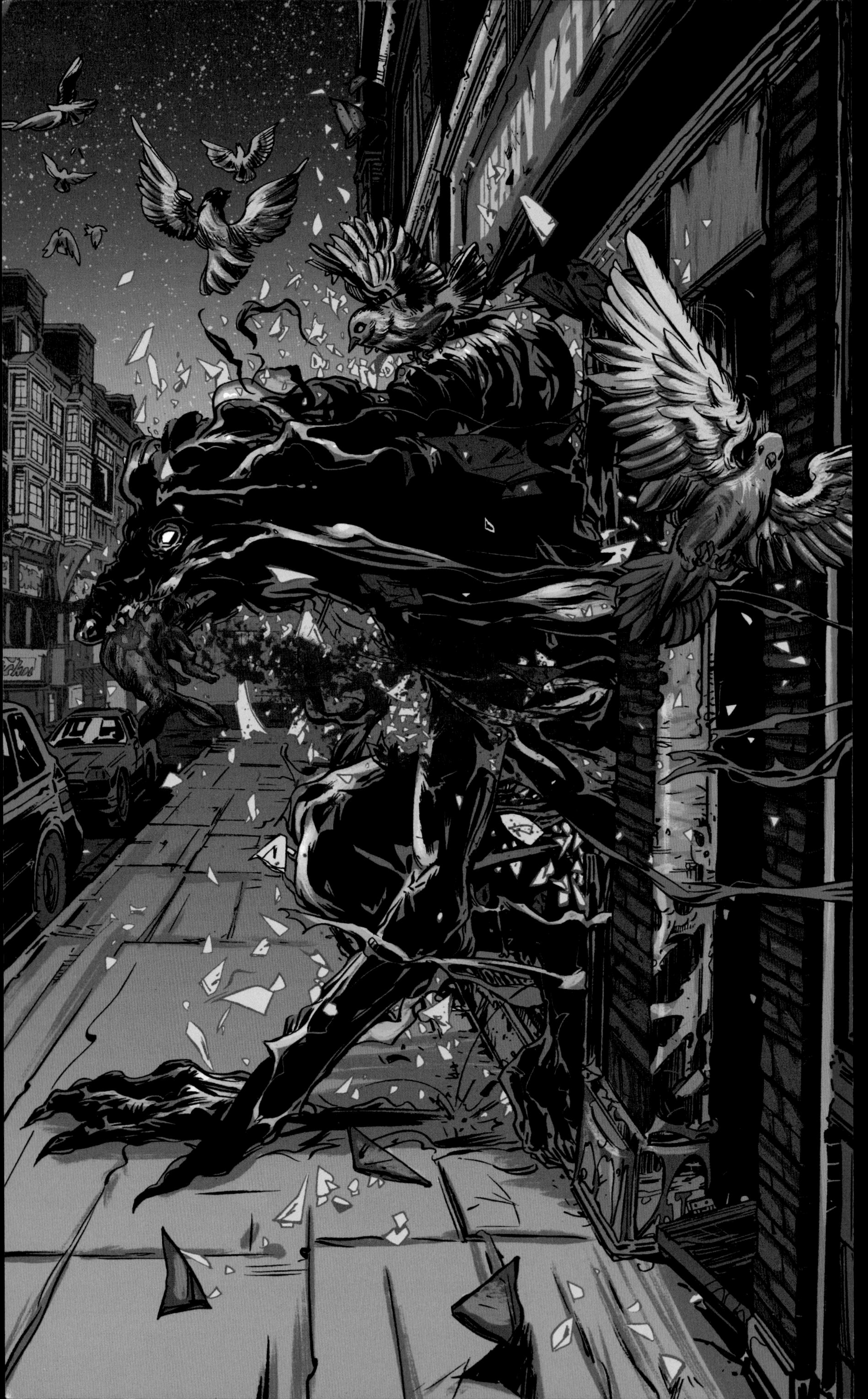

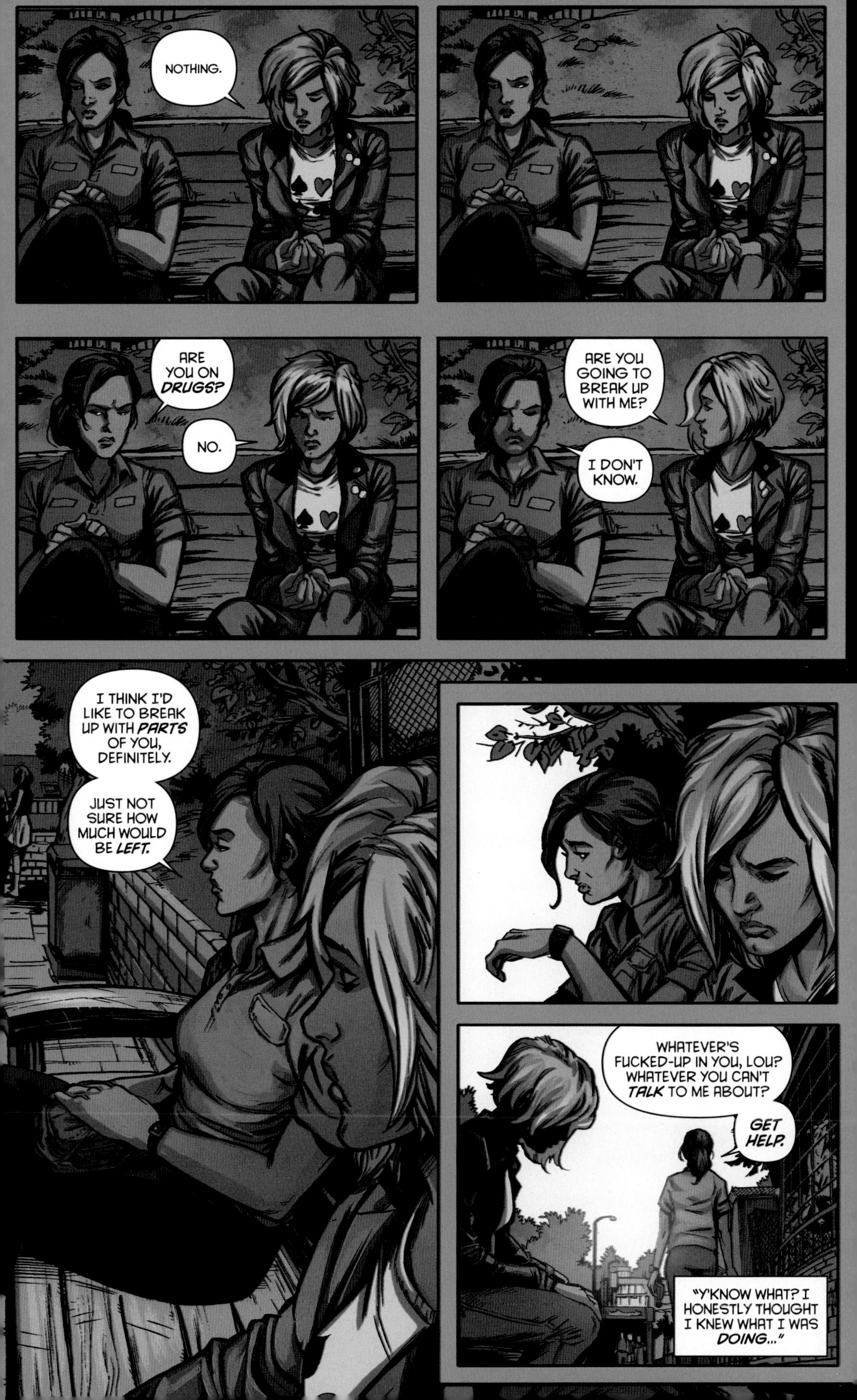
NOTHING.
ARE YOU ON DRUGS?
NO.
ARE YOU GOING TO BREAK UP WITH ME?
I DON'T KNOW.
I THINK I'D LIKE TO BREAK UP WITH PARTS OF YOU, DEFINITELY.
JUST NOT SURE HOW MUCH WOULD BE LEFT.
WHATEVER'S FUCKED-UP IN YOU, LOU? WHATEVER YOU CAN'T TALK TO ME ABOUT?
GET HELP.
"Y'KNOW WHAT? I HONESTLY THOUGHT I KNEW WHAT I WAS DOING..."

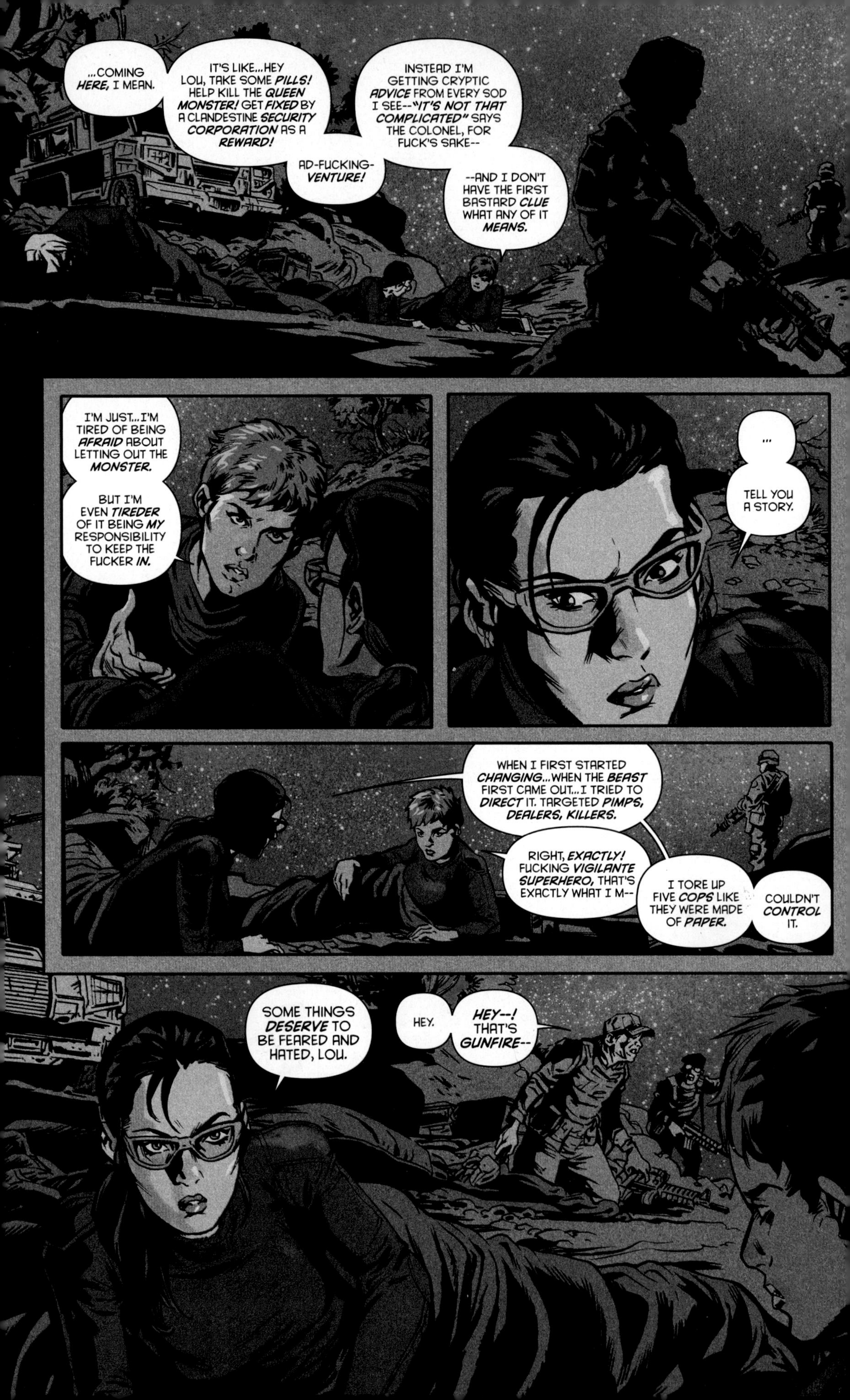
...COMING HERE, I MEAN.
IT'S LIKE...HEY LOU, TAKE SOME PILLS! HELP KILL THE QUEEN MONSTER! GET FIXED BY A CLANDESTINE SECURITY CORPORATION AS A REWARD!
AD-FUCKING-VENTURE!
INSTEAD I'M GETTING CRYPTIC ADVICE FROM EVERY SOD I SEE--"IT'S NOT THAT COMPLICATED" SAYS THE COLONEL, FOR FUCK'S SAKE--
--AND I DON'T HAVE THE FIRST BASTARD CLUE WHAT ANY OF IT MEANS.
I'M JUST...I'M TIRED OF BEING AFRAID ABOUT LETTING OUT THE MONSTER.
BUT I'M EVEN TIREDER OF IT BEING MY RESPONSIBILITY TO KEEP THE FUCKER IN.
...
TELL YOU A STORY.
WHEN I FIRST STARTED CHANGING...WHEN THE BEAST FIRST CAME OUT...I TRIED TO DIRECT IT. TARGETED PIMPS, DEALERS, KILLERS.
RIGHT, EXACTLY! FUCKING VIGILANTE SUPERHERO, THAT'S EXACTLY WHAT I M--
I TORE UP FIVE COPS LIKE THEY WERE MADE OF PAPER.
COULDN'T CONTROL IT.
SOME THINGS DESERVE TO BE FEARED AND HATED, LOU.
HEY.
HEY--! THAT'S GUNFIRE--

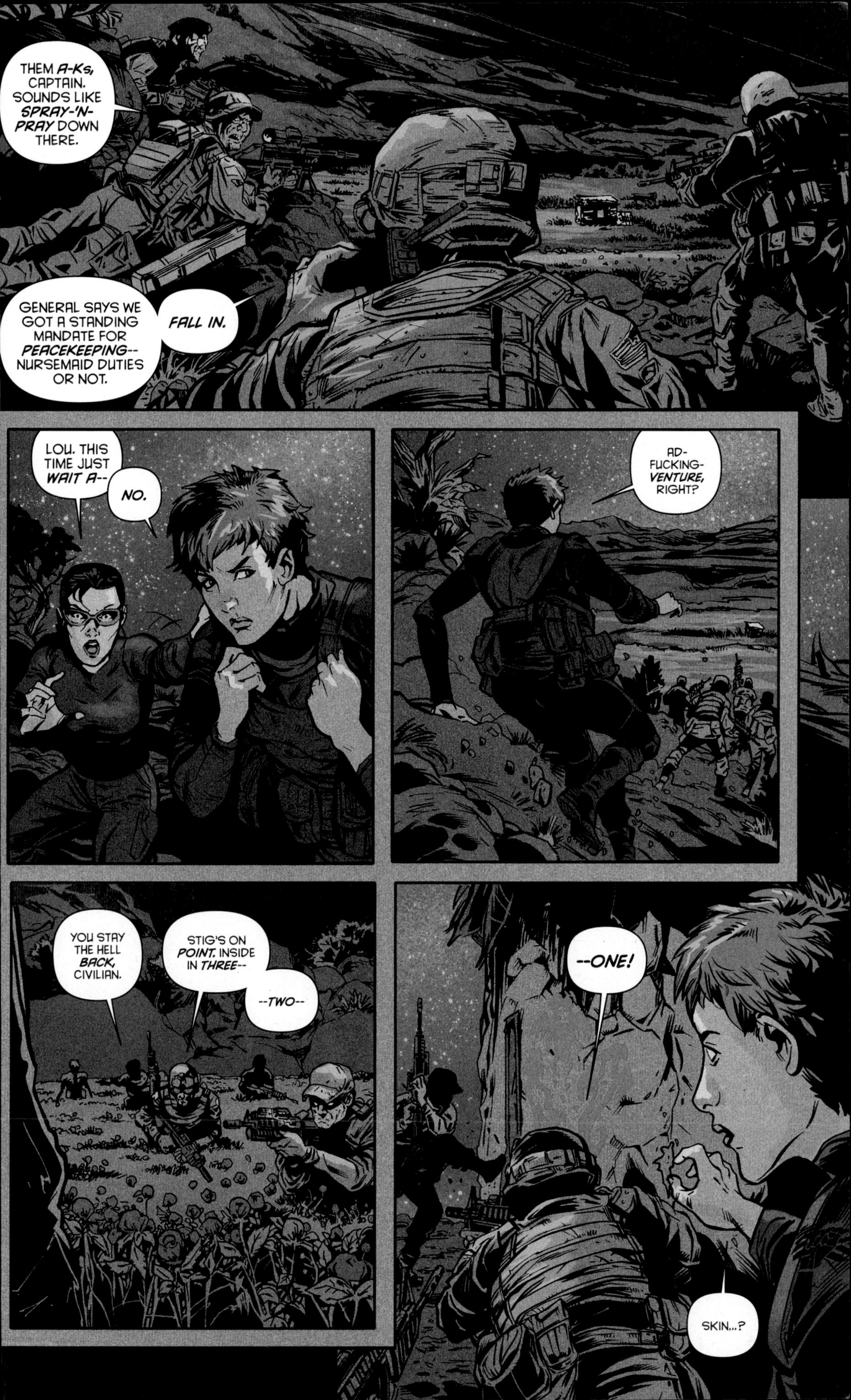
THEM A-Ks, CAPTAIN. SOUNDS LIKE SPRAY-'N-PRAY DOWN THERE.
GENERAL SAYS WE GOT A STANDING MANDATE FOR PEACEKEEPING-- NURSEMAID DUTIES OR NOT.
FALL IN.
LOU. THIS TIME JUST WAIT A--
NO.
AD-FUCKING-VENTURE, RIGHT?
YOU STAY THE HELL BACK, CIVILIAN.
STIG'S ON POINT. INSIDE IN THREE--
--TWO--
--ONE!
SKIN...?

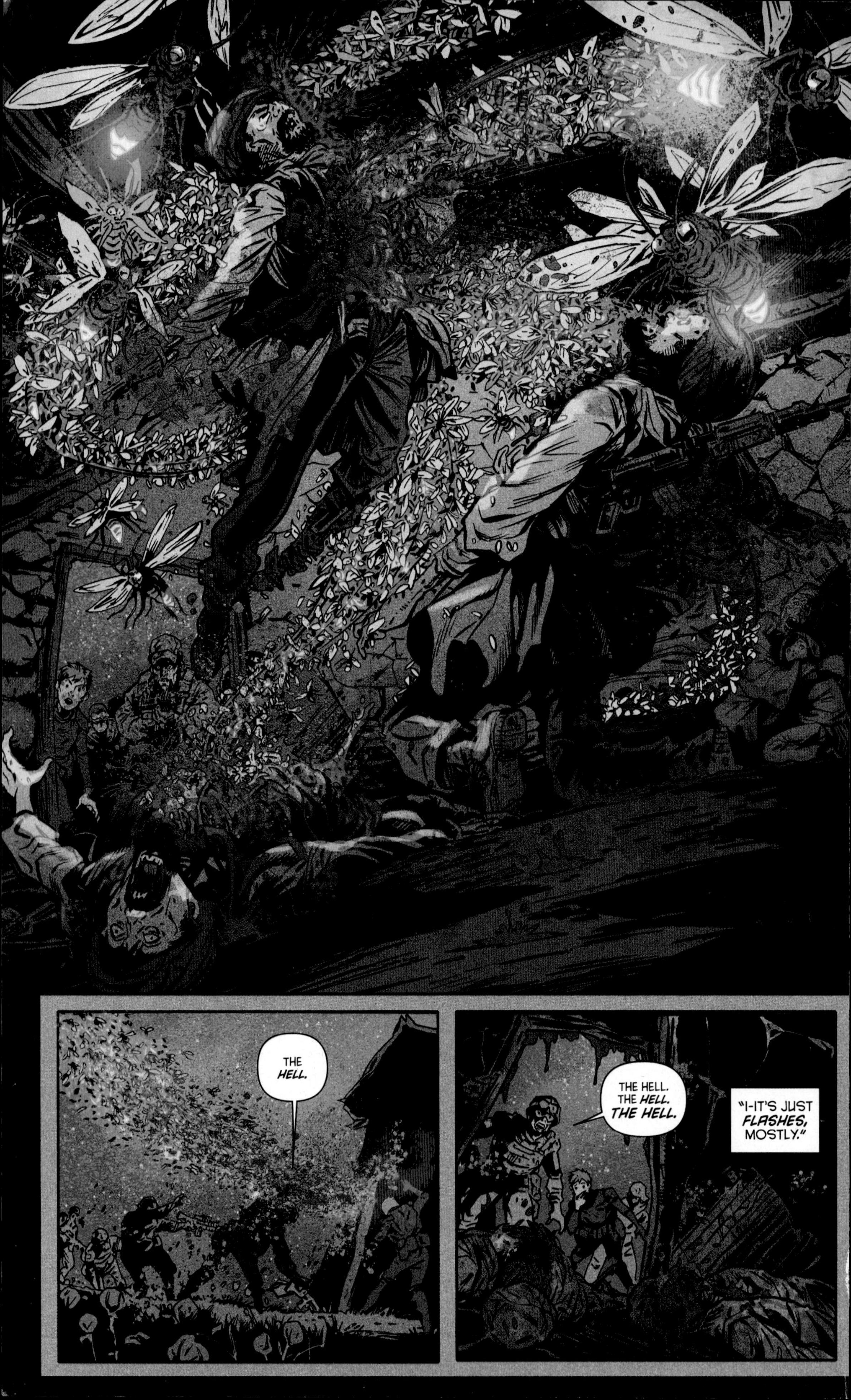
THE *HELL.*
THE HELL. THE *HELL.* ***THE HELL.***
"I-IT'S JUST *FLASHES,* MOSTLY."

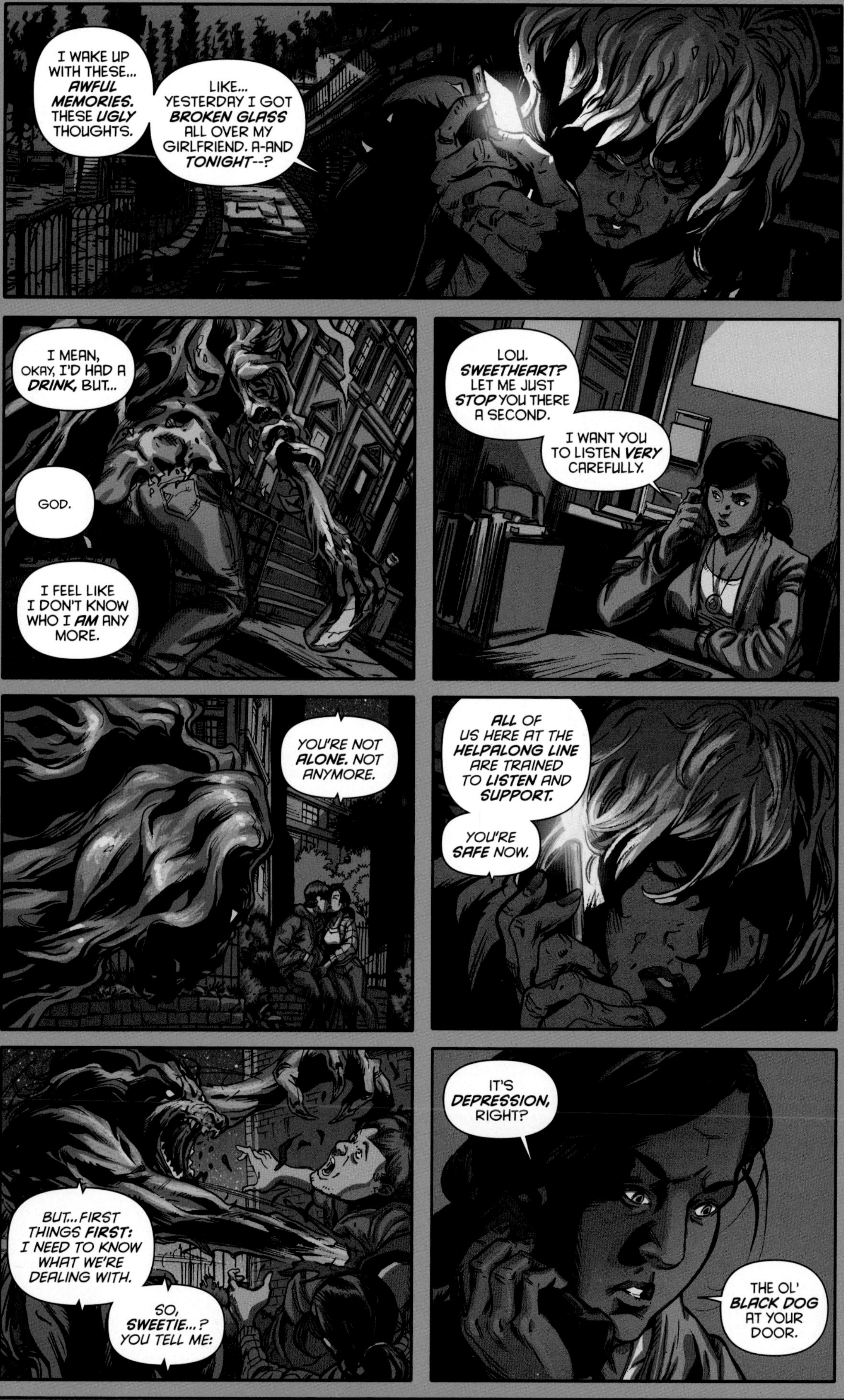
I WAKE UP WITH THESE... AWFUL MEMORIES. THESE UGLY THOUGHTS.
LIKE... YESTERDAY I GOT BROKEN GLASS ALL OVER MY GIRLFRIEND. A-AND TONIGHT--?
I MEAN, OKAY, I'D HAD A DRINK, BUT...
GOD.
I FEEL LIKE I DON'T KNOW WHO I AM ANY MORE.
LOU. SWEETHEART? LET ME JUST STOP YOU THERE A SECOND.
I WANT YOU TO LISTEN VERY CAREFULLY.
YOU'RE NOT ALONE. NOT ANYMORE.
ALL OF US HERE AT THE HELPALONG LINE ARE TRAINED TO LISTEN AND SUPPORT.
YOU'RE SAFE NOW.
BUT...FIRST THINGS FIRST: I NEED TO KNOW WHAT WE'RE DEALING WITH.
SO, SWEETIE...? YOU TELL ME:
IT'S DEPRESSION, RIGHT?
THE OL' BLACK DOG AT YOUR DOOR.

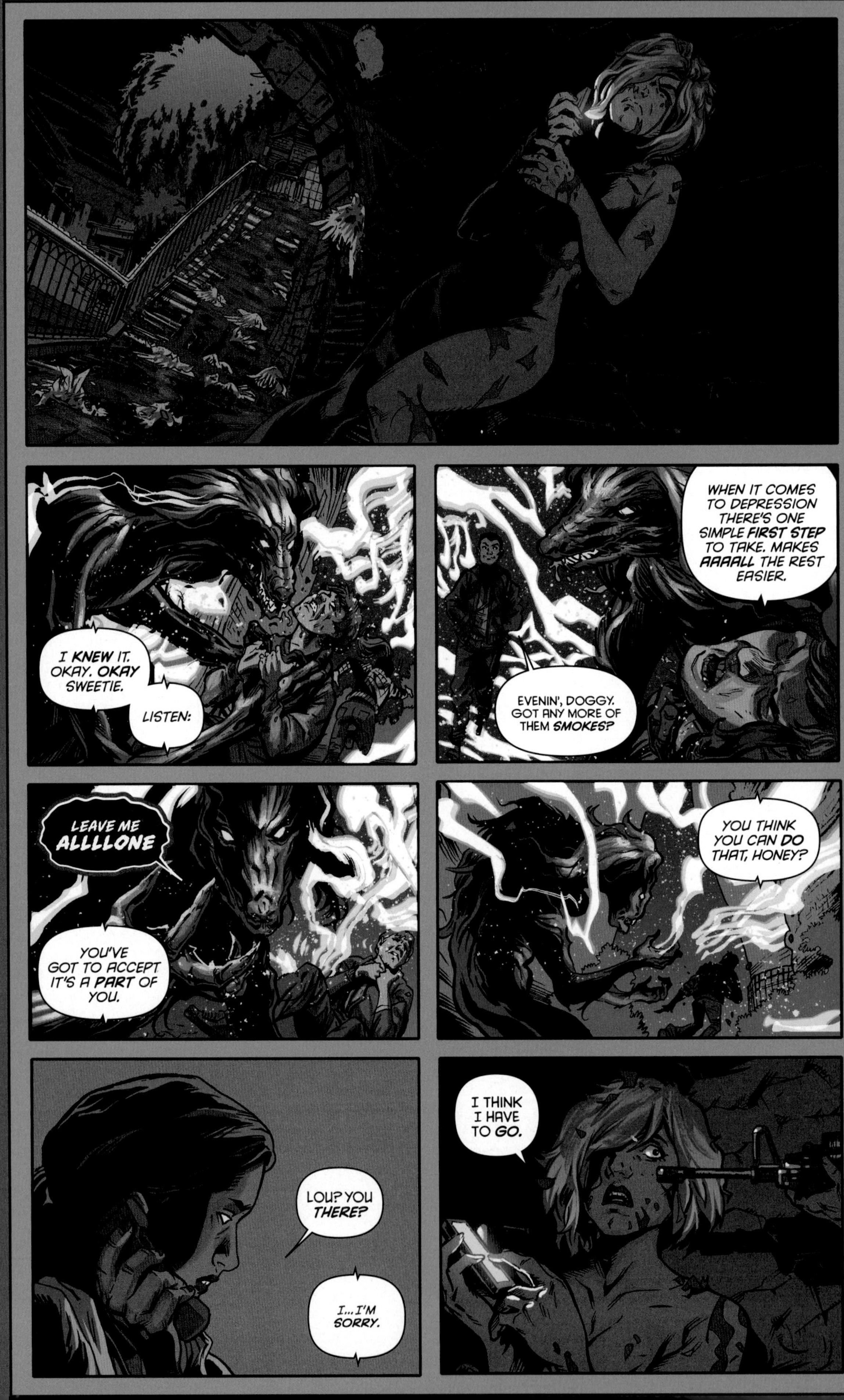
I KNEW IT. OKAY. OKAY SWEETIE.
LISTEN:
WHEN IT COMES TO DEPRESSION THERE'S ONE SIMPLE FIRST STEP TO TAKE. MAKES AAAALL THE REST EASIER.
EVENIN', DOGGY. GOT ANY MORE OF THEM SMOKES?
LEAVE ME ALLLLONE
YOU'VE GOT TO ACCEPT IT'S A PART OF YOU.
YOU THINK YOU CAN DO THAT, HONEY?
LOU? YOU THERE?
I... I'M SORRY.
I THINK I HAVE TO GO.

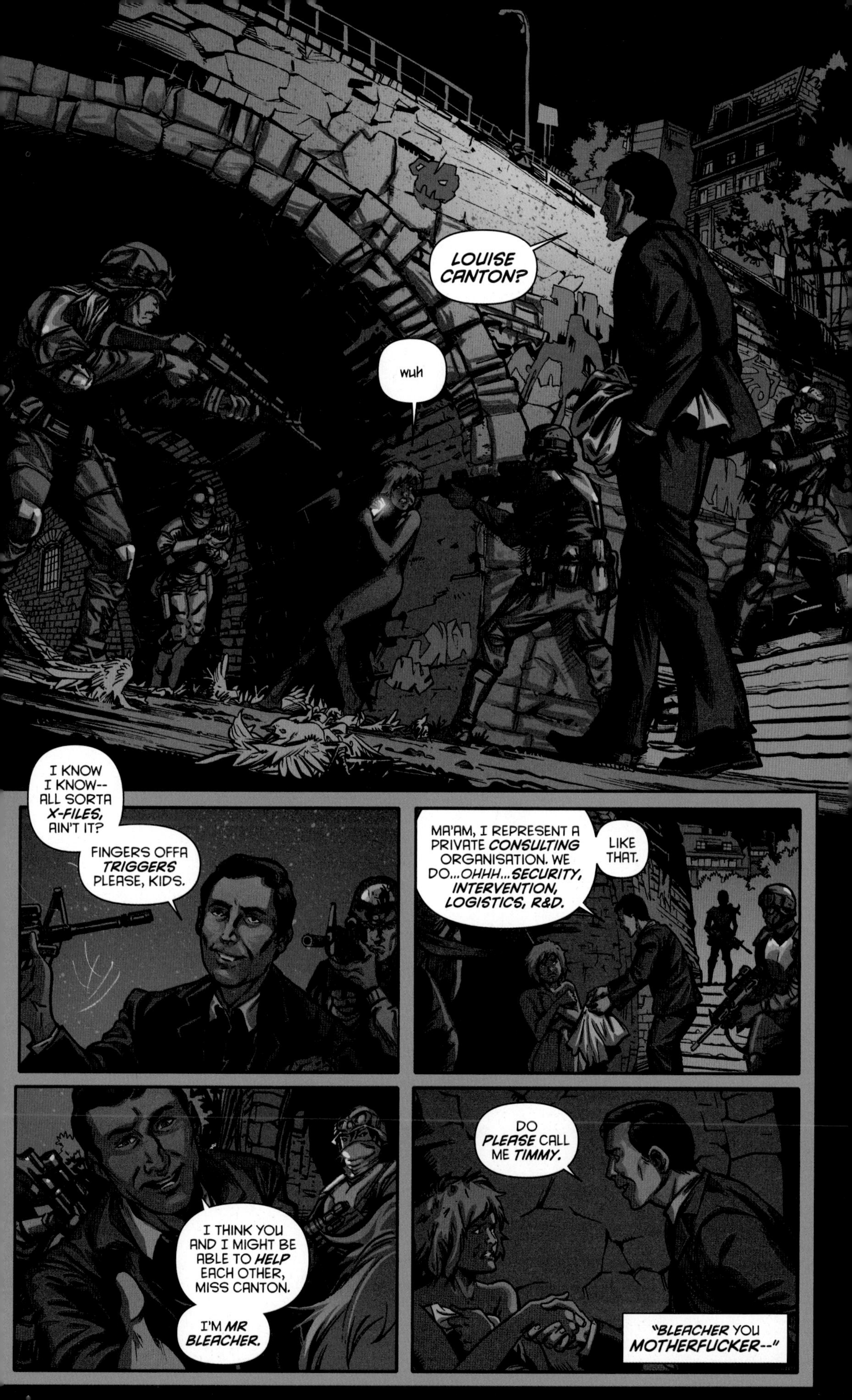
LOUISE CANTON?
wuh
I KNOW I KNOW-- ALL SORTA X-FILES, AIN'T IT?
FINGERS OFFA TRIGGERS PLEASE, KIDS.
MA'AM, I REPRESENT A PRIVATE CONSULTING ORGANISATION. WE DO...OHHH...SECURITY, INTERVENTION, LOGISTICS, R&D.
LIKE THAT.
I THINK YOU AND I MIGHT BE ABLE TO HELP EACH OTHER, MISS CANTON.
I'M MR BLEACHER.
DO PLEASE CALL ME TIMMY.
"BLEACHER YOU MOTHERFUCKER--"

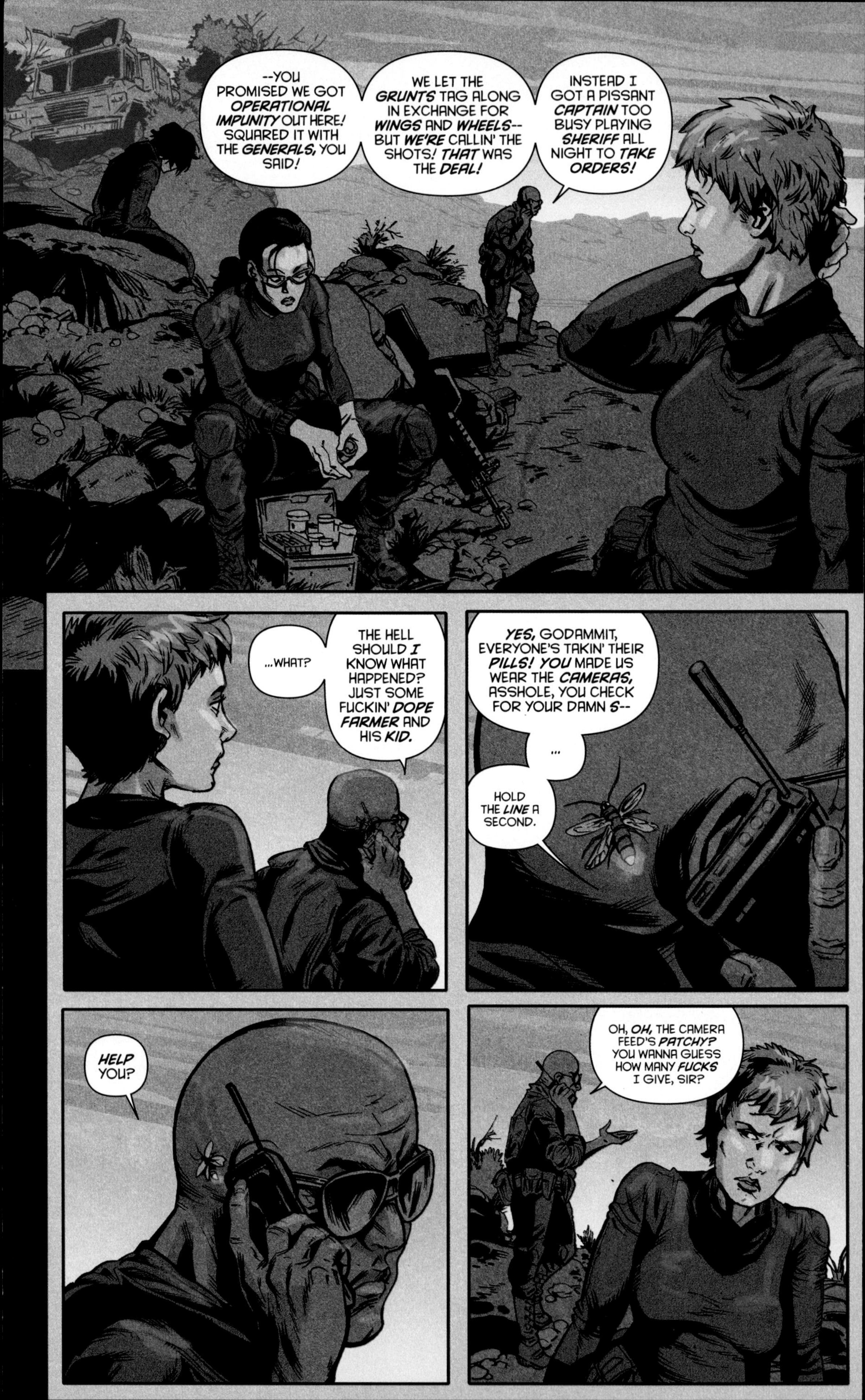
--YOU PROMISED WE GOT OPERATIONAL IMPUNITY OUT HERE! SQUARED IT WITH THE GENERALS, YOU SAID!
WE LET THE GRUNTS TAG ALONG IN EXCHANGE FOR WINGS AND WHEELS-- BUT WE'RE CALLIN' THE SHOTS! THAT WAS THE DEAL!
INSTEAD I GOT A PISSANT CAPTAIN TOO BUSY PLAYING SHERIFF ALL NIGHT TO TAKE ORDERS!
...WHAT?
THE HELL SHOULD I KNOW WHAT HAPPENED? JUST SOME FUCKIN' DOPE FARMER AND HIS KID.
YES, GODAMMIT, EVERYONE'S TAKIN' THEIR PILLS! YOU MADE US WEAR THE CAMERAS, ASSHOLE, YOU CHECK FOR YOUR DAMN S--
...
HOLD THE LINE A SECOND.
HELP YOU?
OH, OH, THE CAMERA FEED'S PATCHY? YOU WANNA GUESS HOW MANY FUCKS I GIVE, SIR?

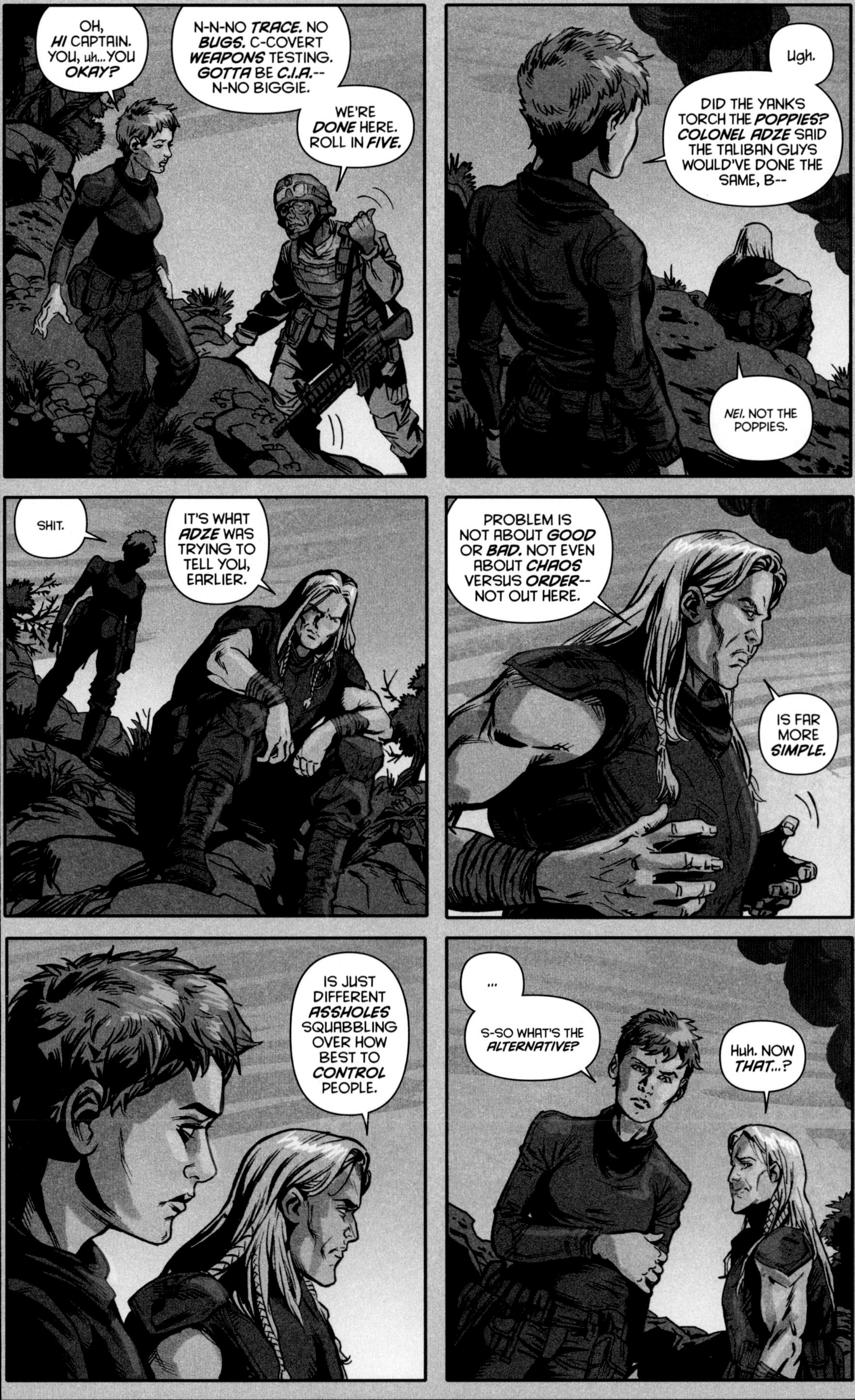
OH, HI CAPTAIN. YOU, uh...YOU OKAY?
N-N-NO TRACE. NO BUGS. C-COVERT WEAPONS TESTING. GOTTA BE C.I.A.-- N-NO BIGGIE.
WE'RE DONE HERE. ROLL IN FIVE.
Ugh.
DID THE YANKS TORCH THE POPPIES? COLONEL ADZE SAID THE TALIBAN GUYS WOULD'VE DONE THE SAME, B--
NEI. NOT THE POPPIES.
SHIT.
IT'S WHAT ADZE WAS TRYING TO TELL YOU, EARLIER.
PROBLEM IS NOT ABOUT GOOD OR BAD. NOT EVEN ABOUT CHAOS VERSUS ORDER-- NOT OUT HERE.
IS FAR MORE SIMPLE.
IS JUST DIFFERENT ASSHOLES SQUABBLING OVER HOW BEST TO CONTROL PEOPLE.
...
S-SO WHAT'S THE ALTERNATIVE?
Huh. NOW THAT...?

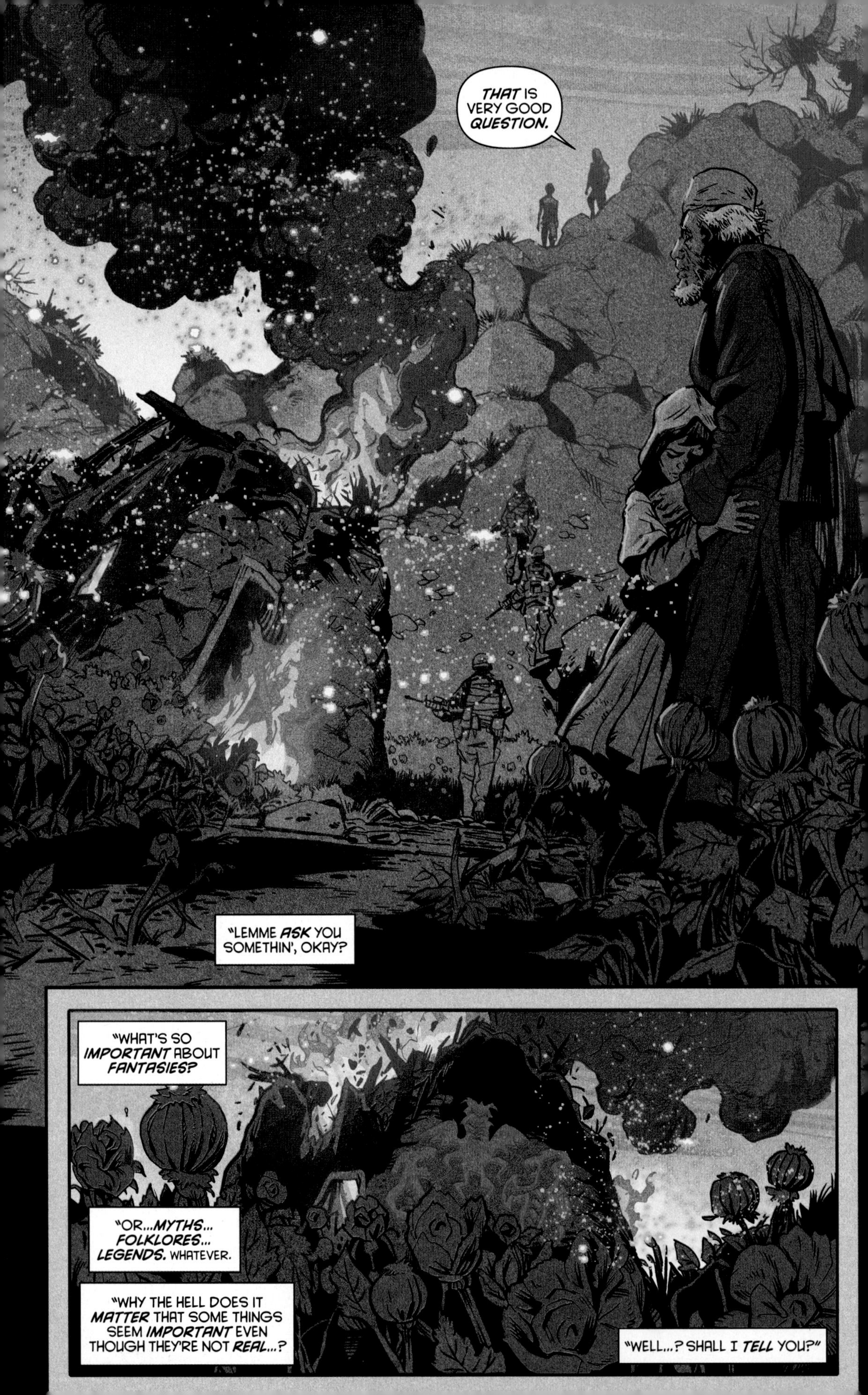
THAT IS VERY GOOD QUESTION.
"LEMME ASK YOU SOMETHIN', OKAY?
"WHAT'S SO IMPORTANT ABOUT FANTASIES?
"OR...MYTHS... FOLKLORES... LEGENDS. WHATEVER.
"WHY THE HELL DOES IT MATTER THAT SOME THINGS SEEM IMPORTANT EVEN THOUGH THEY'RE NOT REAL...?
"WELL...? SHALL I TELL YOU?"

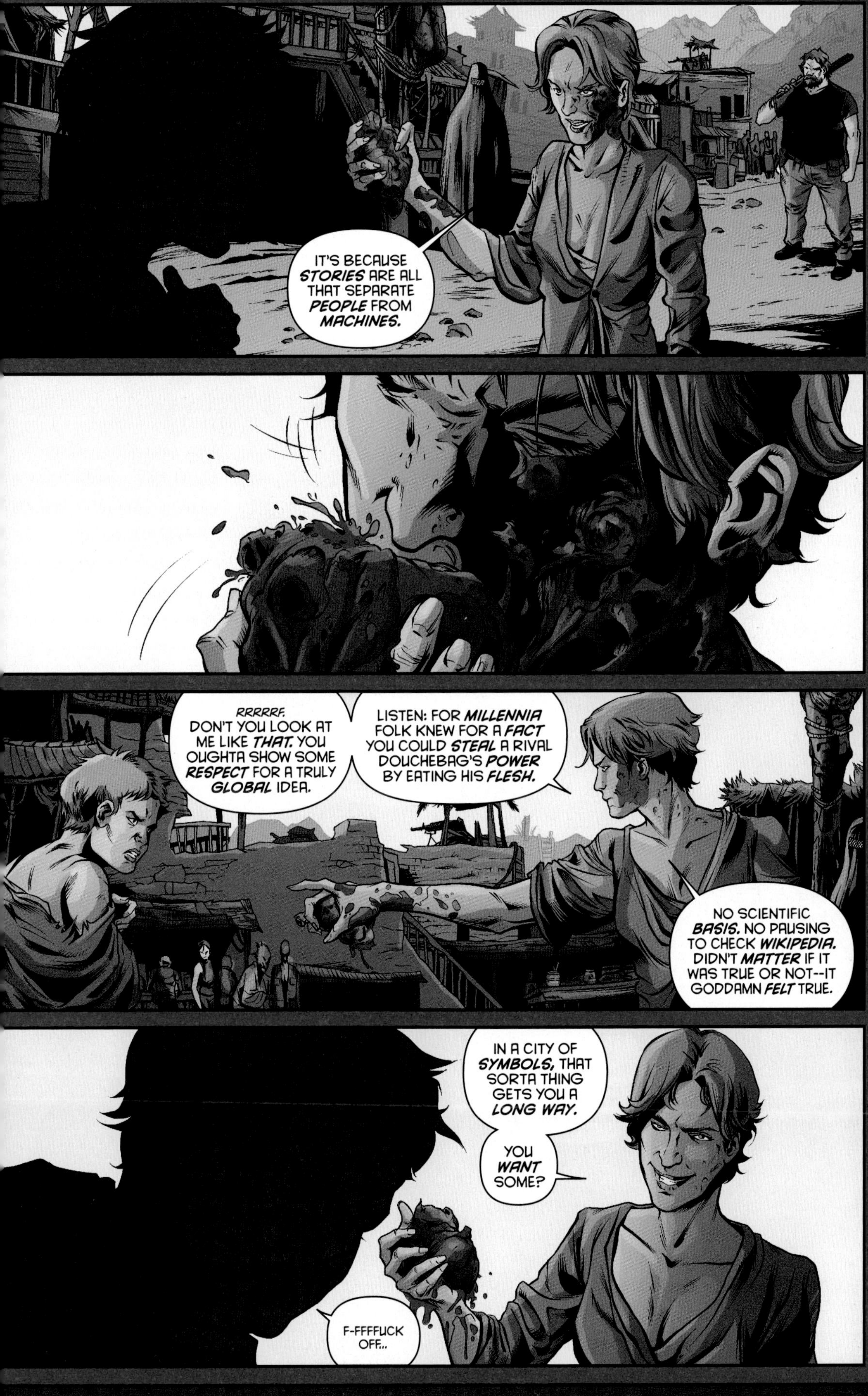
IT'S BECAUSE STORIES ARE ALL THAT SEPARATE PEOPLE FROM MACHINES.
RRRRRF. DON'T YOU LOOK AT ME LIKE THAT. YOU OUGHTA SHOW SOME RESPECT FOR A TRULY GLOBAL IDEA.
LISTEN: FOR MILLENNIA FOLK KNEW FOR A FACT YOU COULD STEAL A RIVAL DOUCHEBAG'S POWER BY EATING HIS FLESH.
NO SCIENTIFIC BASIS. NO PAUSING TO CHECK WIKIPEDIA. DIDN'T MATTER IF IT WAS TRUE OR NOT--IT GODDAMN FELT TRUE.
IN A CITY OF SYMBOLS, THAT SORTA THING GETS YOU A LONG WAY.
YOU WANT SOME?
F-FFFFUCK OFF...

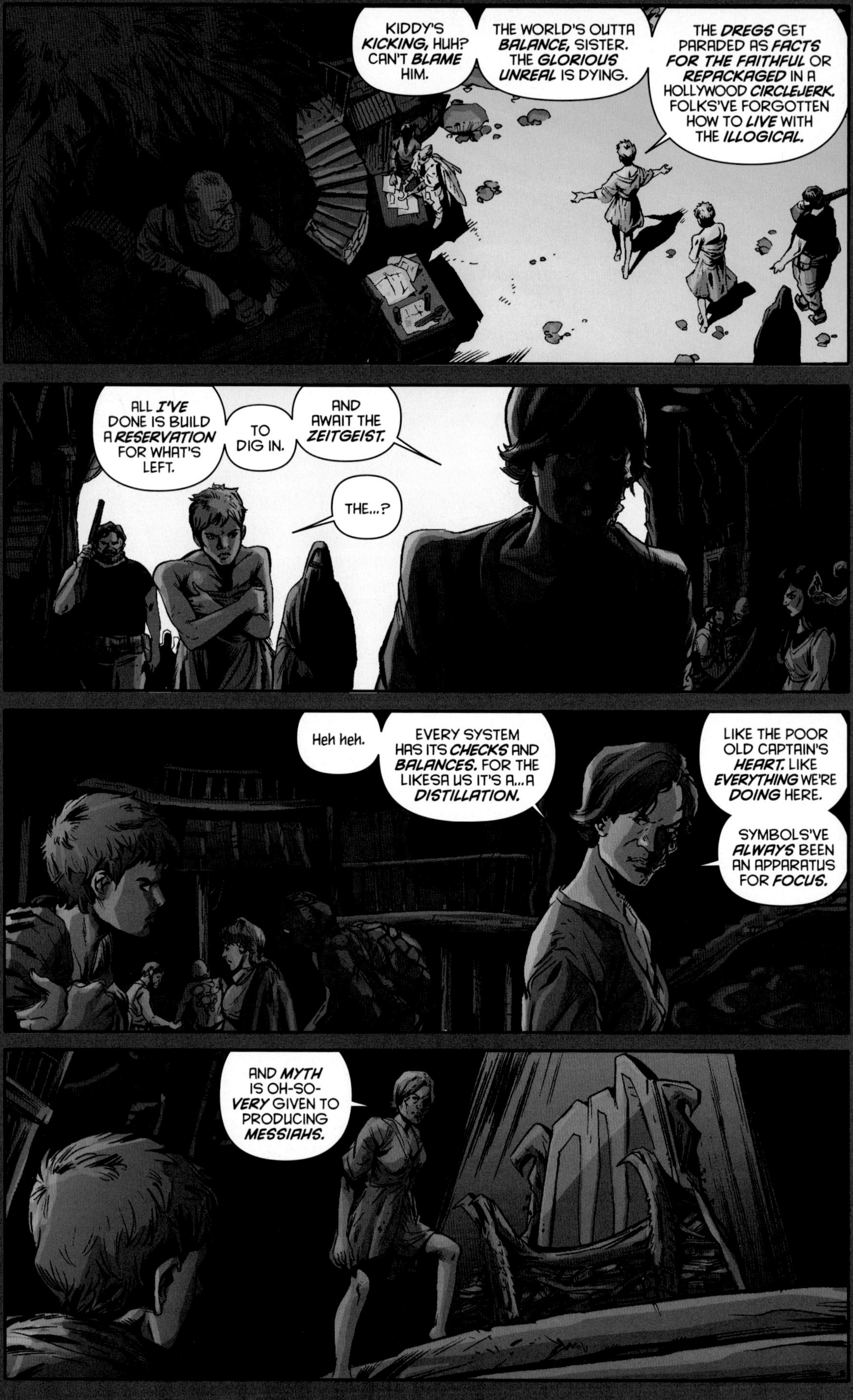
KIDDY'S KICKING, HUH? CAN'T BLAME HIM.
THE WORLD'S OUTTA BALANCE, SISTER. THE GLORIOUS UNREAL IS DYING.
THE DREGS GET PARADED AS FACTS FOR THE FAITHFUL OR REPACKAGED IN A HOLLYWOOD CIRCLEJERK. FOLKS'VE FORGOTTEN HOW TO LIVE WITH THE ILLOGICAL.
ALL I'VE DONE IS BUILD A RESERVATION FOR WHAT'S LEFT.
TO DIG IN.
AND AWAIT THE ZEITGEIST.
THE...?
Heh heh.
EVERY SYSTEM HAS ITS CHECKS AND BALANCES. FOR THE LIKESA US IT'S A...A DISTILLATION.
LIKE THE POOR OLD CAPTAIN'S HEART. LIKE EVERYTHING WE'RE DOING HERE.
SYMBOLS'VE ALWAYS BEEN AN APPARATUS FOR FOCUS.
AND MYTH IS OH-SO-VERY GIVEN TO PRODUCING MESSIAHS.

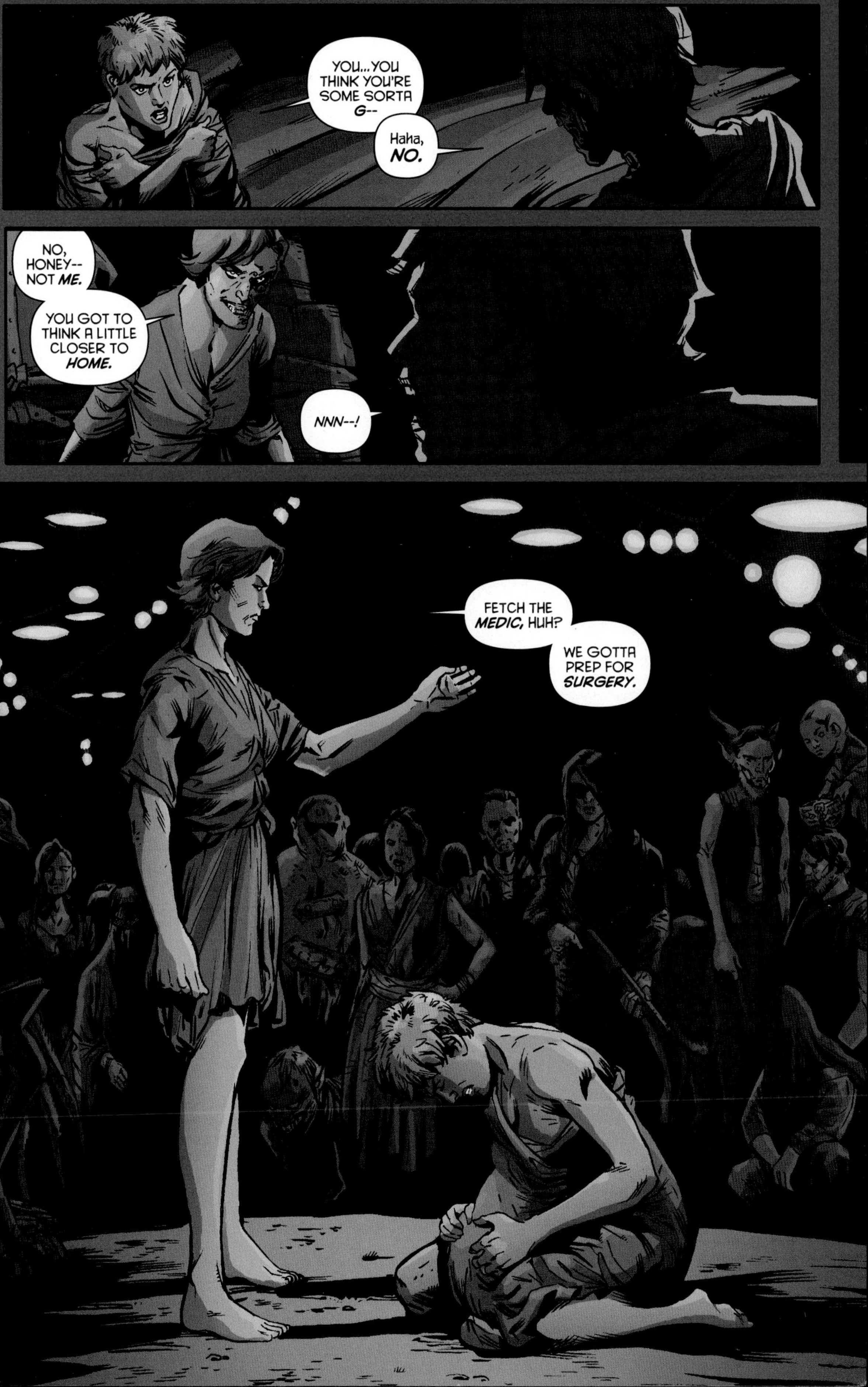
YOU...YOU THINK YOU'RE SOME SORTA G--
Haha, NO.
NO, HONEY-- NOT ME.
YOU GOT TO THINK A LITTLE CLOSER TO HOME.
NNN--!
FETCH THE MEDIC, HUH?
WE GOTTA PREP FOR SURGERY.

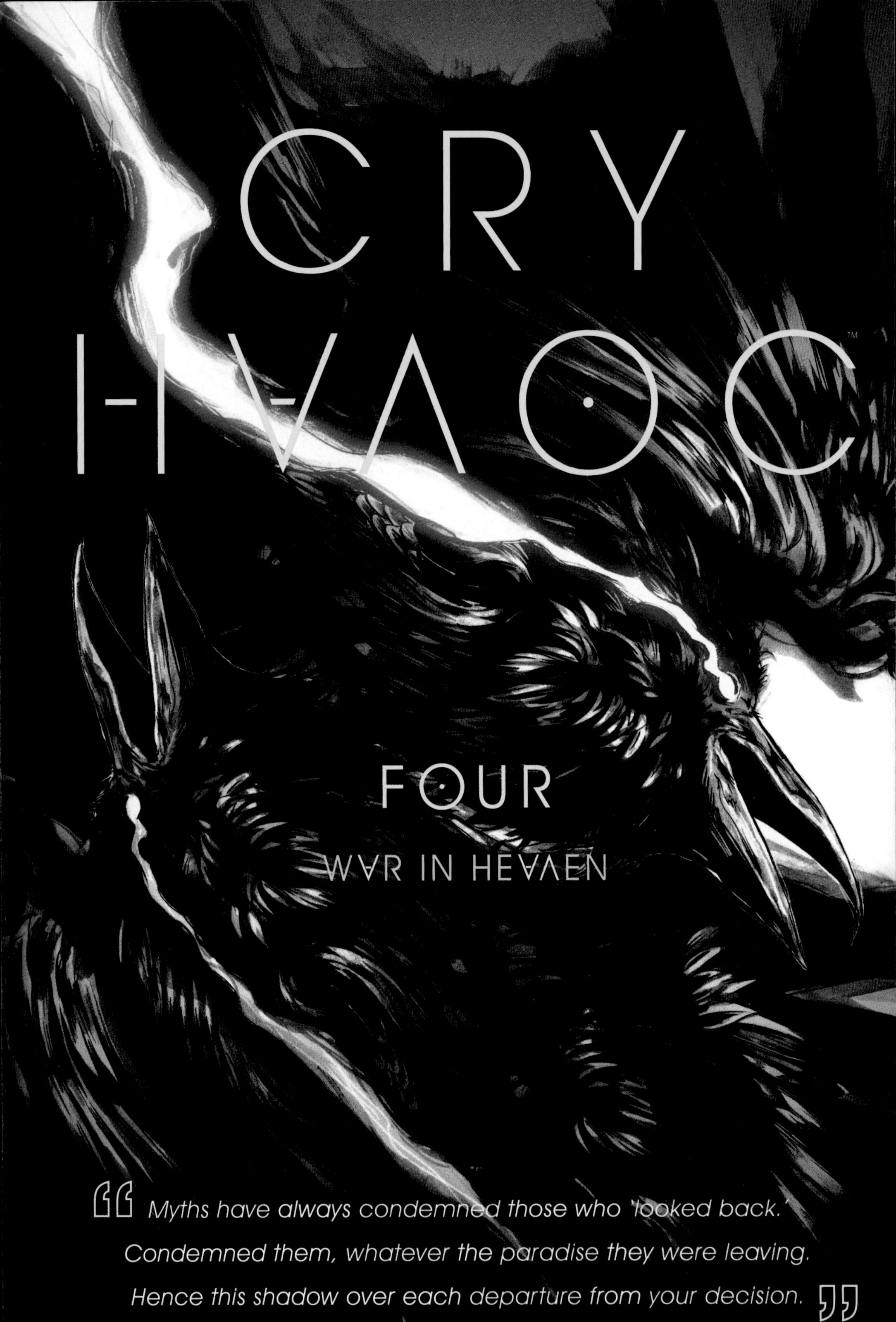
CRY
HAVOC™
FOUR
WAR IN HEAVEN
"Myths have always condemned those who 'looked back.'
Condemned them, whatever the paradise they were leaving.
Hence this shadow over each departure from your decision."

variant cover
DECLAN SHALVEY
JORDIE BELLAIRE

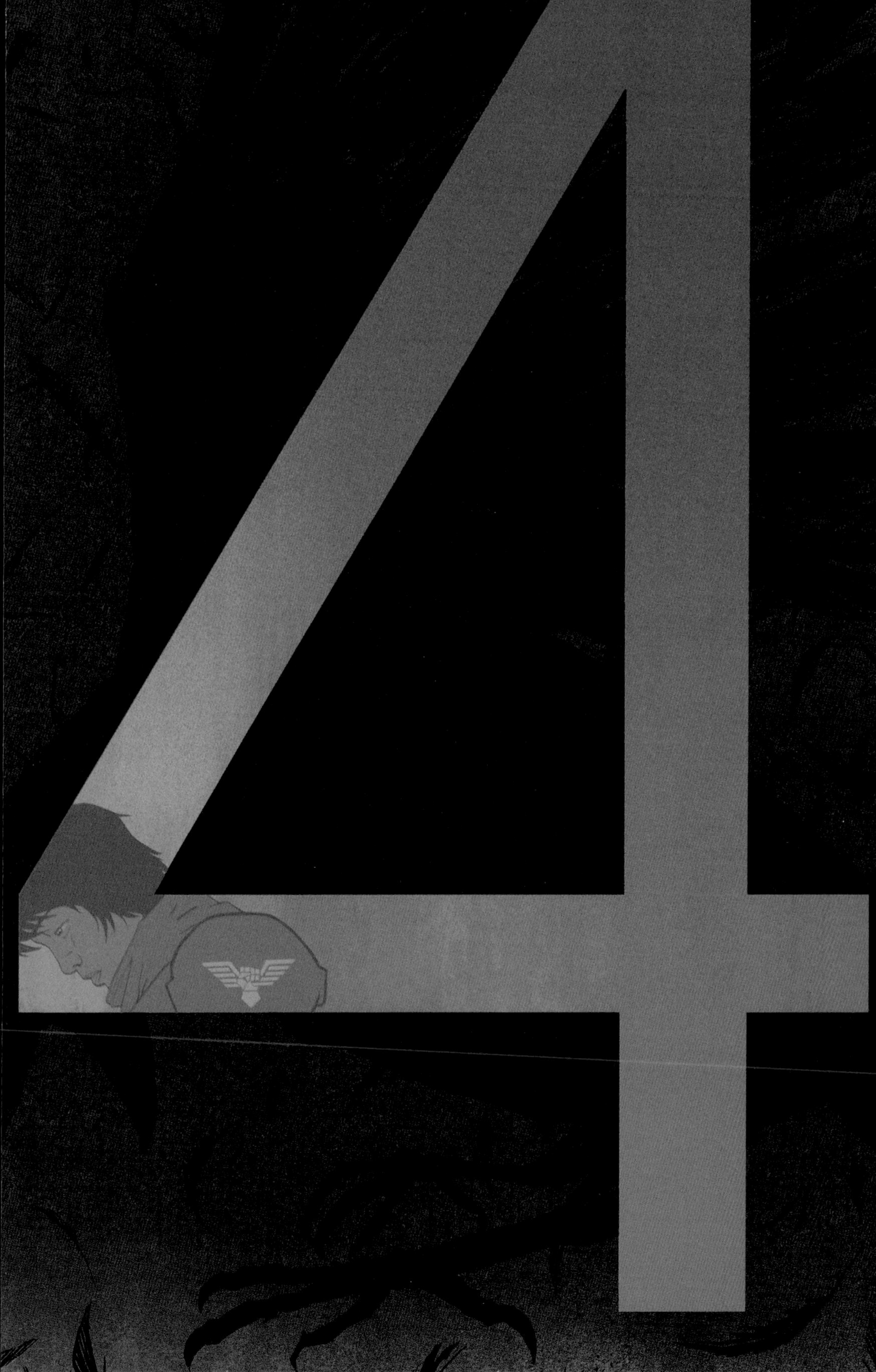

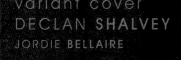

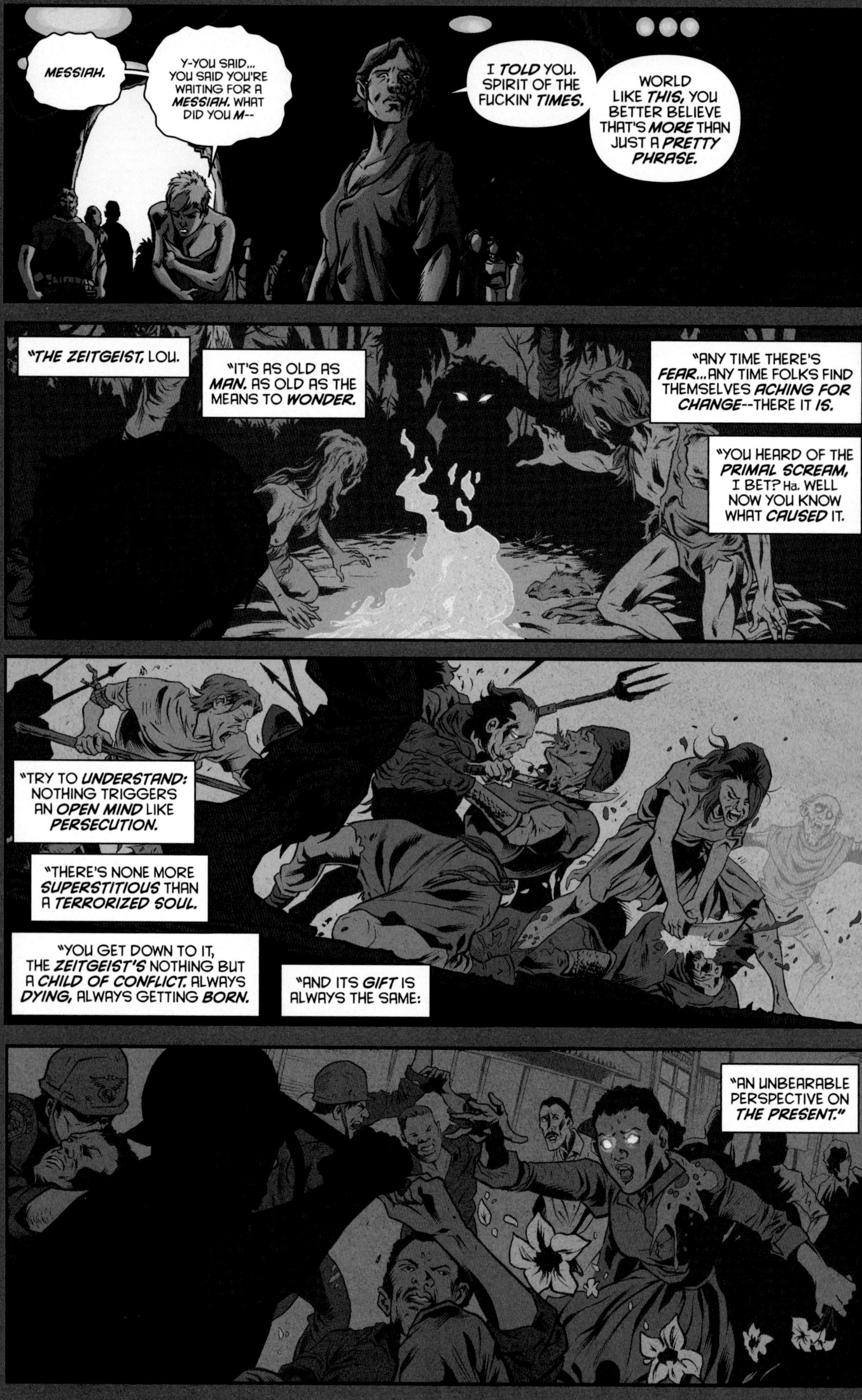
MESSIAH.
Y-YOU SAID... YOU SAID YOU'RE WAITING FOR A MESSIAH. WHAT DID YOU M--
I TOLD YOU. SPIRIT OF THE FUCKIN' TIMES.
WORLD LIKE THIS, YOU BETTER BELIEVE THAT'S MORE THAN JUST A PRETTY PHRASE.
"THE ZEITGEIST, LOU.
"IT'S AS OLD AS MAN. AS OLD AS THE MEANS TO WONDER.
"ANY TIME THERE'S FEAR... ANY TIME FOLKS FIND THEMSELVES ACHING FOR CHANGE--THERE IT IS.
"YOU HEARD OF THE PRIMAL SCREAM, I BET? Ha. WELL NOW YOU KNOW WHAT CAUSED IT.
"TRY TO UNDERSTAND: NOTHING TRIGGERS AN OPEN MIND LIKE PERSECUTION.
"THERE'S NONE MORE SUPERSTITIOUS THAN A TERRORIZED SOUL.
"YOU GET DOWN TO IT, THE ZEITGEIST'S NOTHING BUT A CHILD OF CONFLICT. ALWAYS DYING, ALWAYS GETTING BORN.
"AND ITS GIFT IS ALWAYS THE SAME:
"AN UNBEARABLE PERSPECTIVE ON THE PRESENT."

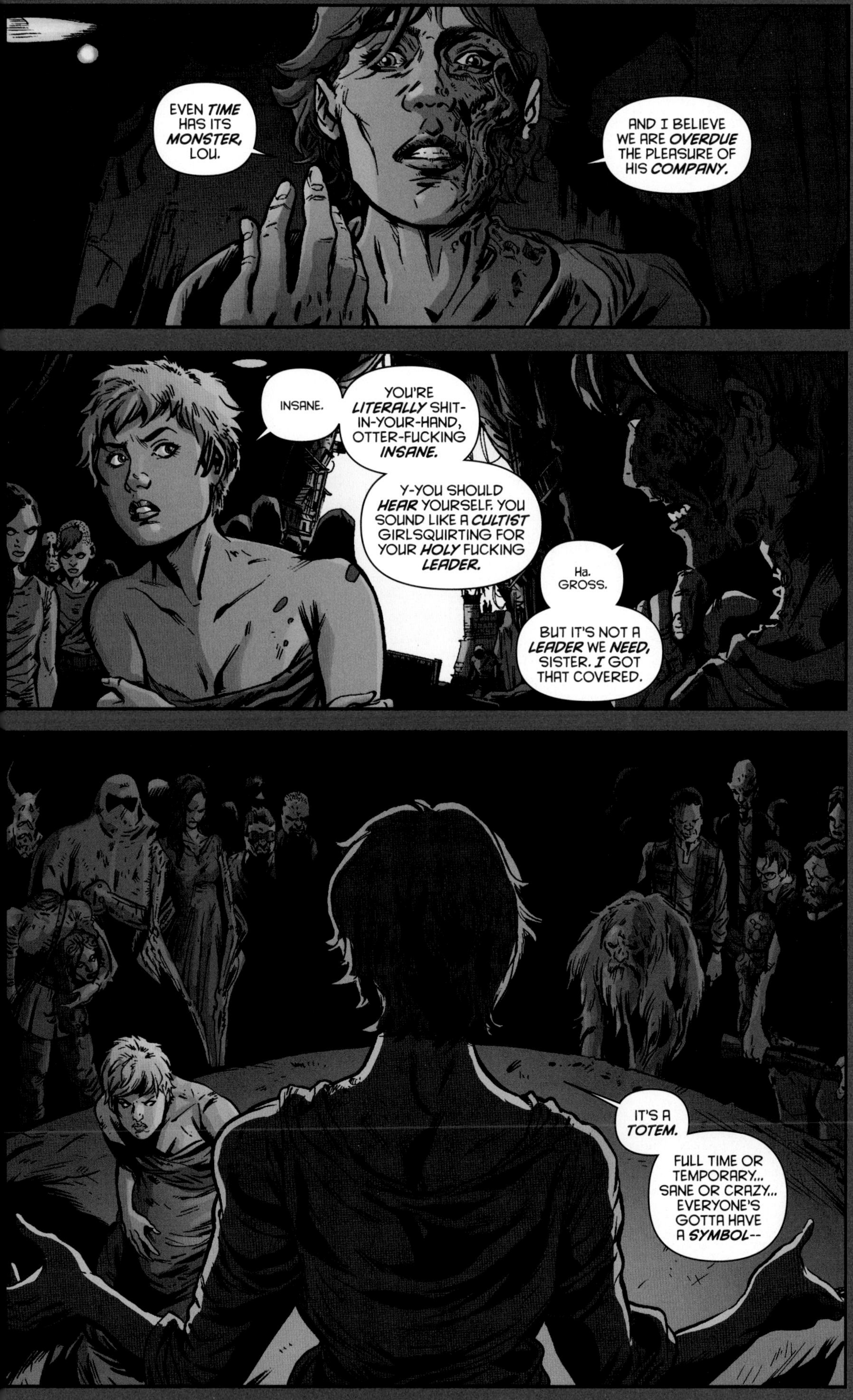
EVEN TIME HAS ITS MONSTER, LOU.
AND I BELIEVE WE ARE OVERDUE THE PLEASURE OF HIS COMPANY.
INSANE.
YOU'RE LITERALLY SHIT-IN-YOUR-HAND, OTTER-FUCKING INSANE.
Y-YOU SHOULD HEAR YOURSELF. YOU SOUND LIKE A CULTIST GIRLSQUIRTING FOR YOUR HOLY FUCKING LEADER.
Ha. GROSS.
BUT IT'S NOT A LEADER WE NEED, SISTER. I GOT THAT COVERED.
IT'S A TOTEM.
FULL TIME OR TEMPORARY... SANE OR CRAZY... EVERYONE'S GOTTA HAVE A SYMBOL--

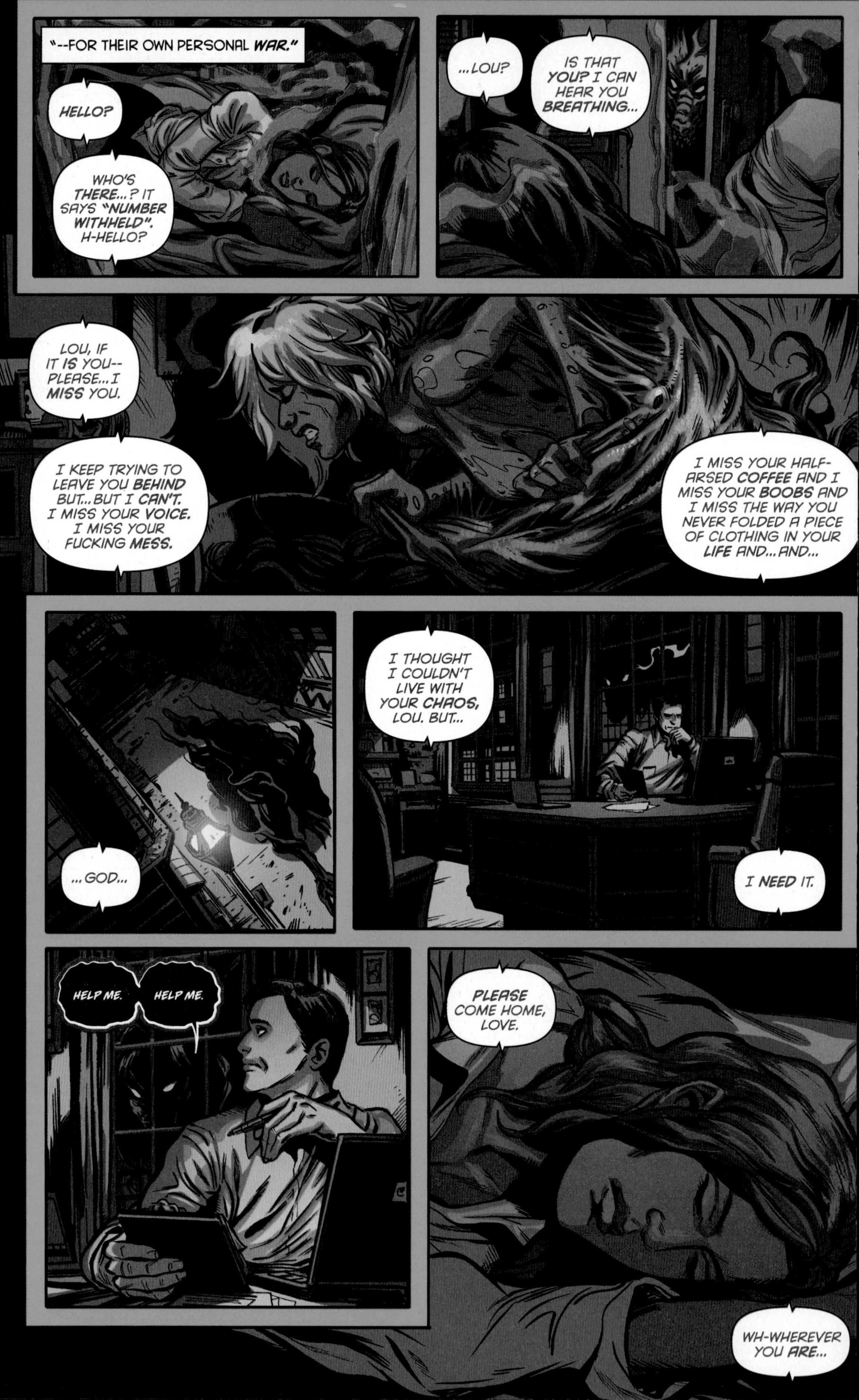
"--FOR THEIR OWN PERSONAL WAR."
HELLO?
WHO'S THERE...? IT SAYS "NUMBER WITHHELD". H-HELLO?
...LOU?
IS THAT YOU? I CAN HEAR YOU BREATHING...
LOU, IF IT IS YOU-- PLEASE...I MISS YOU.
I KEEP TRYING TO LEAVE YOU BEHIND BUT...BUT I CAN'T. I MISS YOUR VOICE. I MISS YOUR FUCKING MESS.
I MISS YOUR HALF-ARSED COFFEE AND I MISS YOUR BOOBS AND I MISS THE WAY YOU NEVER FOLDED A PIECE OF CLOTHING IN YOUR LIFE AND...AND...
...GOD...
I THOUGHT I COULDN'T LIVE WITH YOUR CHAOS, LOU. BUT...
I NEED IT.
HELP ME.
HELP ME.
PLEASE COME HOME, LOVE.
WH-WHEREVER YOU ARE...

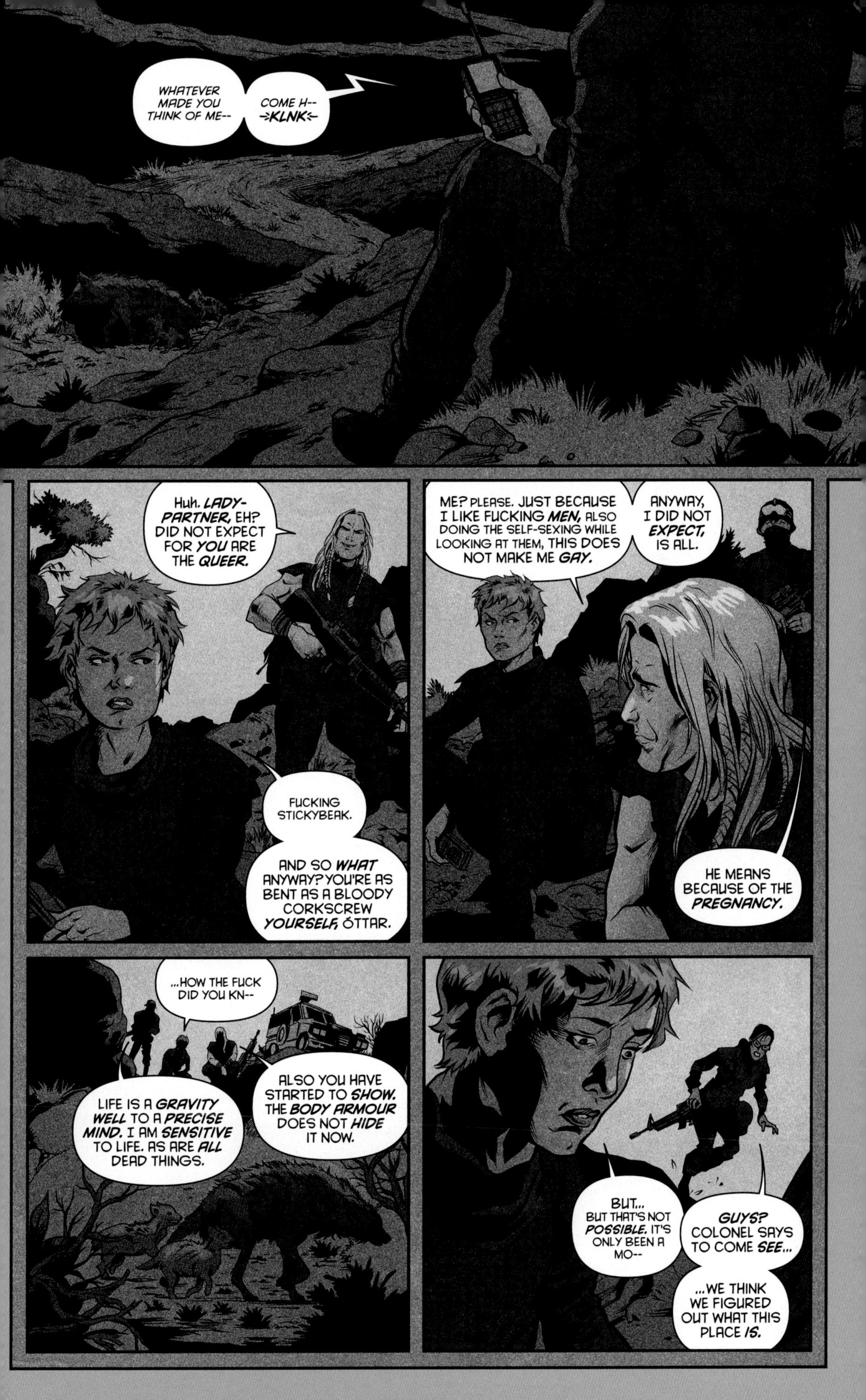

WHATEVER MADE YOU THINK OF ME--
COME H-- ⇥KLNK⇤
Huh. LADY-PARTNER, EH? DID NOT EXPECT FOR YOU ARE THE QUEER.
FUCKING STICKYBEAK.
AND SO WHAT ANYWAY? YOU'RE AS BENT AS A BLOODY CORKSCREW YOURSELF, ÓTTAR.
ME? PLEASE. JUST BECAUSE I LIKE FUCKING MEN, ALSO DOING THE SELF-SEXING WHILE LOOKING AT THEM, THIS DOES NOT MAKE ME GAY.
ANYWAY, I DID NOT EXPECT, IS ALL.
HE MEANS BECAUSE OF THE PREGNANCY.
...HOW THE FUCK DID YOU KN--
LIFE IS A GRAVITY WELL TO A PRECISE MIND. I AM SENSITIVE TO LIFE. AS ARE ALL DEAD THINGS.
ALSO YOU HAVE STARTED TO SHOW. THE BODY ARMOUR DOES NOT HIDE IT NOW.
BUT... BUT THAT'S NOT POSSIBLE. IT'S ONLY BEEN A MO--
GUYS? COLONEL SAYS TO COME SEE...
...WE THINK WE FIGURED OUT WHAT THIS PLACE IS.

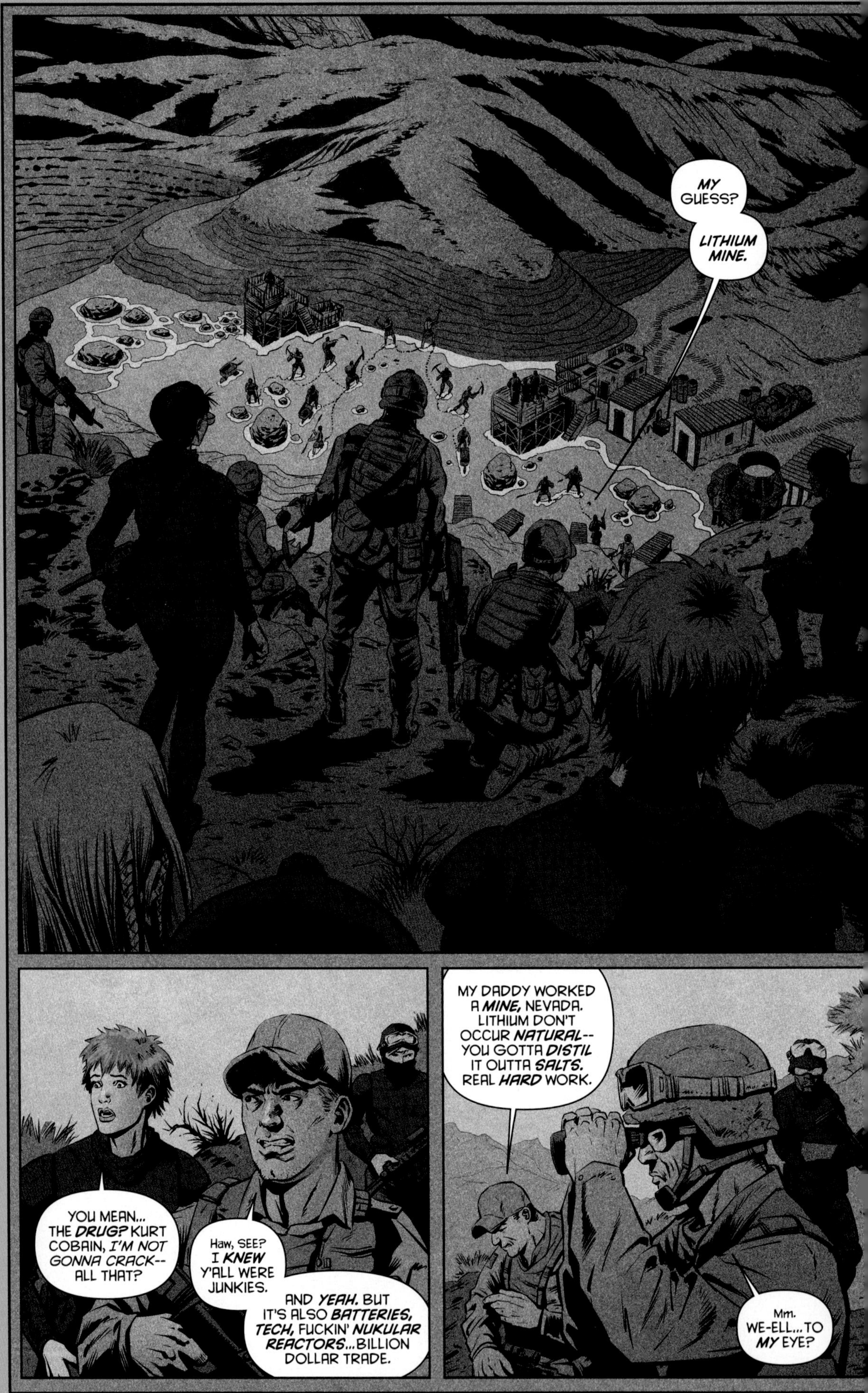
MY GUESS?
LITHIUM MINE.
YOU MEAN... THE DRUG? KURT COBAIN, I'M NOT GONNA CRACK-- ALL THAT?
Haw, SEE? I KNEW Y'ALL WERE JUNKIES.
AND YEAH. BUT IT'S ALSO BATTERIES, TECH, FUCKIN' NUKULAR REACTORS...BILLION DOLLAR TRADE.
MY DADDY WORKED A MINE, NEVADA. LITHIUM DON'T OCCUR NATURAL-- YOU GOTTA DISTIL IT OUTTA SALTS. REAL HARD WORK.
Mm. WE-ELL... TO MY EYE?

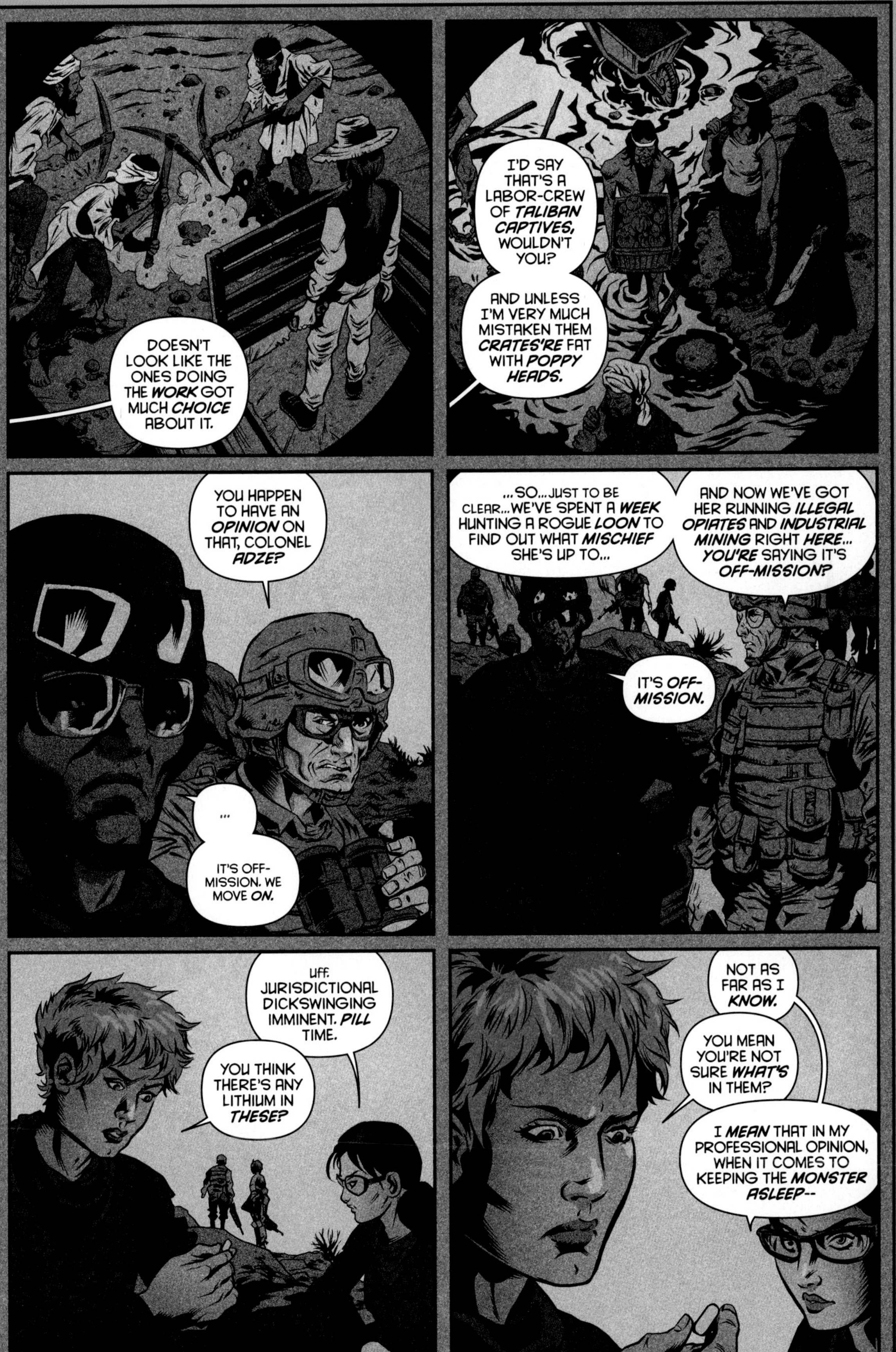
DOESN'T LOOK LIKE THE ONES DOING THE *WORK* GOT MUCH *CHOICE* ABOUT IT.
I'D SAY THAT'S A LABOR-CREW OF *TALIBAN CAPTIVES,* WOULDN'T YOU?
AND UNLESS I'M VERY MUCH MISTAKEN THEM *CRATES'RE* FAT WITH *POPPY HEADS.*
YOU HAPPEN TO HAVE AN *OPINION* ON THAT, COLONEL *ADZE?*
...
IT'S OFF-MISSION. WE MOVE *ON.*
...SO...JUST TO BE CLEAR...WE'VE SPENT A *WEEK* HUNTING A ROGUE *LOON* TO FIND OUT WHAT *MISCHIEF* SHE'S UP TO...
AND NOW WE'VE GOT HER RUNNING *ILLEGAL OPIATES* AND *INDUSTRIAL MINING* RIGHT *HERE... YOU'RE* SAYING IT'S *OFF-MISSION?*
IT'S *OFF-MISSION.*
UFF. JURISDICTIONAL DICKSWINGING IMMINENT. *PILL* TIME.
YOU THINK THERE'S ANY LITHIUM IN *THESE?*
NOT AS FAR AS I *KNOW.*
YOU MEAN YOU'RE NOT SURE *WHAT'S* IN THEM?
I *MEAN* THAT IN MY PROFESSIONAL OPINION, WHEN IT COMES TO KEEPING THE *MONSTER ASLEEP--*

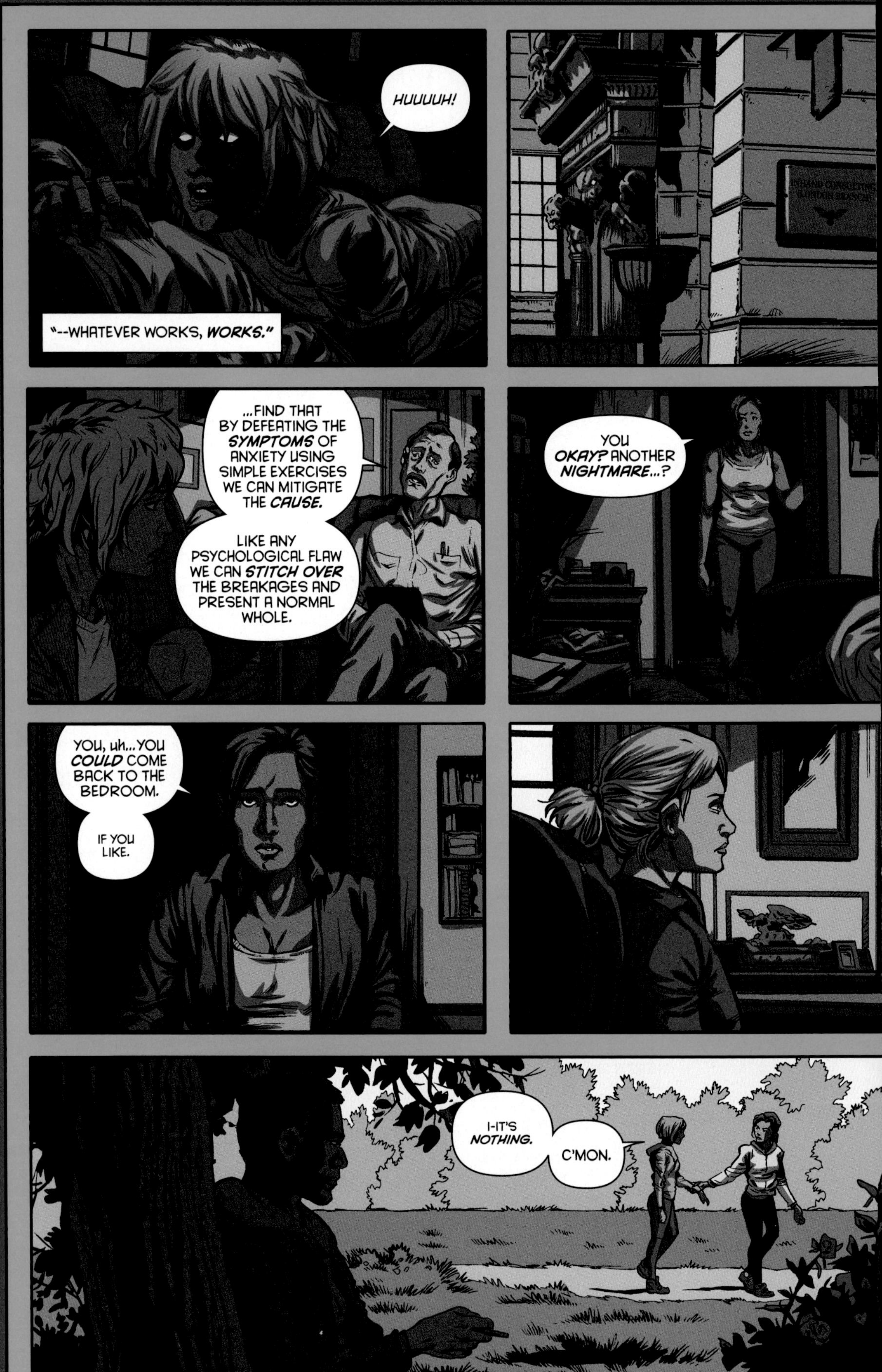
HUUUUH!
"--WHATEVER WORKS, *WORKS.*"
...FIND THAT BY DEFEATING THE *SYMPTOMS* OF ANXIETY USING SIMPLE EXERCISES WE CAN MITIGATE THE *CAUSE.*
LIKE ANY PSYCHOLOGICAL FLAW WE CAN *STITCH OVER* THE BREAKAGES AND PRESENT A NORMAL WHOLE.
YOU *OKAY?* ANOTHER *NIGHTMARE...?*
YOU, uh...YOU *COULD* COME BACK TO THE BEDROOM.
IF YOU LIKE.
I-IT'S *NOTHING.*
C'MON.

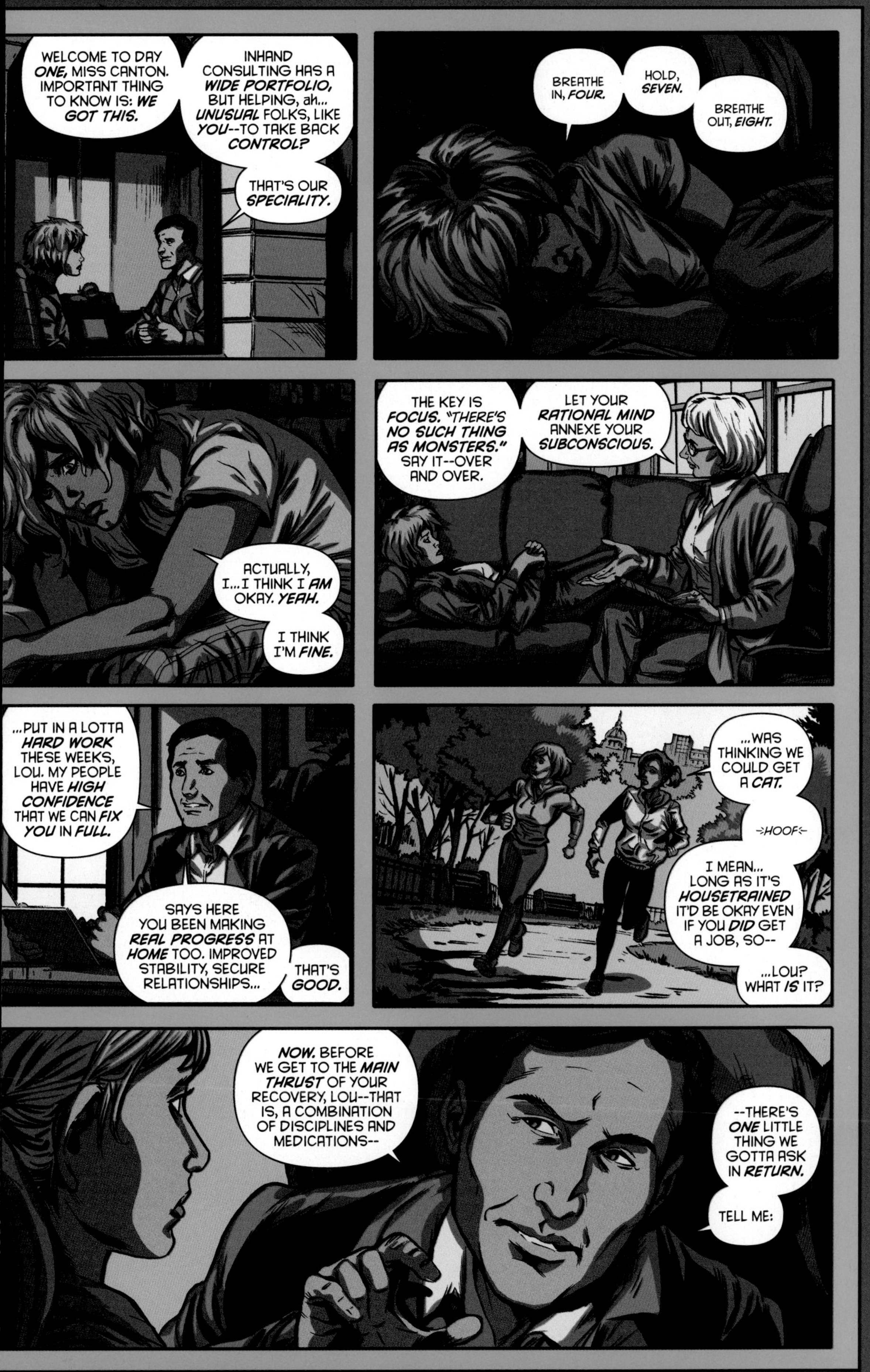
WELCOME TO DAY ONE, MISS CANTON. IMPORTANT THING TO KNOW IS: WE GOT THIS.
INHAND CONSULTING HAS A WIDE PORTFOLIO, BUT HELPING, ah... UNUSUAL FOLKS, LIKE YOU--TO TAKE BACK CONTROL?
THAT'S OUR SPECIALITY.
BREATHE IN, FOUR.
HOLD, SEVEN.
BREATHE OUT, EIGHT.
ACTUALLY, I...I THINK I AM OKAY. YEAH.
I THINK I'M FINE.
THE KEY IS FOCUS. "THERE'S NO SUCH THING AS MONSTERS." SAY IT--OVER AND OVER.
LET YOUR RATIONAL MIND ANNEXE YOUR SUBCONSCIOUS.
...PUT IN A LOTTA HARD WORK THESE WEEKS, LOU. MY PEOPLE HAVE HIGH CONFIDENCE THAT WE CAN FIX YOU IN FULL.
SAYS HERE YOU BEEN MAKING REAL PROGRESS AT HOME TOO. IMPROVED STABILITY, SECURE RELATIONSHIPS...
THAT'S GOOD.
...WAS THINKING WE COULD GET A CAT.
HOOF
I MEAN... LONG AS IT'S HOUSETRAINED IT'D BE OKAY EVEN IF YOU DID GET A JOB, SO--
...LOU? WHAT IS IT?
NOW. BEFORE WE GET TO THE MAIN THRUST OF YOUR RECOVERY, LOU--THAT IS, A COMBINATION OF DISCIPLINES AND MEDICATIONS--
--THERE'S ONE LITTLE THING WE GOTTA ASK IN RETURN.
TELL ME:

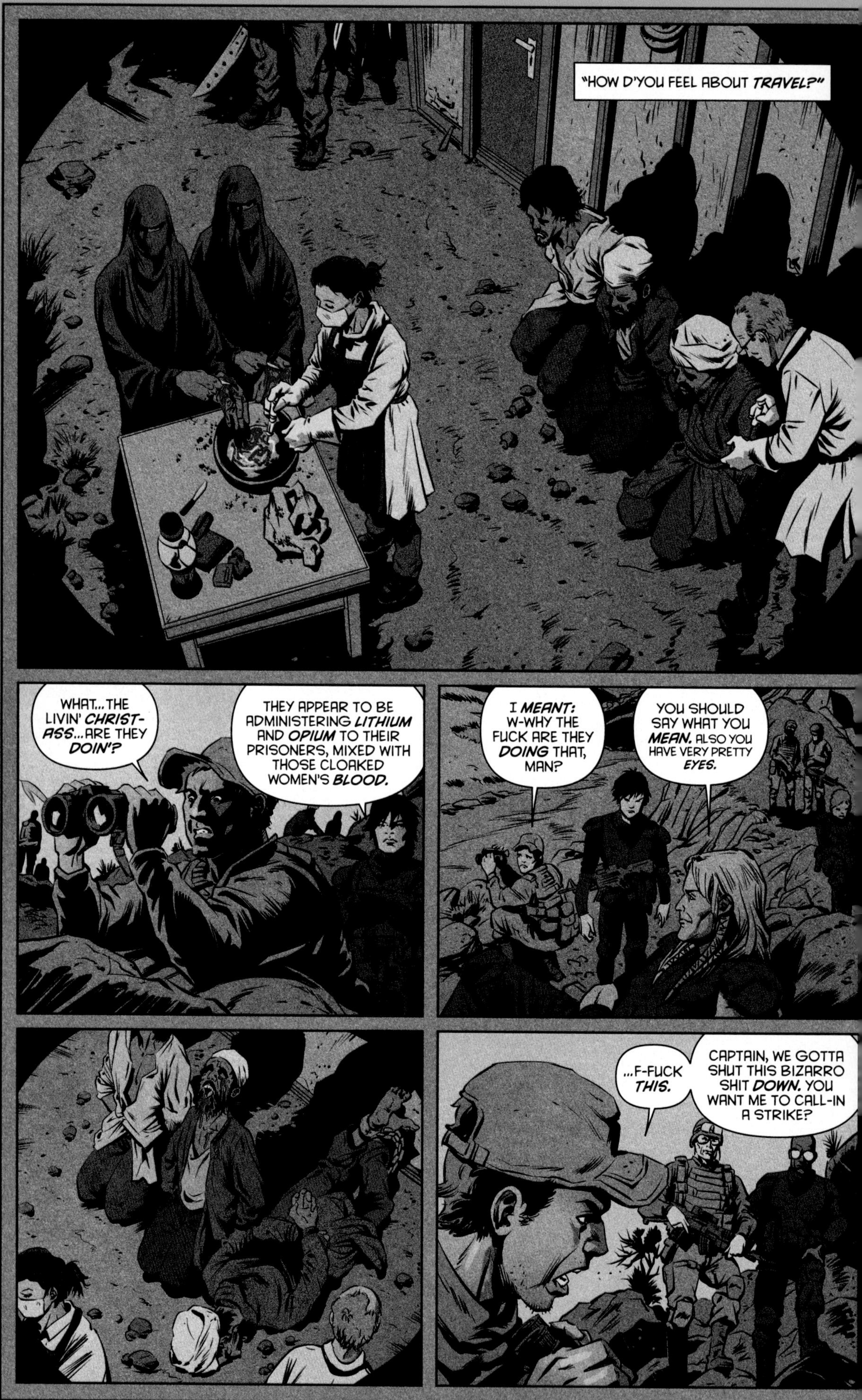
"HOW D'YOU FEEL ABOUT TRAVEL?"
WHAT... THE LIVIN' CHRIST-ASS... ARE THEY DOIN'?
THEY APPEAR TO BE ADMINISTERING LITHIUM AND OPIUM TO THEIR PRISONERS, MIXED WITH THOSE CLOAKED WOMEN'S BLOOD.
I MEANT: W-WHY THE FUCK ARE THEY DOING THAT, MAN?
YOU SHOULD SAY WHAT YOU MEAN. ALSO YOU HAVE VERY PRETTY EYES.
...F-FUCK THIS.
CAPTAIN, WE GOTTA SHUT THIS BIZARRO SHIT DOWN. YOU WANT ME TO CALL-IN A STRIKE?

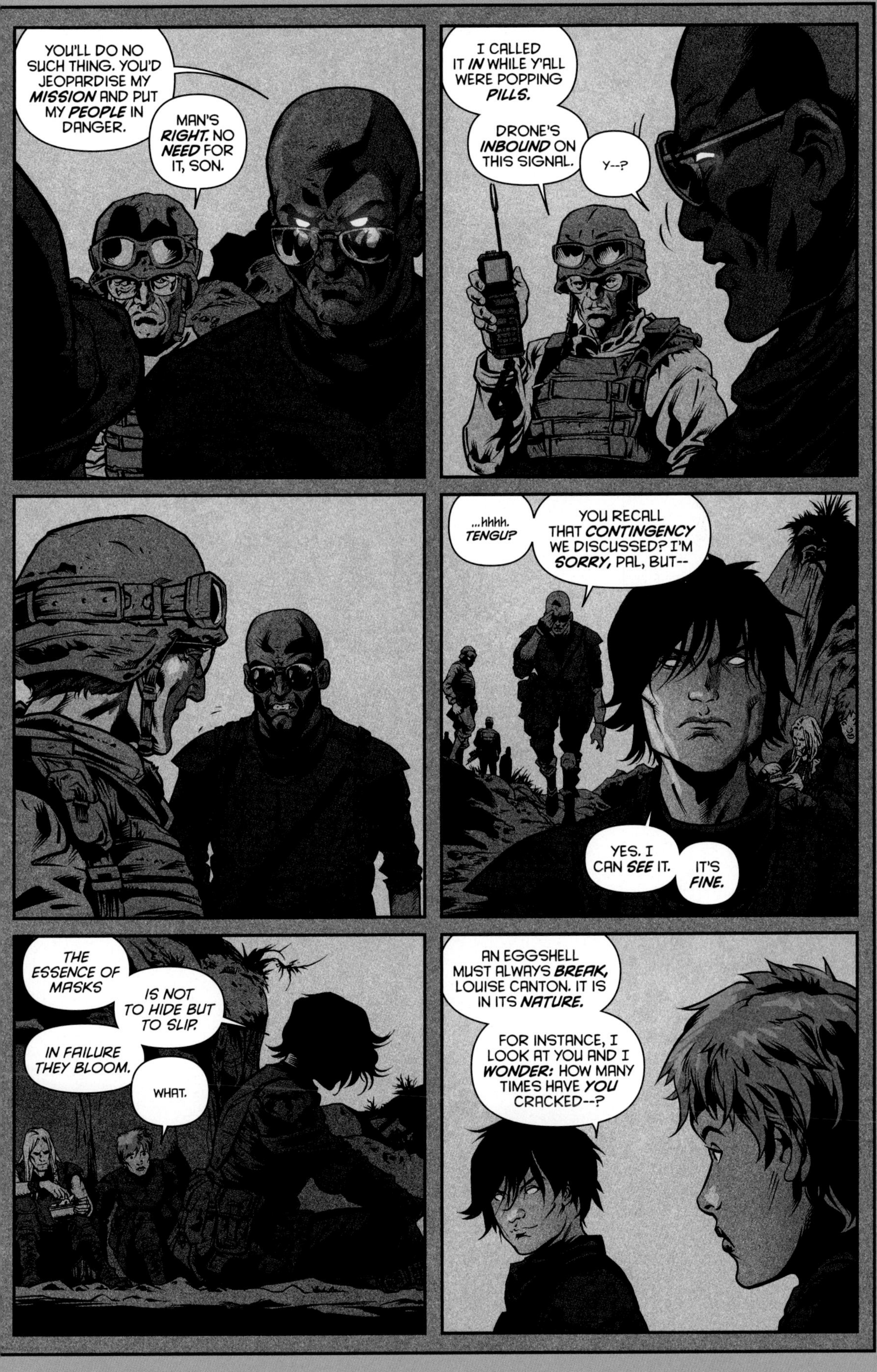

YOU'LL DO NO SUCH THING. YOU'D JEOPARDISE MY MISSION AND PUT MY PEOPLE IN DANGER.
MAN'S RIGHT. NO NEED FOR IT, SON.
I CALLED IT IN WHILE Y'ALL WERE POPPING PILLS.
DRONE'S INBOUND ON THIS SIGNAL.
Y--?
...hhhh. TENGU?
YOU RECALL THAT CONTINGENCY WE DISCUSSED? I'M SORRY, PAL, BUT--
YES. I CAN SEE IT.
IT'S FINE.
THE ESSENCE OF MASKS
IS NOT TO HIDE BUT TO SLIP.
IN FAILURE THEY BLOOM.
WHAT.
AN EGGSHELL MUST ALWAYS BREAK, LOUISE CANTON. IT IS IN ITS NATURE.
FOR INSTANCE, I LOOK AT YOU AND I WONDER: HOW MANY TIMES HAVE YOU CRACKED--?

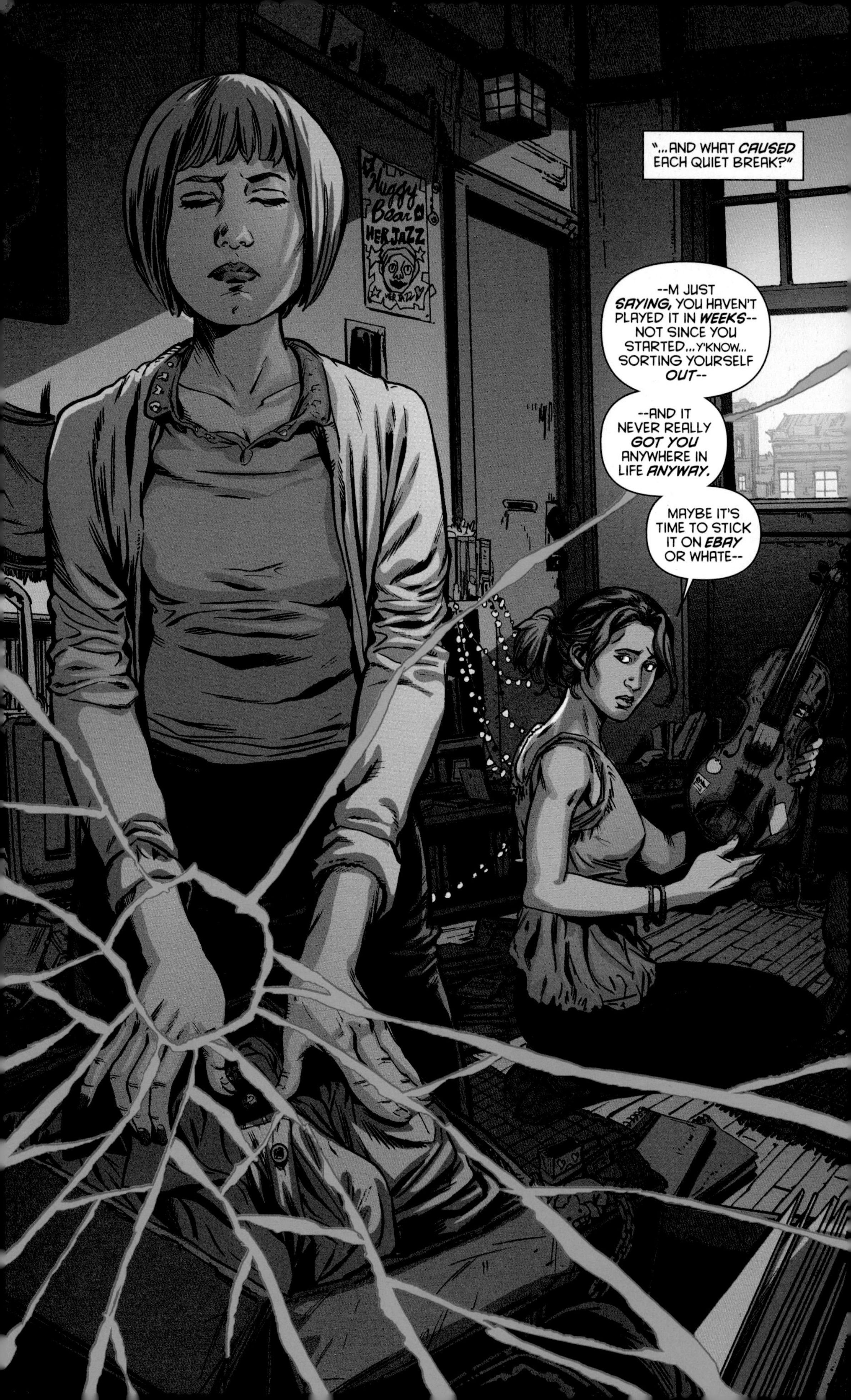
"...AND WHAT CAUSED EACH QUIET BREAK?"
--M JUST SAYING, YOU HAVEN'T PLAYED IT IN WEEKS-- NOT SINCE YOU STARTED...Y'KNOW... SORTING YOURSELF OUT--
--AND IT NEVER REALLY GOT YOU ANYWHERE IN LIFE ANYWAY.
MAYBE IT'S TIME TO STICK IT ON EBAY OR WHATE--

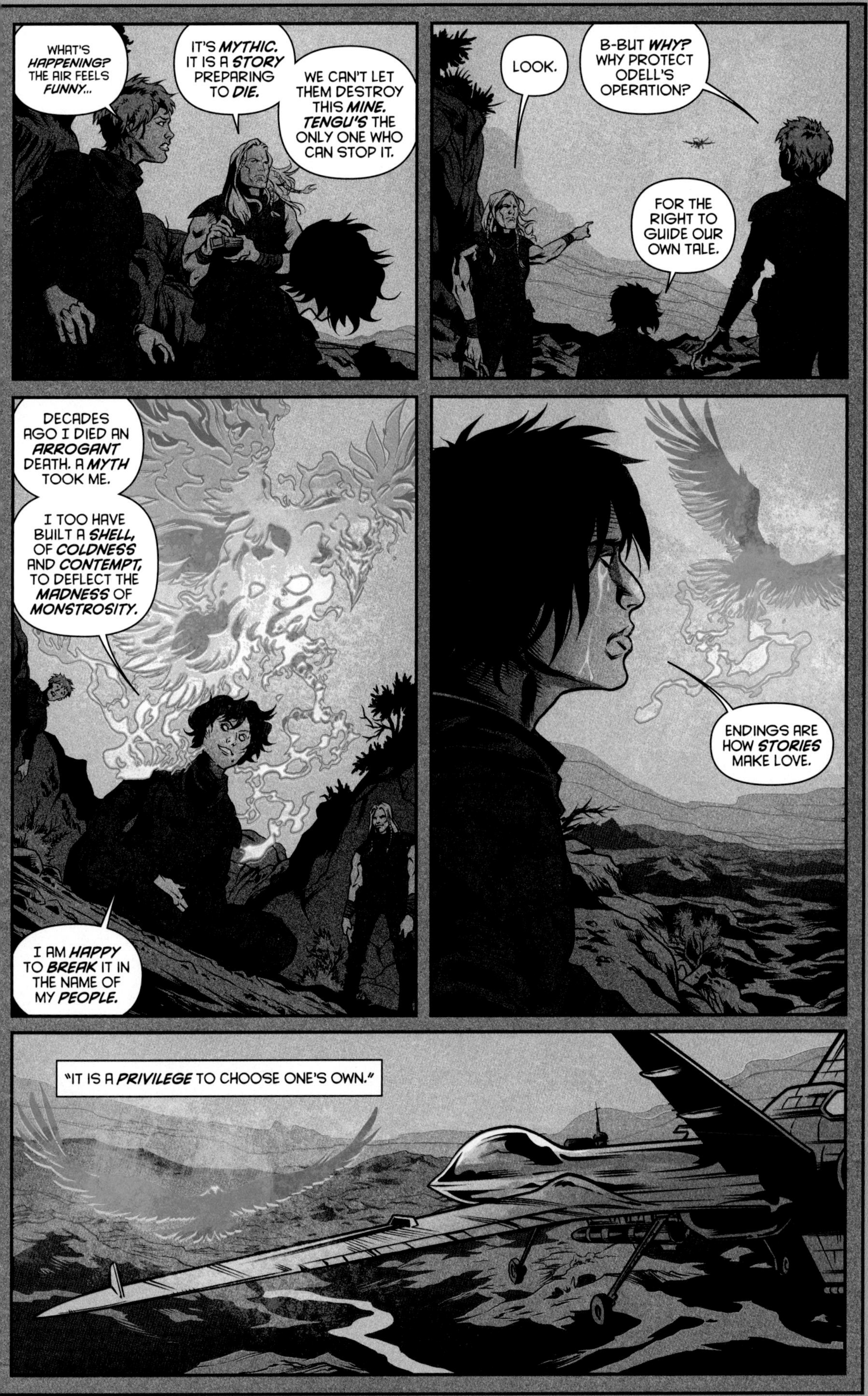
WHAT'S HAPPENING? THE AIR FEELS FUNNY...
IT'S MYTHIC. IT IS A STORY PREPARING TO DIE.
WE CAN'T LET THEM DESTROY THIS MINE. TENGU'S THE ONLY ONE WHO CAN STOP IT.
LOOK.
B-BUT WHY? WHY PROTECT ODELL'S OPERATION?
FOR THE RIGHT TO GUIDE OUR OWN TALE.
DECADES AGO I DIED AN ARROGANT DEATH. A MYTH TOOK ME.
I TOO HAVE BUILT A SHELL, OF COLDNESS AND CONTEMPT, TO DEFLECT THE MADNESS OF MONSTROSITY.
I AM HAPPY TO BREAK IT IN THE NAME OF MY PEOPLE.
ENDINGS ARE HOW STORIES MAKE LOVE.
"IT IS A PRIVILEGE TO CHOOSE ONE'S OWN."

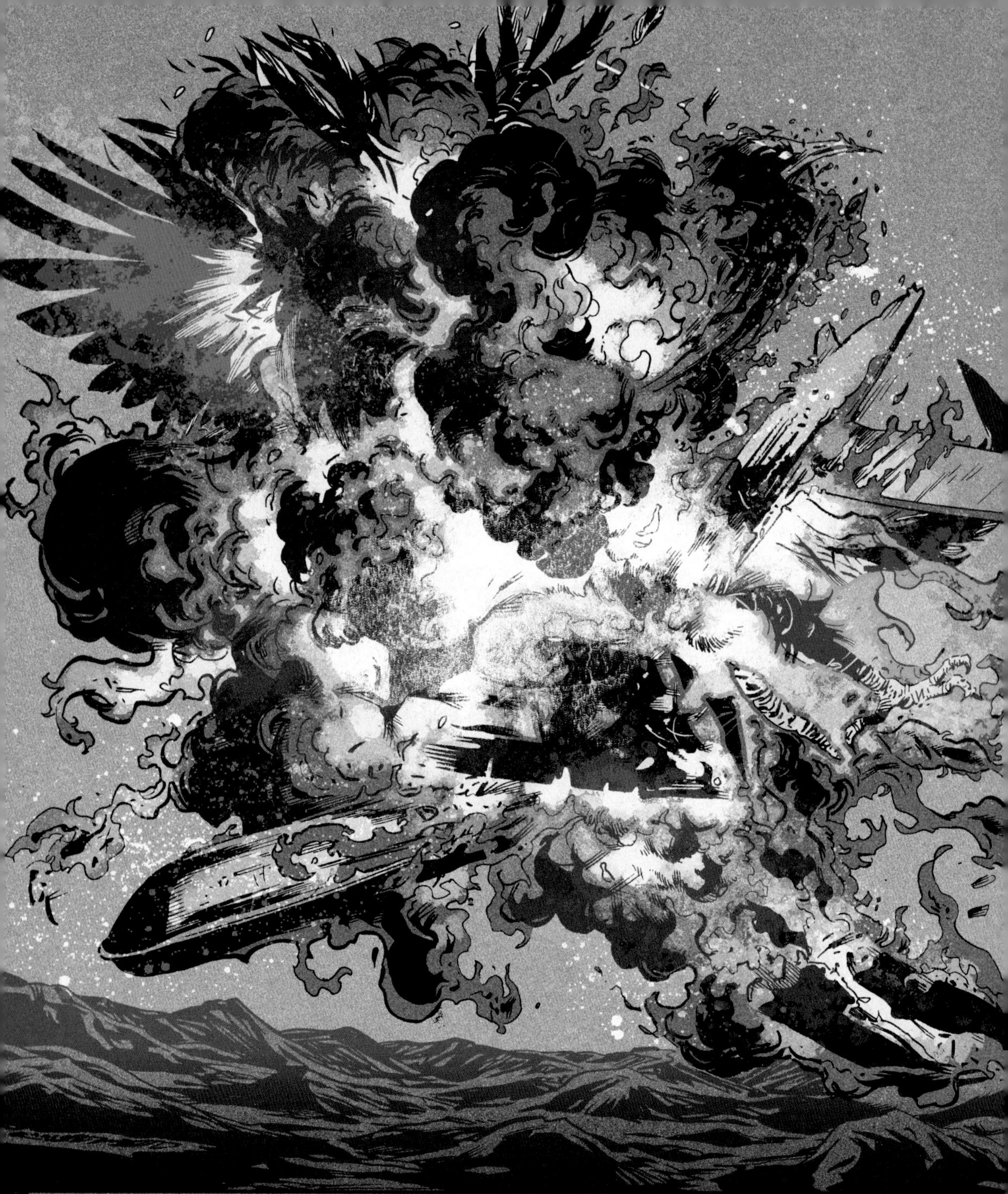
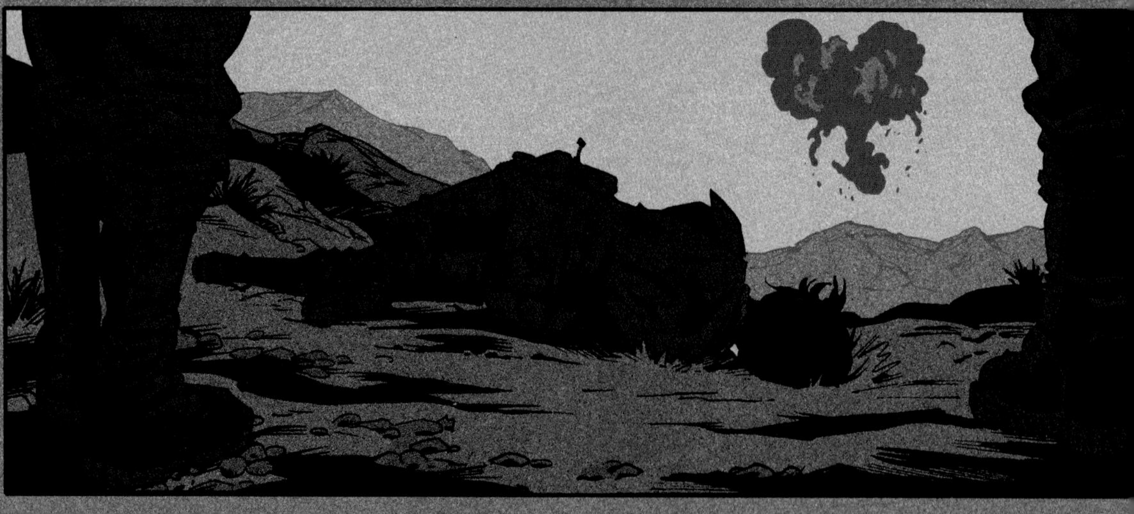

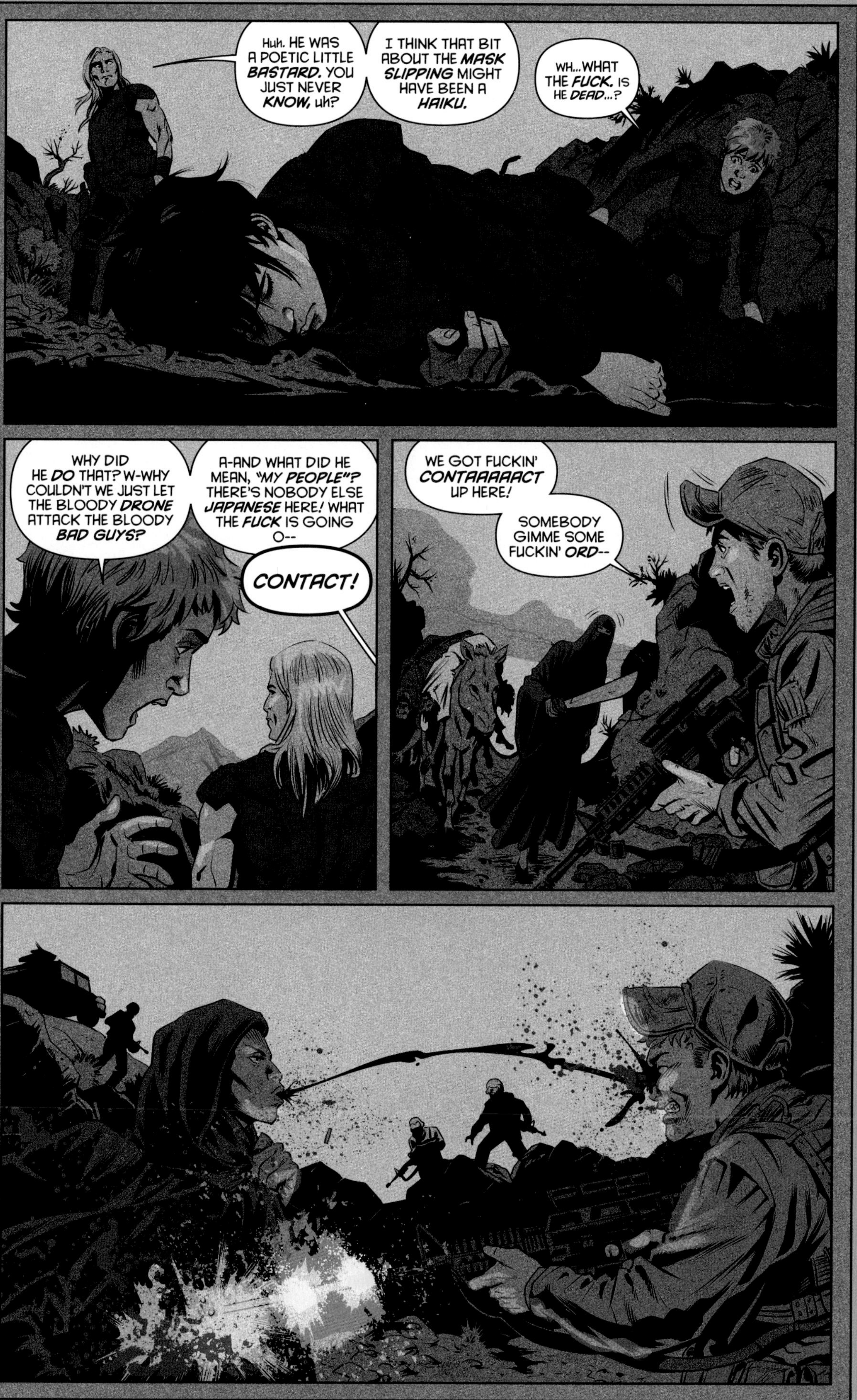
Huh. HE WAS A POETIC LITTLE BASTARD. YOU JUST NEVER KNOW, uh?
I THINK THAT BIT ABOUT THE MASK SLIPPING MIGHT HAVE BEEN A HAIKU.
WH...WHAT THE FUCK. IS HE DEAD...?
WHY DID HE DO THAT? W-WHY COULDN'T WE JUST LET THE BLOODY DRONE ATTACK THE BLOODY BAD GUYS?
A-AND WHAT DID HE MEAN, "MY PEOPLE"? THERE'S NOBODY ELSE JAPANESE HERE! WHAT THE FUCK IS GOING O--
CONTACT!
WE GOT FUCKIN' CONTAAAAACT UP HERE!
SOMEBODY GIMME SOME FUCKIN' ORD--

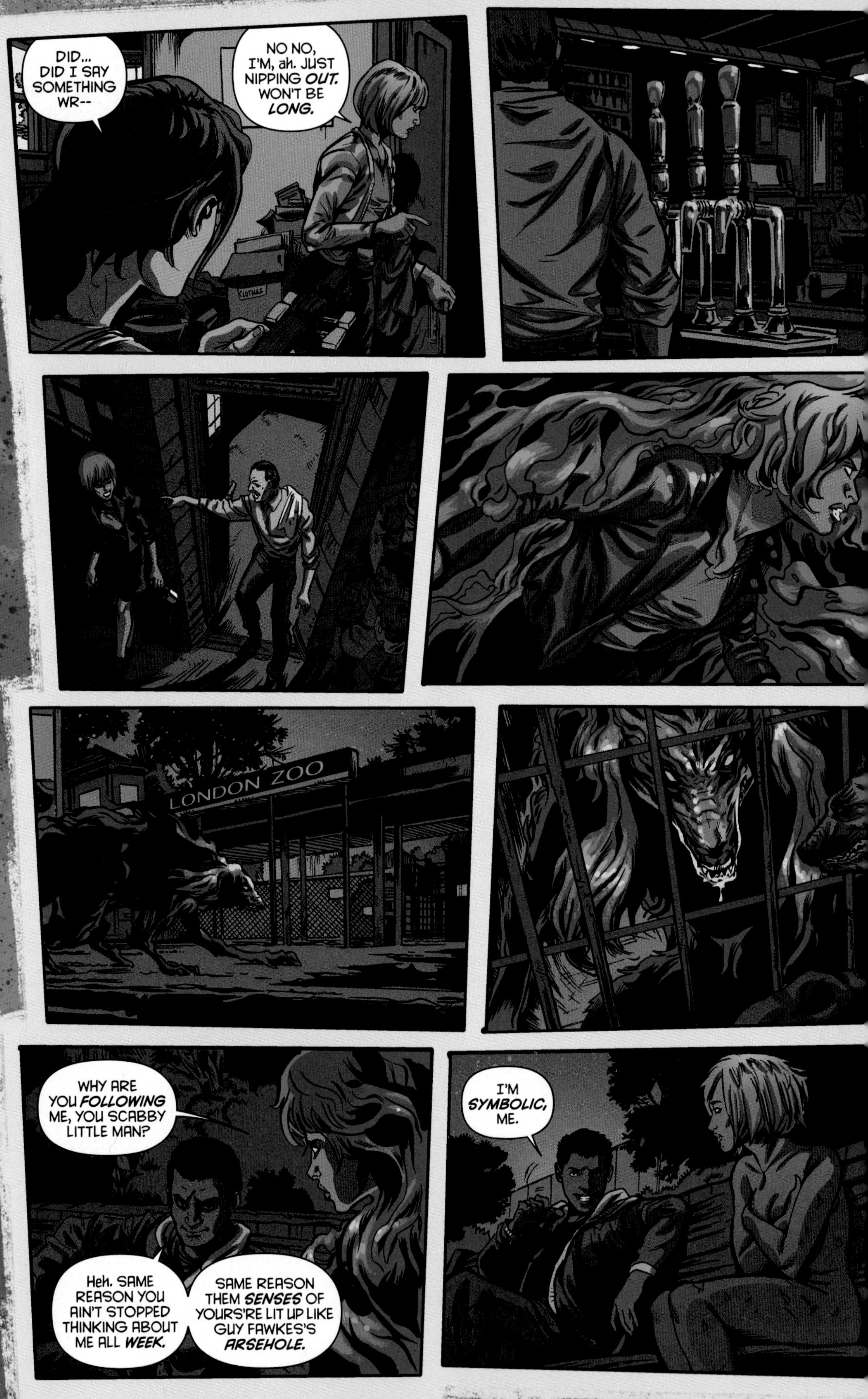
DID... DID I SAY SOMETHING WR--
NO NO, I'M, ah. JUST NIPPING OUT. WON'T BE LONG.
LONDON ZOO
WHY ARE YOU FOLLOWING ME, YOU SCABBY LITTLE MAN?
Heh. SAME REASON YOU AIN'T STOPPED THINKING ABOUT ME ALL WEEK.
SAME REASON THEM SENSES OF YOURS'RE LIT UP LIKE GUY FAWKES'S ARSEHOLE.
I'M SYMBOLIC, ME.

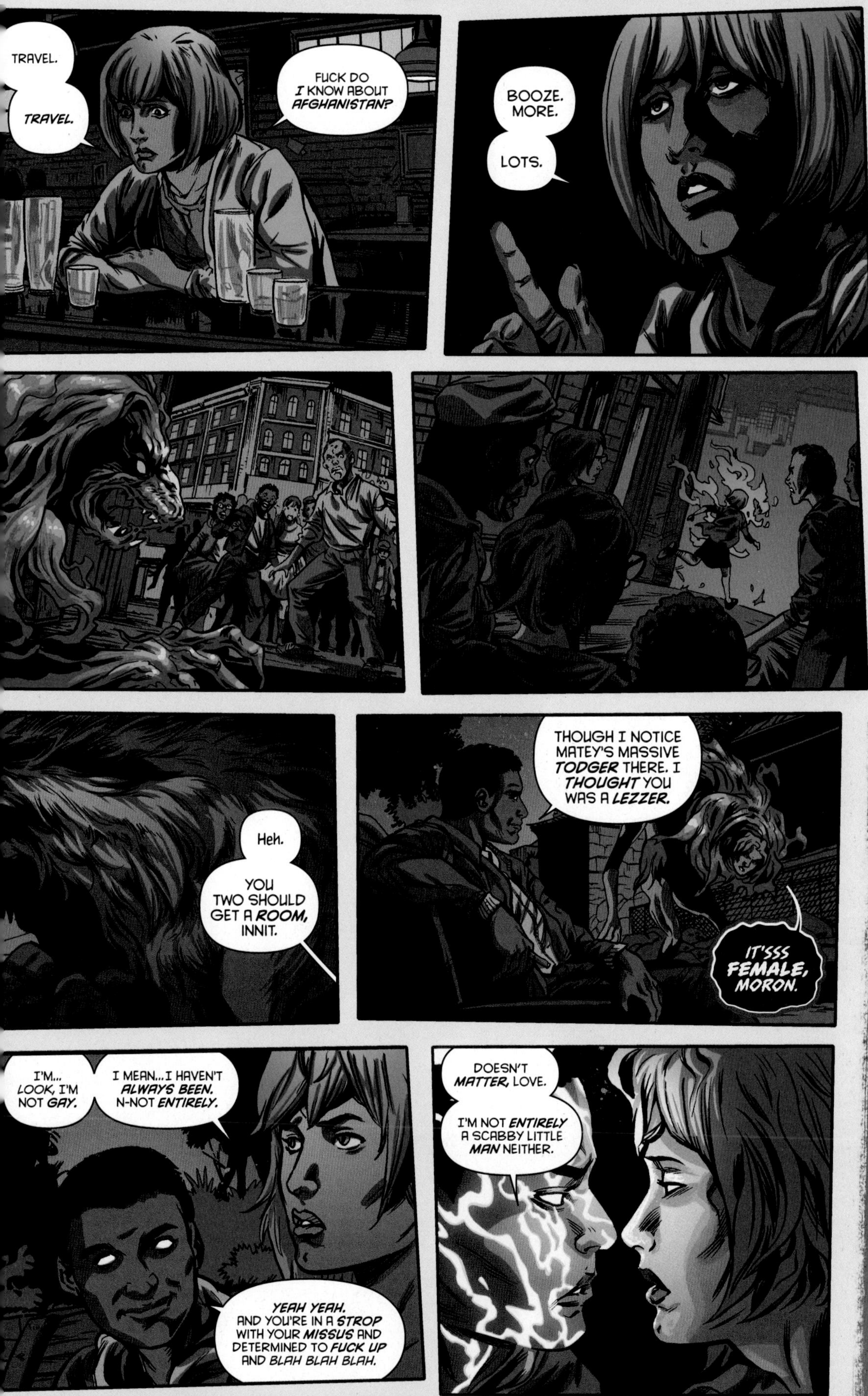
TRAVEL.
TRAVEL.
FUCK DO I KNOW ABOUT AFGHANISTAN?
BOOZE. MORE.
LOTS.
Heh.
YOU TWO SHOULD GET A ROOM, INNIT.
THOUGH I NOTICE MATEY'S MASSIVE TODGER THERE. I THOUGHT YOU WAS A LEZZER.
IT'SSS FEMALE, MORON.
I'M... LOOK, I'M NOT GAY.
I MEAN...I HAVEN'T ALWAYS BEEN. N-NOT ENTIRELY.
YEAH YEAH. AND YOU'RE IN A STROP WITH YOUR MISSUS AND DETERMINED TO FUCK UP AND BLAH BLAH BLAH.
DOESN'T MATTER, LOVE.
I'M NOT ENTIRELY A SCABBY LITTLE MAN NEITHER.

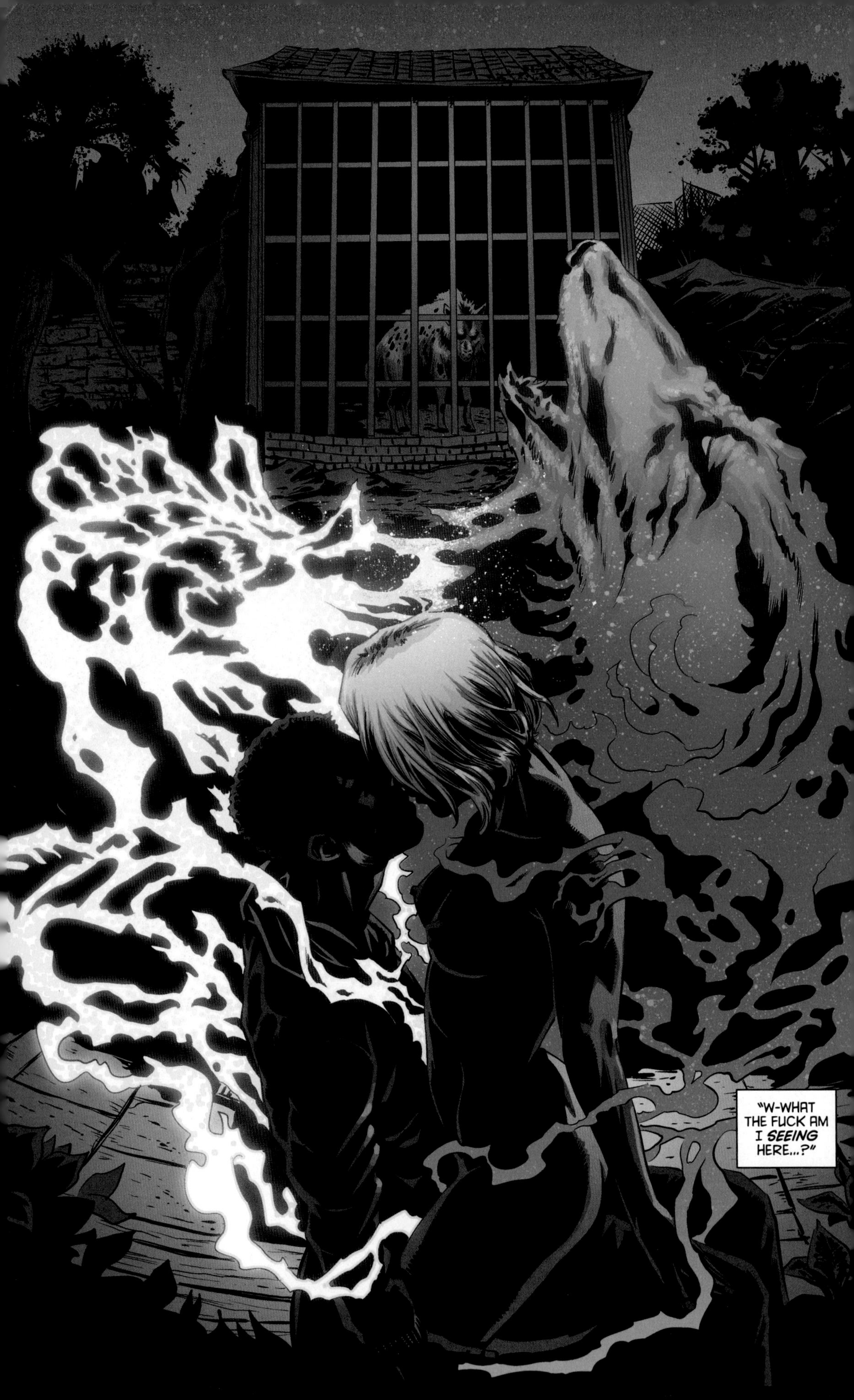
"W-WHAT THE FUCK AM I *SEEING* HERE...?"

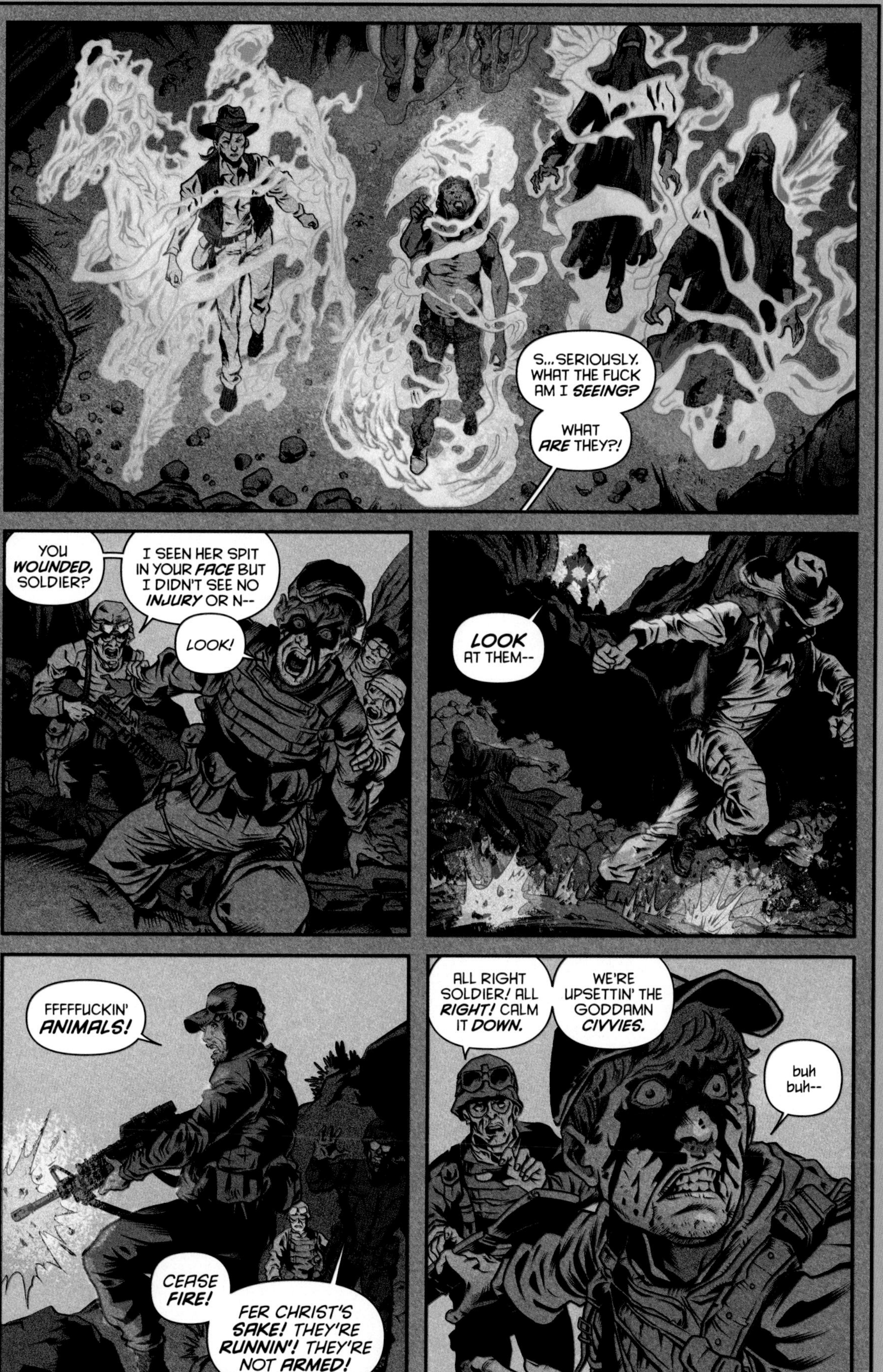
S...SERIOUSLY. WHAT THE FUCK AM I SEEING?
WHAT ARE THEY?!
YOU WOUNDED, SOLDIER?
I SEEN HER SPIT IN YOUR FACE BUT I DIDN'T SEE NO INJURY OR N--
LOOK!
LOOK AT THEM--
FFFFFUCKIN' ANIMALS!
CEASE FIRE!
FER CHRIST'S SAKE! THEY'RE RUNNIN'! THEY'RE NOT ARMED!
ALL RIGHT SOLDIER! ALL RIGHT! CALM IT DOWN.
WE'RE UPSETTIN' THE GODDAMN CIVVIES.
buh buh--

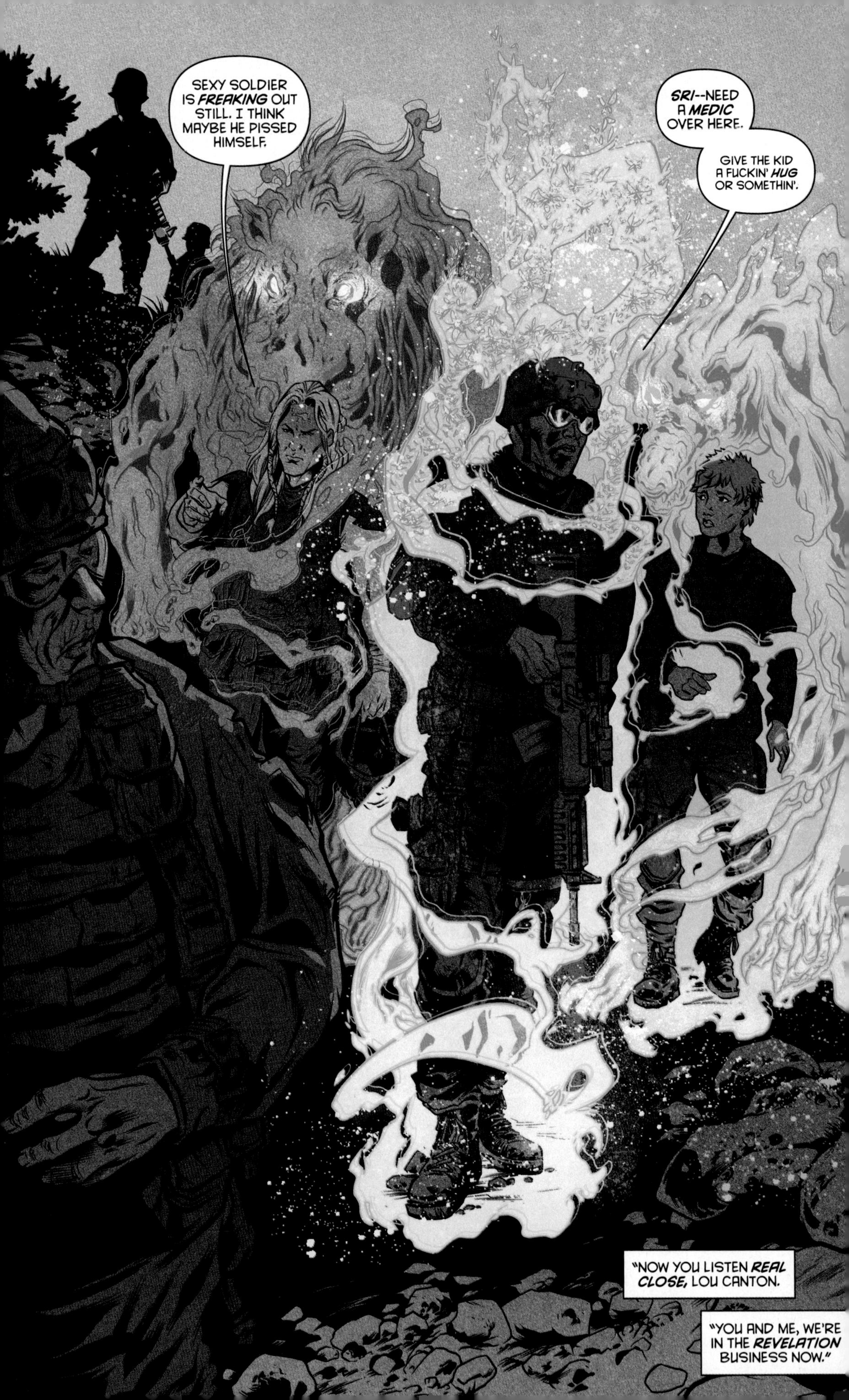
SEXY SOLDIER IS FREAKING OUT STILL. I THINK MAYBE HE PISSED HIMSELF.
SRI--NEED A MEDIC OVER HERE.
GIVE THE KID A FUCKIN' HUG OR SOMETHIN'.
"NOW YOU LISTEN REAL CLOSE, LOU CANTON.
"YOU AND ME, WE'RE IN THE REVELATION BUSINESS NOW."

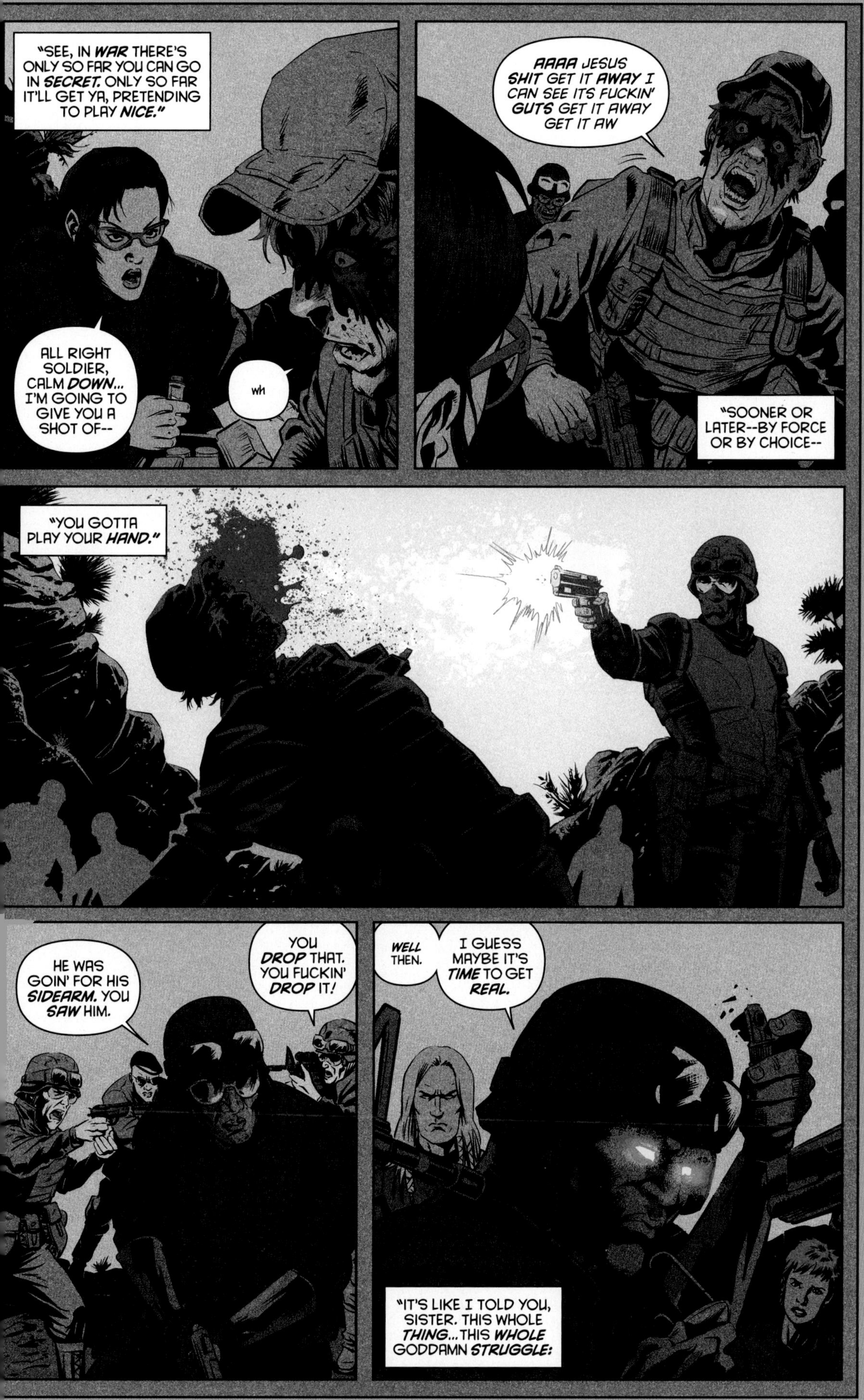
"SEE, IN WAR THERE'S ONLY SO FAR YOU CAN GO IN SECRET. ONLY SO FAR IT'LL GET YA, PRETENDING TO PLAY NICE."
ALL RIGHT SOLDIER, CALM DOWN... I'M GOING TO GIVE YOU A SHOT OF--
wh
AAAA JESUS SHIT GET IT AWAY I CAN SEE ITS FUCKIN' GUTS GET IT AWAY GET IT AW
"SOONER OR LATER--BY FORCE OR BY CHOICE--
"YOU GOTTA PLAY YOUR HAND."
HE WAS GOIN' FOR HIS SIDEARM. YOU SAW HIM.
YOU DROP THAT. YOU FUCKIN' DROP IT!
WELL THEN.
I GUESS MAYBE IT'S TIME TO GET REAL.
"IT'S LIKE I TOLD YOU, SISTER. THIS WHOLE THING...THIS WHOLE GODDAMN STRUGGLE:

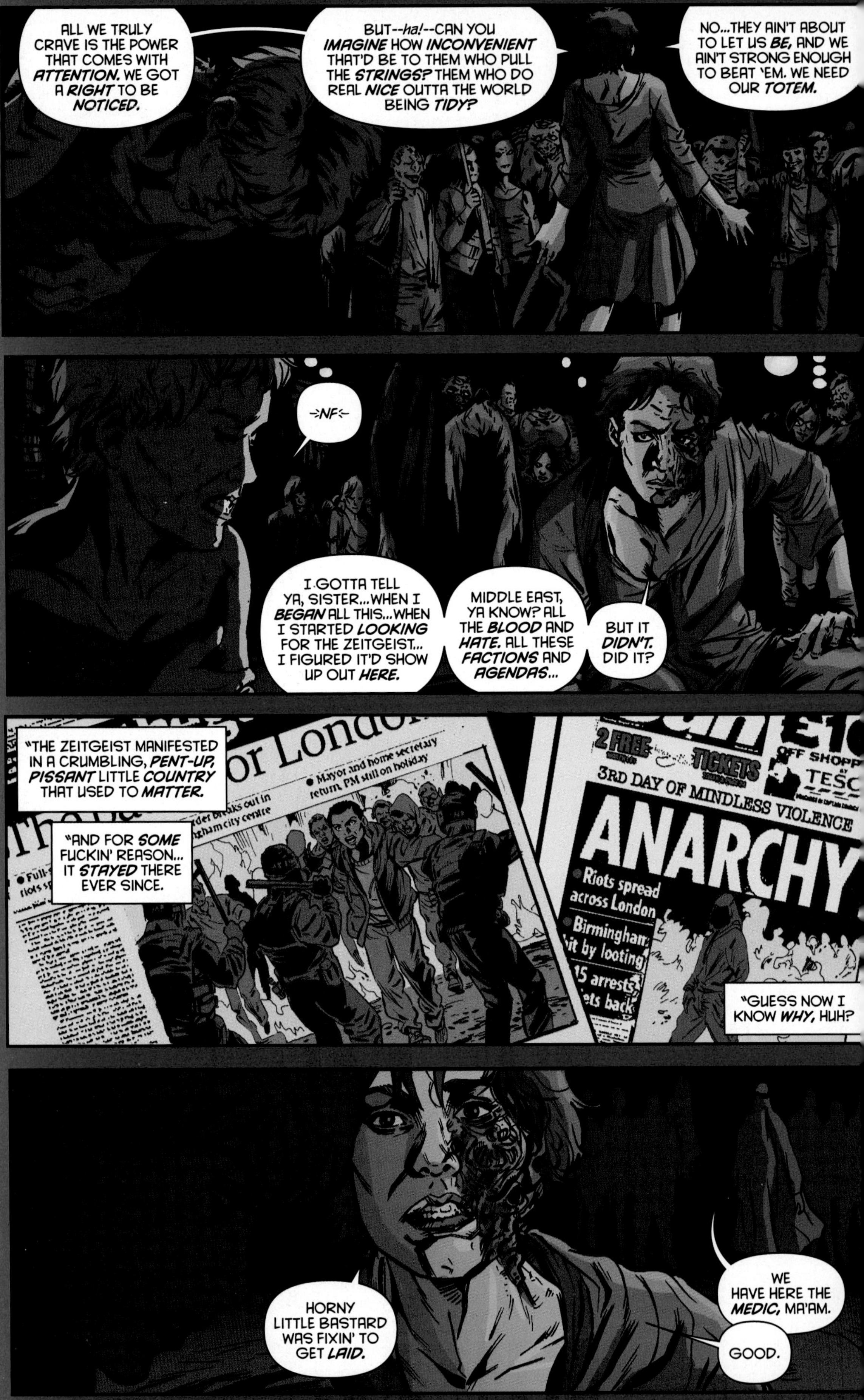

ALL WE TRULY CRAVE IS THE POWER THAT COMES WITH *ATTENTION.* WE GOT A *RIGHT* TO BE *NOTICED.*
BUT--*ha!*--CAN YOU *IMAGINE* HOW *INCONVENIENT* THAT'D BE TO THEM WHO PULL THE *STRINGS?* THEM WHO DO REAL *NICE* OUTTA THE WORLD BEING *TIDY?*
NO...THEY AIN'T ABOUT TO LET US *BE,* AND WE AIN'T STRONG ENOUGH TO BEAT 'EM. WE NEED OUR *TOTEM.*
NF
I GOTTA TELL YA, SISTER...WHEN I *BEGAN* ALL THIS...WHEN I STARTED *LOOKING* FOR THE ZEITGEIST... I FIGURED IT'D SHOW UP OUT *HERE.*
MIDDLE EAST, YA KNOW? ALL THE *BLOOD* AND *HATE.* ALL THESE *FACTIONS* AND *AGENDAS*...
BUT IT *DIDN'T.* DID IT?
"THE ZEITGEIST MANIFESTED IN A CRUMBLING, *PENT-UP, PISSANT* LITTLE *COUNTRY* THAT USED TO *MATTER.*
"AND FOR *SOME* FUCKIN' REASON... IT *STAYED* THERE EVER SINCE.
or London
Mayor and home secretary return, PM still on holiday
3RD DAY OF MINDLESS VIOLENCE
ANARCHY
Riots spread across London
Birmingham
15 arrests
"GUESS NOW I KNOW *WHY,* HUH?
HORNY LITTLE BASTARD WAS FIXIN' TO GET *LAID.*
WE HAVE HERE THE *MEDIC,* MA'AM.
GOOD.

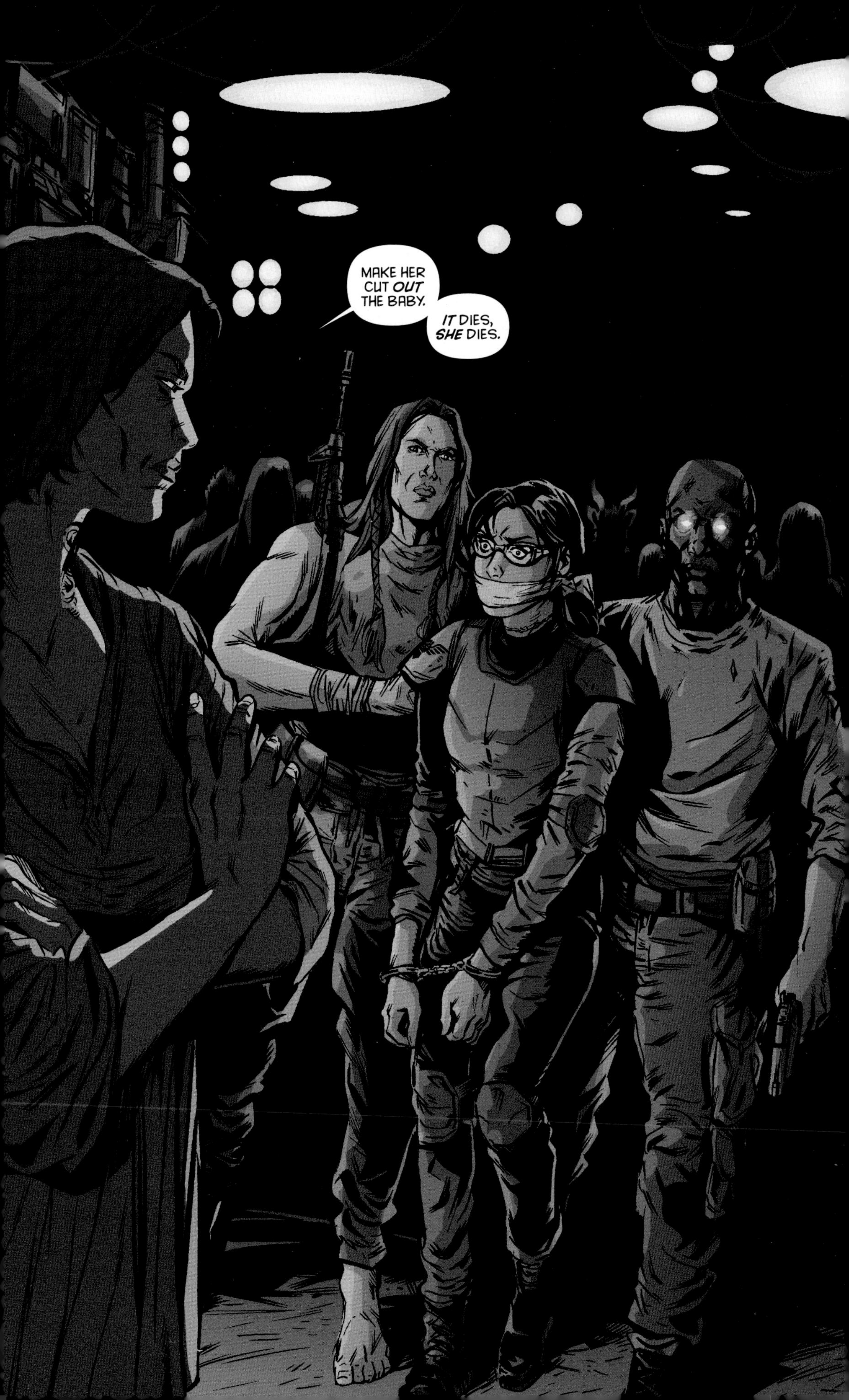
MAKE HER CUT *OUT* THE BABY.
IT DIES, *SHE* DIES.

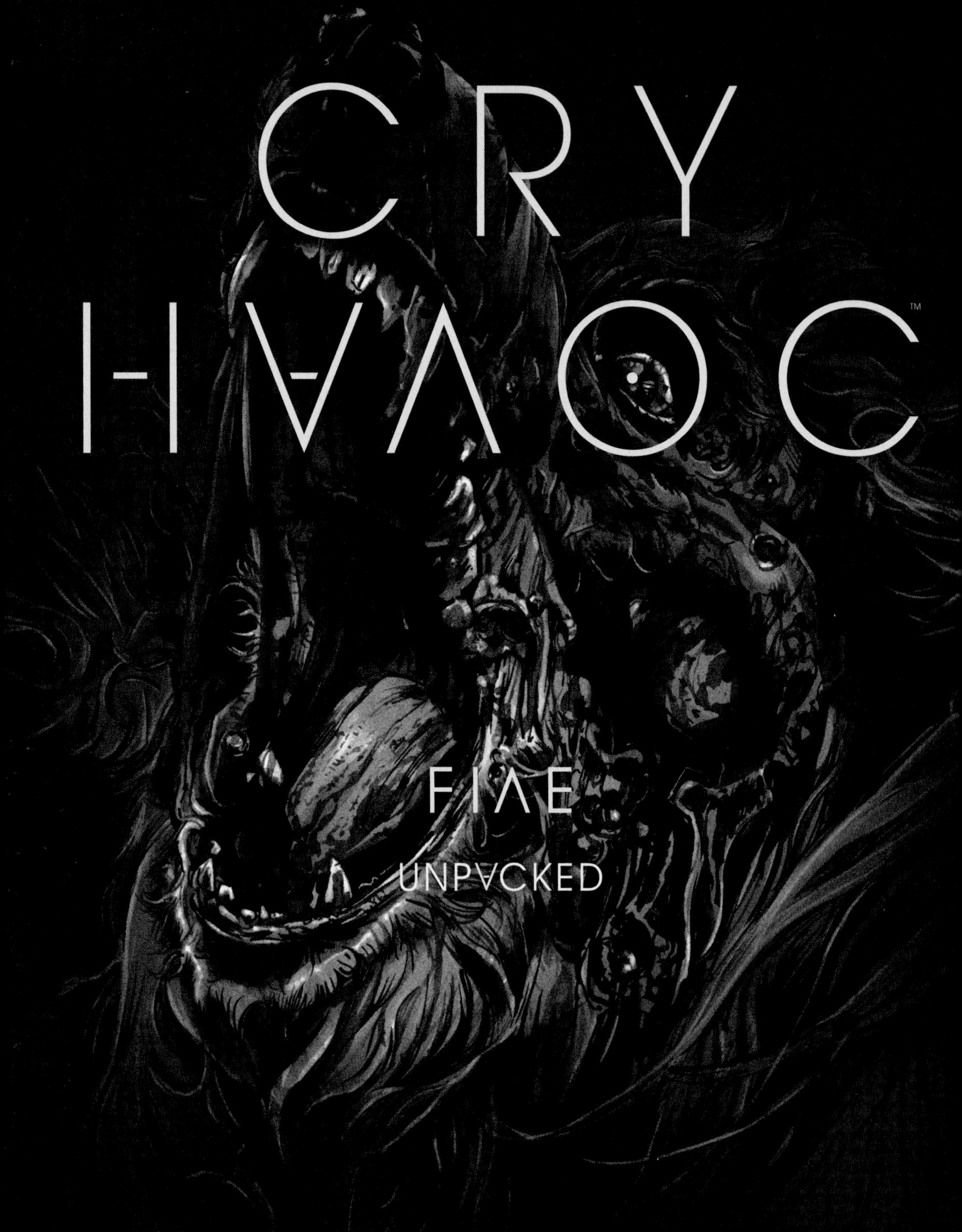
CRY HAVOC™
FIVE
UNPACKED

> *I have often had the fancy that there is some one Myth for every man, which, if we but knew it, would make us understand all he did and thought.*

WILLIAM BUTLER YEATS

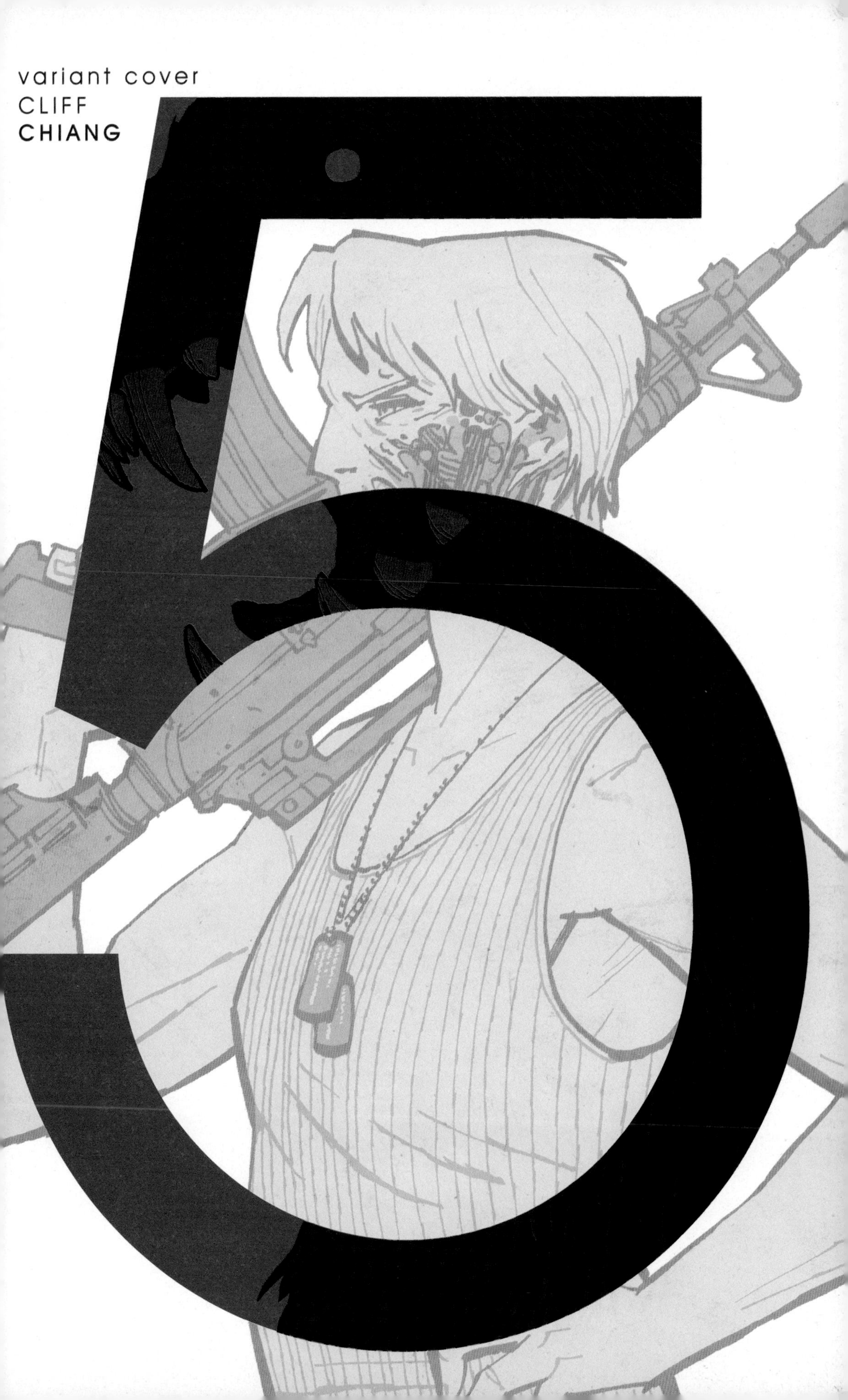
variant cover
CLIFF
CHIANG

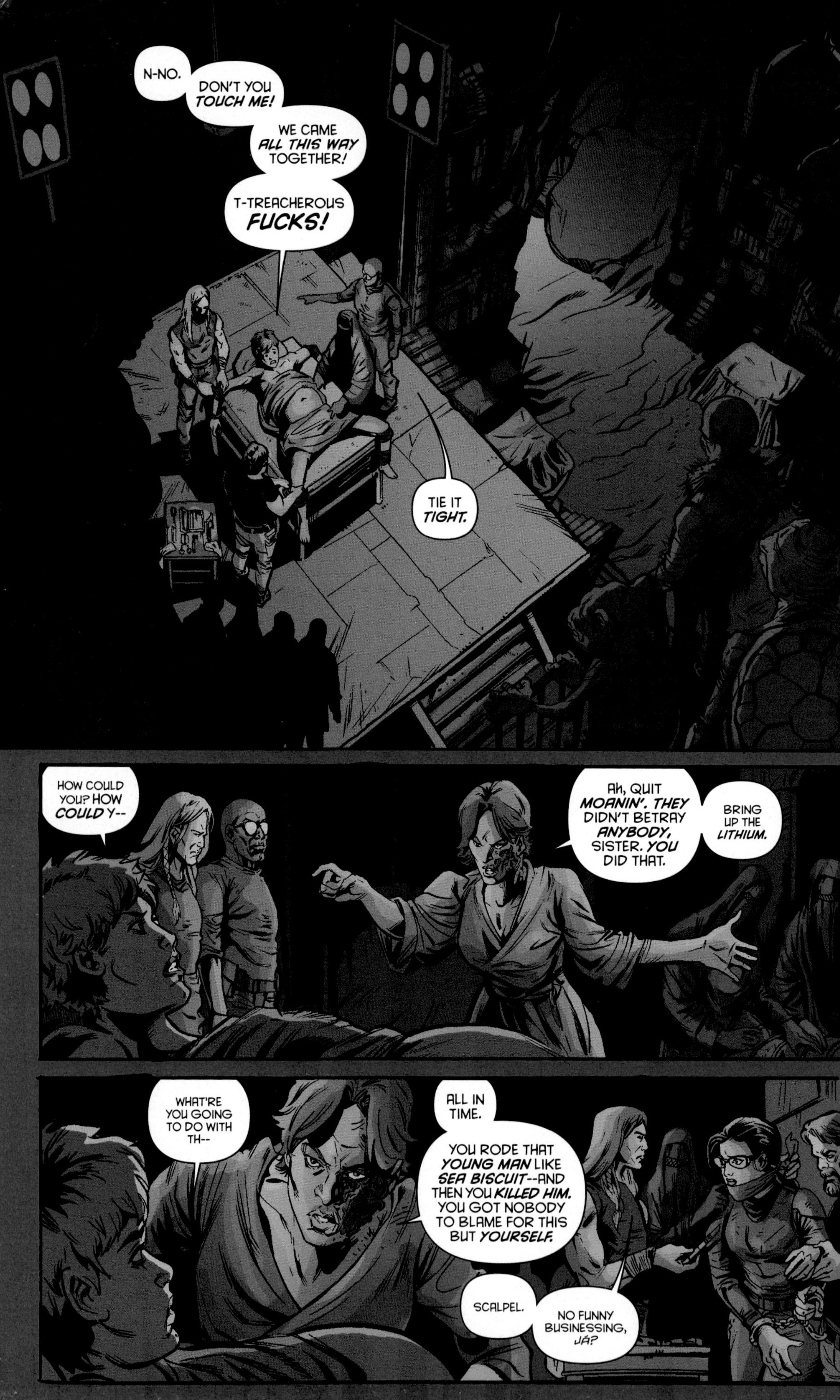
N-NO.
DON'T YOU TOUCH ME!
WE CAME ALL THIS WAY TOGETHER!
T-TREACHEROUS FUCKS!
TIE IT TIGHT.
HOW COULD YOU? HOW COULD Y--
Ah, QUIT MOANIN'. THEY DIDN'T BETRAY ANYBODY, SISTER. YOU DID THAT.
BRING UP THE LITHIUM.
WHAT'RE YOU GOING TO DO WITH TH--
ALL IN TIME.
YOU RODE THAT YOUNG MAN LIKE SEA BISCUIT--AND THEN YOU KILLED HIM. YOU GOT NOBODY TO BLAME FOR THIS BUT YOURSELF.
SCALPEL.
NO FUNNY BUSINESSING, JA?

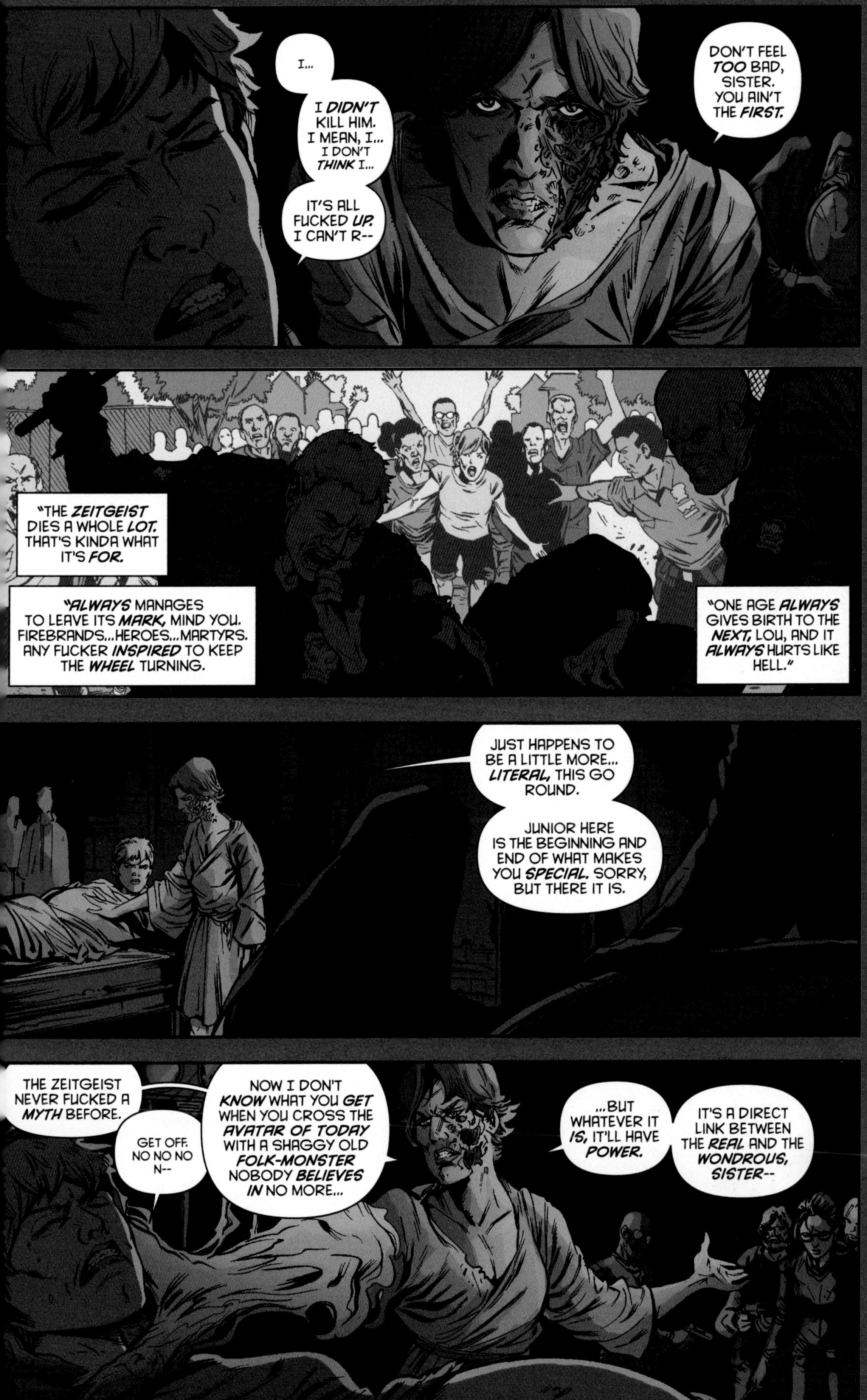

I...
I DIDN'T KILL HIM. I MEAN, I... I DON'T THINK I...
IT'S ALL FUCKED UP. I CAN'T R--
DON'T FEEL TOO BAD, SISTER. YOU AIN'T THE FIRST.
"THE ZEITGEIST DIES A WHOLE LOT. THAT'S KINDA WHAT IT'S FOR.
"ALWAYS MANAGES TO LEAVE ITS MARK, MIND YOU. FIREBRANDS...HEROES...MARTYRS. ANY FUCKER INSPIRED TO KEEP THE WHEEL TURNING.
"ONE AGE ALWAYS GIVES BIRTH TO THE NEXT, LOU, AND IT ALWAYS HURTS LIKE HELL."
JUST HAPPENS TO BE A LITTLE MORE... LITERAL, THIS GO ROUND.
JUNIOR HERE IS THE BEGINNING AND END OF WHAT MAKES YOU SPECIAL. SORRY, BUT THERE IT IS.
THE ZEITGEIST NEVER FUCKED A MYTH BEFORE.
GET OFF. NO NO NO N--
NOW I DON'T KNOW WHAT YOU GET WHEN YOU CROSS THE AVATAR OF TODAY WITH A SHAGGY OLD FOLK-MONSTER NOBODY BELIEVES IN NO MORE...
...BUT WHATEVER IT IS, IT'LL HAVE POWER.
IT'S A DIRECT LINK BETWEEN THE REAL AND THE WONDROUS, SISTER--

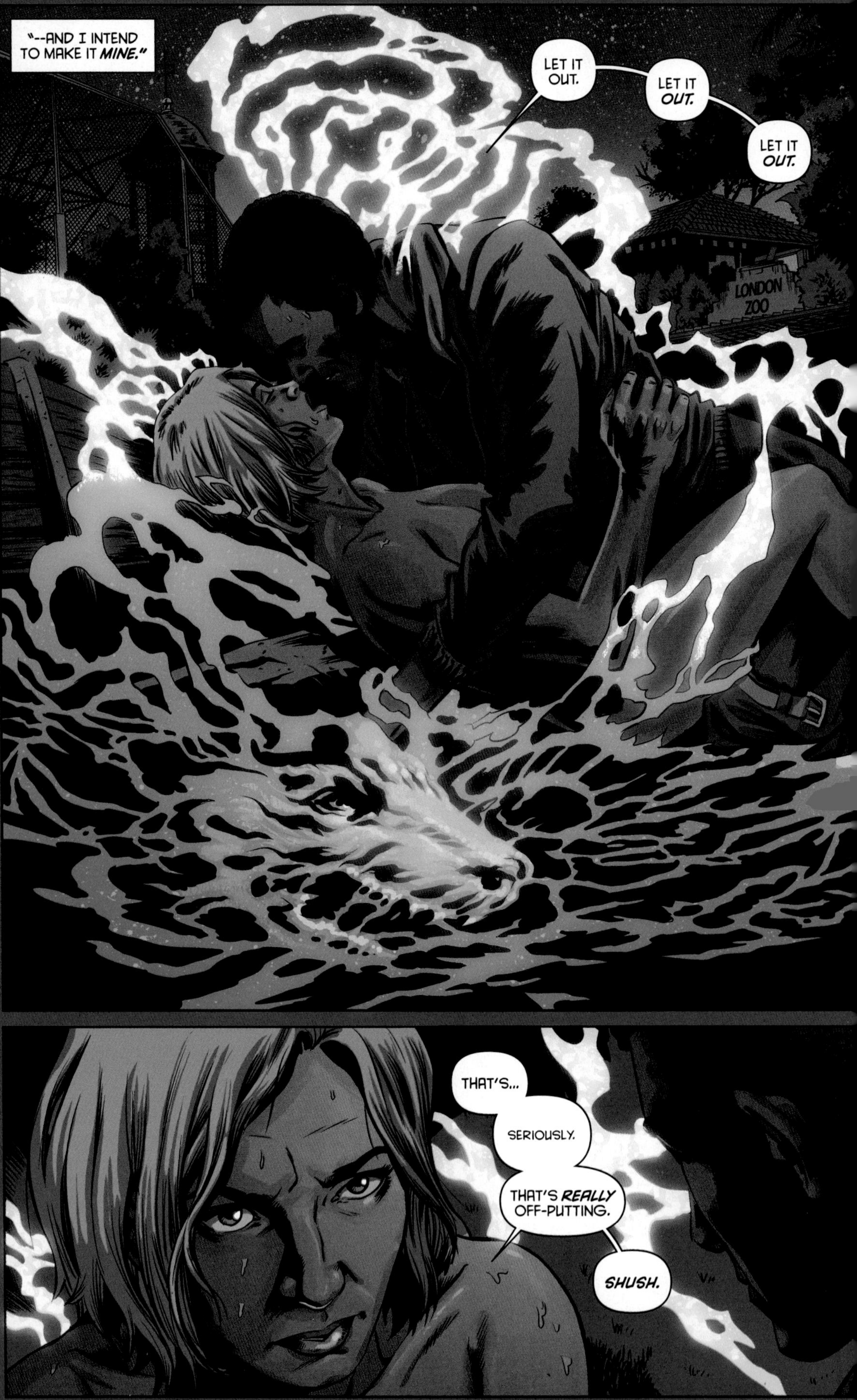
"--AND I INTEND TO MAKE IT *MINE.*"
LET IT OUT.
LET IT *OUT.*
LET IT *OUT.*
LONDON ZOO
THAT'S...
SERIOUSLY.
THAT'S *REALLY* OFF-PUTTING.
SHUSH.

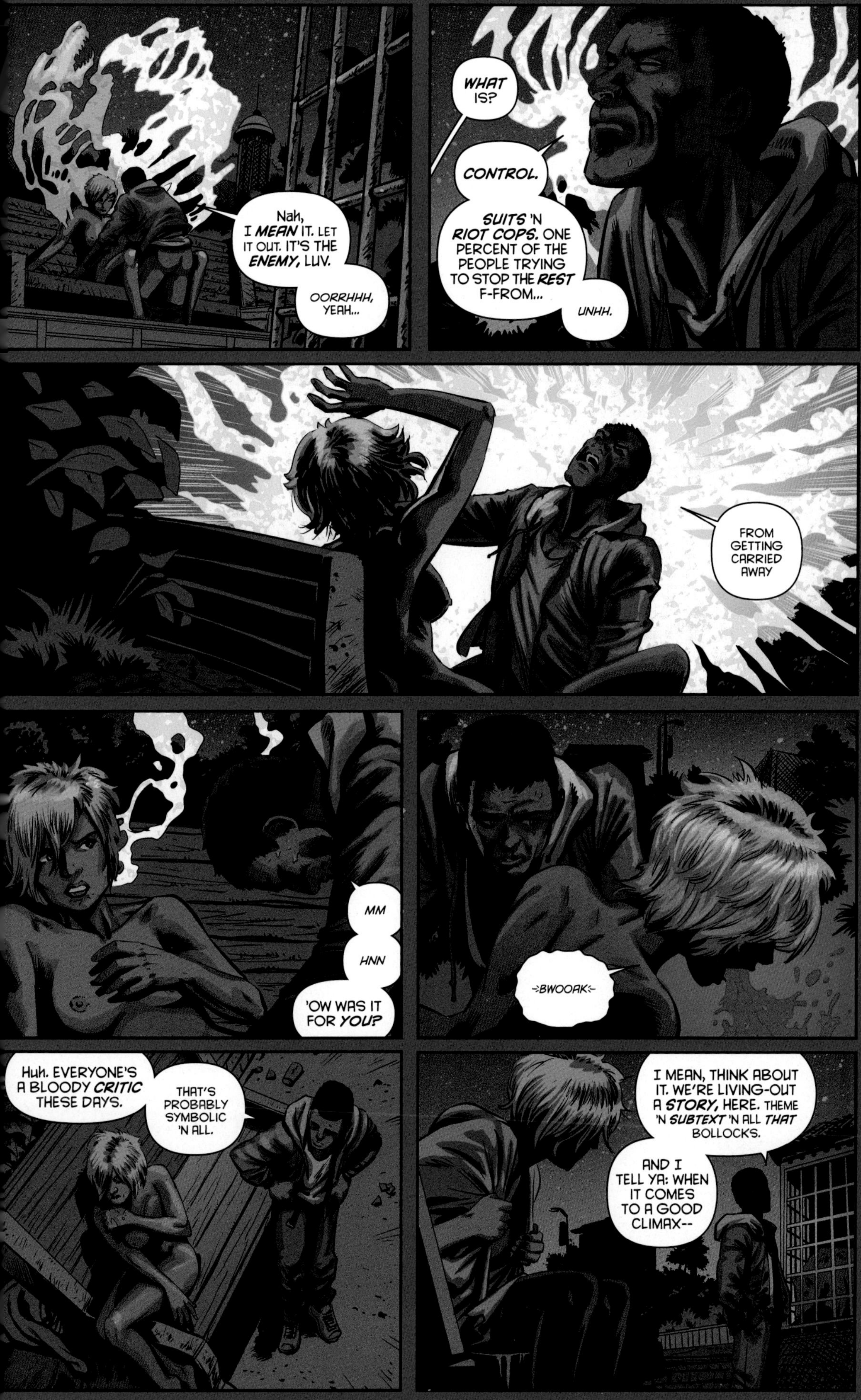

Nah, I MEAN IT. LET IT OUT. IT'S THE ENEMY, LUV.
OORRHHH, YEAH...
WHAT IS?
CONTROL.
SUITS 'N RIOT COPS. ONE PERCENT OF THE PEOPLE TRYING TO STOP THE REST F-FROM...
UNHH.
FROM GETTING CARRIED AWAY
MM
HNN
'OW WAS IT FOR YOU?
BWOOAK
Huh. EVERYONE'S A BLOODY CRITIC THESE DAYS.
THAT'S PROBABLY SYMBOLIC 'N ALL.
I MEAN, THINK ABOUT IT. WE'RE LIVING-OUT A STORY, HERE. THEME 'N SUBTEXT 'N ALL THAT BOLLOCKS.
AND I TELL YA: WHEN IT COMES TO A GOOD CLIMAX--

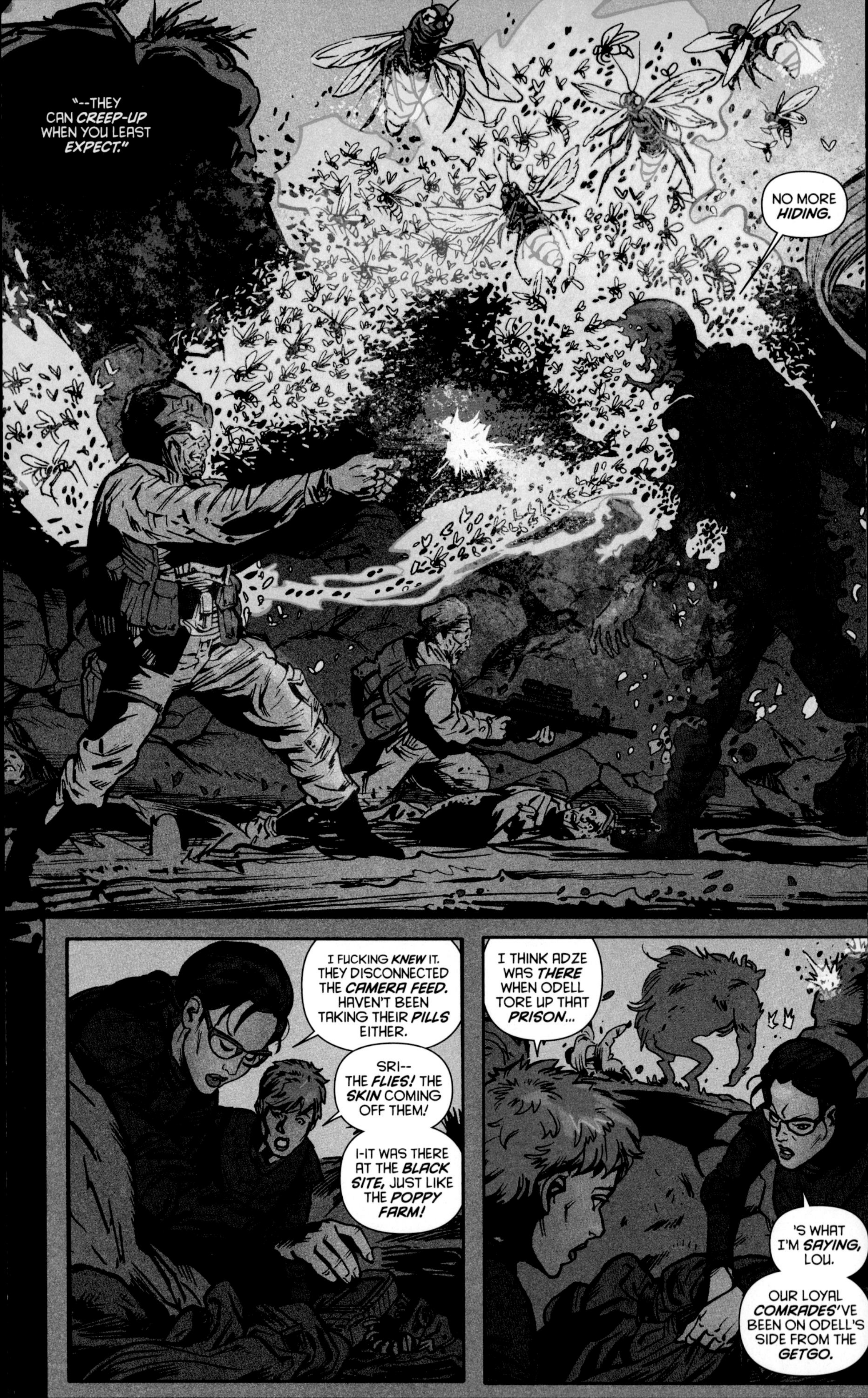
"--THEY CAN CREEP-UP WHEN YOU LEAST EXPECT."
NO MORE HIDING.
I FUCKING KNEW IT. THEY DISCONNECTED THE CAMERA FEED. HAVEN'T BEEN TAKING THEIR PILLS EITHER.
SRI-- THE FLIES! THE SKIN COMING OFF THEM!
I-IT WAS THERE AT THE BLACK SITE, JUST LIKE THE POPPY FARM!
I THINK ADZE WAS THERE WHEN ODELL TORE UP THAT PRISON...
'S WHAT I'M SAYING, LOU.
OUR LOYAL COMRADES'VE BEEN ON ODELL'S SIDE FROM THE GETGO.

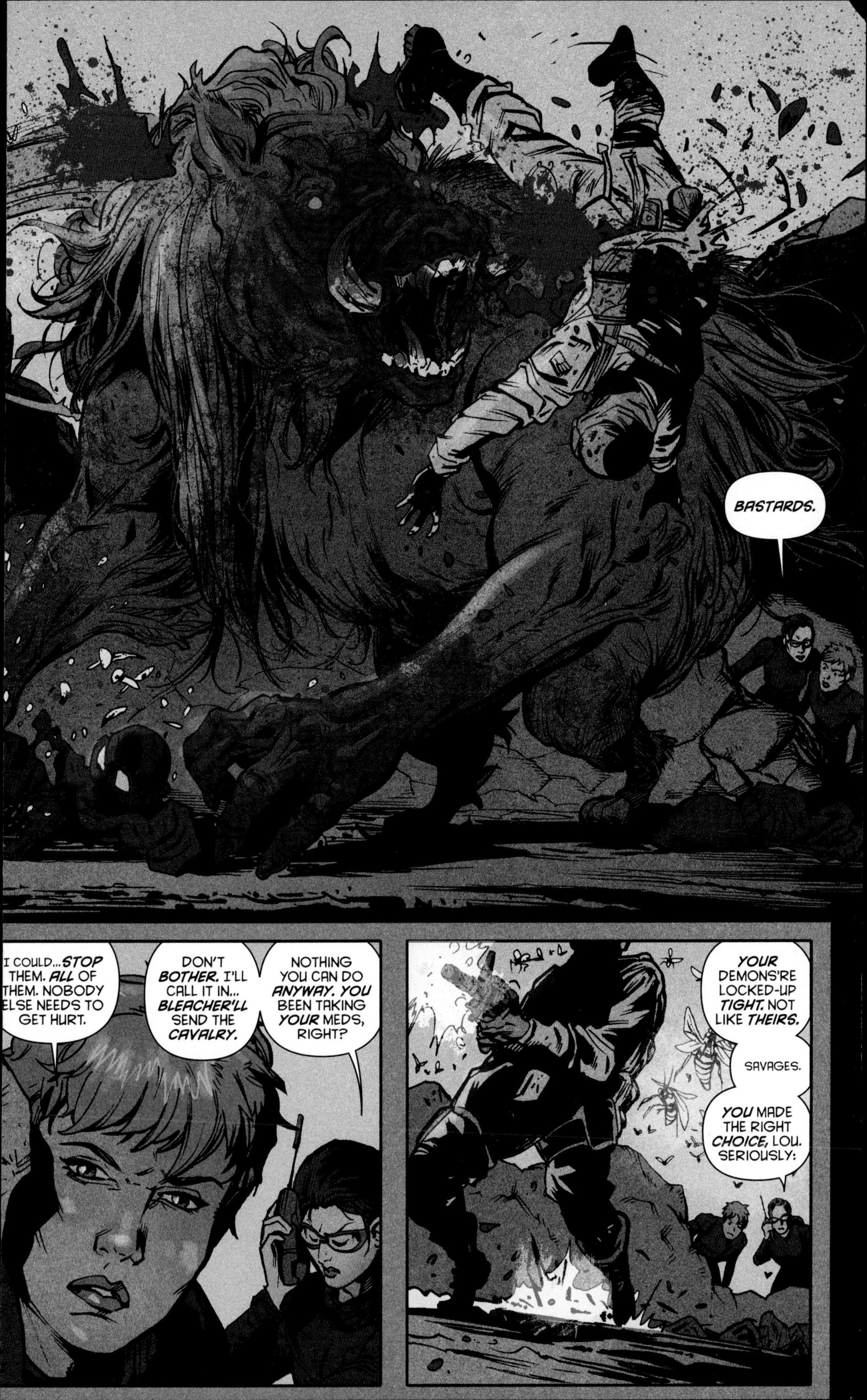
BASTARDS.
I COULD...STOP THEM. ALL OF THEM. NOBODY ELSE NEEDS TO GET HURT.
DON'T BOTHER. I'LL CALL IT IN... BLEACHER'LL SEND THE CAVALRY.
NOTHING YOU CAN DO ANYWAY. YOU BEEN TAKING YOUR MEDS, RIGHT?
YOUR DEMONS'RE LOCKED-UP TIGHT. NOT LIKE THEIRS.
SAVAGES.
YOU MADE THE RIGHT CHOICE, LOU. SERIOUSLY:

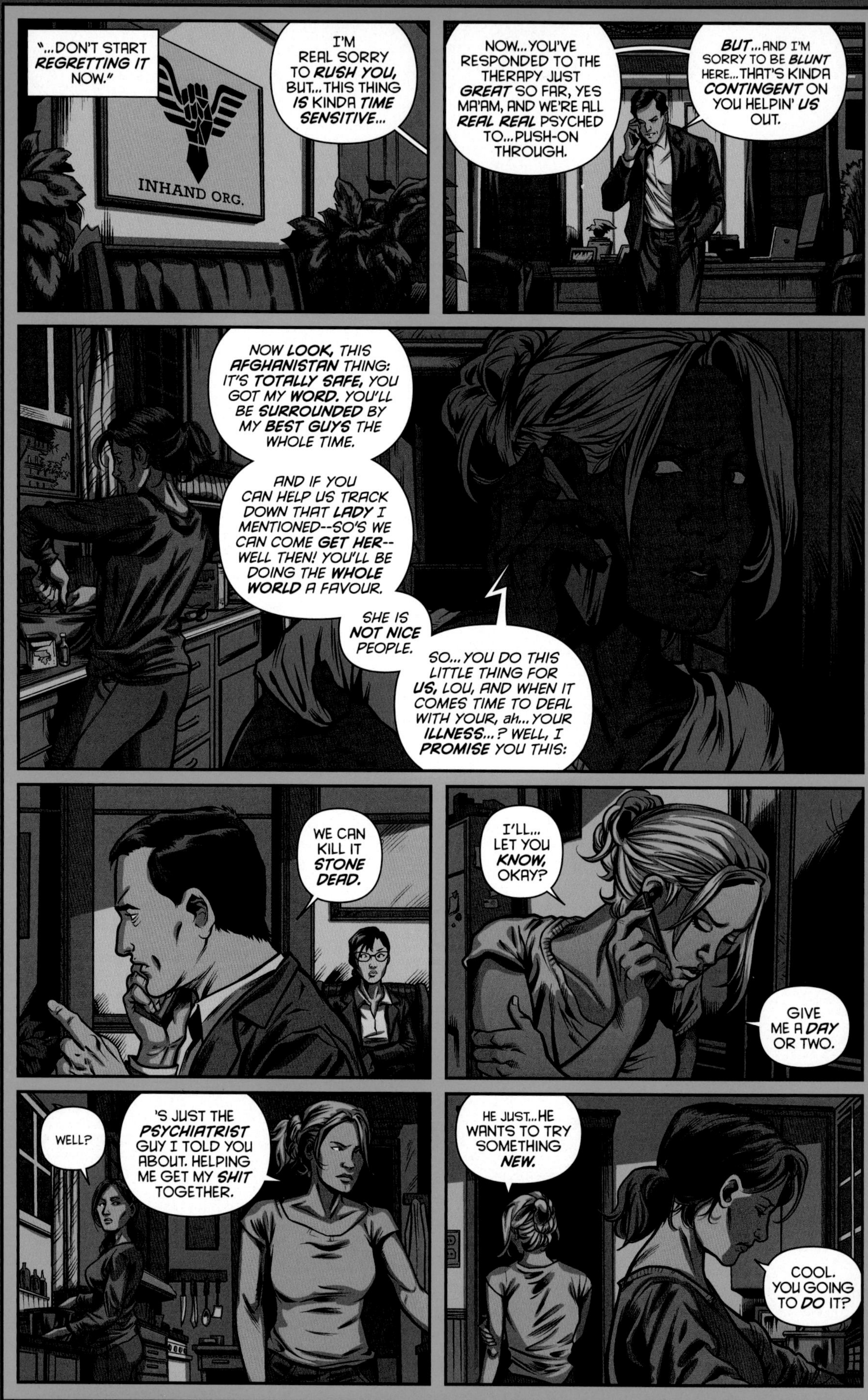
"...DON'T START REGRETTING IT NOW."
I'M REAL SORRY TO RUSH YOU, BUT...THIS THING IS KINDA TIME SENSITIVE...
INHAND ORG.
NOW...YOU'VE RESPONDED TO THE THERAPY JUST GREAT SO FAR, YES MA'AM, AND WE'RE ALL REAL REAL PSYCHED TO...PUSH-ON THROUGH.
BUT...AND I'M SORRY TO BE BLUNT HERE...THAT'S KINDA CONTINGENT ON YOU HELPIN' US OUT.
NOW LOOK, THIS AFGHANISTAN THING: IT'S TOTALLY SAFE, YOU GOT MY WORD. YOU'LL BE SURROUNDED BY MY BEST GUYS THE WHOLE TIME.
AND IF YOU CAN HELP US TRACK DOWN THAT LADY I MENTIONED--SO'S WE CAN COME GET HER--WELL THEN! YOU'LL BE DOING THE WHOLE WORLD A FAVOUR.
SHE IS NOT NICE PEOPLE.
SO...YOU DO THIS LITTLE THING FOR US, LOU, AND WHEN IT COMES TIME TO DEAL WITH YOUR, ah...YOUR ILLNESS...? WELL, I PROMISE YOU THIS:
WE CAN KILL IT STONE DEAD.
I'LL... LET YOU KNOW, OKAY?
GIVE ME A DAY OR TWO.
WELL?
'S JUST THE PSYCHIATRIST GUY I TOLD YOU ABOUT. HELPING ME GET MY SHIT TOGETHER.
HE JUST...HE WANTS TO TRY SOMETHING NEW.
COOL. YOU GOING TO DO IT?

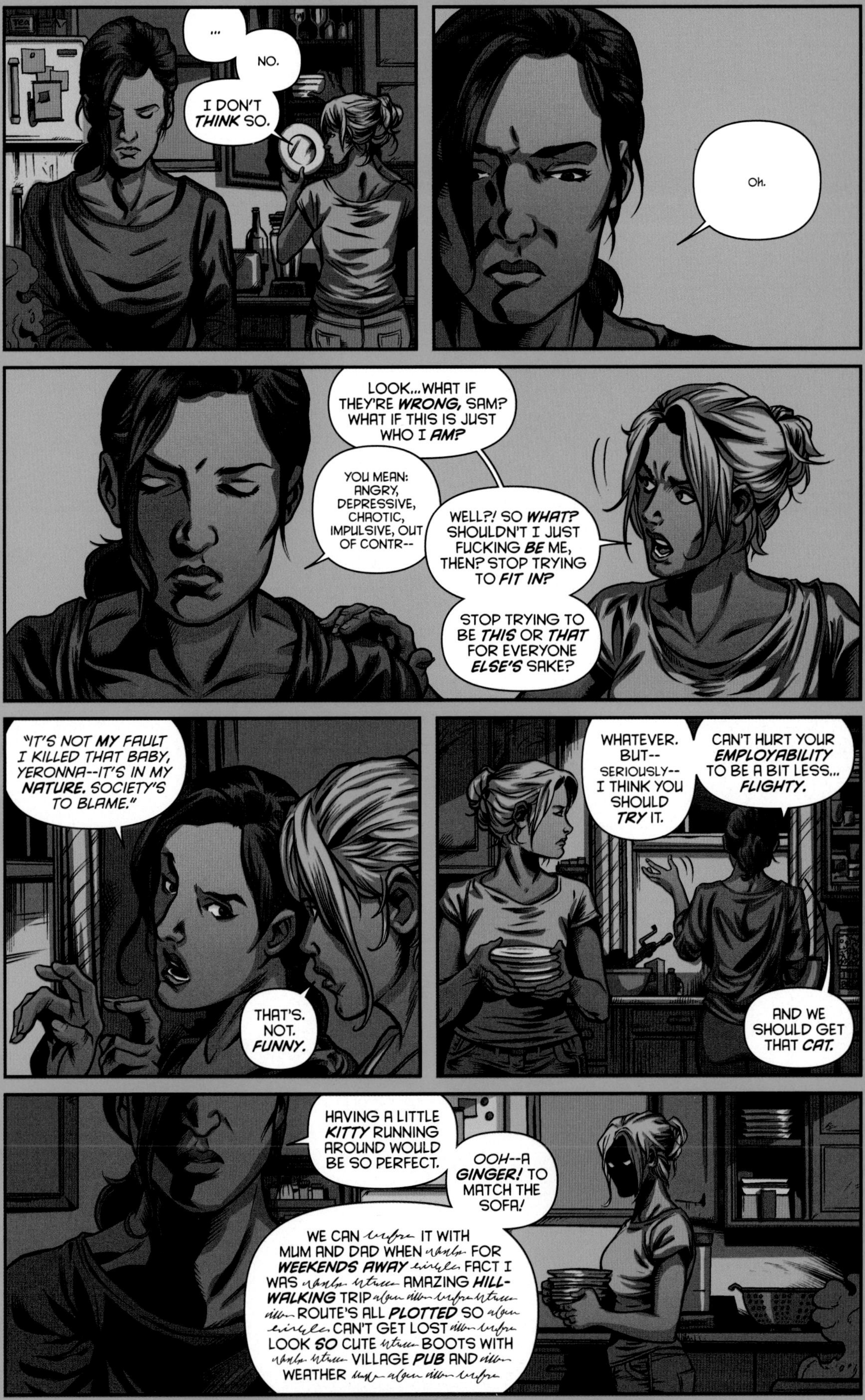

...
NO.
I DON'T *THINK* SO.
Oh.
LOOK...WHAT IF THEY'RE *WRONG*, SAM? WHAT IF THIS IS JUST WHO I *AM?*
YOU MEAN: ANGRY, DEPRESSIVE, CHAOTIC, IMPULSIVE, OUT OF CONTR--
WELL?! SO *WHAT?* SHOULDN'T I JUST FUCKING *BE* ME, THEN? STOP TRYING TO *FIT IN?*
STOP TRYING TO BE *THIS* OR *THAT* FOR EVERYONE *ELSE'S* SAKE?
"IT'S NOT *MY* FAULT I KILLED THAT BABY, YERONNA--IT'S IN MY *NATURE.* SOCIETY'S TO BLAME."
THAT'S. NOT. *FUNNY.*
WHATEVER. BUT-- SERIOUSLY-- I THINK YOU SHOULD *TRY* IT.
CAN'T HURT YOUR *EMPLOYABILITY* TO BE A BIT LESS... *FLIGHTY.*
AND WE SHOULD GET THAT *CAT.*
HAVING A LITTLE *KITTY* RUNNING AROUND WOULD BE SO PERFECT.
OOH--A *GINGER!* TO MATCH THE SOFA!
WE CAN IT WITH MUM AND DAD WHEN FOR *WEEKENDS AWAY* FACT I WAS AMAZING *HILL-WALKING* TRIP ROUTE'S ALL *PLOTTED* SO CAN'T GET LOST LOOK *SO* CUTE BOOTS WITH VILLAGE *PUB* AND WEATHER

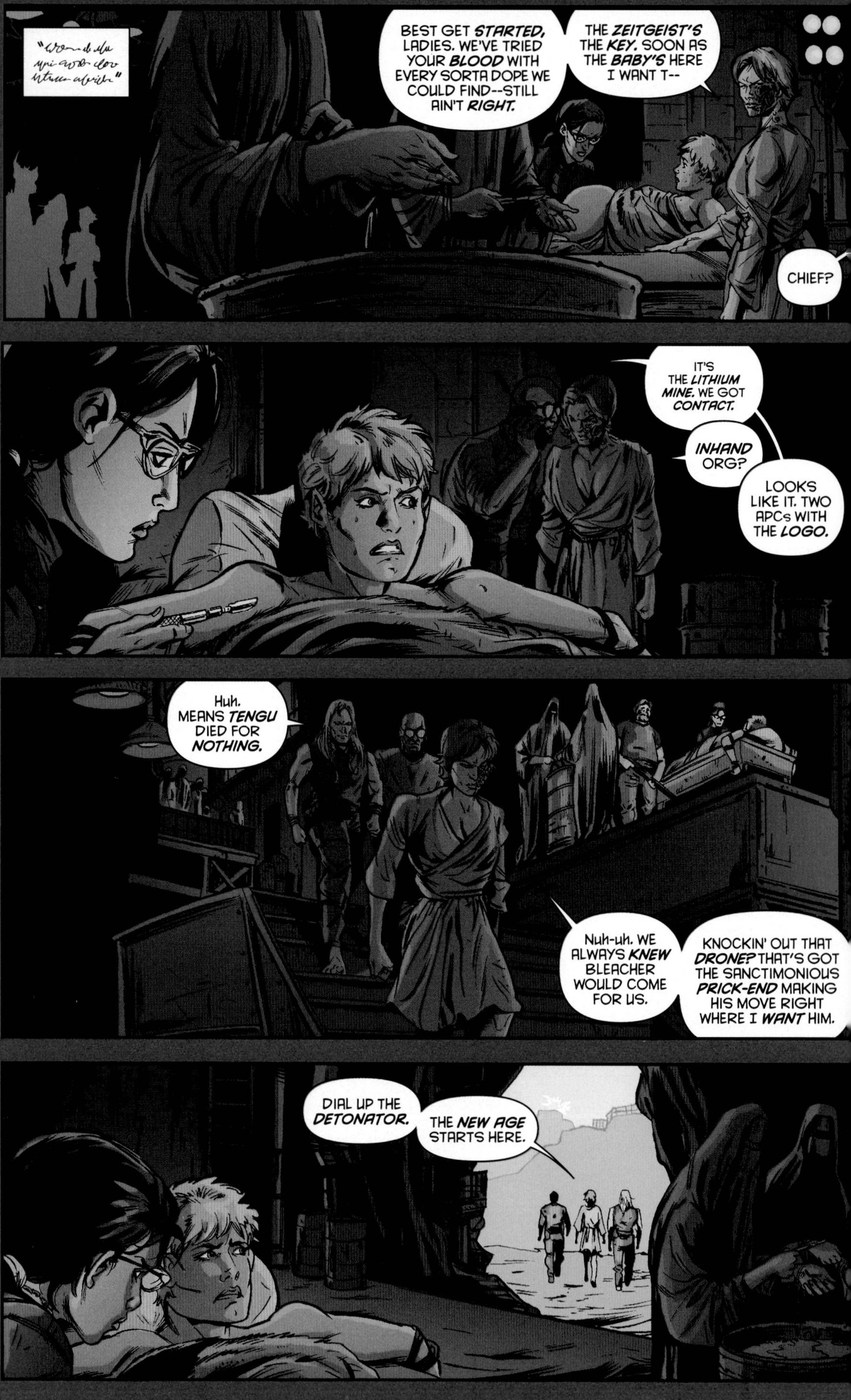
BEST GET STARTED, LADIES. WE'VE TRIED YOUR BLOOD WITH EVERY SORTA DOPE WE COULD FIND--STILL AIN'T RIGHT.
THE ZEITGEIST'S THE KEY. SOON AS THE BABY'S HERE I WANT T--
CHIEF?
IT'S THE LITHIUM MINE. WE GOT CONTACT.
INHAND ORG?
LOOKS LIKE IT. TWO APCs WITH THE LOGO.
Huh. MEANS TENGU DIED FOR NOTHING.
Nuh-uh. WE ALWAYS KNEW BLEACHER WOULD COME FOR US.
KNOCKIN' OUT THAT DRONE? THAT'S GOT THE SANCTIMONIOUS PRICK-END MAKING HIS MOVE RIGHT WHERE I WANT HIM.
DIAL UP THE DETONATOR.
THE NEW AGE STARTS HERE.

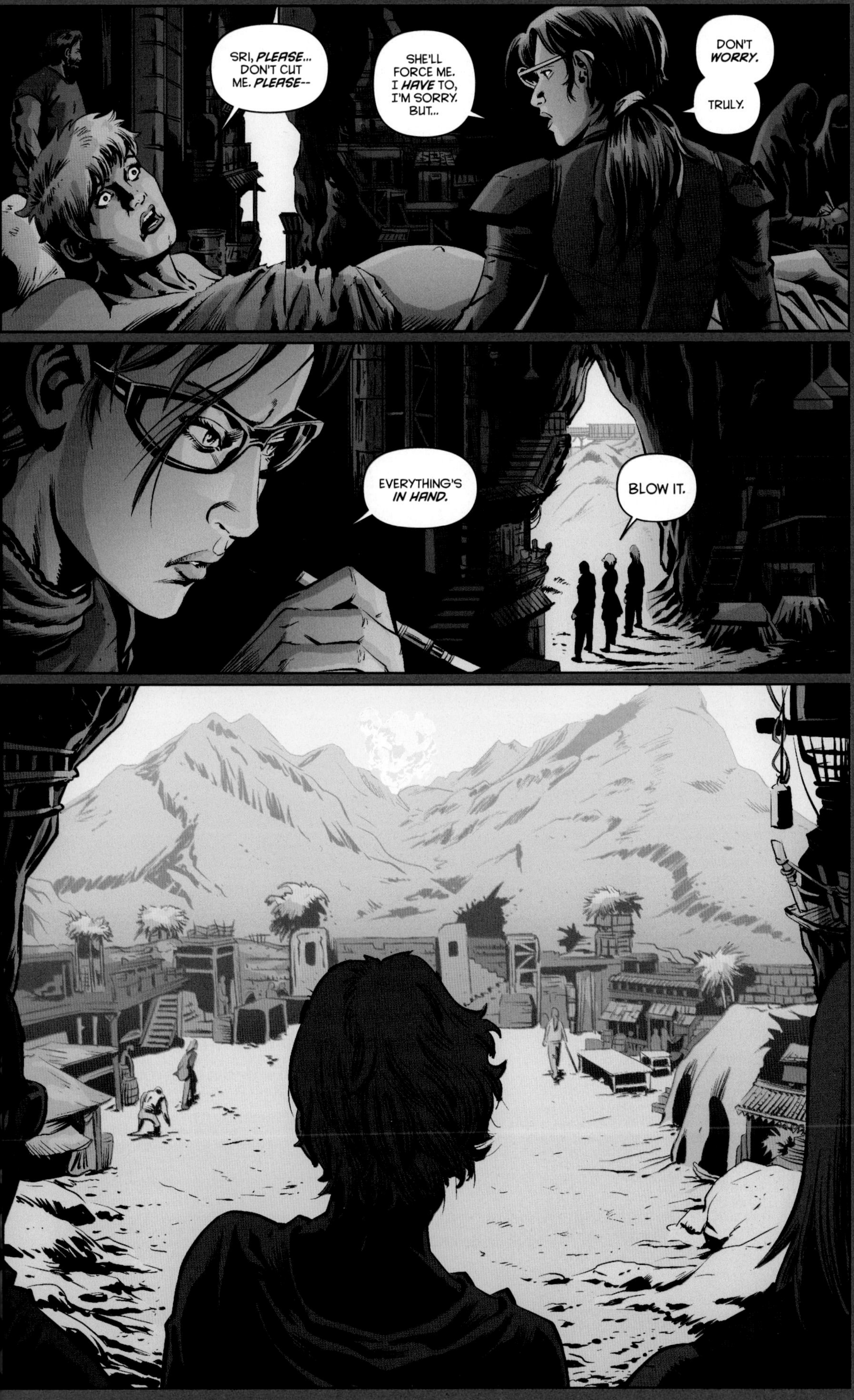
SRI, PLEASE... DON'T CUT ME. PLEASE--
SHE'LL FORCE ME. I HAVE TO, I'M SORRY. BUT...
DON'T WORRY.
TRULY.
EVERYTHING'S IN HAND.
BLOW IT.

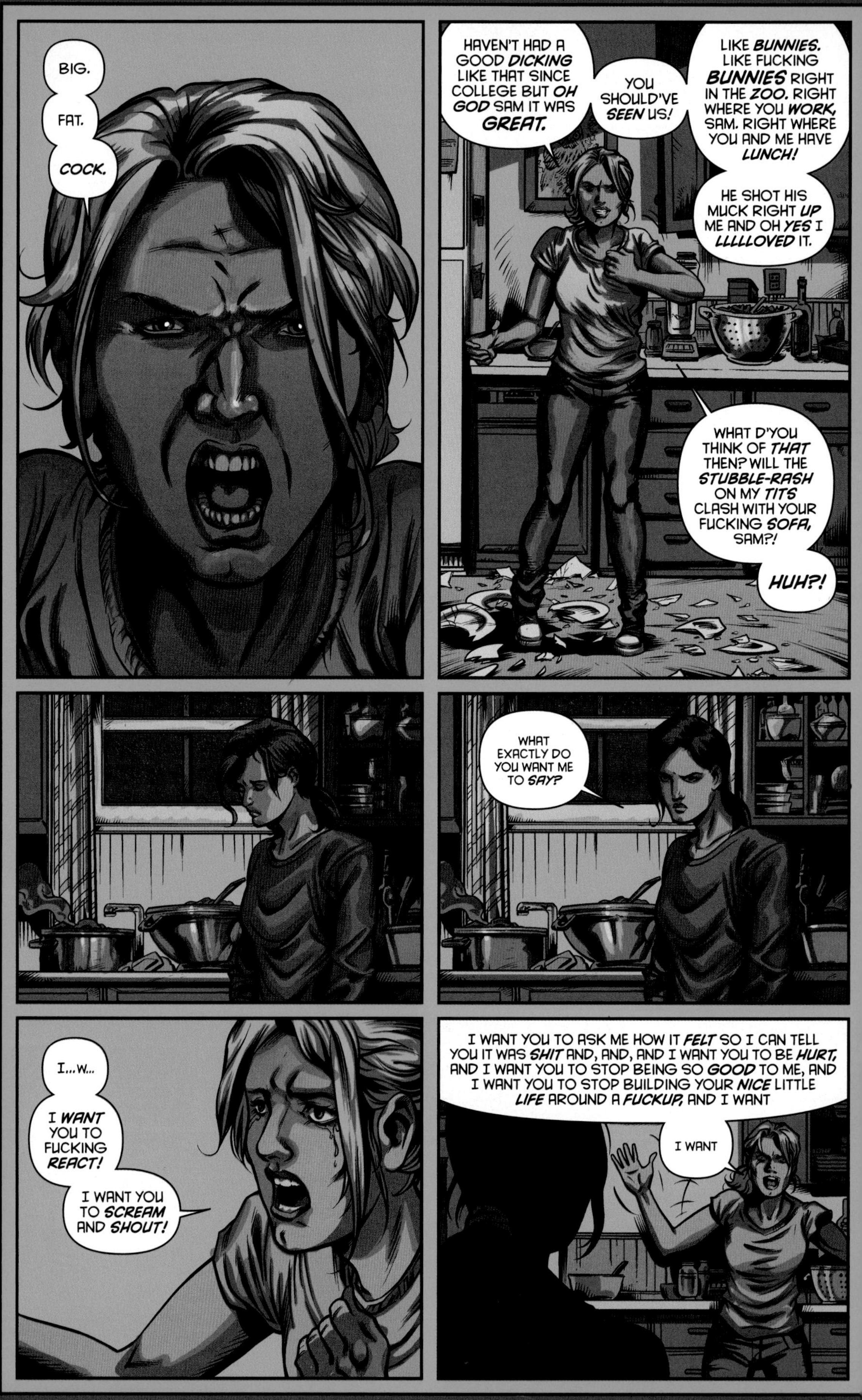
BIG.
FAT.
COCK.
HAVEN'T HAD A GOOD DICKING LIKE THAT SINCE COLLEGE BUT OH GOD SAM IT WAS GREAT.
YOU SHOULD'VE SEEN US!
LIKE BUNNIES. LIKE FUCKING BUNNIES RIGHT IN THE ZOO. RIGHT WHERE YOU WORK, SAM. RIGHT WHERE YOU AND ME HAVE LUNCH!
HE SHOT HIS MUCK RIGHT UP ME AND OH YES I LLLLLOVED IT.
WHAT D'YOU THINK OF THAT THEN? WILL THE STUBBLE-RASH ON MY TITS CLASH WITH YOUR FUCKING SOFA, SAM?!
HUH?!
WHAT EXACTLY DO YOU WANT ME TO SAY?
I...W...
I WANT YOU TO FUCKING REACT!
I WANT YOU TO SCREAM AND SHOUT!
I WANT YOU TO ASK ME HOW IT FELT SO I CAN TELL YOU IT WAS SHIT AND, AND, AND I WANT YOU TO BE HURT, AND I WANT YOU TO STOP BEING SO GOOD TO ME, AND I WANT YOU TO STOP BUILDING YOUR NICE LITTLE LIFE AROUND A FUCKUP, AND I WANT
I WANT

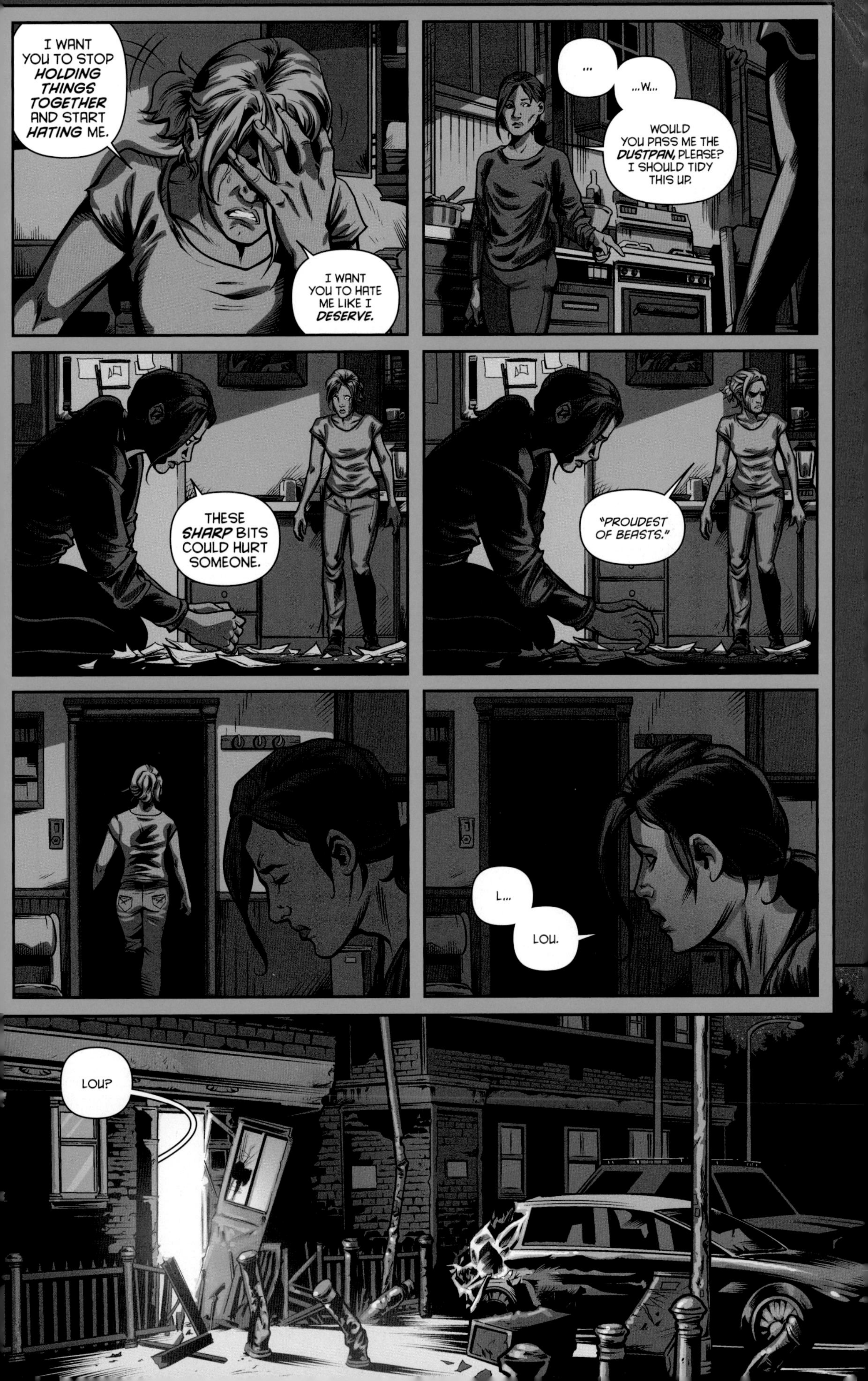
I WANT YOU TO STOP HOLDING THINGS TOGETHER AND START HATING ME.
I WANT YOU TO HATE ME LIKE I DESERVE.
...
...W...
WOULD YOU PASS ME THE DUSTPAN, PLEASE? I SHOULD TIDY THIS UP.
THESE SHARP BITS COULD HURT SOMEONE.
"PROUDEST OF BEASTS."
L...
LOU.
LOU?

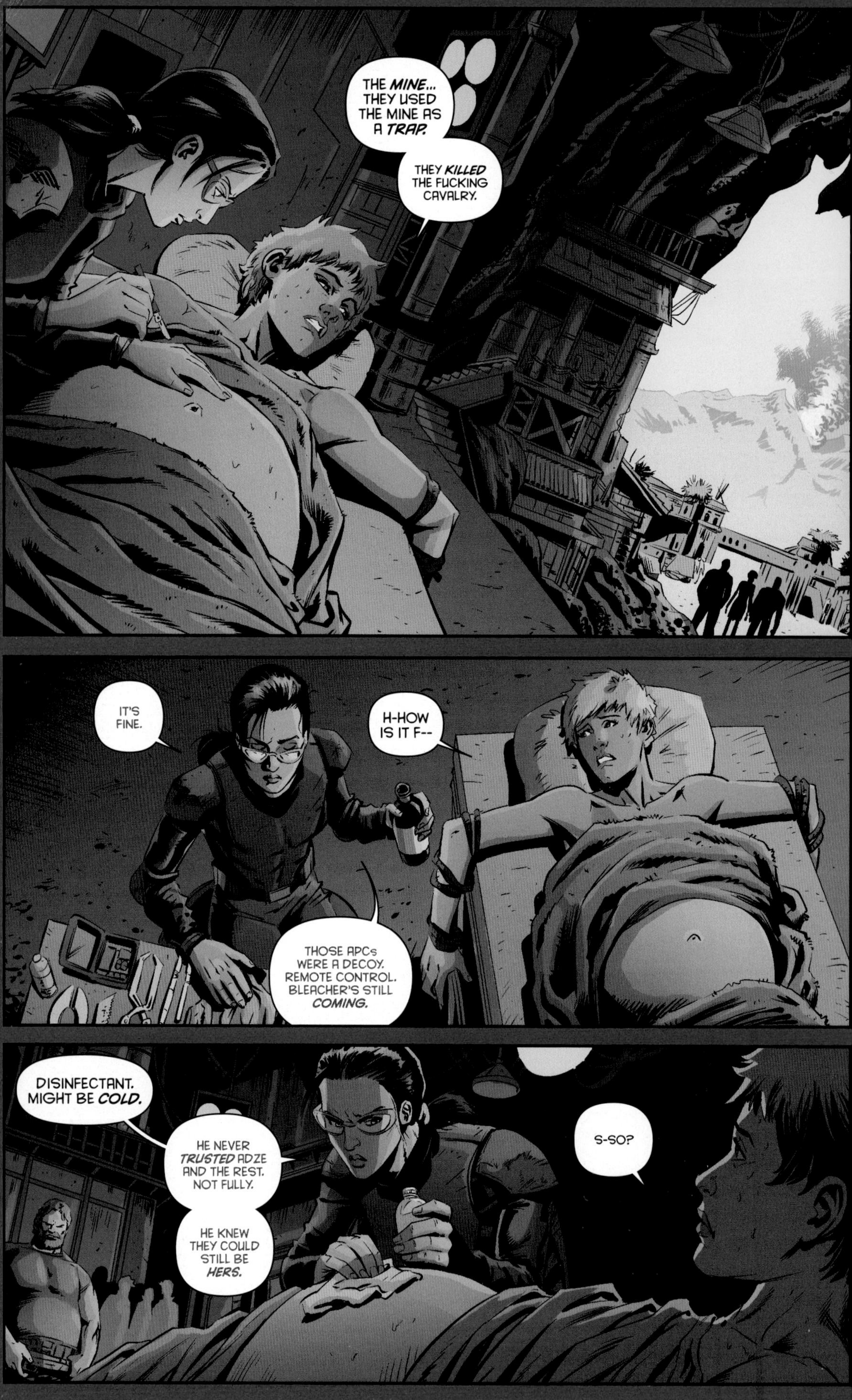
THE *MINE*... THEY USED THE MINE AS A *TRAP.*
THEY *KILLED* THE FUCKING CAVALRY.
IT'S FINE.
H-HOW IS IT F--
THOSE APCs WERE A DECOY. REMOTE CONTROL. BLEACHER'S STILL *COMING.*
DISINFECTANT. MIGHT BE *COLD.*
HE NEVER *TRUSTED* ADZE AND THE REST. NOT FULLY.
S-SO?
HE KNEW THEY COULD STILL BE *HERS.*

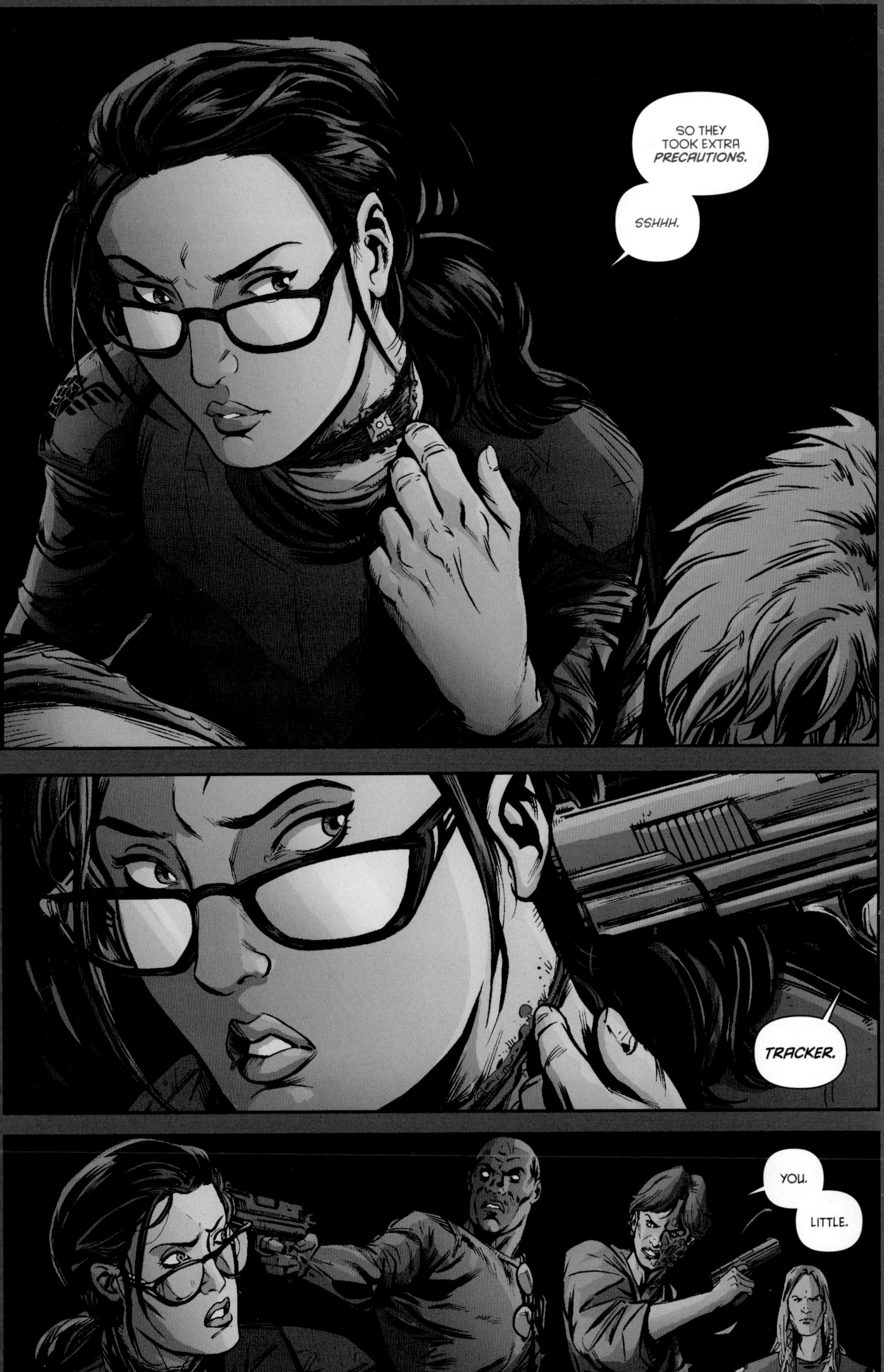
SO THEY TOOK EXTRA *PRECAUTIONS.*
SSHHH.
TRACKER.
YOU.
LITTLE.

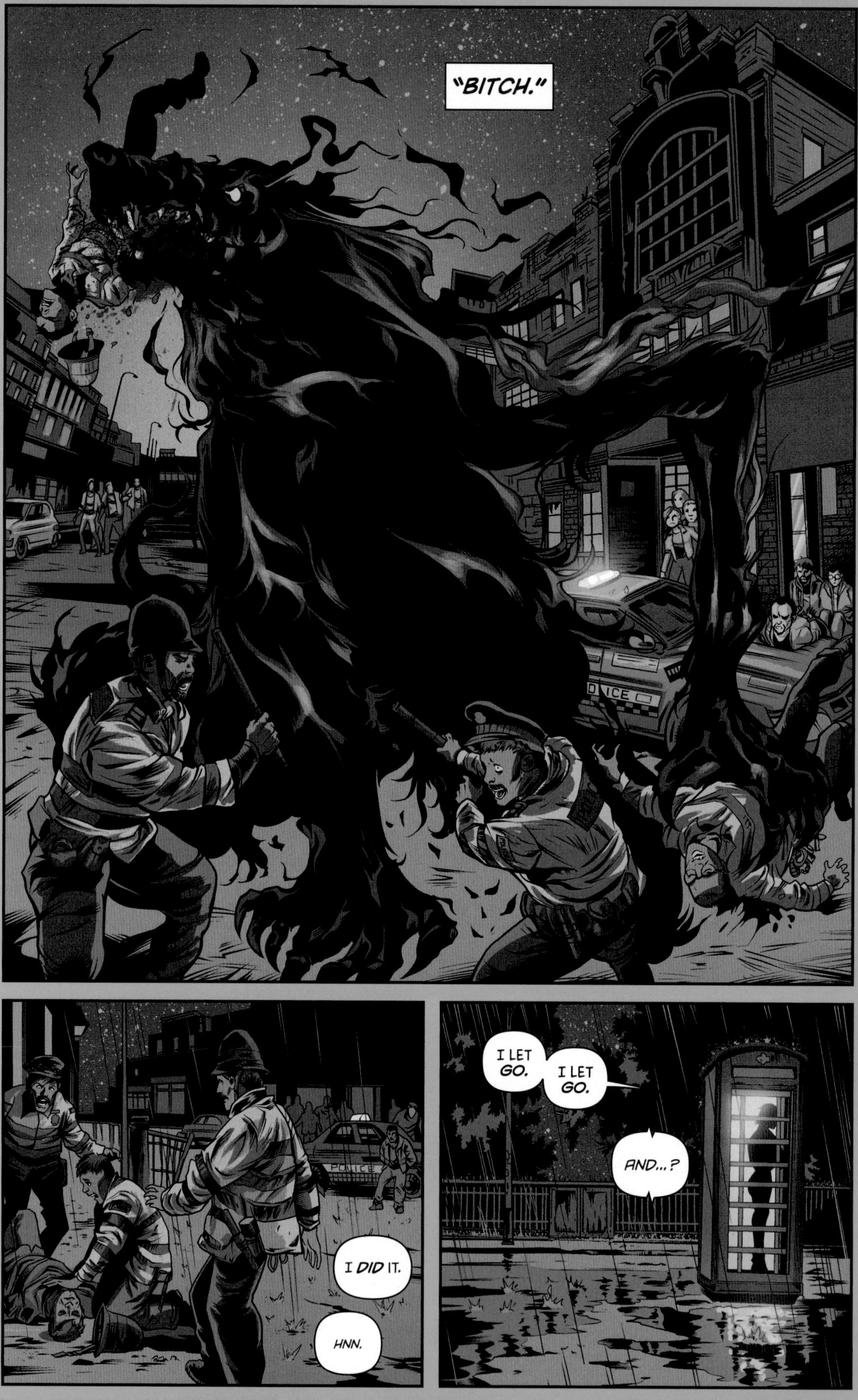
"BITCH."
POLICE
POLICE
I DID IT.
HNN.
I LET GO.
I LET GO.
AND...?

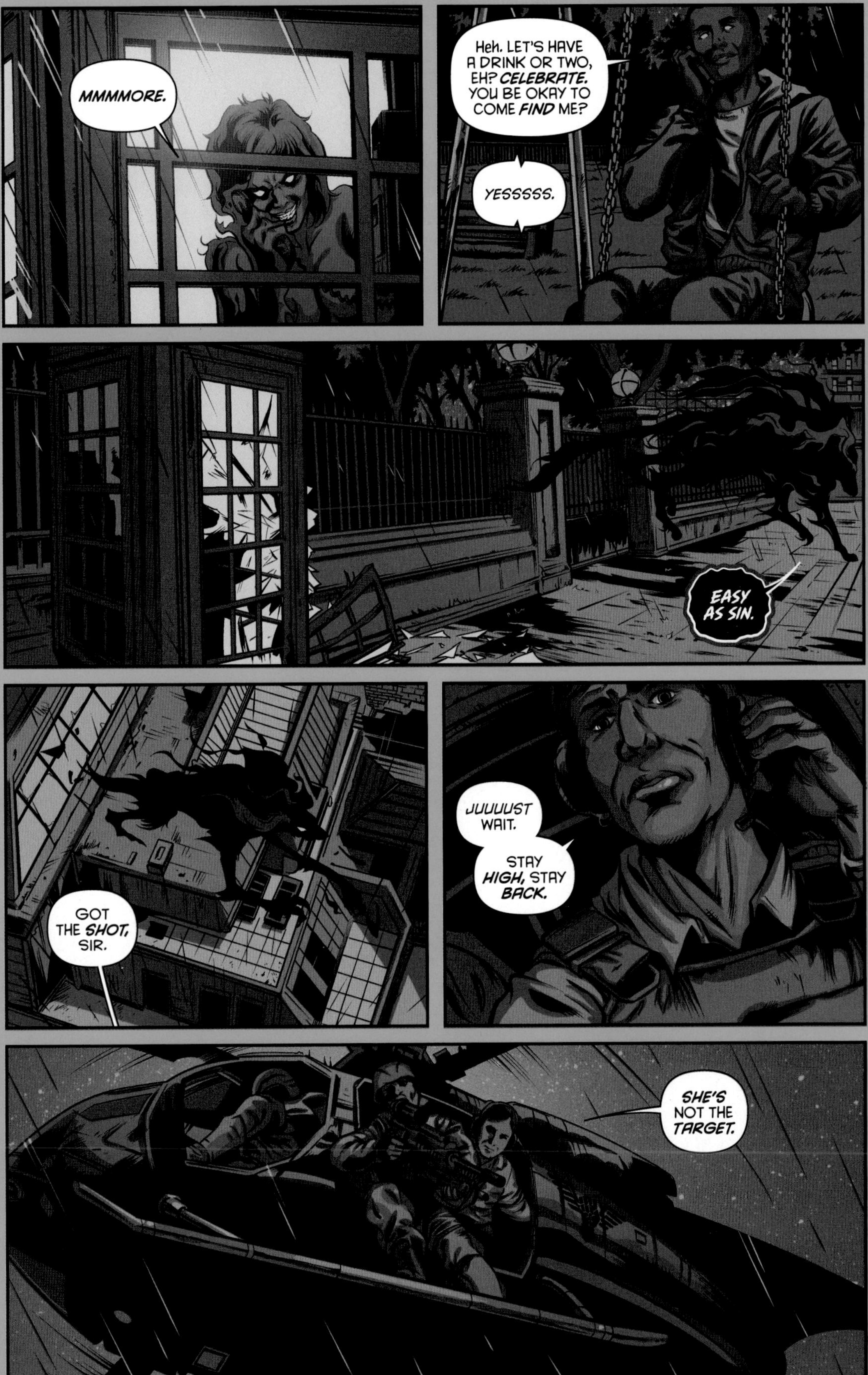
MMMMORE.
Heh. LET'S HAVE A DRINK OR TWO, EH? CELEBRATE. YOU BE OKAY TO COME FIND ME?
YESSSSS.
EASY AS SIN.
GOT THE SHOT, SIR.
JUUUUST WAIT.
STAY HIGH, STAY BACK.
SHE'S NOT THE TARGET.

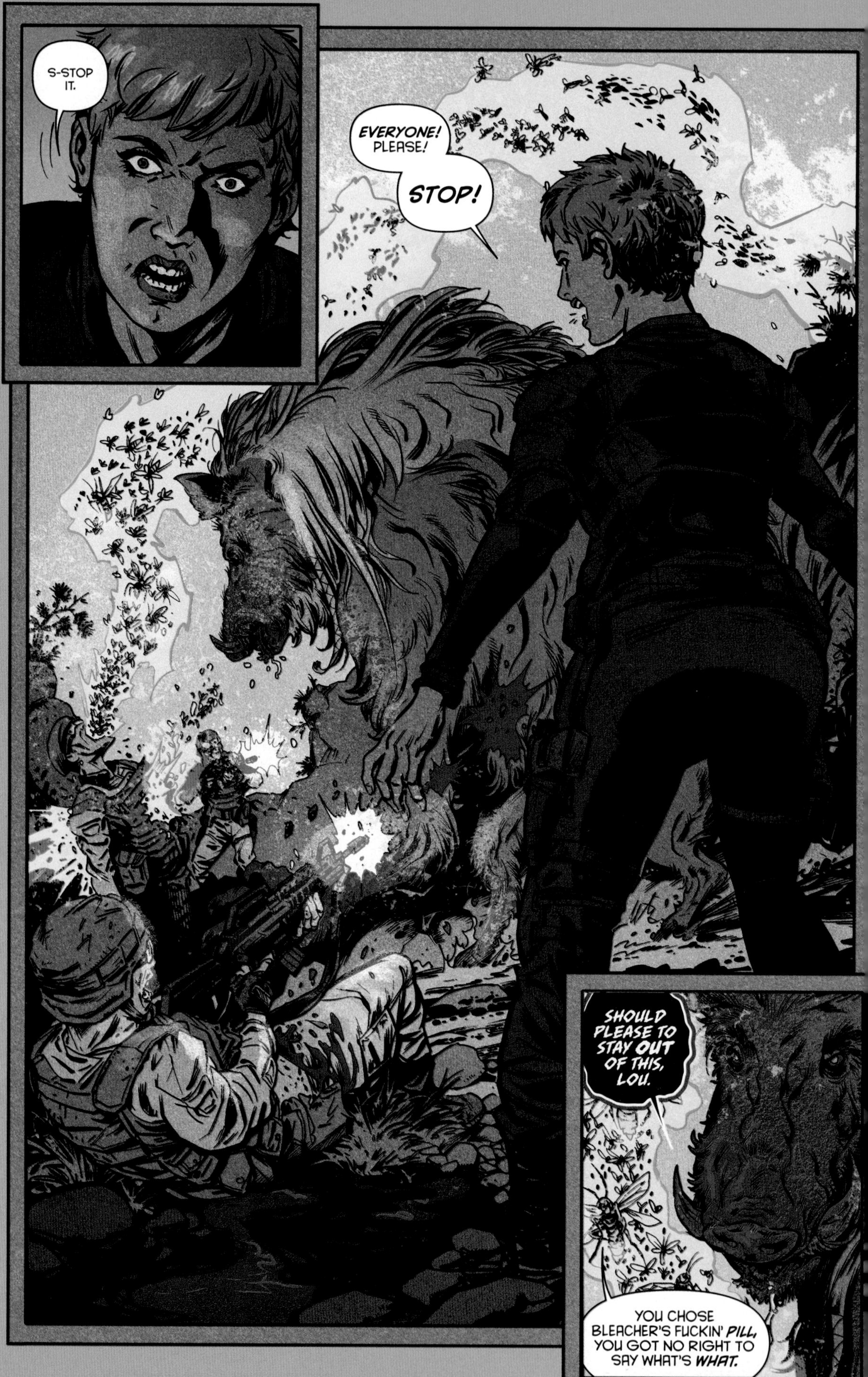
S-STOP IT.
EVERYONE! PLEASE!
STOP!
SHOULD PLEASE TO STAY OUT OF THIS, LOU.
YOU CHOSE BLEACHER'S FUCKIN' PILL, YOU GOT NO RIGHT TO SAY WHAT'S WHAT.

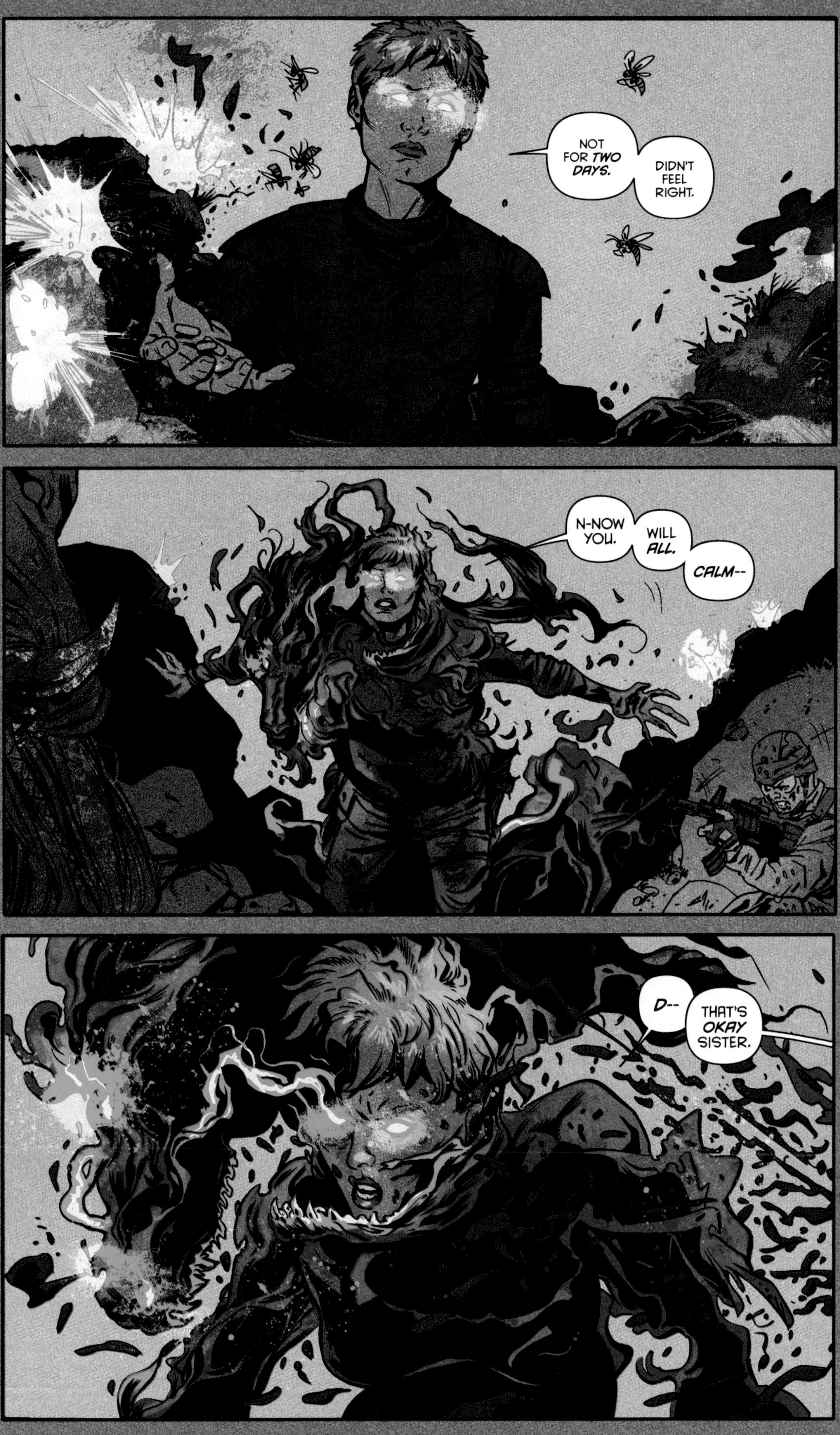
NOT FOR TWO DAYS.
DIDN'T FEEL RIGHT.
N-NOW YOU.
WILL ALL.
CALM--
D--
THAT'S OKAY SISTER.

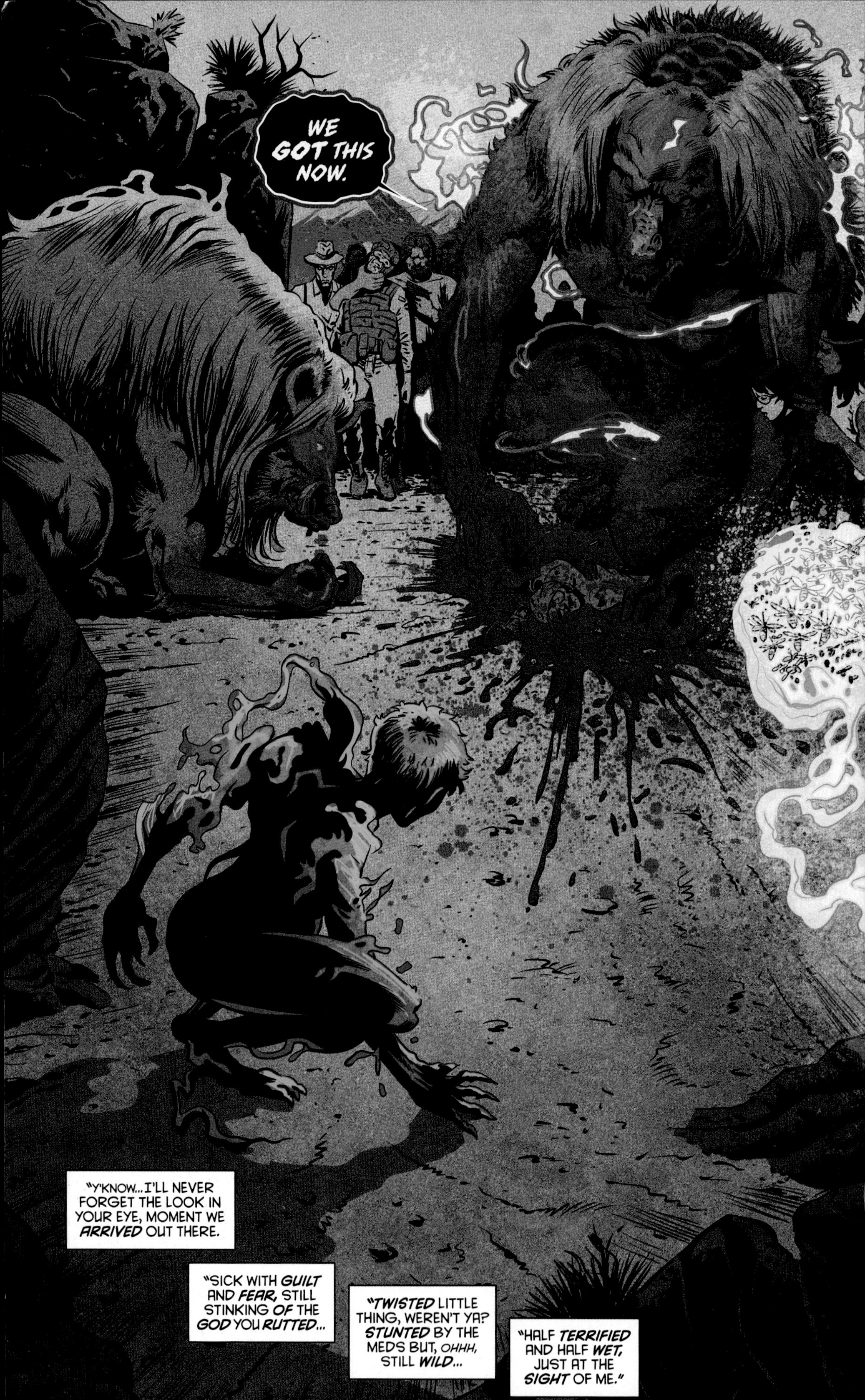
WE GOT THIS NOW.
"Y'KNOW...I'LL NEVER FORGET THE LOOK IN YOUR EYE, MOMENT WE ARRIVED OUT THERE.
"SICK WITH GUILT AND FEAR, STILL STINKING OF THE GOD YOU RUTTED...
"TWISTED LITTLE THING, WEREN'T YA? STUNTED BY THE MEDS BUT, OHHH, STILL WILD...
"HALF TERRIFIED AND HALF WET, JUST AT THE SIGHT OF ME."

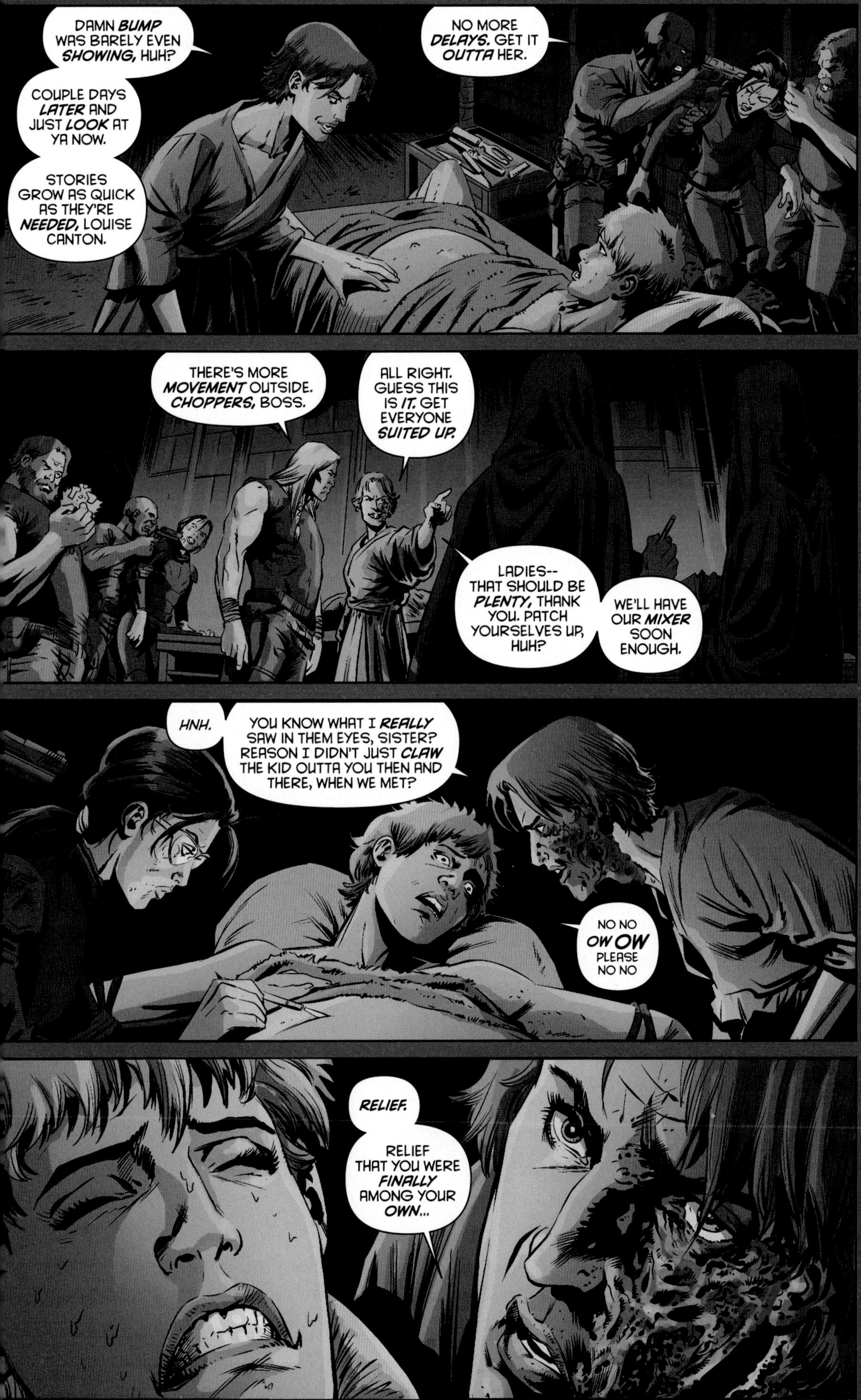
DAMN BUMP WAS BARELY EVEN SHOWING, HUH?
COUPLE DAYS LATER AND JUST LOOK AT YA NOW.
STORIES GROW AS QUICK AS THEY'RE NEEDED, LOUISE CANTON.
NO MORE DELAYS. GET IT OUTTA HER.
THERE'S MORE MOVEMENT OUTSIDE. CHOPPERS, BOSS.
ALL RIGHT. GUESS THIS IS IT. GET EVERYONE SUITED UP.
LADIES-- THAT SHOULD BE PLENTY, THANK YOU. PATCH YOURSELVES UP, HUH?
WE'LL HAVE OUR MIXER SOON ENOUGH.
HNH.
YOU KNOW WHAT I REALLY SAW IN THEM EYES, SISTER? REASON I DIDN'T JUST CLAW THE KID OUTTA YOU THEN AND THERE, WHEN WE MET?
NO NO OW OW PLEASE NO NO
RELIEF.
RELIEF THAT YOU WERE FINALLY AMONG YOUR OWN...

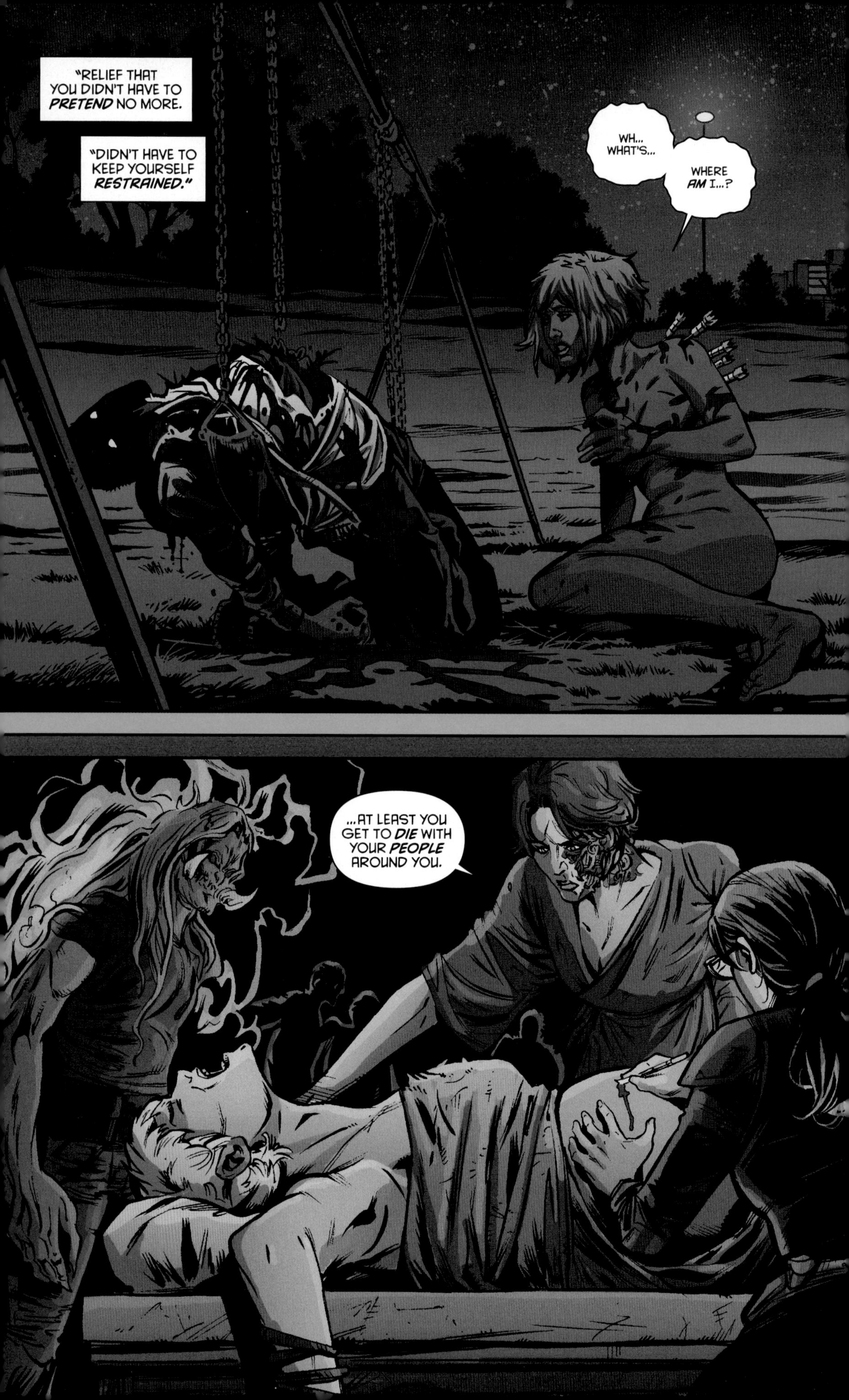

"RELIEF THAT YOU DIDN'T HAVE TO PRETEND NO MORE.
"DIDN'T HAVE TO KEEP YOURSELF RESTRAINED."
WH... WHAT'S...
WHERE AM I...?
...AT LEAST YOU GET TO DIE WITH YOUR PEOPLE AROUND YOU.

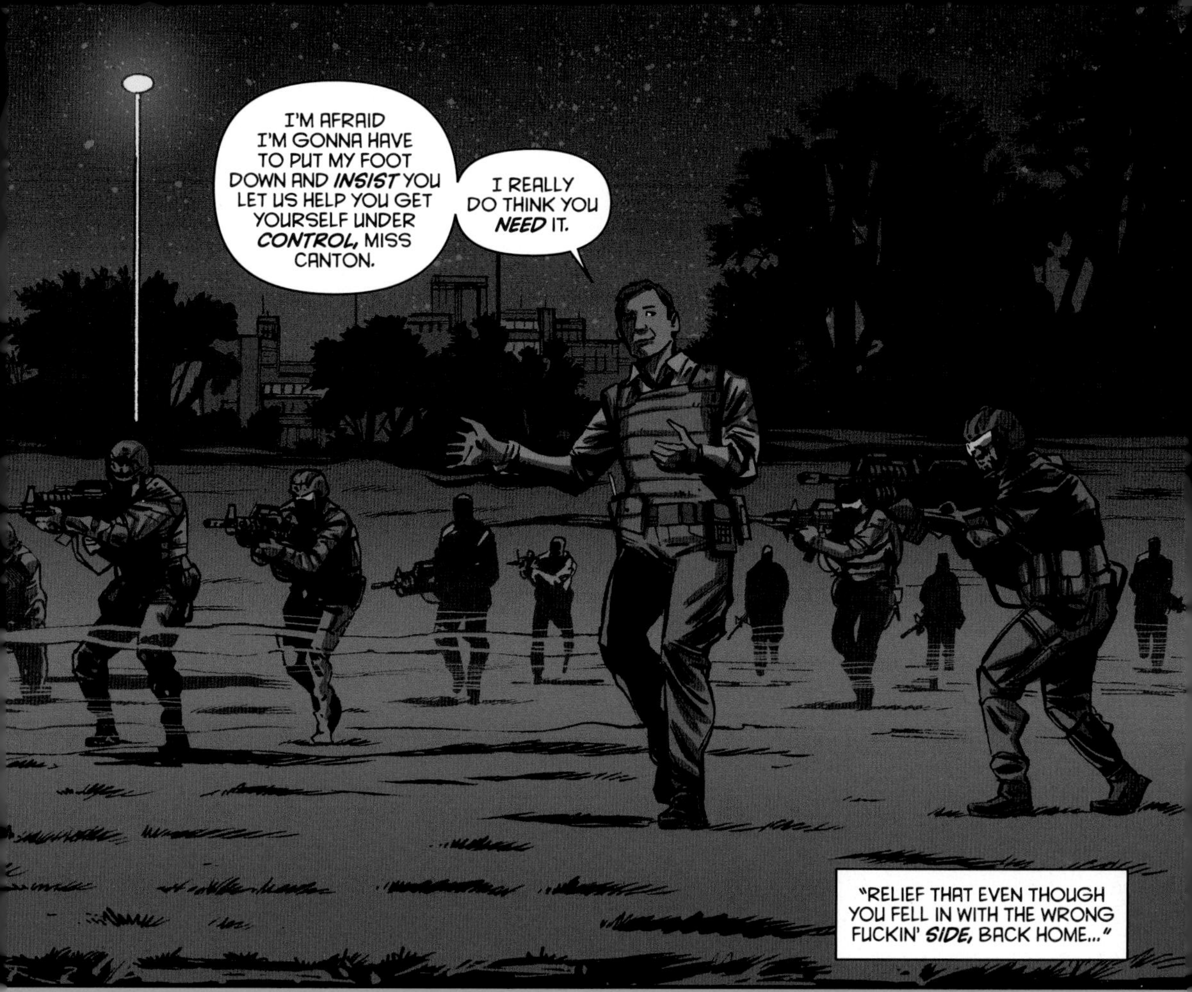
I'M AFRAID I'M GONNA HAVE TO PUT MY FOOT DOWN AND *INSIST* YOU LET US HELP YOU GET YOURSELF UNDER *CONTROL,* MISS CANTON.
I REALLY DO THINK YOU *NEED* IT.
"RELIEF THAT EVEN THOUGH YOU FELL IN WITH THE WRONG FUCKIN' *SIDE,* BACK HOME..."

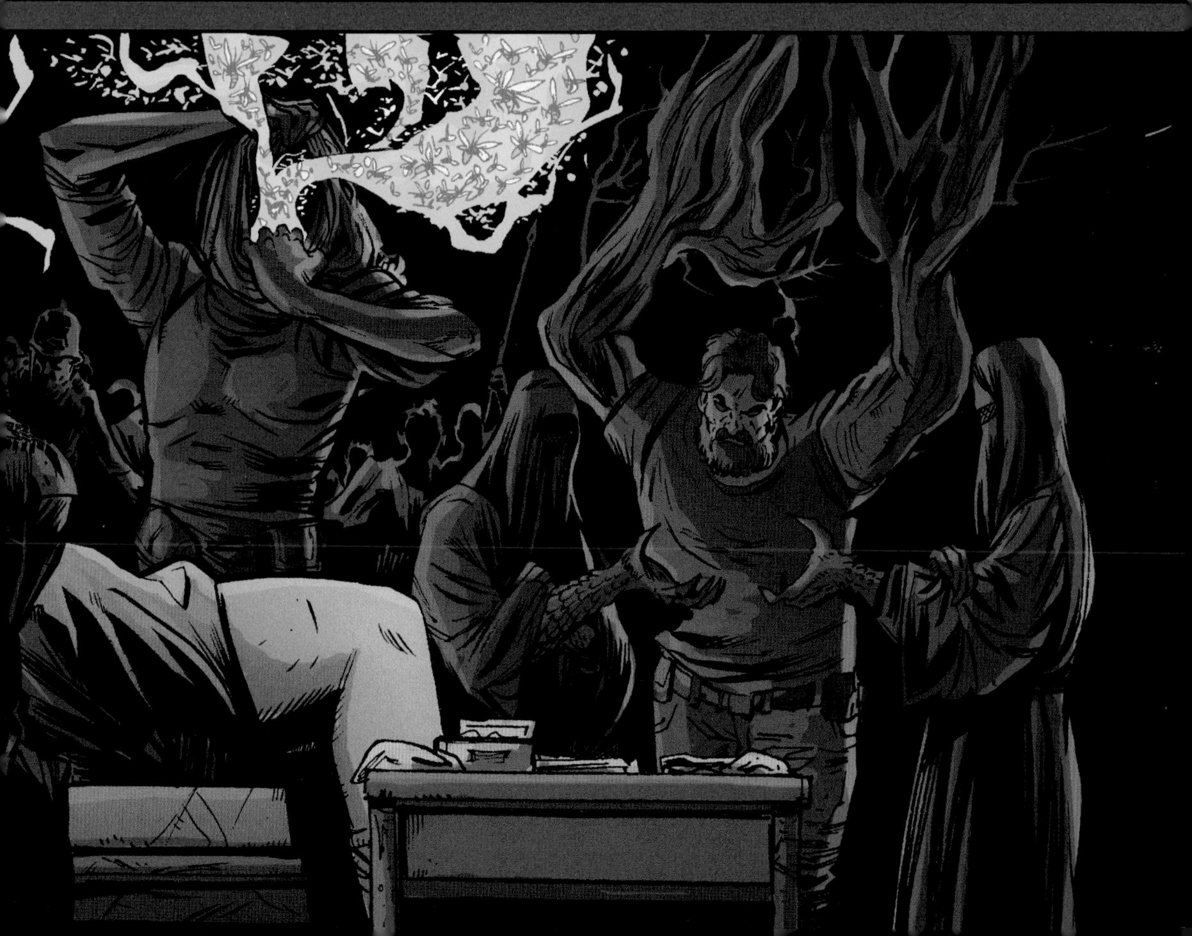

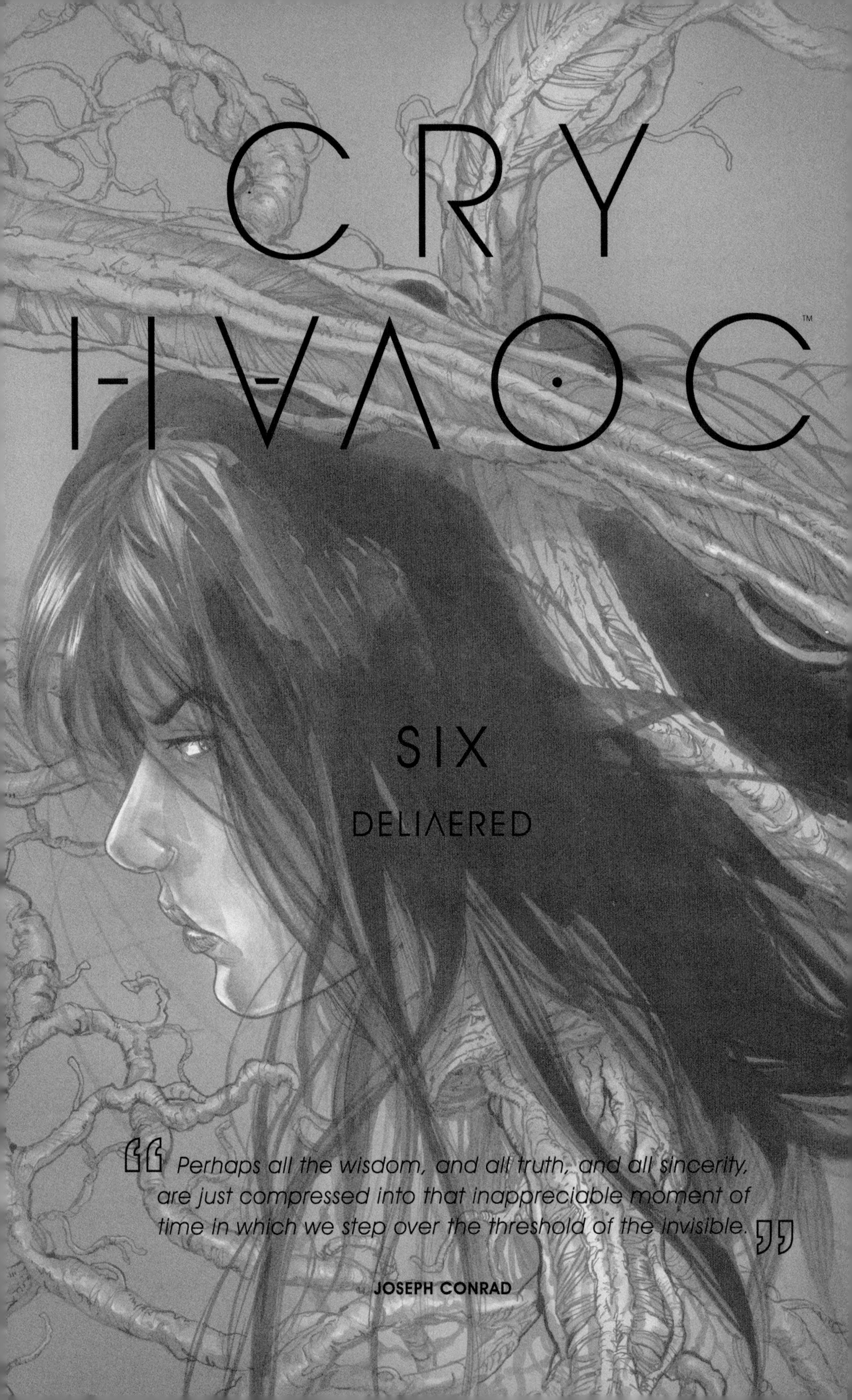
CRY HAVOC™
SIX
DELIVERED
"Perhaps all the wisdom, and all truth, and all sincerity, are just compressed into that inappreciable moment of time in which we step over the threshold of the invisible."
JOSEPH CONRAD

variant cover
SEAN **PHILLIPS**

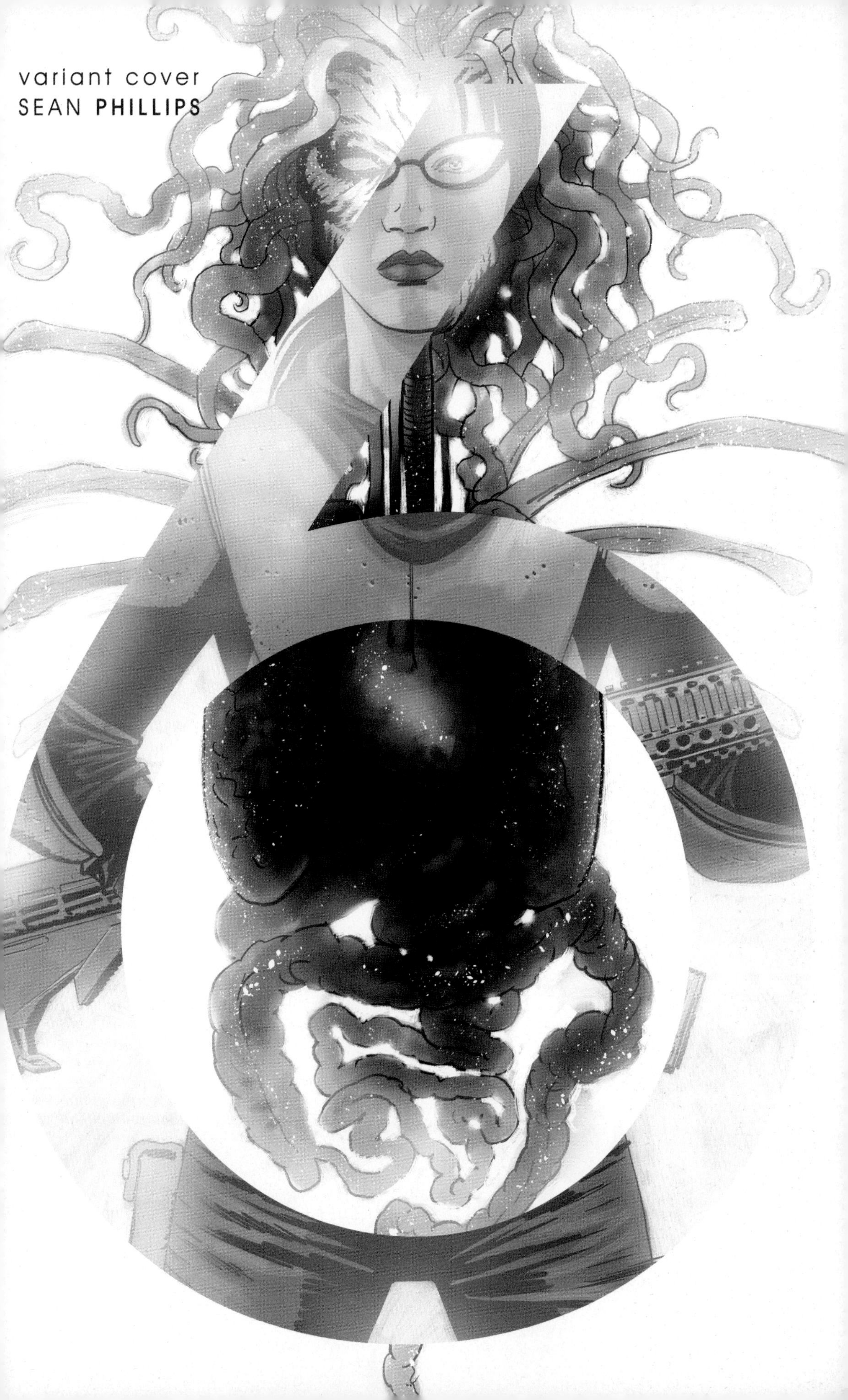

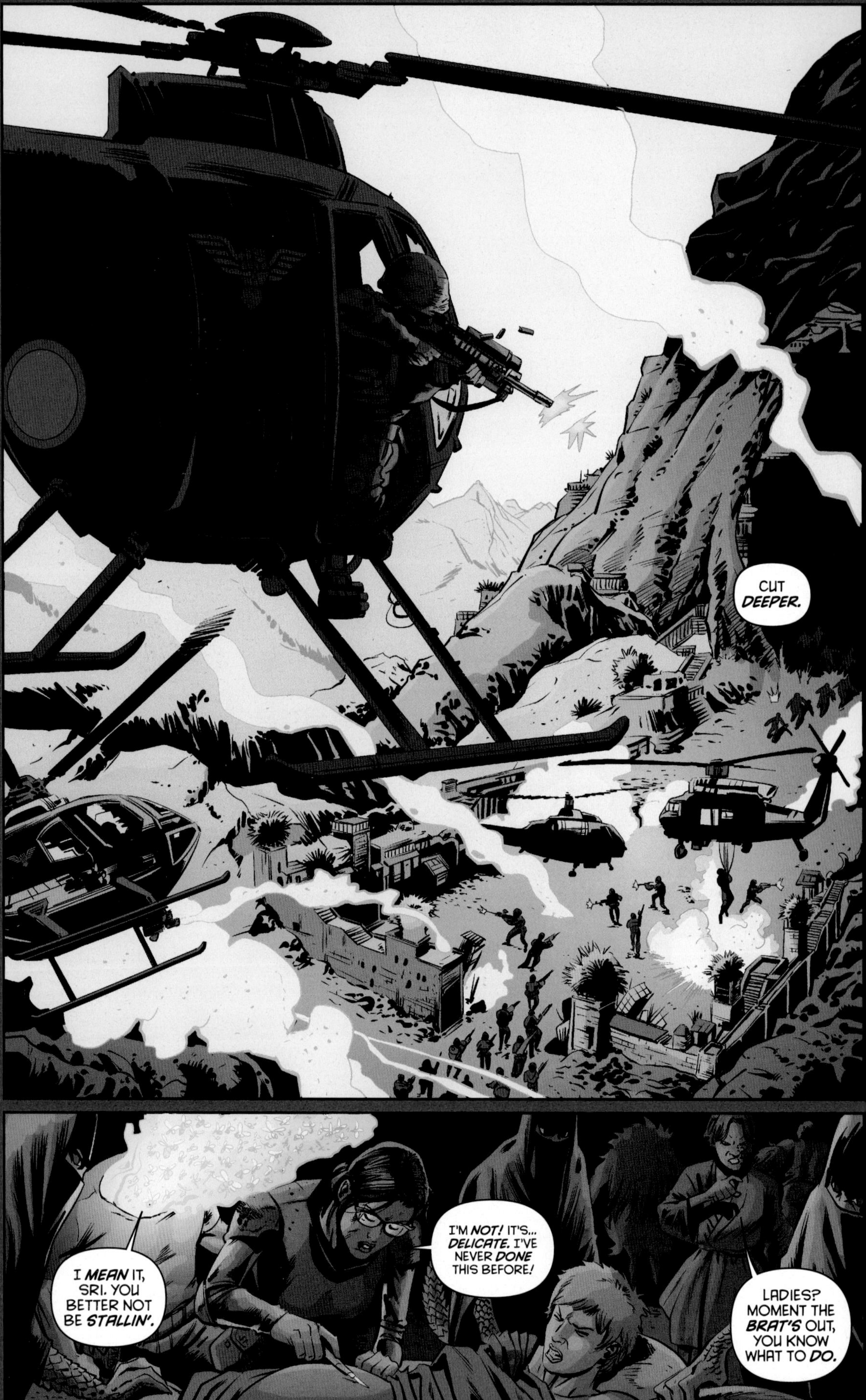
CUT DEEPER.
I MEAN IT, SRI. YOU BETTER NOT BE STALLIN'.
I'M NOT! IT'S... DELICATE. I'VE NEVER DONE THIS BEFORE!
LADIES? MOMENT THE BRAT'S OUT, YOU KNOW WHAT TO DO.

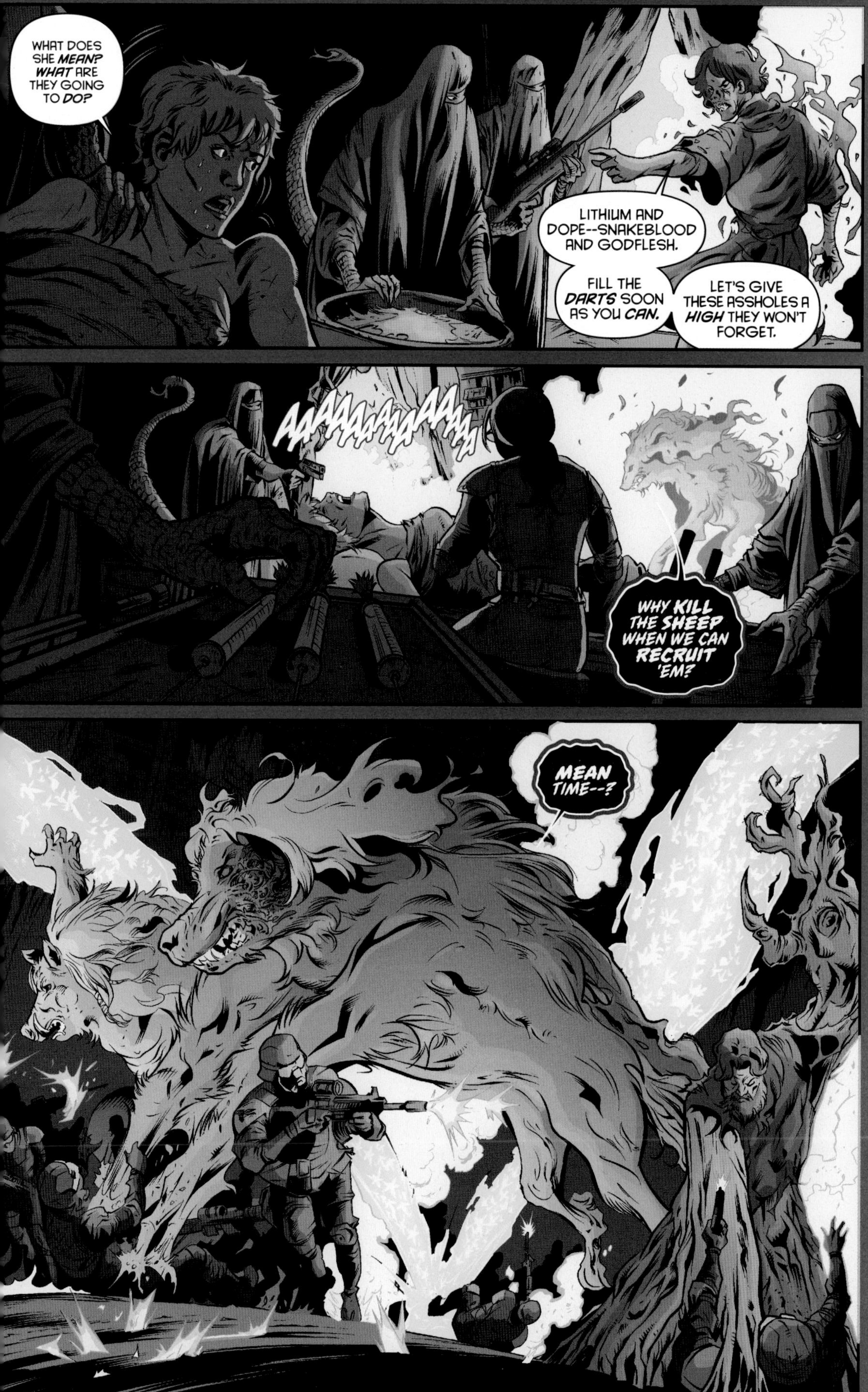
WHAT DOES SHE MEAN? WHAT ARE THEY GOING TO DO?
LITHIUM AND DOPE--SNAKEBLOOD AND GODFLESH.
FILL THE DARTS SOON AS YOU CAN.
LET'S GIVE THESE ASSHOLES A HIGH THEY WON'T FORGET.
AAAAAAAAAAAAAA
WHY KILL THE SHEEP WHEN WE CAN RECRUIT 'EM?
MEAN TIME--?

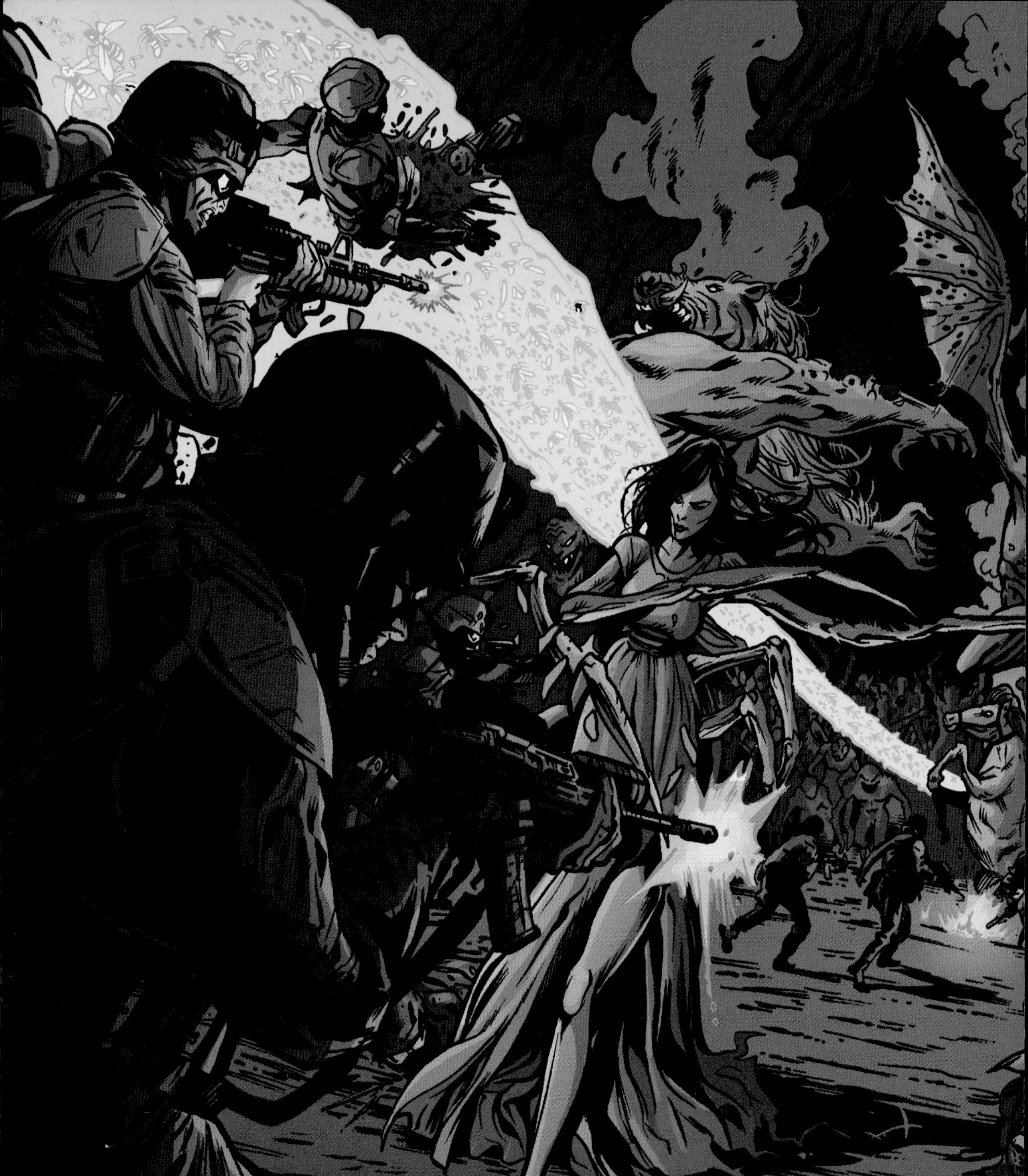

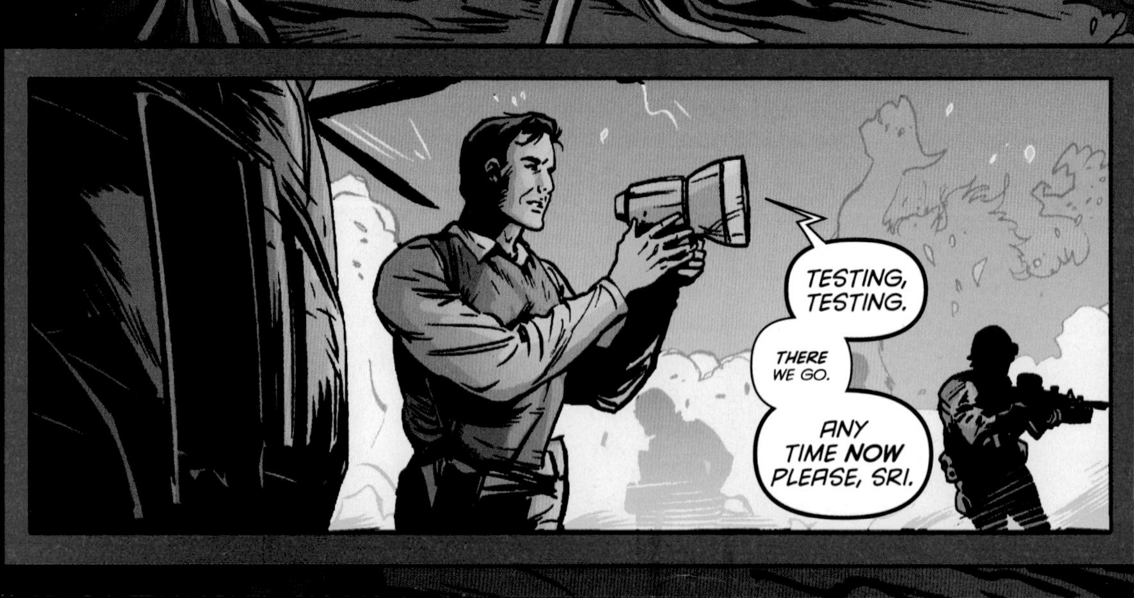
TESTING, TESTING.
THERE WE GO.
ANY TIME NOW PLEASE, SRI.

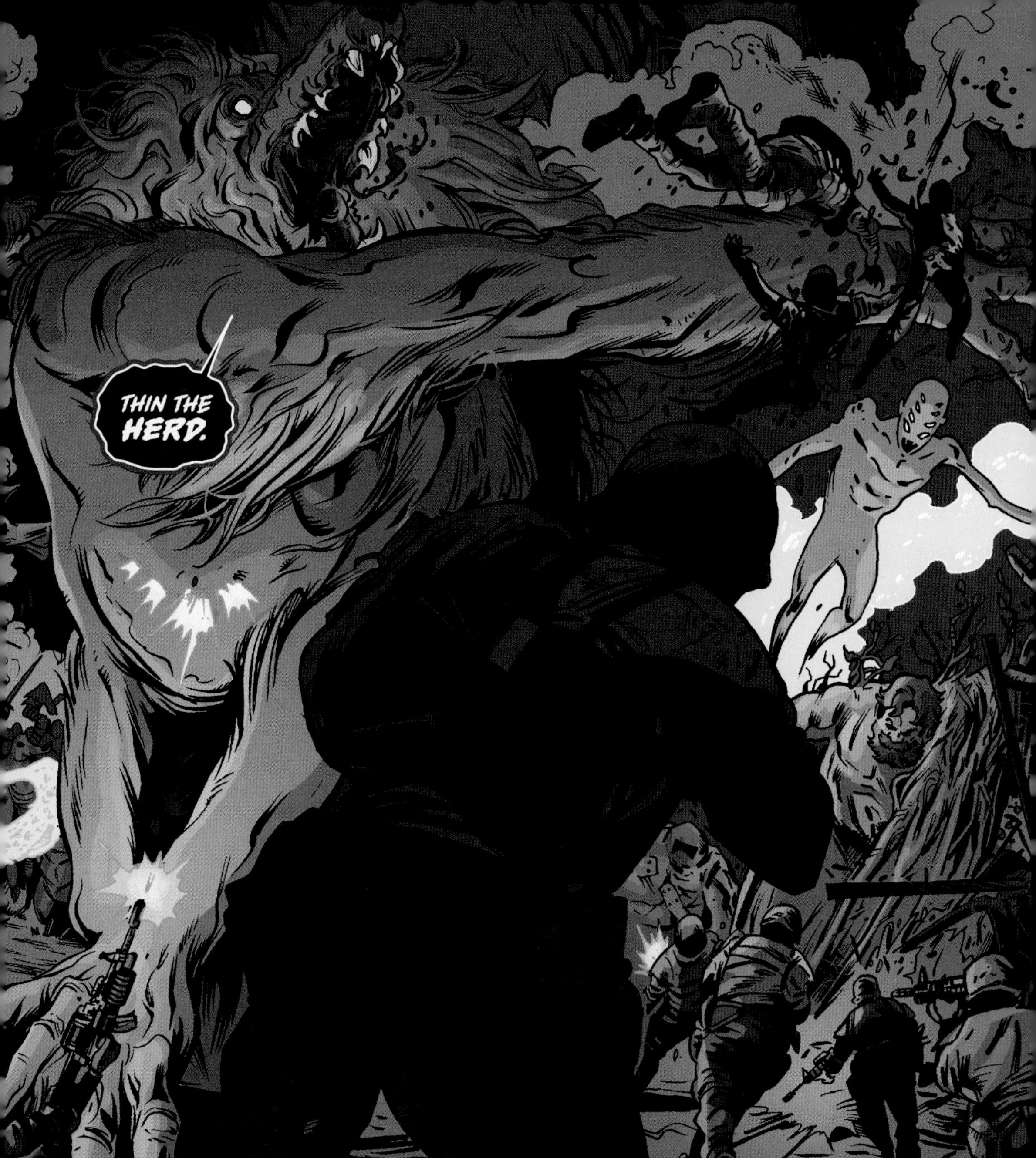
THIN THE HERD.

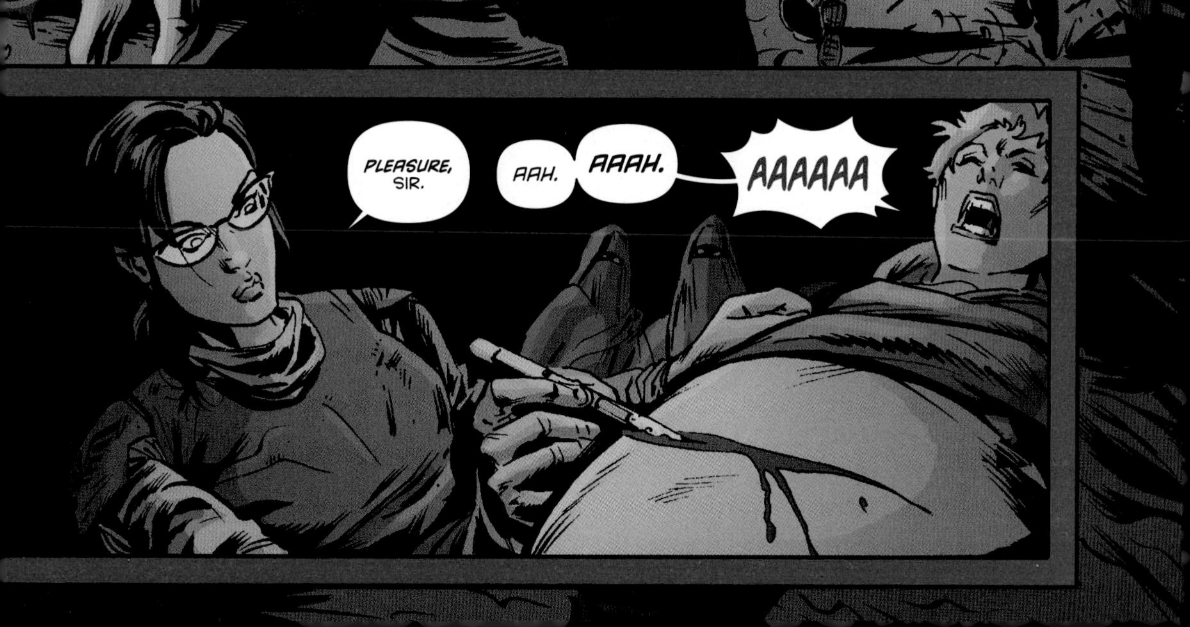
PLEASURE, SIR.
AAH.
AAAH.
AAAAAA

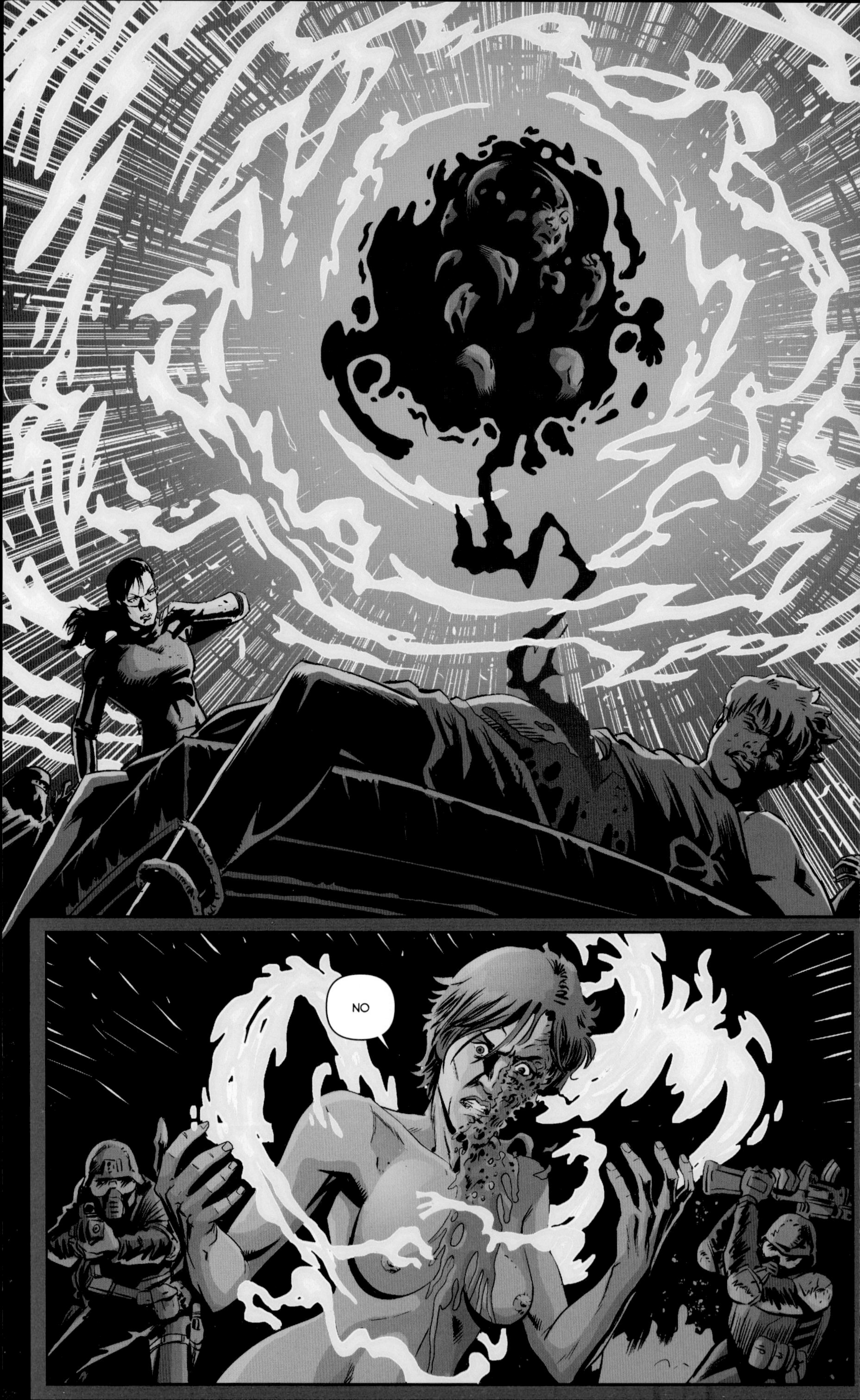
NO

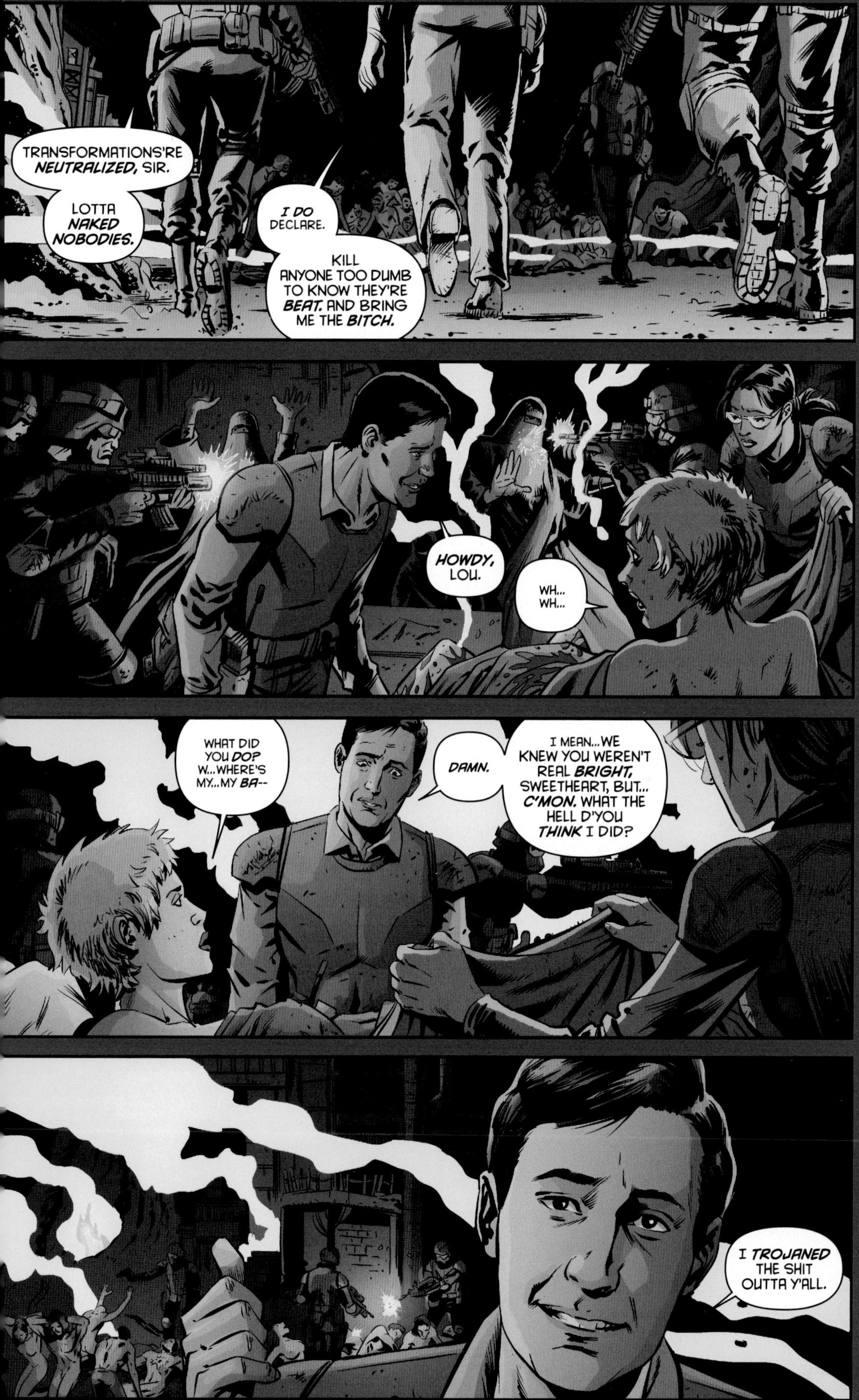
TRANSFORMATIONS'RE NEUTRALIZED, SIR.
LOTTA NAKED NOBODIES.
I DO DECLARE.
KILL ANYONE TOO DUMB TO KNOW THEY'RE BEAT. AND BRING ME THE BITCH.
HOWDY, LOU.
WH... WH...
WHAT DID YOU DO? W...WHERE'S MY...MY BA--
DAMN.
I MEAN...WE KNEW YOU WEREN'T REAL BRIGHT, SWEETHEART, BUT... C'MON. WHAT THE HELL D'YOU THINK I DID?
I TROJANED THE SHIT OUTTA Y'ALL.

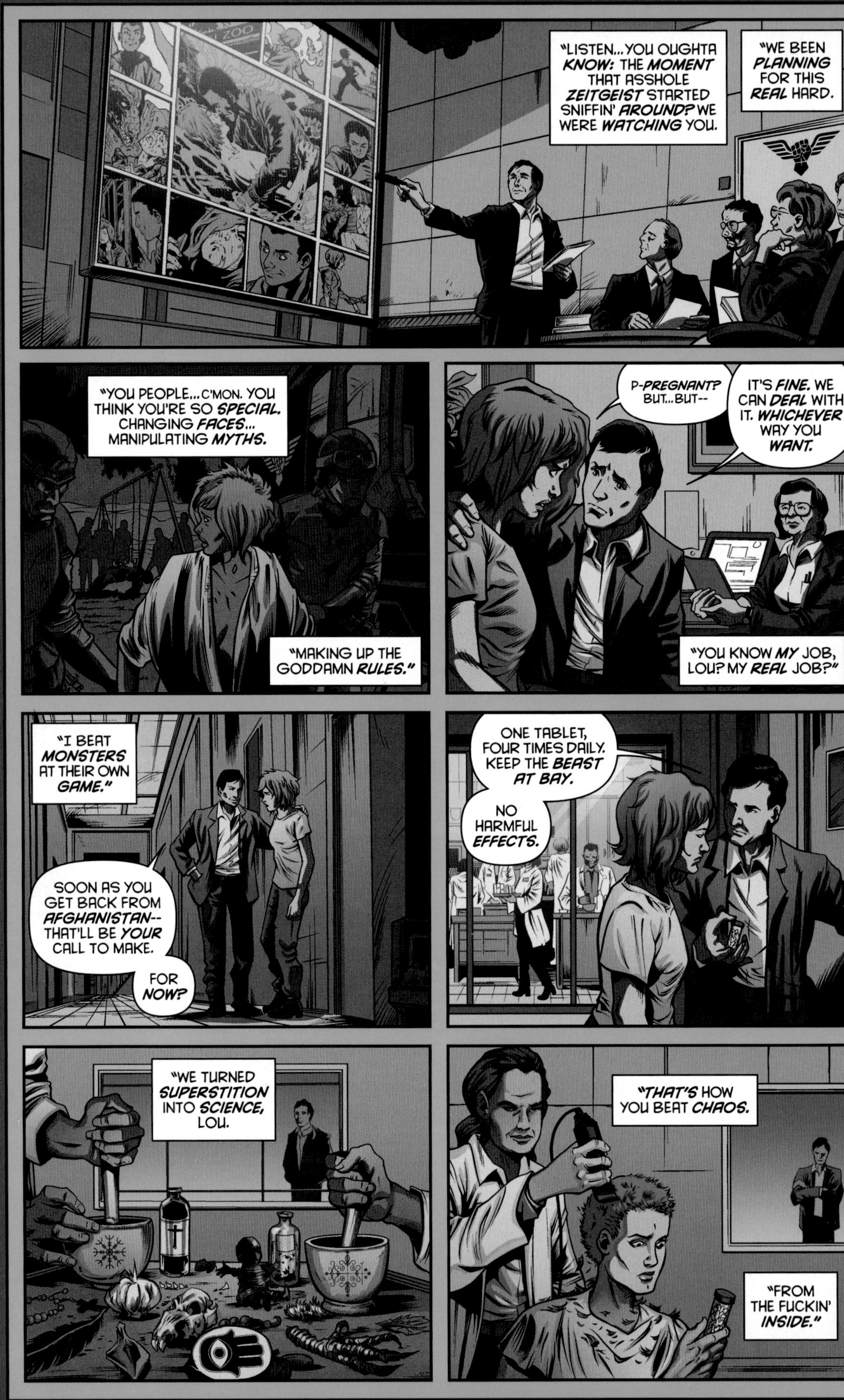
"LISTEN...YOU OUGHTA KNOW: THE MOMENT THAT ASSHOLE ZEITGEIST STARTED SNIFFIN' AROUND? WE WERE WATCHING YOU.
"WE BEEN PLANNING FOR THIS REAL HARD.
"YOU PEOPLE... C'MON. YOU THINK YOU'RE SO SPECIAL. CHANGING FACES... MANIPULATING MYTHS.
"MAKING UP THE GODDAMN RULES."
P-PREGNANT? BUT...BUT--
IT'S FINE. WE CAN DEAL WITH IT. WHICHEVER WAY YOU WANT.
"YOU KNOW MY JOB, LOU? MY REAL JOB?"
"I BEAT MONSTERS AT THEIR OWN GAME."
SOON AS YOU GET BACK FROM AFGHANISTAN-- THAT'LL BE YOUR CALL TO MAKE.
FOR NOW?
ONE TABLET, FOUR TIMES DAILY. KEEP THE BEAST AT BAY.
NO HARMFUL EFFECTS.
"WE TURNED SUPERSTITION INTO SCIENCE, LOU.
"THAT'S HOW YOU BEAT CHAOS.
"FROM THE FUCKIN' INSIDE."

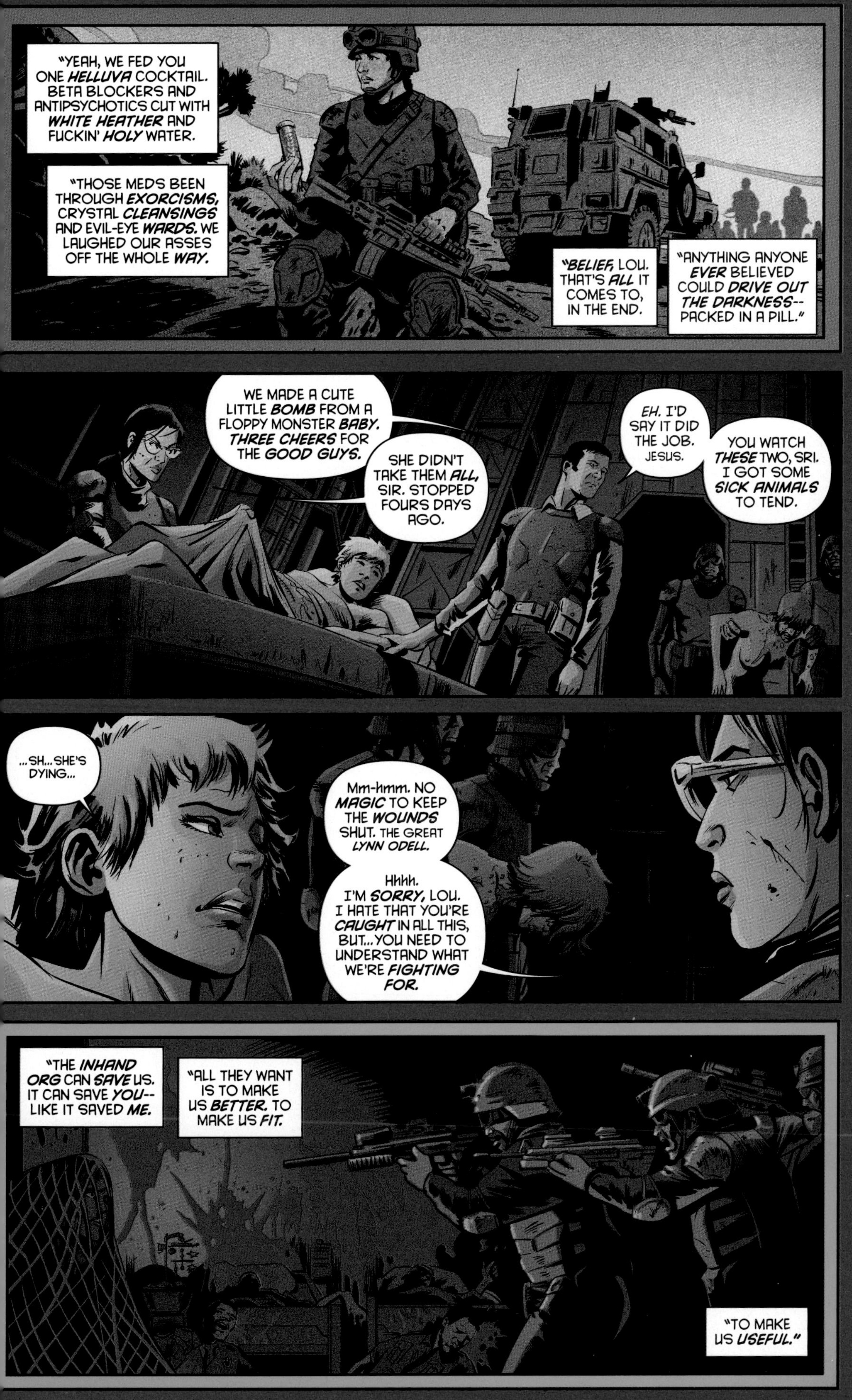

"YEAH, WE FED YOU ONE HELLUVA COCKTAIL. BETA BLOCKERS AND ANTIPSYCHOTICS CUT WITH WHITE HEATHER AND FUCKIN' HOLY WATER.
"THOSE MEDS BEEN THROUGH EXORCISMS, CRYSTAL CLEANSINGS AND EVIL-EYE WARDS. WE LAUGHED OUR ASSES OFF THE WHOLE WAY.
"BELIEF, LOU. THAT'S ALL IT COMES TO, IN THE END.
"ANYTHING ANYONE EVER BELIEVED COULD DRIVE OUT THE DARKNESS--PACKED IN A PILL."
WE MADE A CUTE LITTLE BOMB FROM A FLOPPY MONSTER BABY. THREE CHEERS FOR THE GOOD GUYS.
SHE DIDN'T TAKE THEM ALL, SIR. STOPPED FOURS DAYS AGO.
EH. I'D SAY IT DID THE JOB. JESUS.
YOU WATCH THESE TWO, SRI. I GOT SOME SICK ANIMALS TO TEND.
...SH...SHE'S DYING...
Mm-hmm. NO MAGIC TO KEEP THE WOUNDS SHUT. THE GREAT LYNN ODELL.
Hhhh. I'M SORRY, LOU. I HATE THAT YOU'RE CAUGHT IN ALL THIS, BUT...YOU NEED TO UNDERSTAND WHAT WE'RE FIGHTING FOR.
"THE INHAND ORG CAN SAVE US. IT CAN SAVE YOU--LIKE IT SAVED ME.
"ALL THEY WANT IS TO MAKE US BETTER. TO MAKE US FIT.
"TO MAKE US USEFUL."

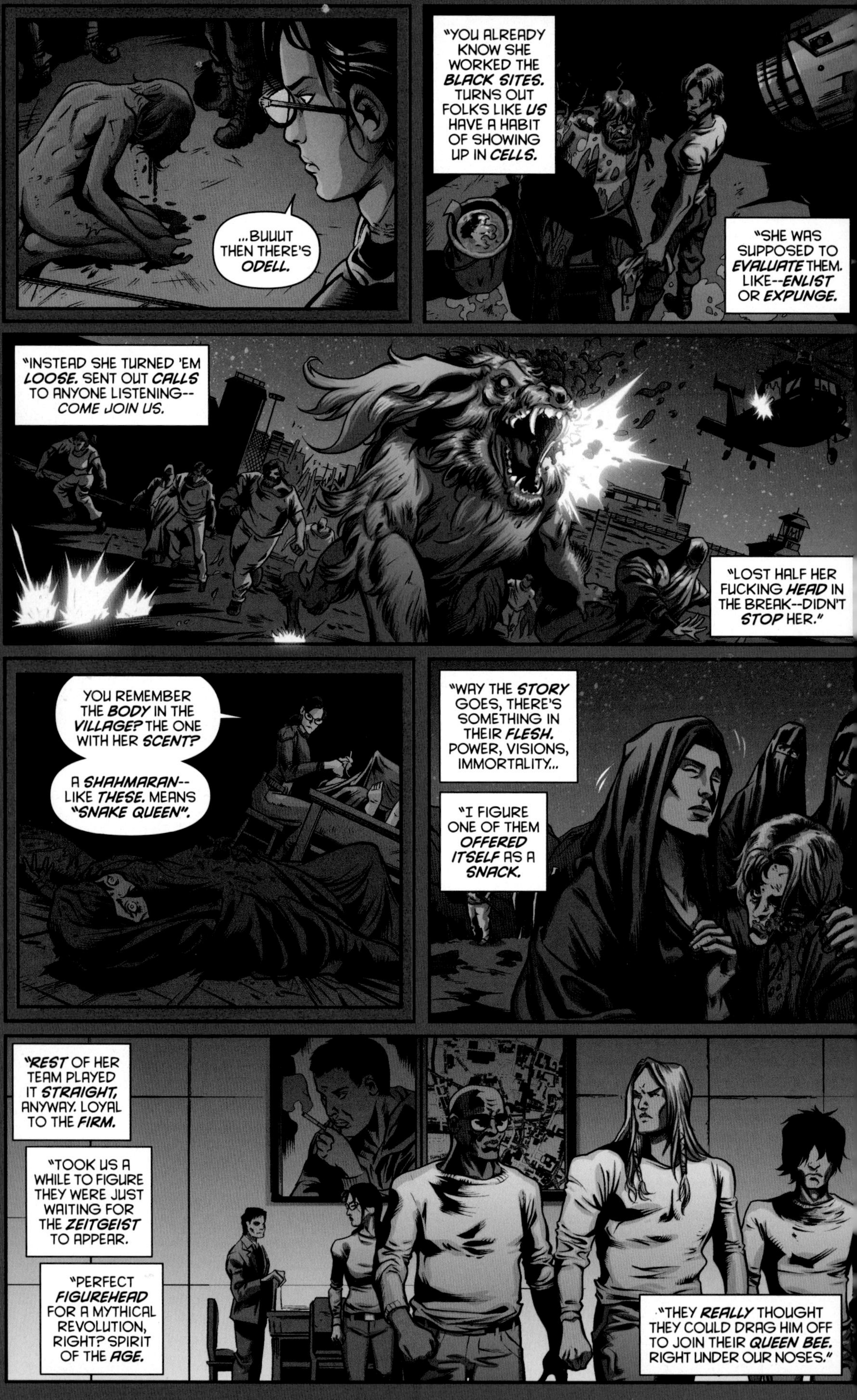
...BUUUT THEN THERE'S ODELL.
"YOU ALREADY KNOW SHE WORKED THE BLACK SITES. TURNS OUT FOLKS LIKE US HAVE A HABIT OF SHOWING UP IN CELLS.
"SHE WAS SUPPOSED TO EVALUATE THEM. LIKE--ENLIST OR EXPUNGE.
"INSTEAD SHE TURNED 'EM LOOSE. SENT OUT CALLS TO ANYONE LISTENING-- COME JOIN US.
"LOST HALF HER FUCKING HEAD IN THE BREAK--DIDN'T STOP HER."
YOU REMEMBER THE BODY IN THE VILLAGE? THE ONE WITH HER SCENT?
A SHAHMARAN-- LIKE THESE. MEANS "SNAKE QUEEN".
"WAY THE STORY GOES, THERE'S SOMETHING IN THEIR FLESH. POWER, VISIONS, IMMORTALITY...
"I FIGURE ONE OF THEM OFFERED ITSELF AS A SNACK.
"REST OF HER TEAM PLAYED IT STRAIGHT, ANYWAY. LOYAL TO THE FIRM.
"TOOK US A WHILE TO FIGURE THEY WERE JUST WAITING FOR THE ZEITGEIST TO APPEAR.
"PERFECT FIGUREHEAD FOR A MYTHICAL REVOLUTION, RIGHT? SPIRIT OF THE AGE.
"THEY REALLY THOUGHT THEY COULD DRAG HIM OFF TO JOIN THEIR QUEEN BEE. RIGHT UNDER OUR NOSES."

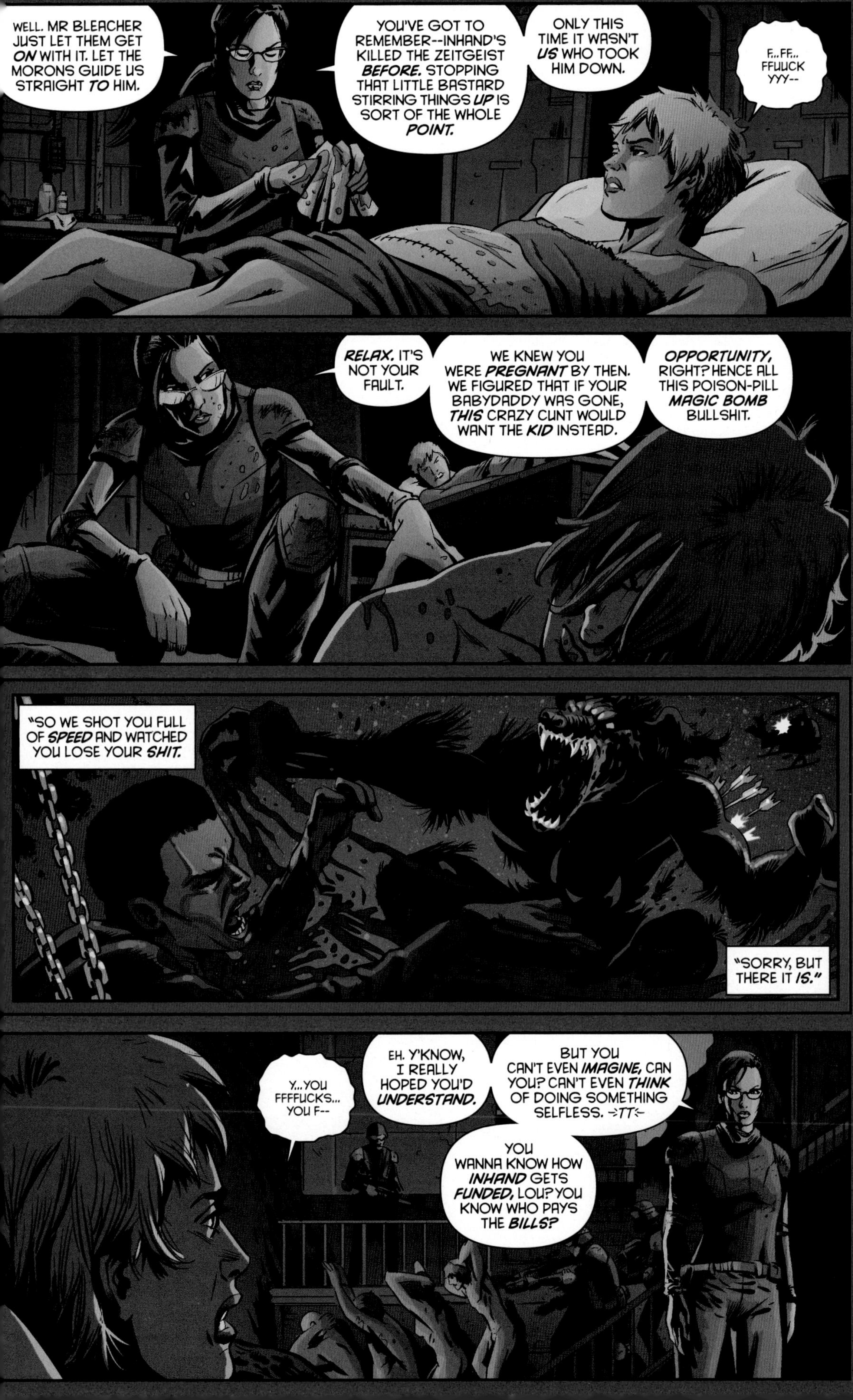
WELL. MR BLEACHER JUST LET THEM GET ON WITH IT. LET THE MORONS GUIDE US STRAIGHT TO HIM.
YOU'VE GOT TO REMEMBER--INHAND'S KILLED THE ZEITGEIST BEFORE. STOPPING THAT LITTLE BASTARD STIRRING THINGS UP IS SORT OF THE WHOLE POINT.
ONLY THIS TIME IT WASN'T US WHO TOOK HIM DOWN.
F...FF... FFUUCK YYY--
RELAX. IT'S NOT YOUR FAULT.
WE KNEW YOU WERE PREGNANT BY THEN. WE FIGURED THAT IF YOUR BABYDADDY WAS GONE, THIS CRAZY CUNT WOULD WANT THE KID INSTEAD.
OPPORTUNITY, RIGHT? HENCE ALL THIS POISON-PILL MAGIC BOMB BULLSHIT.
"SO WE SHOT YOU FULL OF SPEED AND WATCHED YOU LOSE YOUR SHIT.
"SORRY, BUT THERE IT IS."
Y...YOU FFFFUCKS... YOU F--
EH. Y'KNOW, I REALLY HOPED YOU'D UNDERSTAND.
BUT YOU CAN'T EVEN IMAGINE, CAN YOU? CAN'T EVEN THINK OF DOING SOMETHING SELFLESS. =TT=
YOU WANNA KNOW HOW INHAND GETS FUNDED, LOU? YOU KNOW WHO PAYS THE BILLS?

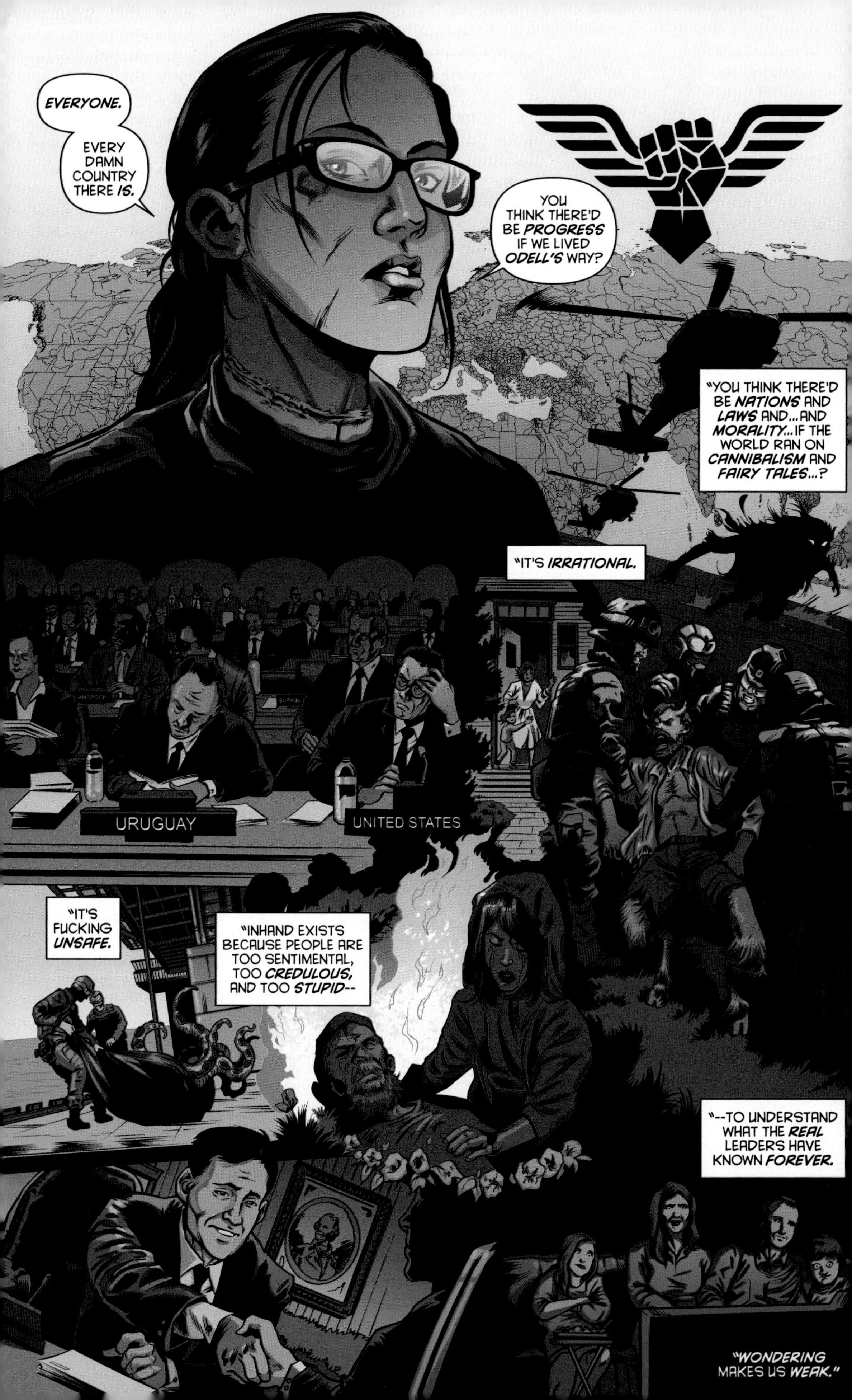

EVERYONE.
EVERY DAMN COUNTRY THERE IS.
YOU THINK THERE'D BE PROGRESS IF WE LIVED ODELL'S WAY?
"YOU THINK THERE'D BE NATIONS AND LAWS AND...AND MORALITY...IF THE WORLD RAN ON CANNIBALISM AND FAIRY TALES...?
"IT'S IRRATIONAL.
URUGUAY
UNITED STATES
"IT'S FUCKING UNSAFE.
"INHAND EXISTS BECAUSE PEOPLE ARE TOO SENTIMENTAL, TOO CREDULOUS, AND TOO STUPID--
"--TO UNDERSTAND WHAT THE REAL LEADERS HAVE KNOWN FOREVER.
"WONDERING MAKES US WEAK."

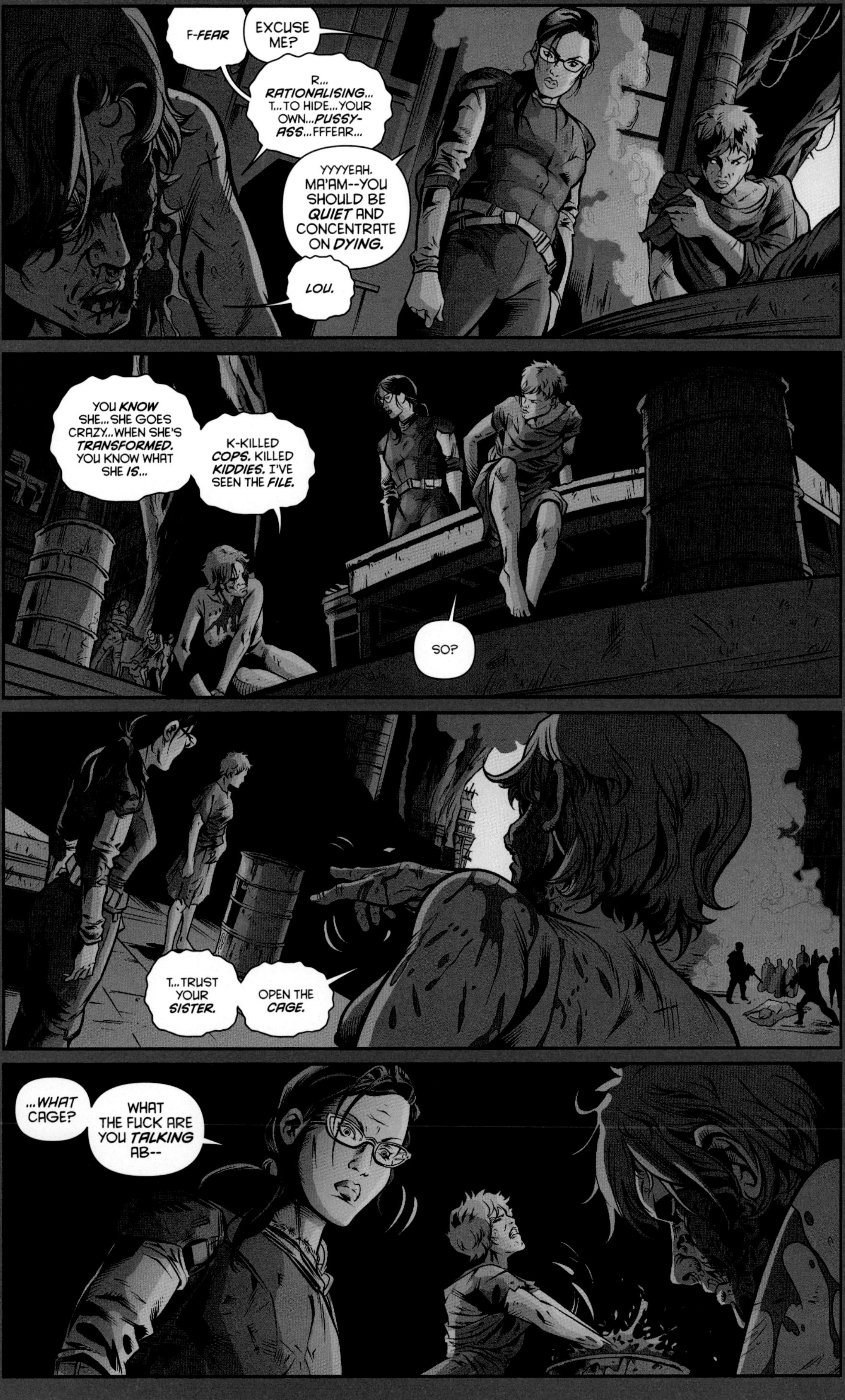
F-FEAR
EXCUSE ME?
R... RATIONALISING... T...TO HIDE...YOUR OWN...PUSSY-ASS...FFFEAR...
YYYYEAH. MA'AM--YOU SHOULD BE QUIET AND CONCENTRATE ON DYING.
LOU.
YOU KNOW SHE...SHE GOES CRAZY...WHEN SHE'S TRANSFORMED. YOU KNOW WHAT SHE IS...
K-KILLED COPS. KILLED KIDDIES. I'VE SEEN THE FILE.
SO?
T...TRUST YOUR SISTER.
OPEN THE CAGE.
...WHAT CAGE?
WHAT THE FUCK ARE YOU TALKING AB--

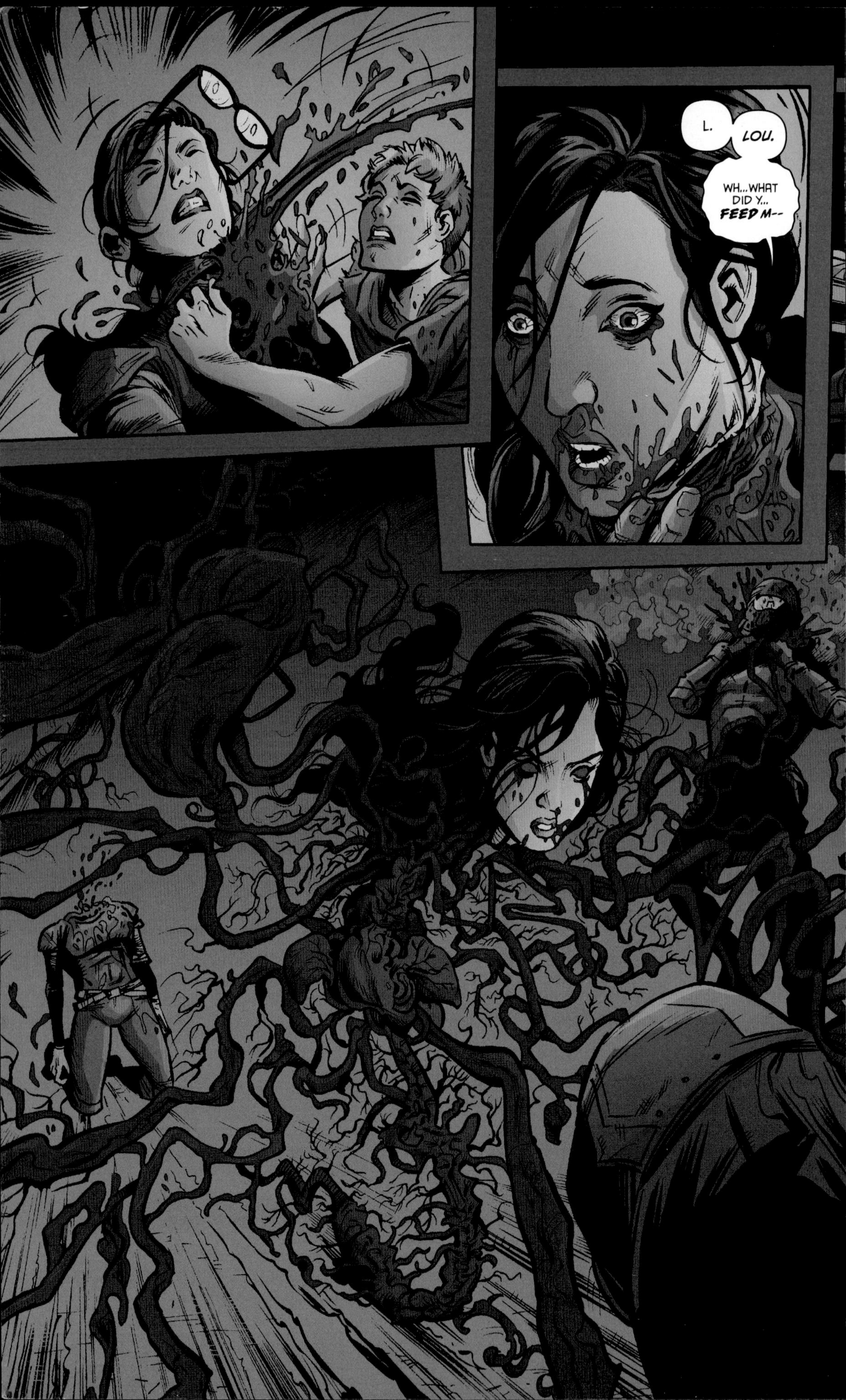
L.
LOU.
WH...WHAT DID Y... FEED M--

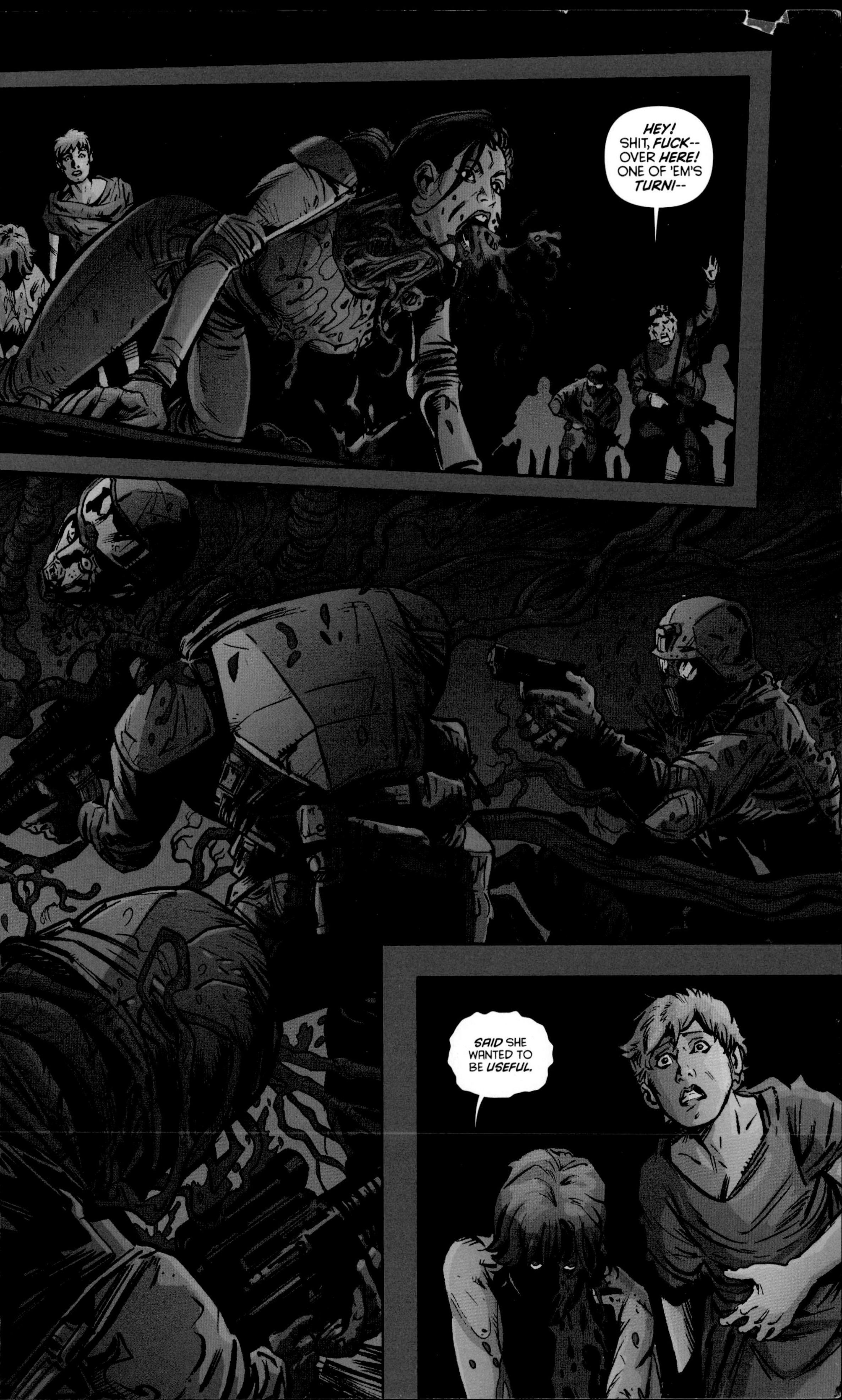
HEY! SHIT, FUCK-- OVER HERE! ONE OF 'EM'S TURNI--
SAID SHE WANTED TO BE USEFUL.

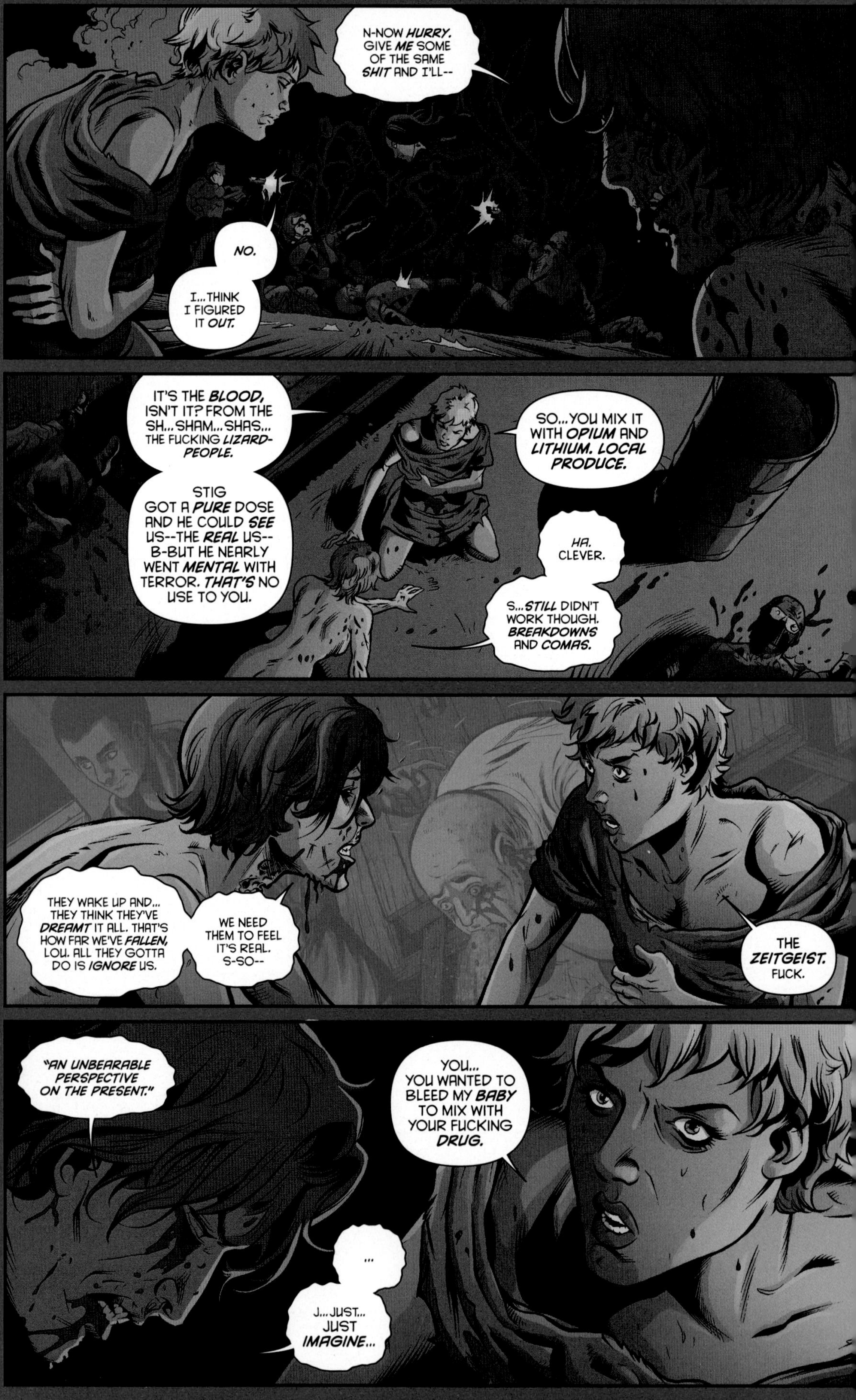
N-NOW HURRY. GIVE ME SOME OF THE SAME SHIT AND I'LL--
NO.
I... THINK I FIGURED IT OUT.
IT'S THE BLOOD, ISN'T IT? FROM THE SH... SHAM... SHAS... THE FUCKING LIZARD-PEOPLE.
STIG GOT A PURE DOSE AND HE COULD SEE US--THE REAL US--B-BUT HE NEARLY WENT MENTAL WITH TERROR. THAT'S NO USE TO YOU.
SO... YOU MIX IT WITH OPIUM AND LITHIUM. LOCAL PRODUCE.
HA. CLEVER.
S... STILL DIDN'T WORK THOUGH. BREAKDOWNS AND COMAS.
THEY WAKE UP AND... THEY THINK THEY'VE DREAMT IT ALL. THAT'S HOW FAR WE'VE FALLEN, LOU. ALL THEY GOTTA DO IS IGNORE US.
WE NEED THEM TO FEEL IT'S REAL. S-SO--
THE ZEITGEIST. FUCK.
"AN UNBEARABLE PERSPECTIVE ON THE PRESENT."
YOU... YOU WANTED TO BLEED MY BABY TO MIX WITH YOUR FUCKING DRUG.
...
J... JUST... JUST IMAGINE...

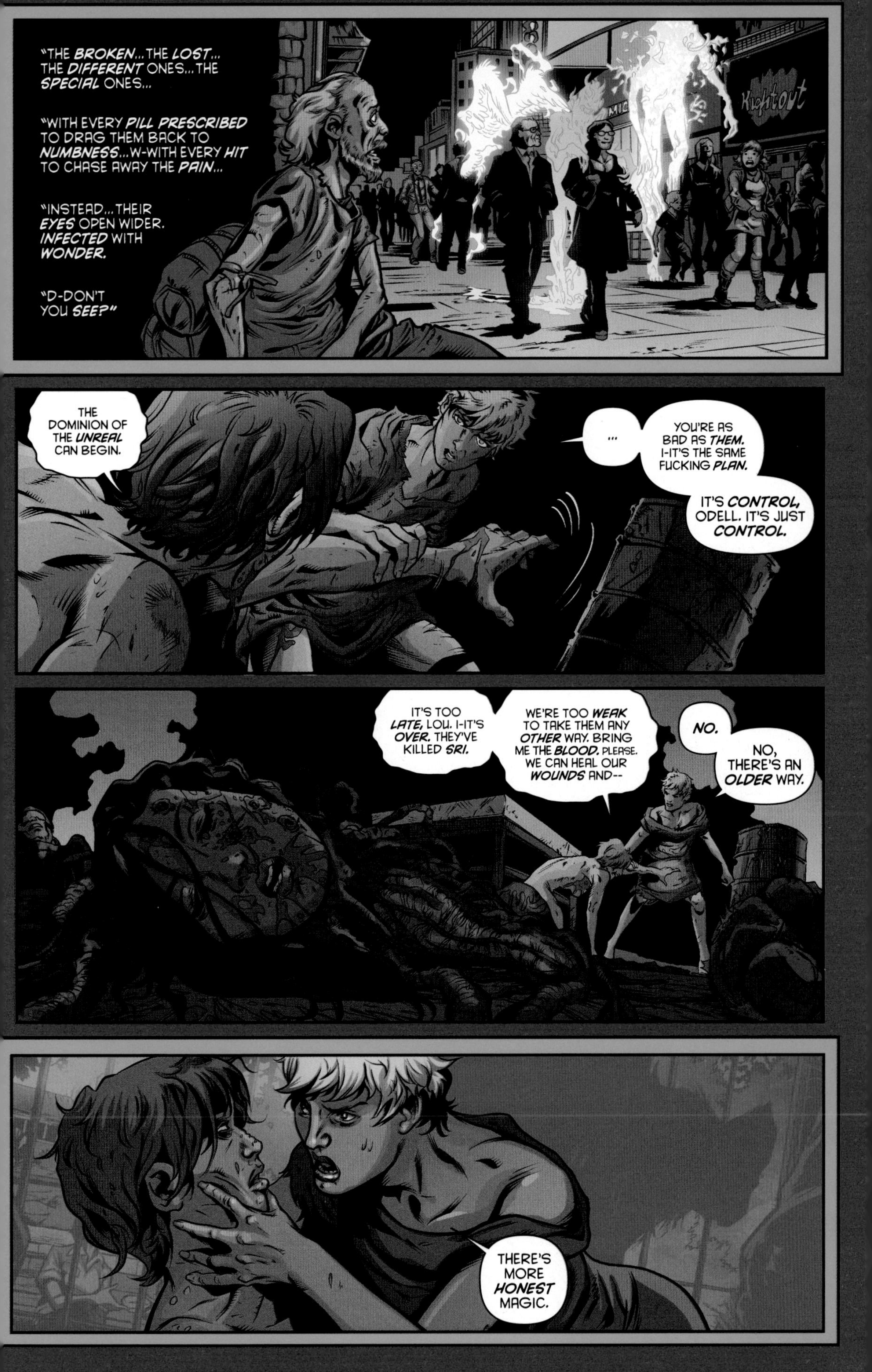
"THE BROKEN... THE LOST... THE DIFFERENT ONES... THE SPECIAL ONES...
"WITH EVERY PILL PRESCRIBED TO DRAG THEM BACK TO NUMBNESS... W-WITH EVERY HIT TO CHASE AWAY THE PAIN...
"INSTEAD... THEIR EYES OPEN WIDER. INFECTED WITH WONDER.
"D-DON'T YOU SEE?"
THE DOMINION OF THE UNREAL CAN BEGIN.
...
YOU'RE AS BAD AS THEM. I-IT'S THE SAME FUCKING PLAN.
IT'S CONTROL, ODELL. IT'S JUST CONTROL.
IT'S TOO LATE, LOU. I-IT'S OVER. THEY'VE KILLED SRI.
WE'RE TOO WEAK TO TAKE THEM ANY OTHER WAY. BRING ME THE BLOOD. PLEASE. WE CAN HEAL OUR WOUNDS AND--
NO.
NO, THERE'S AN OLDER WAY.
THERE'S MORE HONEST MAGIC.

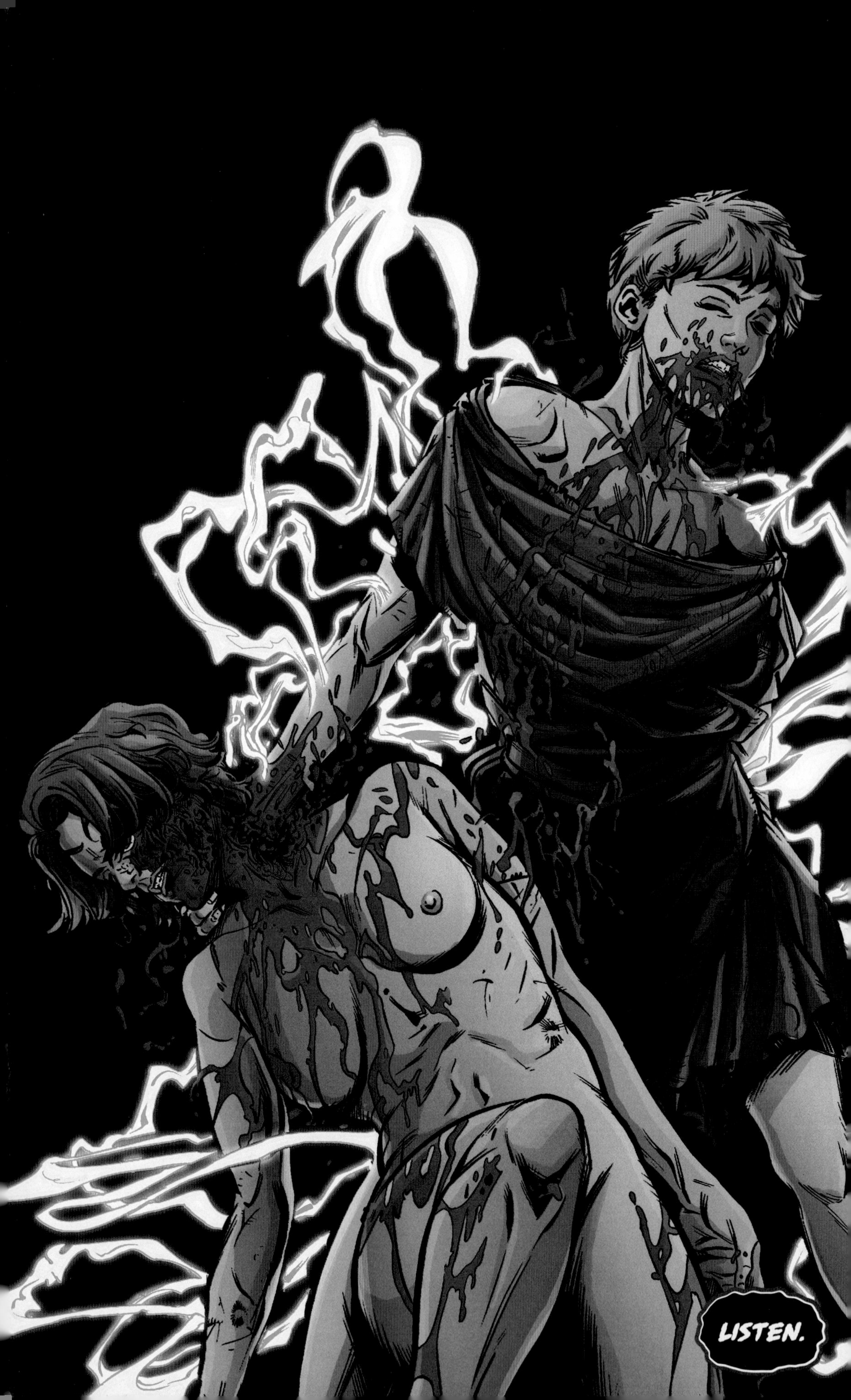
LISTEN.

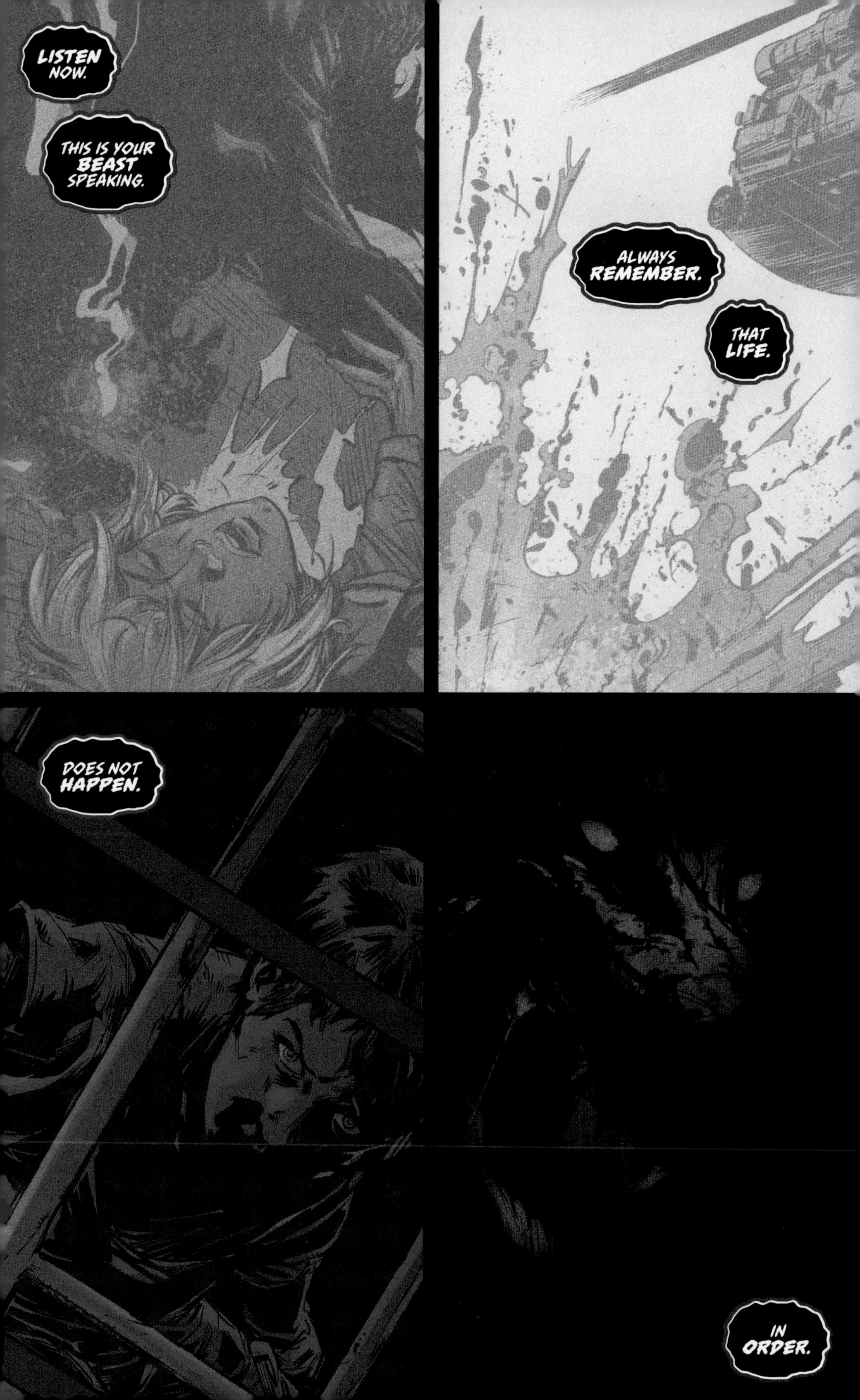
LISTEN NOW.
THIS IS YOUR BEAST SPEAKING.
ALWAYS REMEMBER.
THAT LIFE.
DOES NOT HAPPEN.
IN ORDER.

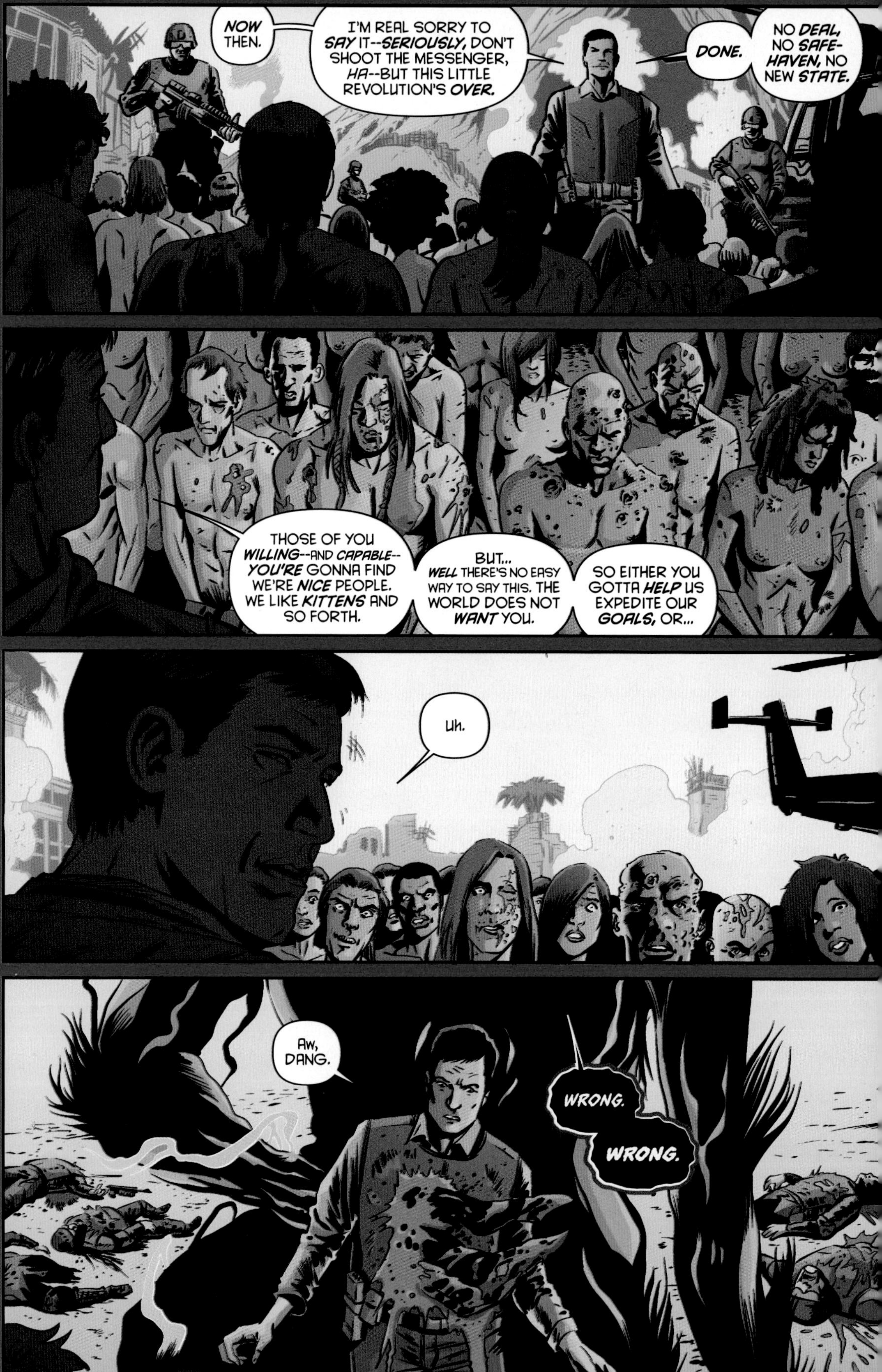
NOW THEN.
I'M REAL SORRY TO SAY IT--SERIOUSLY, DON'T SHOOT THE MESSENGER, HA--BUT THIS LITTLE REVOLUTION'S OVER.
DONE.
NO DEAL, NO SAFE-HAVEN, NO NEW STATE.
THOSE OF YOU WILLING--AND CAPABLE--YOU'RE GONNA FIND WE'RE NICE PEOPLE. WE LIKE KITTENS AND SO FORTH.
BUT... WELL THERE'S NO EASY WAY TO SAY THIS. THE WORLD DOES NOT WANT YOU.
SO EITHER YOU GOTTA HELP US EXPEDITE OUR GOALS, OR...
UH.
AW, DANG.
WRONG.
WRONG.

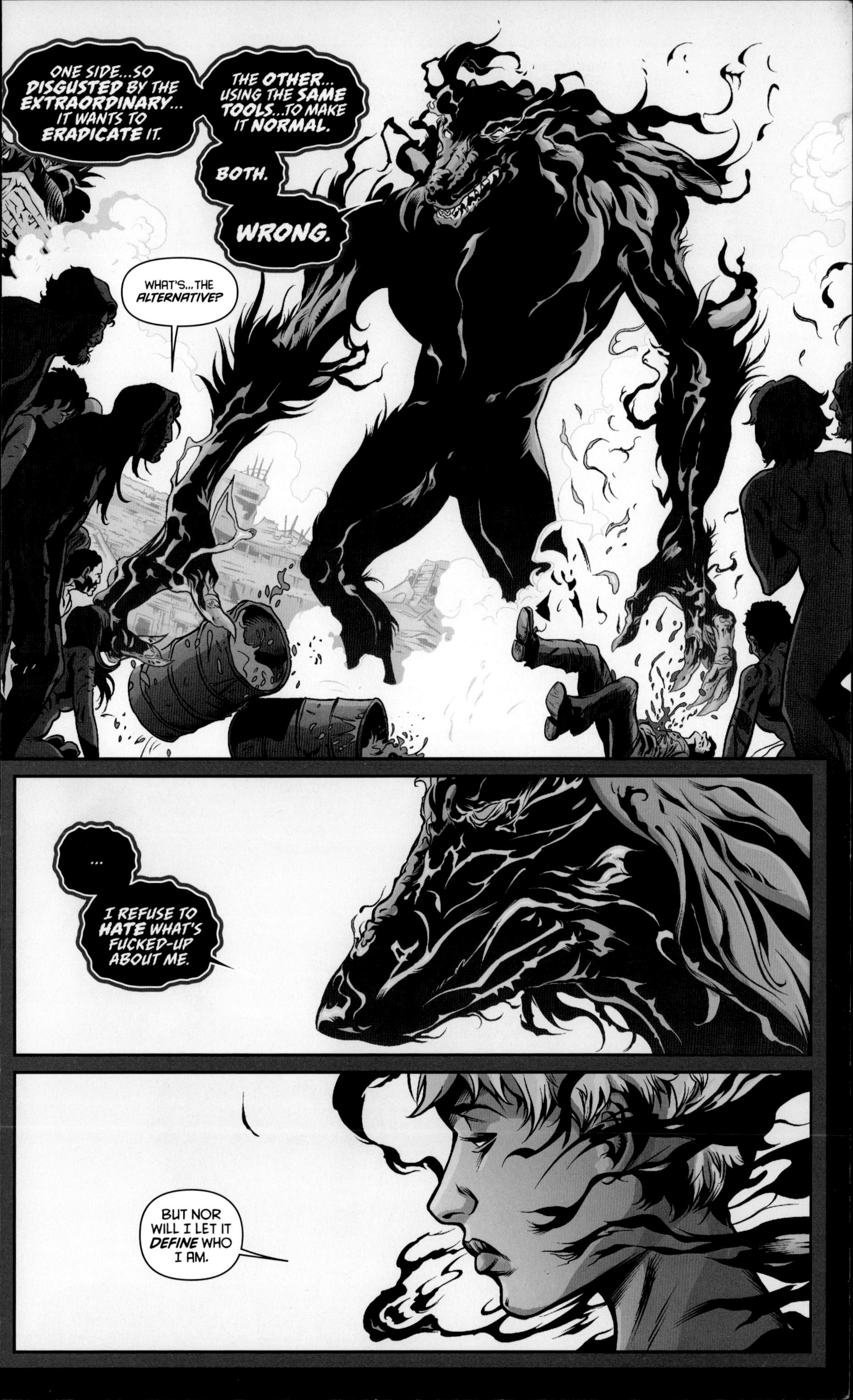
ONE SIDE...SO DISGUSTED BY THE EXTRAORDINARY... IT WANTS TO ERADICATE IT.
THE OTHER... USING THE SAME TOOLS...TO MAKE IT NORMAL.
BOTH.
WRONG.
WHAT'S...THE ALTERNATIVE?
...
I REFUSE TO HATE WHAT'S FUCKED-UP ABOUT ME.
BUT NOR WILL I LET IT DEFINE WHO I AM.

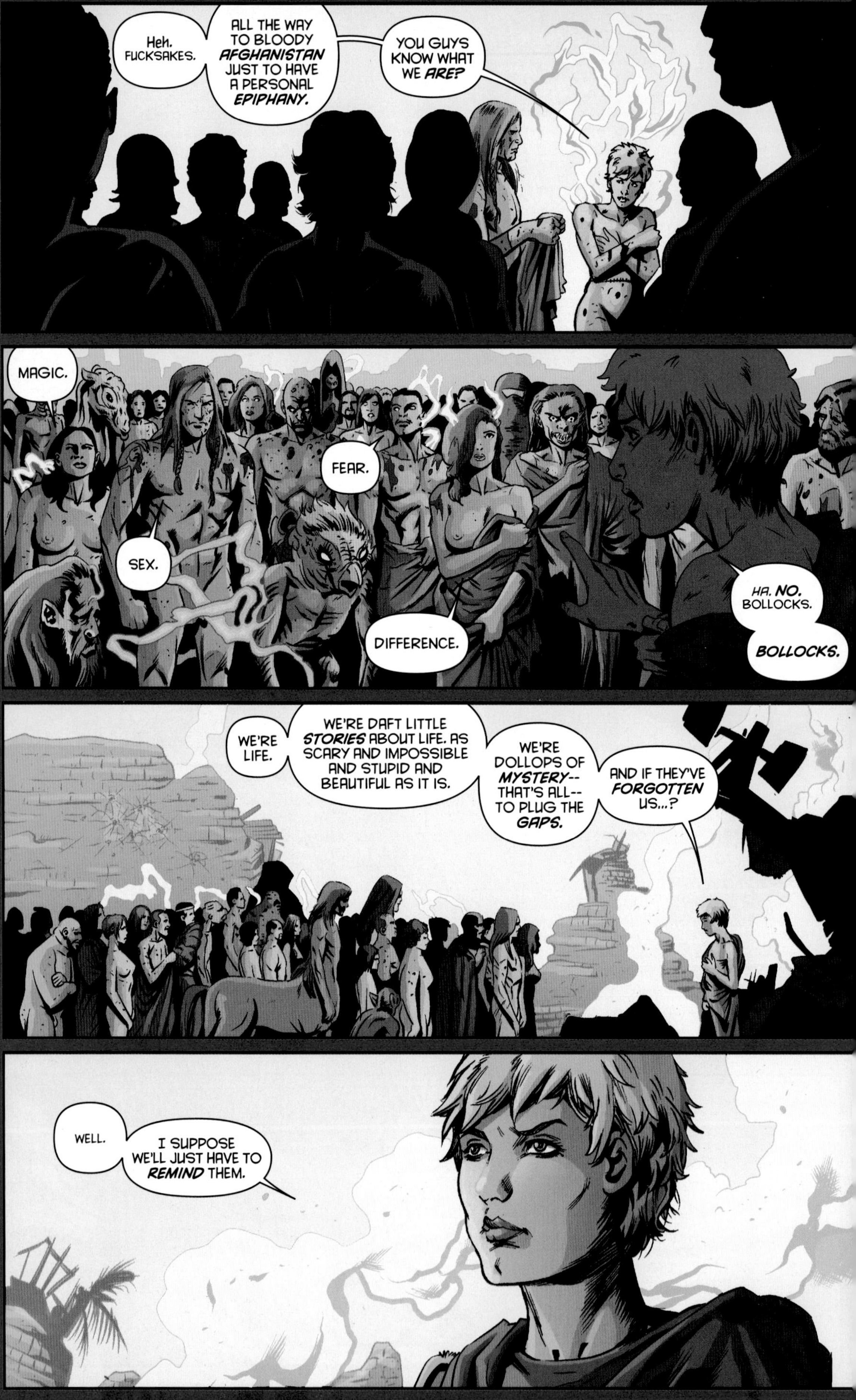
Heh. FUCKSAKES.
ALL THE WAY TO BLOODY *AFGHANISTAN* JUST TO HAVE A PERSONAL *EPIPHANY.*
YOU GUYS KNOW WHAT WE *ARE?*
MAGIC.
SEX.
FEAR.
DIFFERENCE.
HA. **NO.** BOLLOCKS.
BOLLOCKS.
WE'RE LIFE.
WE'RE DAFT LITTLE *STORIES* ABOUT LIFE. AS SCARY AND IMPOSSIBLE AND STUPID AND BEAUTIFUL AS IT IS.
WE'RE DOLLOPS OF *MYSTERY*-- THAT'S ALL-- TO PLUG THE *GAPS.*
AND IF THEY'VE *FORGOTTEN* US...?
WELL.
I SUPPOSE WE'LL JUST HAVE TO *REMIND* THEM.

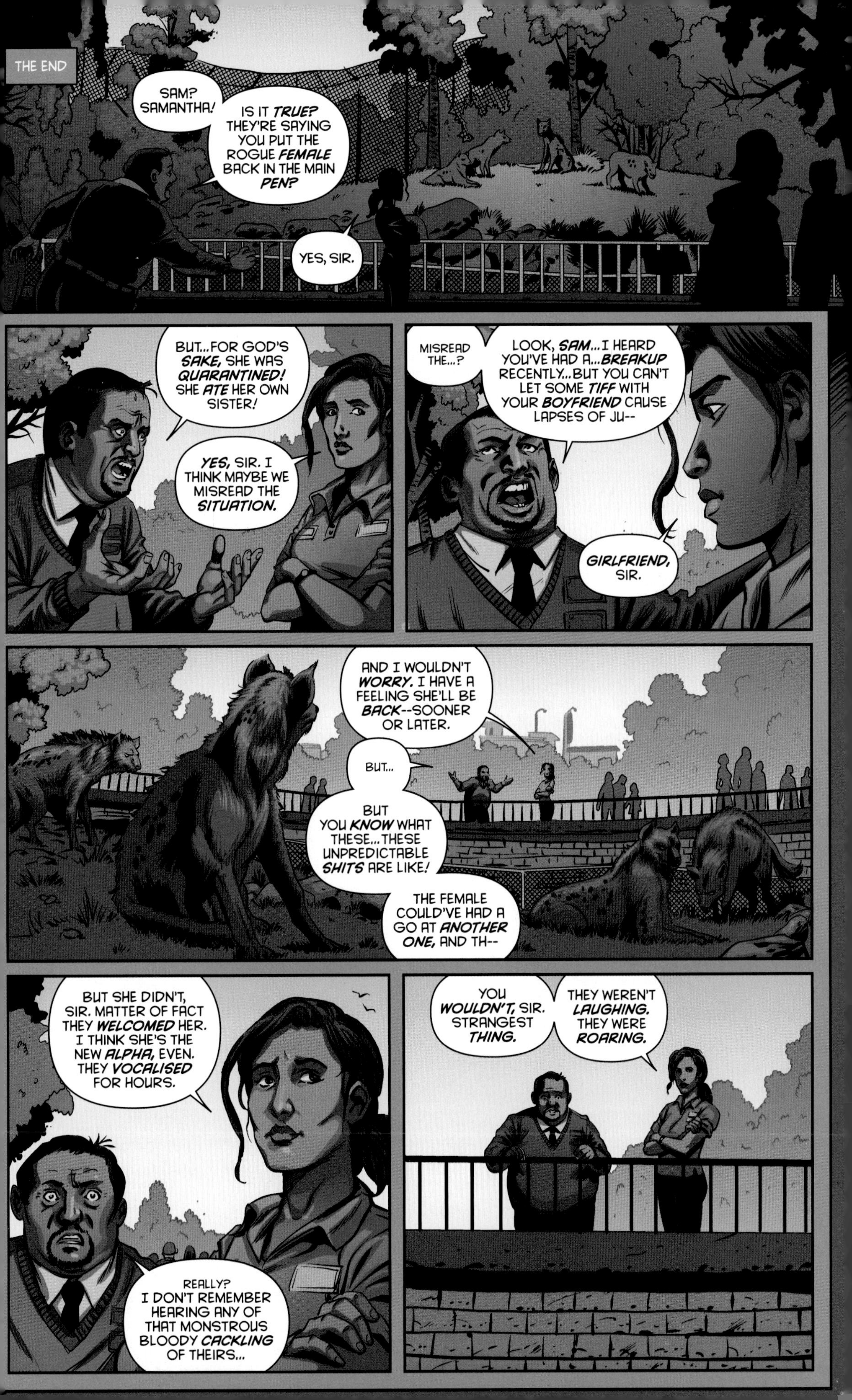
THE END
SAM? SAMANTHA!
IS IT TRUE? THEY'RE SAYING YOU PUT THE ROGUE FEMALE BACK IN THE MAIN PEN?
YES, SIR.
BUT...FOR GOD'S SAKE, SHE WAS QUARANTINED! SHE ATE HER OWN SISTER!
YES, SIR. I THINK MAYBE WE MISREAD THE SITUATION.
MISREAD THE...?
LOOK, SAM...I HEARD YOU'VE HAD A...BREAKUP RECENTLY...BUT YOU CAN'T LET SOME TIFF WITH YOUR BOYFRIEND CAUSE LAPSES OF JU--
GIRLFRIEND, SIR.
AND I WOULDN'T WORRY. I HAVE A FEELING SHE'LL BE BACK--SOONER OR LATER.
BUT...
BUT YOU KNOW WHAT THESE...THESE UNPREDICTABLE SHITS ARE LIKE!
THE FEMALE COULD'VE HAD A GO AT ANOTHER ONE, AND TH--
BUT SHE DIDN'T, SIR. MATTER OF FACT THEY WELCOMED HER. I THINK SHE'S THE NEW ALPHA, EVEN. THEY VOCALISED FOR HOURS.
REALLY? I DON'T REMEMBER HEARING ANY OF THAT MONSTROUS BLOODY CACKLING OF THEIRS...
YOU WOULDN'T, SIR. STRANGEST THING.
THEY WEREN'T LAUGHING. THEY WERE ROARING.

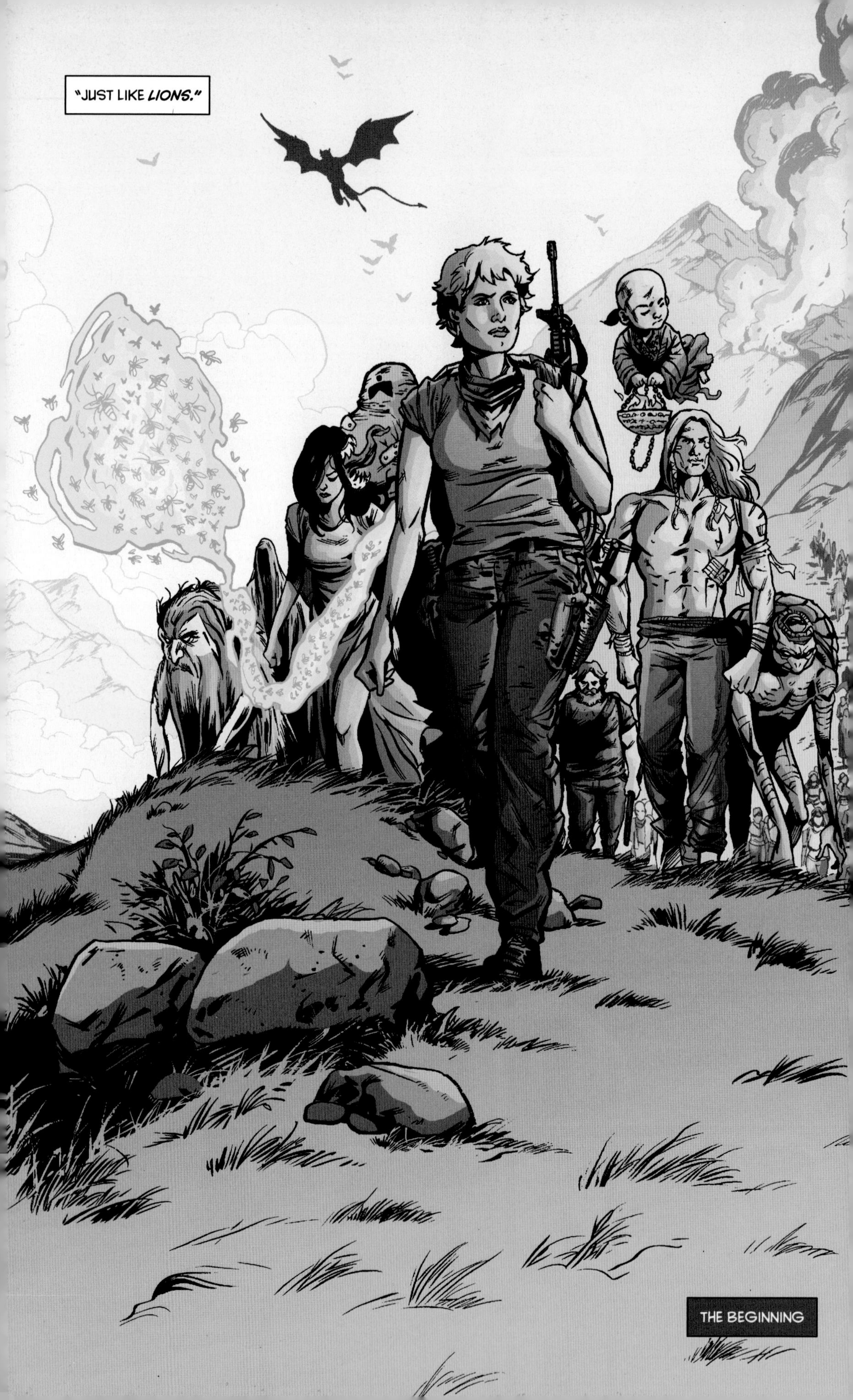
"JUST LIKE *LIONS.*"
THE BEGINNING

ANNOTATIONS

The following notes and references are compiled from the backmatter of the monthly comic. We contemplated re-numbering each entry to correspond with the pagination of this collected volume, but – to avoid splattering the original art with superimposed page numbers – decided against. We hope you'll be able to follow along by simply counting forward from each interstitial chapter break.

⊙NE

Page 1 – Bloody-minded to a fault, let's start at the end. Our first look here at what we shall, for now, call simply "the red place," at least until our truculent story decides to give us some more information.

Incidentally, I'm assuming you've read the preceding comic by this point, hence you'll know what I'm talking about when I mention this is also our introduction to the color palette chosen by our first superstar colorist: Lee Loughridge. We hit upon the idea of using three different hue-wranglers when pondering ways to differentiate between the phases of Lou's story. Colorists often get a raw deal in the comicbook world, so it's a pleasure to be showcasing how much of an impact their different voices can have on a single artist's work. We'll meet the other two in due course.

This is also, of course, our first introduction to the magnificent Louise Canton, although, alas, not presently in great shape. Quite literally.

Page 2 – Our first look at the "London" phase of Lou's story, it being chronologically the first, and at the blue-favoring palette of our second colorist, Nick Filardi. Artists will often tell you blue tones recede while red tones advance, so it seemed a fitting assignation for the "beginning" and "end" phases of our story.

For precision, the beastie there is *Crocuta crocuta*, the Spotted Hyena, and what a remarkable critter she is.

Page 3 – The Tubular Ladyparts thing here is entirely true, as is the unique social/pack behaviour which derives. It's also, rather depressingly, the subject of a huge amount of history, lore and metaphor, almost all of which casts the poor hyena as a cowardly androgyne whose remarkable

junk is good for nothing but folk-medicine curatives and floppycock treatments.

Aristotle tried to set the record straight 2,300 years ago, but the 3rd-century AD *Physiologus* came along to set the trend for endless Christian bestiaries, throughout the Middle Ages, describing the Hyena with its dangerously unorthodox tackle as a duplicitous sex-changer and devil. In truth, despite the insistences of a certain Disney film, Hyenas are significantly better parents, far more sociably peaceful, and (I'm told) significantly less stinky, than the unreasonably favored Lion.

Page 4 – Sam's story about Persian hunters believing that Hyenas would submit to flattery (presumably these would be the smaller "Striped" variety, *Hyaena hyaena*, which are indigenous to the Middle East, and have far less interesting genitals) is taken from *The Standard Natural History, Vol. V: Mammals*, by John Sterling Kinglsey, written 1884. A beautiful, fully illustrated version is online at: **www.archive.org/details/standardnaturalh05king**

Other hyena myths abound, by the way, not least the human/hyena hybrid Kaftar. There does however seem to be a particular belief in the ability to propitiate these creatures using carefully chosen language. In *The Magicality of the Hyena*, Jürgen W. Frembgen describes hunters local to Kandahar, Afghanistan, entering dens with nothing but a noose. By murmuring the magic formula – "turn into dust, turn into stone" – the animal can be made docile enough to be collared.

I mention all this – apart from it being a lovely bit of fluff – simply to establish that when we arrive in the Middle East, next page, the acid-tone skies and unsentimental military toys shouldn't be allowed to disguise a land *seething* with myth.

Page 5 – And here's our first look at the third and final phase of Lou's story, chronologically "the middle", as colored by the masterful Matt Wilson.

That airborne behemoth is a CH47-F Chinook Helicopter. Two just like it go thundering over my house every week, presumably on their way to the royal artillery at Woolwich, and I can fully attest that when Stig describes their "unnatural state of 'hover'" on the next page, he ain't shitting.

Page 6 – Let the record state that the interior space of a CH47-F Chinook was most definitely not designed with dialogue progressions in mind. These next few pages involved endless diagrams in the script and numerous headaches for poor Ryan.

The bit of kit stowed at the stern is an RG-31 Nyala APC. More on that next episode.

Page 7 – Now that we've introduced each of the three time zones in Lou's story, here's a good chance to point out a secondary tool to help differentiate the story threads (and hence help readers to not get lost in the jumps), in addition to our triply-distinguished colorists.

Look carefully and you'll notice that the "blue" pages from the start of Lou's story never exceed two columns of four stacked rows. Panels are frequently merged, but in essence these pages are all scripted around the principal of an eight-panel grid. The same is true of the "middle" pages, in Afghanistan, except using a six-panel grid. In the final "red place" stages of the story, we're down to a maximum of four panels, always full-page width.

The hope is that these distinctions not only aid in differentiation, but control the pace of the tale in a way that speaks to the themes at the heart of the story. About which I'm saying nothing just yet.

Page 8 – Our first spot of overt spookiness here, courtesy of the unassuming chap known as Tengu. I'll say a little more about him and his halo of kami (godly) and yōkai (spirit) associations when we come to showcase him more closely. For now I'll simply mention that I've been fascinated by the Karasu Tengu – often associated with corvids and kites – since finding a mask in the British Museum depicting what appeared to be an angry man with a cock for a nose. Academia, thy name is smut.

You can pre-empt my future wafflings about these crow-spirits by checking out *The Tengu* by Marinus Willem de Visser, but it's a cute coincidence – given the title of this series and the species of myth infecting Lou – that the name originally comes from the Chinese "tiangou", meaning a dog-like demon.

The tattoo on Óttar's arm is the Fehu rune – abstractly it's just

an "F" – which we'll talk about next episode when we get to know Óttar better.

Page 10 – The Old Bailey, with its famous golden sculpture by F.W. Pomeroy. Here we're specifically interested in a little gated alley off Warwick Lane called "Amen Court", supposedly named for monks reaching the final line of their pater nosters as they processed past on Feast Days. Before that the lane was known, rather unimaginatively, as "Deadman's Walk."

Unimaginatively, that is, because this is also the former site of the infamous Newgate Gaol, remembered by 18th-century writer Henry Fielding as a "prototype of hell". Having held famous prisoners ranging from Giacomo Casanova to William Penn (he of "~sylvania"), it was London's official place of public execution after the Tyburn gallows were decommissioned in 1783 – hence the "deadman's walk". You'd expect a lot of ghosts in a place like this, but we're interested in one in particular...

Page 11 – A 17th-century booklet, written by a convicted highwayman named Luke Hutton during his (terminal) stay in Newgate, proposes one origin for the myth which has haunted it for centuries: a ghastly black dog, slinking and slobbering, attending those doomed to die.

According to Hutton's piece, a scholar was imprisoned in Newgate in 1596 for witchcraft, but was killed and eaten by his starving cellmates before his trial. The unfortunate wizard was even "deemed passing good meate". The dog appeared soon after, and although the guilty cannibals managed to escape the gaol, the hound pursued them wherever they went, ultimately exacting its bloody (or in some accounts, purely psychological) revenge.

 I won't go too much further into this stuff, because the notion of Monstrous Black Dogs is a folkloric Pandora's Box which dwarfs this mere one example. Werewolves really are just the tip of the Canine Gribbly iceberg, although Lou's conclusion on the next page – "I've

been mugged by a werewolf" – is perhaps forgivable given how little known the proto-mythology truly is.

Page 13 – (...a proto-myth, by the way, which is almost named by Óttar just here. More on that next episode.) Anyway, here we are arriving at our first ground-location in Afghanistan. This is based on reams of photos of US-run prisons in Kandahar Province, which I mentioned earlier. "Turn into dust... turn into stone." There are no coincidences in myth.

I won't say much here about Adze, the glow-eyed leader of Lou's present companions, but I daresay a little homework into the word itself might provide some hints.

Page 14 – The interior reference here was based round the frequently sickening images which have trickled out from inside some of the CIA's most notorious black sites, most notably the Abu Ghraib prison west of Baghdad. We know that a lot of these places were mothballed after Obama's "Executive Order 13491", which restricted the kinds of "enhanced interrogation" previously used within them.

Page 15 – As per the above descriptions on Black Sites, it felt like a nice dollop of justice to imply a literal monster blew the lid on a monstrous system.

Page 17 – Our first look here at the distinctive psychedelic aesthetic of Lou's heightened senses, which for the time being is our one hint that she's become something other than human. We worried it would be a challenge to match up this sort of detail between three very different colorists, but – as you'll see next page – these guys have a spooky synchronicity.

Page 18 – Dalston. To the uninitiated, a spot in East London which kneejerked from a poor street-market hub dominated by Turkish and Egyptian businesses to a latte-swilling, cat cafe-visiting, quinoa-guzzling, cocktail-quaffing paradise for scrawny white hipster-boys with enormous moustaches and no hips. So profound was the transformation that it's become the archetype for similar regeneration – "the scruffy arty crowd = profit", basically – all over London. My own (currently) wonderful market neighbourhood, for instance, is apparently doomed to become "the next Dalston". I tingle.

Sam's comment – "a morgue without a corpse" – is shamelessly pinched from (if memory serves) Bill Bryson describing Las Vegas.

Page 20 – Americans: for "kebab shop", read "schwarma joint". Noble culinary wizardry in which Levantine gentlemen use whacking great knives to slice juicy scab-like peelings of reformed lamb off what can only be described as an elephant's leg. Food of the gods, and a requisite going-home-time snack for any pissed Brit.

Page 22 – And at last we meet the enigmatic Lynn Odell, subject of so much setup, about whom I intend to say nothing at all.

TWO ⊙

Page 1 – Let's start this second chapter with the key to all magic and myth: names. Our new friend Lynn Odell rattles off a barrage of the things, all variations on a theme: enormous monster Dogs.

Of all the prototypical Spectral Hounds, the best known is probably the East Anglian "Black Shuck", but even the most courageous attempt to taxonomise these creatures (as in the highly recommended *Lore of the Land*, by Westwood & Simpson) never quite convinces. For me, in amongst the shifting continuum of names – pwc, puck, shuck, shock, shag, shough – there lies a denominator: the ubiquitous shaggy beast with glittering eyes, just outside the fire's glow.

Interesting fact: despite the English speaking world's fondness for depicting these gribblies as mastiffs, pinschers and rottweilers, similar myths from Europe often give the role to the giant poodle. No, really.

Page 2 – Odell's little rant here is a truncated version of a lecture I give about stories and comics. The basic thesis is that the human brain can only parse life experience in the form of narrative units, and comics are the most perfectly engineered medium to satisfy that predisposition. Congratulations on your wise purchase.

Page 3 – As mentioned last time, our pimpin' ride here is an RG-31 NYALA or, if you prefer, a "category 1 Mine Resistant Ambush Protected (MRAP) vehicle". One exciting fact about these machines is that they're considered to have a "non aggressive appearance", so as well as military use they're operated by several considerate Police Forces around the world. Looks pretty fucking aggressive to me.

Page 5 – A moment to delight in Ryan's design of the barghest. I mentioned above how effortless it feels to syncretise all Folkloric Hounds into a single primal blur, though it must be said that if any resists the stew pot it's the archetypal Werewolf, which has become arguably more distinct in today's cultural canon. And less interesting, I think. Despite leaning heavily on *Cry Havoc's* most simple précis during marketing ("Lesbian werewolf goes to war") we also wanted our central Shaggy Dog to be just that. Not a wolf, not a rubber suit, but a lean and rangy hound with long matted fur, dangling ears and gracile limbs. Even from these few glimpses it's clear Ryan's nailed it.

Page 9 – For our readers in future years: Lou's reference to "teacup cocktails" here refers to a fad, hopefully long since passed by whatever blessed age you presently occupy, rampant in East London at the time of writing, for speakeasy-style bars emulating those of Prohibition-Era USA, for no particular reason, by serving overpriced concoctions in jam jars, teapots and mugs. "Mugs", coincidentally, also being a useful noun for said establishments' patrons.

Page 10 – Appropriately, given all the above pontification about nomenclature, the runic word being spoken by Óttar is another name. He's calling out to his patron Goddess – the heart and soul of the myth which defines him, in fact – and we'll learn more about that in just a moment. The word is **FREYJA**.

Page 11 – So then. Óttar. Golly. His story derives from the *Hyndluljóð*, the "Lay of Hyndla," from the Poetic Edda: one of the racier parts of the profoundly violent and sexy canon of tales which chronicle the myths and legends of the Norse religion. The hero of the piece, "Óttar the Simple", pleads with his patron Goddess Freyja to help him learn about his own ancestry, which she achieves by smuggling him into the lair of a giant seeress, Hyndla. This being a Norse legend she does so by turning him into an animal, in this case "Hildisvini": literally, "battle pig". (Best band name ever.) Likewise, this being a Norse legend, when we're told Freyja rode her battle pig wherever she went, it doesn't necessarily mean As A Means Of Transport.

I'm not even reaching here. In his *Essays on Eddic Poetry* John McKinnell makes a strong case for Óttar and Freyja being lovers (in fact he argues the whole *Hyndluljóð* is sopping with sexy rivalry between Freyja and Hyndla, both presumably after a good hard oinking. Sorry). Freyja certainly has a reputation for being a bit of a goer, having

bedded four dwarfs in the *Sörla þáttr* and been accused by Loki (in the *Lokasenna*) of being basically an Asgardian bicycle. (Which is a bit rich coming from Loki: a serial sex pest who turned himself into a mare, raised his tail for a super-powered stallion and gave birth to an eight-legged foal.) Like I said: racy stuff.

What's really great about Freyja is that she wears her reputation for eroticism without shame, and indeed all the Eddic canon seems quite pleased to let her. In the Loki-being-a-dick episode mentioned above even Njörðr, Freyja's dad, just shrugs and says it's normal for a hot-blooded lass with her pig of the boys – sorry, pick, *pick* – to take lovers.

I mention all this to explain why our current conception of Óttar, still able to shift into Battle Pig at will, has been dedicating so much time to, ahem, self relief. Simply put: he needs to have a horribly overcharged sexdrive just to keep up with his holy benefactress.

Raging physical transformations are a long-standing staple of comics, of course, and I've often wondered if sexual frustration doesn't make a more fitting trigger than the rather vague "rage" approach. Please therefore accept this grisly page as a characteristically Eddic take on the quintessential "**Hulk Smash!**"

Page 12 – The Job Centre: a common sight on any British high street. We've rather fictionalised the scale of waiting line, if only to identify the scene with the one other occasion our US readers might have encountered a Job Centre in fiction: the famous "dancing in line" scene from *The Full Monty*. The pub at the bottom is based on the Cellars – formerly The Edinburgh – of Newington Green, Islington.

Page 14 – The mysterious and half-eaten corpse there, as we shall later discover, belongs to a very particular type of Turkish entity. Discovering it was a huge last-minute relief, replacing an earlier (somewhat fudged) attempt to make use of the Mahabharatic Hindu demons known as Raksasha, whose only point of relevance in this context was that they were apparently enthusiastic cannibals. Finding myths about edible monsters was more challenging than expected.

Page 16 – The Germans famously have a term for everything. In as much as there *can* be a single nominative description for anything as sprawling, contradictory, irrational and plain bloody marvellous as folklore, "time ghost" gets my vote.

Page 20 – It feels churlish to tease you with a description of something without depicting it ("show not tell" being the cardinal rule of comics), but good things come to those who wait.

The Penanggalan is a real thing (at least, a real myth, if you see what I mean), and since we'll be encountering it in the flesh, as it were, in due course, I'll say nothing more about it now... except to note in passing that Sri pretty much covers all the basics with her flippant description – detachable head, dangling bowels, Feasting On The Flesh Of The Living, yadda yadda – but mysteriously neglects to mention that Penanggalans are often found lurking close to pregnant women. That may be important.

Page 22 – See above note.

THREE

Page 1 – Welcome to Newfolk. Amidst the better-known beings actively showing their true selves here, the dedicated monsterist may spot a Jorōgumo (sexy Japanese honeytrap spider-woman), a gangly bubak (quintessential Polish bogeyman), an Abura-Akago (oil-drinking fiery baby ghost) and the genuinely horrible Popobawa: a one-eyed bat monster from Tanzania with a penchant for forced sodomy. That last one, by the way, didn't enter the annals of folklore (I said "annals", jeez) until 1965. Myth-making is alive and well.

Page 2 – Our swarthy bearded henchman reveals a little of his inner nature, here. He's a Leshy: a woodland guardian-spirit from Russia. Think Swamp Thing with a sexy accent. Oh, and check out panel 3, where everybody's favourite rabbinic homunculus, a golem, is chatting with a Slavic tutelary dwarf called a domovoy (or a d'edek, in Czech). I've got this whole ridiculous headcanon about these two being old lovers from Prague, the only place with myths about both, divided by racism, reunited at last.

Page 4 – Many sections of the Islamic community espouse aniconism: a prohibition on depictions of living things. The precise terms of the rule vary, with some of its strictest adherents among Sunni extremists like the Taliban. By their interpretation of Sharia it's not only depictions of holy persons which are idolatrous, but attempts to draw or sculpt any living creature. Interestingly the *Quran* itself gives no such directive, but there are plenty of examples in the *Hadith* (that is: post-Quranic transcriptions of the prophet's words) of Muhammad being annoyed by drawings and sculptures, and in one case a comfy cushion, which look like animals. Whatever you may think of the proscription itself (in my opinion no more or less relevant in today's world than injunctions on eating pork or pre-marital sexytimes) at least it's given us some of the most extraordinary geometric art in the world.

I mention all this because the present tale is inherently bound with notions of control and chaos, and this particular scene was one of the first that occurred to me. It's easy to dismiss violent extremists (as Sri does this issue) as "primitive" or "barbarous" – both of which adjectives I've literally just heard in a TV report about Islamic fundamentalists. But such words, connoting chaos and savagery, mislead deeply. The example on this page is about as pure a vision of *control* as you can get. A child, thoughtlessly driven to express herself, being prevented from doing so by adult men. Because they're frightened of her.

A mischievous aside: even at its most orthodox, aniconism only prohibits depictions of living things. One rather wonders at the theological implications of drawing mythical monsters. How does one define "living"?

Page 7 – *Papaver somniferum*, the opium poppy, from which flows everything from *Kubla Kahn* to *The Wire*. Also: lots of dead people.

White, pink or red, it grows like hell in the Afghan sun. Whatever you may have heard, the core Taliban do not make their money selling sweet heretical heroin to foolish Western imperialists. In fact in July 2000, when the group controlled much of the country, Taliban leader Mullah Mohammed Omar declared growing poppies "un-Islamic" and oversaw one of, if not *the* most successful anti-drug campaigns in history. Implementing some pretty horrifying tactics, opium production fell by 99% in Taliban-controlled areas. Three quarters of the world's supply of heroin, wiped out. Evil totalitarian fuckheads they may be, but corrupt, inefficient or chaotic they most certainly are not.

The ban didn't last, of course. Since 2002, when the likes of Captain MacManus and Sergeant Stig boldly liberated the region, opium farming has swelled to bumper levels, now accounting for 92% of the illicit opiates bought and sold across the world. Whatever this conflict is, it ain't a war on drugs.

Page 10 – There is no situation so tragic that I can't be made to laugh via the inclusion of an inquisitive llama in the background.

Page 13 – Ah, the swarm. Probably *Luciola discicollis Castelnau*, to any avid entomologists. The West African firefly to the rest of us.

There is a monster – a spirit, actually – found among the Ewe people of Southern Ghana and Togo. It's a shapeshifter and a blood-sucker. It takes the form of a single firefly, or sometimes a swarm, and I first heard of it years ago when researching vampires for a different project. It's stuck with me ever since, so much so that even though I can find little extra information about it today (a faded copy of Matthew Bunson's *Vampire Encyclopaedia* is the nearest I can get, and he doesn't cite sources) nonetheless I couldn't resist using it here. This type of monster, for those who haven't twigged yet, is called an Adze.

Page 14 – The "Helpalong Line" is a total invention, riffing on real organisations offering the same service: listen, support, comfort. The best known of which, in the UK, is probably the Samaritans. (I've always been slightly iffy about that name. The whole point of the biblical parable being referenced was that the Samaritans utterly *loathed* the Israelites, making a charitable deed by a "good" one so much more impressive. In context, this is rather like naming your counselling service WE HATE YOU BUT WE MIGHT BE NICE TODAY.)

"Black Dog" has had a surprisingly long career, etymologically, as a negative abstraction. Plutarch writes that 400 years before him (which puts us around 450BC) the appearance of a black dog was understood to foretell disaster. The term crops up more than once in Medieval then Tudor literature as a metaphor for death or disease, and by the time of Queen Anne has taken a turn slangwards: now a colloquialism for a poorly stamped shilling.

Winston Churchill is often assumed to have first deployed the phrase as a euphemism for his depression, but (according to Megan McKinlay's strong paper on this topic) its use predates him by 150 years. Hence in letters between literary giant Samuel Johnson and diarist Hester Thrale in the late 18th century, we find the latter writing of her gloomy husband Henry: "I hope he shall soon shake off the black dog and come home as light as a feather".

Page 16 – Meet Mr Bleacher, of the Inhand Org. We'll be seeing a lot more of him, so let me just mention in passing that I loved the idea of the archetypal untrustworthy suit being a cheery chap called Timmy.

Page 20 – Exocannibalism: the eating of enemies. There's little point trying to trace the origins of the practice: it appears in basically every place where humanity has prehistory. For a few cultures – the Aztec, notably – the act was a sophisticated religious affair (in their case a propitiation of the sun). For most others the link between consuming flesh and absorbing the owners' characteristics was regarded as self-evident. Generally speaking the logic followed an anatomical utilitarianism, hence eating an enemy's tongue would improve your voice, feasting on his feet would make you run faster, noshing on his naughtybits would... well. You get the gist.

What's really weird is how many ancient cultures identify the heart specifically as the seat of a person's inner-self. In multiple languages we find words – the Hebrew *lebab*, the Sanskrit *hRd*, the Chinese *xTn*, the Egyptian *ib* – which refer interchangeably to either a throbbing cardiac muscle or abstractions like "mind", "spirit" and "centre-of-being".

Incidentally, lest we think exocannibalism is gone from the world, allow me to grimly remind you of Liberian President Charles Taylor, who ordered his troops to eat the flesh of captured enemies during the Sierra-Leonean wars of the nineties, or indeed Syrian rebel commander Abu Sakkar, who in 2013 was filmed eating the raw ventricles of a dead government soldier. Eat your heart out, ancient world.

FOUR

Page 1 – A couple of historical vignettes. The third panel samples the Peasant's Revolt in 1381, in which Wat Tyler & co induced an uprising against English serfdom, during which a handful of angry ploughmen came within a gnat's tit of ending the monarchic Plantagenets. The fourth panel takes us to 1992 LA and the race-riots which boiled there, after four LAPD officers needlessly tasered, batoned and kicked the living shit out of African-American Rodney King, and were promptly acquitted of all excess by a jury with zero black faces. These apparently disparate episodes, separated by 611 years, impinge on the present tale to make a simple point: for all that we like to think culture evolves to reflect the times, humanity's binary condition has *always* been that those in charge abhor change, those in the gutter crave it.

Page 4 – The critters at the foot of the hill are striped hyenas: adorable animals with the dreary taxonomic cognomen *Hyaena hyaena*. Unlike their larger spotted cousins these guys are lacking in any exciting genital adaptations. On the other hand they're practitioners of lifelong monogamy with the particular twist that whereas the male is expected to provide food for the pups, he's not allowed *near* them. Basically: hyenas have been tinkering with conventional approaches to society and gender for millions of years, and they seem to laugh a lot more than the basic human. "Proudest of beasts", remember?

Page 5 – Lithium is indeed big business, and Afghanistan is lousy with it. A 2007 geological survey suggested that one third of the country's untapped resources could be worth $3 trillion. Bear this in mind next time you see Western leaders looking believably earnest whilst denying they're only fighting wars because of oil revenue.

The problem is that lithium's a bastard to extract. It's so reactive that exposure to air makes it throw a wobbler, so when Stig talks about "mining" he's actually describing distillation and concentration. Clay is mixed into solar brine pools which are allowed to evaporate over months. What's left is a chemically stable salt – lithium chloride – which will eventually get mixed with potassium chloride and separated through electrolysis. A huge number of the modern world's edgiest gadgets, and the industrial processes used to make them, rely on lithium and similarly tough-to-extract minerals. In many cases the term "rare earth materials" doesn't actually signify the chemical's in short supply, but that it's super-hard and often dangerous to fetch. Hence countries with an attitude of disposability towards its workers are leaders in the field. Don't be surprised if the global economy over the next century is shaped by leaders' willingness to condemn multitudes to the mines.

All of which is very interesting, and cogent to the misty subtexts gathering in the background of our tale, but for now let us note that, yes, Lithium – in fact its ionic component Li+ – is indeed widely used as a mood stabilizer, and a treatment for everything from depression to bipolar disorder by way of cluster headaches.

Page 12 – The wretched silhouette of the General Atomics MQ-9 Reaper Drone. Which, just so you know, can travel 1000 miles and loiter for 25 hours above literally anywhere it pleases, during which it kills time auto-plotting firing solutions on anything that moves with its AGM-114 Hellfire Missiles and 500lb bombs. Armaments which, by the way, were a featured upgrade from the drones' predecessors back when we all stopped pretending there's any difference between surveillance and combat. The shadow of the drone will, I think, go down in history as the defining icon of this era.

Page 13 – Fare thee well, Karasu Tengu, we barely knew you.

Just about every culture under the sun has an impressive suite of stored-up myths revolving around birds, often in roles either psychopompic (ie: an escort into the afterlife) or interlocutory (ie: as intermediaries between the divine and the mundane). It's easy to understand why, too. Quite apart from obvious associations between flying and unearthliness, to pre-global societies migrating birds must have seemed especially magical, travelling beyond the known world every year, returning to herald a new season. It's therefore perhaps no great surprise that legends revolving around non-migratory birds often characterise them as sly, mischievous, unpredictable or downright murderous; something especially true of the much-maligned *Corvidae*. That is, crows, ravens, rooks, magpies and jays. It doesn't help that these are some of the cleverest animals on the planet (seriously, their brain-to-body weight ratio is up there with apes and dolphins), with a penchant for mimicry of human voices and a neat sideline in eating dead people. If snowy white swans are the honking fuckwitted boyscouts of the heavens, crows are the slinking cackling bastards of the lower spheres.

Hence we find crows conforming to trickster-archetypes in both Australian and Native American indigenous mythologies; likewise it's a raven who plays the role of the smartass which finds land (and hence doesn't come home) in pre-biblical accounts of the flood (*Epic of Gilgamesh*, especially); the wandering God-Sage Odin employs the ravens Huginn and Muninn to spy on his earthly domains; and the celtic war-goddess Badb chooses a crow's form to accept bloody propitiation. In fact the Japanese Karasu Tengu is something of an outlier in this class, having started-out as something completely different, and slowly morphed into a wise but minacious crowlike entity.

The first mention of the Tengu appears in the *Nihon Shoki* in 720 AD, in which a shooting star is identified as a "heavenly dog" (borrowing the Chinese term "tiāngoǔ"). The meteor served as an ill omen preceding a military uprising, and over the following centuries was inducted into the endless role of Japanese spirits, imps and ghosts. At some uncertain stage the asteroidal dog became a bird – first a buzzard, then a crow – and I rather like the current hypothesis that the Garuda is to blame: the fabulous Hindu eagle-man who ferries around Vishnu on his shoulders, which Buddhist scholars were keen to appropriate and pluralize as a race of warlike winged entities.

For me the beauty of the Tengu is that its folkloric history so perfectly tallies with one common conception of crows: as frantic collectors of shiny nonsense. The Tengu has accumulated and discarded a bewildering kaleidoscope of meanings and aesthetics during its 1300 years: from Chinese portent to raptor-demon, from tutelary mountain spirit to wise adherent of the ascetic Shungendō practice. Somewhere along the way the long beak of the crow has become blurred with the long nose of the shinto god Sarutahiko, so that in modern Japan the Tengu is most closely associated with scowling masks featuring enormous and unmistakably penis-like probosces.

I mention all this delicious and eternally changing color simply to underline something which our current tale's Tengu – who we've chosen to imagine as a lifeless body hosting a great and ghostly spirit – has just realised: no matter how cold and dead a story may seem, it gains new life with every telling.

Page 18 – A swift note to introduce the concept of second sight, or true sight, most commonly known to folklorists in its Scottish/Gaelic conception as "an da shealladh". There are literally dozens of stories, from Iceland to New Zealand, in which a lowly mortal – often as a consequence of having helped or liberated magical creatures – is accidentally blessed with the proscribed ability to see into the magical dimension. This extrasensory perception seems like a jolly useful skill, at first, but when the denizens of [Insert Mythical Realm Here] realise they're being spied on, it all goes horribly wrong. Quite possibly this all belongs in the same canon of disciplinarian myth as the tale of Orpheus and Eurydice, or indeed Lot's salty wife. It arises here in connection with the same enigmatic niqab-wearing women we've had occasion to meet several times already, and whose mystery will be unravelled in the coming issues.

FIVE

Page 1 – Another rollicking round of Spot The Obscure Monster here, and Ryan's spoiled me by including three of my favourites all in the same place.

The lady on the left, with a toothy surprise waiting for any unwary hair stylist, is a futakuchi-onna, a Japanese yokai whose name literally means "two-mouthed woman." The origin stories vary for this unhappy creature – in some versions the second mouth is a punishment levied on its host, in others the woe is targeted at her husband – but in all forms it cautions against the sin of miserliness. Put simply, he or she who withholds food is destined to require twice as much.

The lumpy little fellow with (look closely) suckers instead of fingers is a Yara-Ma-Yha-Who, a wonderfully creative form of vampire indigenous to Australia. Their preferred method of exsanguination is to drop upon victims from a tree, leech them dry through their suckers, then swallow the body. And then puke it back up. And then swallow it again. This occurs several times, until the prey has shrunk down to the same size as the predator and become another Yara-Ma-Yha-Who.

(While I'm on the topic: there is almost no culture in the world that doesn't have some form of vampire-analogue in its lore. I find it eternally vexing that the most popularly known species, the cape-wearing, widow's-peak-sporting archetype beloved of Hollywood, is literally the most boring of the lot.)

Lastly, the turtle-shelled chap at the bottom right corner is a Kappa: a charming Japanese water-creature with a fondness for cucumbers (hence sushi rolls featuring that noble vegetable are known as *kappa maki*). Kappas are generally benevolent, but will waylay and occasionally drown those who stray near dangerous waters. With typical Japanese efficiency this chelonian charybdis has also been co-opted as an occult motivator towards politeness. According to lore the Kappa's monstrous power derives from water, which it carries with it wherever it goes, in a shallow depression on top of its head. If, however, the Kappa is greeted by its potential victims with the requisite formality – a respectful bow – it cannot help but reciprocate: spilling the water and forcing it to rush off to the local pond to re-up. In other words: *always watch your manners, kids, or the cucumber-gobbling turtle-man will get you.*

Page 7 – A word on the Inhand Org logo, which has been quietly appearing on our heroes' uniforms (and indeed the backs of the comic) throughout. Composed by our designer Emma Price, it stands in my opinion as an exemplar of intelligent symbology. What seems at first a familiar device – the flighted fist, ubiquitous iconography of macho paramilitary dickery – reveals to the closer inspector that the wings emerge from inside, not behind, the hand. Note again the company's name, remind yourself of a popular aphorism about birds and bushes, and you know everything you need about the organisation's remit and attitude towards control.

Like so much in *Cry Havoc*, knowing this stuff isn't remotely critical. But it speaks volumes about the attention to detail and dedication to the controlling idea which drives the entire team. They are a cracking bunch.

Pages 11&12 – There's a rumor going around that breaking up is hard to do. Writing about it isn't much fun either.

Conflicts of the heart are some of the most uncomfortable sequences to script. Partly that's because art will always emote where text will always encode, lacking the ragged component of voice-tone (picture your humble writer performing this all aloud in his office, much to his neighbors' annoyance); and partly because romantic arguments are by definition irrational. People *do* act out of character, people *will* say awful things for the worst reasons. You can't write this stuff unless you've seen it.

I mention this with reference to Lou's brutal tirade in hopes of preserving at least a little sympathy for her. As she pelts her lover with news of her infidelity, and announces the betrayal of her own supposedly rigid sexuality, remember that Lou's real target here is herself. Devastating those who love you is one of the most comprehensive forms of self-harm there is. Likewise, Sam's dull adherence to keeping things tidy (that dustpan line kills me) is not a sign that she's cold.

Emotional coping-strategies are among the most poorly-evolved software we have. Control and chaos at war, even here.

Page 16 – The chopper, for the milporn-minded, is an MD530F, modified with a sniper port. It's based on identical vehicles operated by real-life "private security consultancy" Academi, formerly and famously known as Blackwater.

Our present story's Inhand Org are shamelessly modelled on that same company, and whilst their emphasis on mysticism and folklore may set them apart – about which more next episode – their off-grid, unregulated, multi-discipline approach to Hired Shadiness is pure Blackwater.

Founded in 1997 by former Navy SEAL Erik Prince, and named after the 7000 acres of the Great Dismal Swamp where it has its not-at-all-like-a-super-secret-villain's-lair-honest headquarters, Blackwater (which later became Xe Services, which later became Academi, which wound-up as a division of Constellis Holdings, but you'd be a fool and a liar to claim they're sensitive to brand toxicity) is one of those real life entities too absurdly vile to support its own analysis. You can't discuss this company without feeling like a hack novelist.

Put simply: Blackwater was, and its descendant companies still are, paid billions of dollars every year by western governments to perform military activities. Activities which, let's be clear, those same governments could've done an awful lot cheaper if they'd instead used, ohhh, I don't know, their own soldiers.

In theory, bringing in Blackwater frees up the *real* troops to do the important stuff. In practice it absolves the real troops from having to do all the morally reprehensible bullying, top-tier skullduggery and outright illegal bullshit that might look a bit icky on their commanders' records.

The catalogue of Blackwater's [alleged] dubiousness is too long to go into. Check out Jeremy Scahill's *Blackwater: The Rise Of The World's Most Powerful Mercenary Army* (2008, Serpent's Tail) for a worryingly detailed look. But know that the Best Hits compilation features such crowd-pleasers as the [alleged] slaughter of 17 unarmed Iraqis in 2007, the [alleged] arming of vigilantes in post-Katrina New Orleans, and a [not alleged; this one's public record] death-threat aimed at a State Department Investigator. An investigator who, not incidentally, had recently dared describe BW as operating with "an environment of liability and negligence."

These guys have access to the highest levels of security, owe allegiance to nothing but the monthly paycheck, and their history is a litany of bloodstained notes marked "Nobody Held Accountable."

Blackwater is the ultimate expression of capitalist imperium: *we kill the fuckers who don't fit, so you don't have to. Now pay up.*

Your tax dollars at work.

SIX

Page 2 – Time at last to explicate our niqab-wearing (and abruptly scaly) friends. They are Shahmarans: pre-Islamic beings of the Anatolian plateau, whose name means "Queen of the Snakes." Plenty of scholars associate them with even older legends – the Hittite monster Illuyanka seem popular – but it's depressingly common for female folk-figures to be recast as duplicitous fiends, so let's stick to the kinder conception of the core fable (as per Tomris Uyar's *Ödeşmeler ve Şahmeran Hikâyesi*).

One day a desert traveller encounters the wise and gentle Shahmaran – half woman, half snake – and, falling in love, lives with her. Being just a fickle human, alas, he eventually gets bored and heads home, where he's tricked into betraying her whereabouts. This would be bad enough if not for an ambitious local vizier (there's always one), who claims the flesh of a Shahmaran will bestow healing and enlightenment on its eater. By various means the unhappy traveller is himself induced to partake of the grisly meal. Just before dying the Shahmaran explains some of her flesh is poisoned, some is miraculous – but lies about which part is which. Hence the evil Vizier comes to a sticky end while the traveller gains immortality, perception and power, all thanks to the fidelity and self-sacrifice of the lover he betrayed.

Myths about consuming magical flesh are weirdly rare, but there are notable examples in loftier circles. That notoriously boozy ancient Greek god Dionysus, for example, was once torn apart and eaten, by which act he was "born again." If that all sounds uncomfortably familiar then yes, I'm afraid there really is a graphic precedent for the transubstantiation of bread and wine in modern churches every Sunday. Theophagy – the act of eating one's god – is as old as the hills, and Sir James Frazer draws a direct line between Dionysus and Jesus in *The Golden Bough*. Any Catholic reading this might in future spare a thought, as they take Communion, for the Queen of the Snakes who surrendered her flesh for love.

Page 7 – The paraphernalia in the sixth panel is a panoply of apotropaics. That is, objects and symbols for warding, dispelling or destroying evil. Plenty of classics here – rosaries, holy water, garlic and iron filings – but the more dedicated ogler will recognise also a First Nations arrowhead, a chicken's foot, a black feather, a rodent-skull and the symbolic Hamsa (whose gazing "hand" deflects the evil eye). The symbols on the mortars are the Eddic Helm Of Awe, and the Veve of that fine old transplane Loa, Papa Legba. All are associated with the ritual defeat of monstrosity (except perhaps the Veve, but we figured if we were trying to mix drugs and dreams we'd throw a nod towards the gatekeeper of the realms too). This is superstition-as-convenience writ large, and beyond the sinister M.O. of the Inhand Org it is utterly, quintessentially and uniquely human.

Pages 13 & 14 – At last we meet the Penanggalan, Malaysia's visceral vampire. Best described in the 1845 Malay work *Hikayat Abdullah*, the Penanggalan is a cursed woman – usually a midwife. Fuelled by an irresistible blood-lust, at night she undergoes a terrible transformation. With the pop of wet skin her head, rising upwards, detaches from its neck. As it lifts into the air it drags with it her spinal cord, her lungs, her heart, and finally the great thrashing cords of her viscera, dripping poison, dangling like the toxic fronds of a jellyfish, as she hovers through the night.

A few neat extra flourishes from the same text: the Penanggalan often comes complete with an obvious whiff of vinegar (for eminently logical reasons: her viscera swell up while outside the body, so she has to undertake some mild self-pickling to cram them back down the throat-hole); her worst enemy is a thorn bush (nothing worse than getting your own pendulous guts snagged on an ill-placed thistle); and she enjoys nothing so much as wriggling up through the floorboards to feast during a child's birth, being partial to infant and placenta alike.

As has been remarked, it's astonishing how obsessed we are in the West by our dreary vampire figure, when his global cousins are so very much more inventive. Southeast Asia boasts a particularly demented creativity on this score.

By the way, there's a worryingly high incidence among international folklores of monsters identified with midwives. The Filipino Aswang – which is clearly an ancestor of the similar but nastier Penaggalan – is another one among many. As Damon L. Woods explains in *The Philippines: ACSH*, the arrival of Catholicism in the 16th and 17th centuries brought with it the sudden imposition of centralised – and exclusively male – governments. These replaced agrarian village communities guided by female priests and cunning-women, amongst whose duties was the delivery of babies. By simply associating these rural figureheads with existing bogeymen, the missionary friars overthrew centuries of matriarchal authority at the drop of a rumor. One senses it's not reaching too far to assume the same, or something similar, happened all over the world.

In folklore, as in all other walks of life, women of skill and learning have been easy targets, especially for men of ambition and control, since time immemorial.

Page 16 – Odell is far from unique in proposing earthly substances as a means to access wondrous worlds (though I imagine her industrial-scale approach is, at least, novel). In fact there's an ages-old tradition of heavenly highs, with pretty much all the big faiths having had at least cult-cells, and often majority orthodoxies, devoted to the pursuit of chemical epiphany. From the fly agaric chomping Berserkers to the modern União do Vegetal (mixing Christianity with the legally-loopholed right to guzzle a fuckton of ayahuasca), it's perhaps unsurprising that a 2011 study (Móró, Simon, Bárd, & Rácz) found that users of psychedelics regard "spirituality as more personally important compared to non-drug users." Spiritually being defined here as "one's relationship to God, or whatever you perceive to be the Ultimate Transcendence." One suspects a cult devoted to The Pizza-Delivery Dude can't be far away.

The granddaddy of all metaphysical mindbenders is the Proto-Indo/Iranian "Soma": a yellow flower producing a trip of such reality-haemorrhaging oneness that in both Vedic and Zoroastrian tradition the name of the plant and the drink are synonymous with a divine principle. It is said, tantalisingly, "to roar."

Annoyingly – but perhaps inevitably – the human race has absentmindedly forgotten what the principal ingredient of Soma actually *is*, requiring modern practitioners to offer expiatory prayers to apologise for using a substitute dope. I can't help feeling this tells you literally everything you need to know about humanity and the functionality of faith.

And that, as they say, is that – at least for this phase of Lou's tale. If one thing above all has emerged from her peregrinations, or indeed my own ramblings back here, I hope it is this: that the relative realness of a thing is unimportant beside its capacity to inspire transformations. There is nothing in the human heart more open to abuse than the twin urges to take literally that which is wondrous, and to control that which is wild.

It remains only for me to thank you, on behalf of the team, for your time and your patience.

Until the next beginning,

– **Si Spurrier**

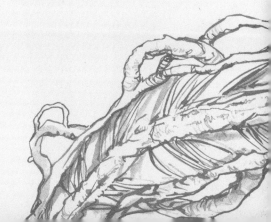

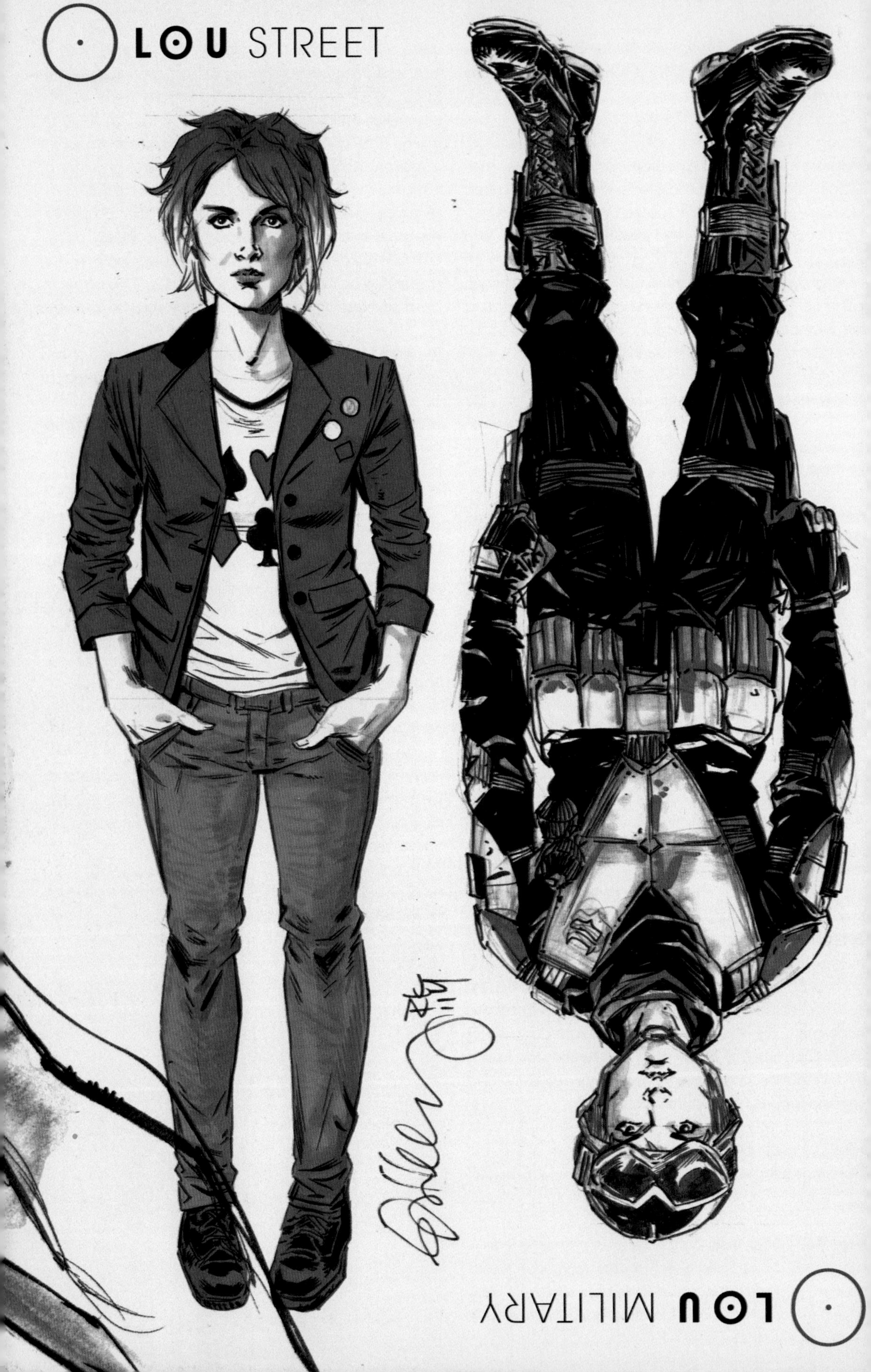
LOU STREET
LOU MILITARY

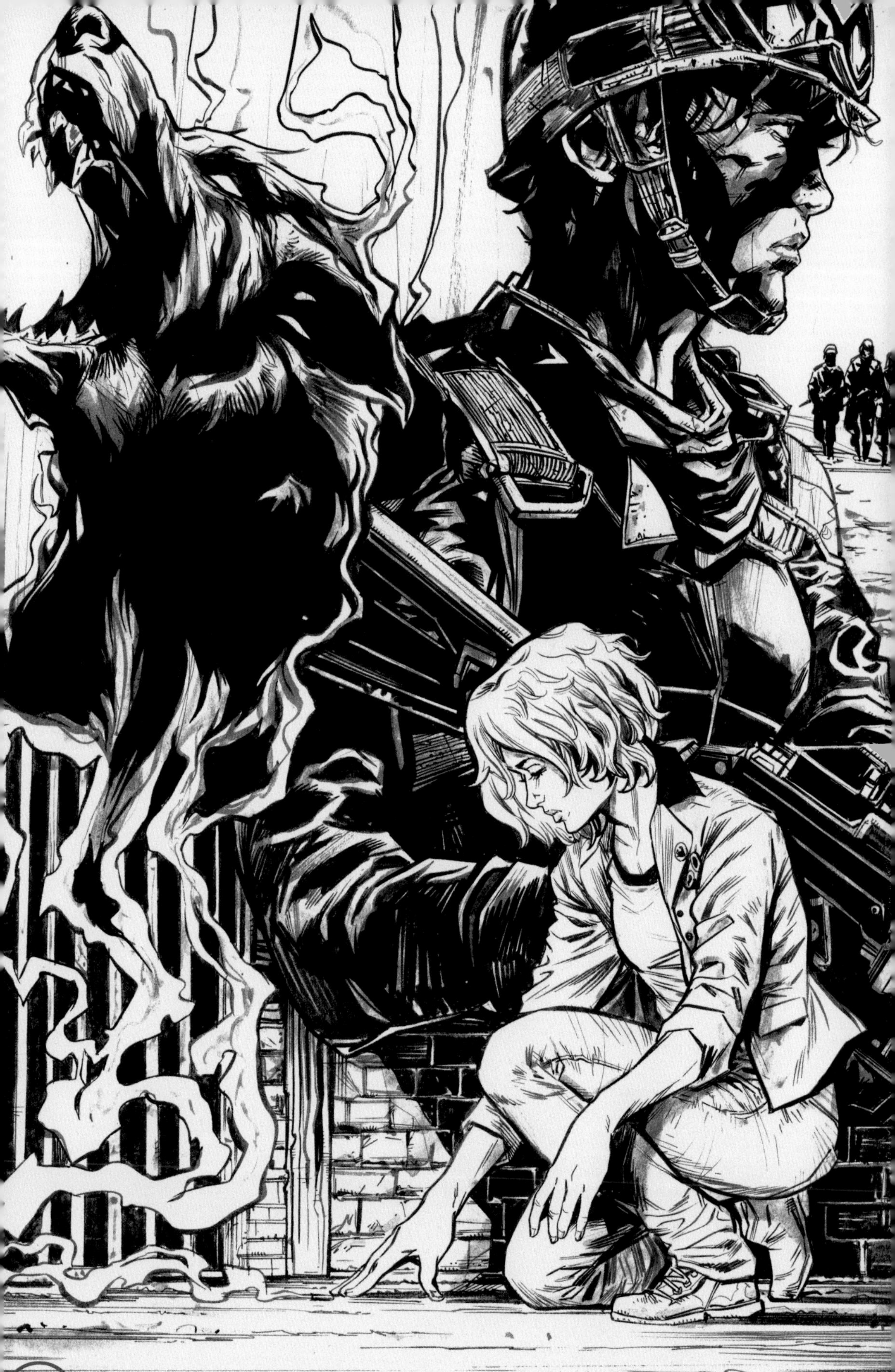

EARLY **CONCEPT**

by RYAN KELLY

HAVOC
ONLINE

CryHavocComic.tumblr.com

Si Spurrier   @sispurrier

Ryan Kelly   @funrama

Nick Filardi   @nickfil

Lee Loughridge   @leeloughridge

Matt Wilson   @colornmatt

Simon Bowland   @simonbowland

Emma Price   @tinymaster

[FOR MORE INFORMATION
REREAD COMIC]